Quick Analysis
for Busy
Decision Makers

Quick Analysis for Busy Decision Makers

ROBERT D. BEHN

&

JAMES W. VAUPEL

Basic Books, Inc., Publishers   New York

Library of Congress Cataloging in Publication Data

Behn, Robert D.
  Quick analysis for busy decision makers.

  Includes bibliographical references and index.
  1. Decision-making. I. Vaupel, James W. II. Title.
HD30.23.B43   658.4'0354   81–68402
ISBN 0–465–06787–5 (cloth)   AACR2
ISBN 0–465–06788–3 (paper)

TO

Victor D. and Nona H. Behn

AND

Edward W. and Gertrude W. Vaupel

With Love and Thanks

CONTENTS

PART III
Complications and Dynamics

ACKNOWLEDGMENTS

YEARS in the making. With a cast of thousands. If this book were a movie, it would have to be billed as a Cecil B. deMille production.

For it has literally had a cast of thousands. Since 1973, students who have taken the course from which this book emerged have contributed immensely to the final product. Indeed, those who took early versions of the course—and thus used early drafts of some of the chapters—will barely recognize most of the book. Their questions, complaints, and ideas forced us to revise it, and revise it, and revise it. Similarly, our teaching assistants in these courses independently have provided invaluable assessments of our ideas and their presentation. For their assistance, and for their patience with those early drafts, we thank them all.

We have benefited from the support, encouragement, criticisms, and suggestions of an army of colleagues and friends: William H. Behn, Colin C. Blaydon, Randall R. Bovbjerg, Anthony C. Broh, Rex V. Brown, Philip J. Cook, Peter R. Decker, Harvey V. Fineberg, Gregory Fischer, Joel L. Fleishman, Willis D. Hawley, Clinton W. Kelly III, Bruce R. Kuniholm, Howard C. Kunreuther, Joseph Lipscomb, Jr., Kenneth R. MacCrimmon, Duncan MacRae, Jr., Jerry Mechling, Mark H. Moore, M. Granger Morgan, David E. Price, Howard Raiffa, Michael Rosenberg, Donald Shepard, Deborah A. Stone, Paul Slovic, Nancy G. Vaupel, Milton C. Weinstein, and Richard Zeckhauser. We thank them individually and collectively. They have tried to help us with the score but are not responsible for the music. If the melody is cacophonous to your intellectual ears, it is we, as both the composers and the musicians, who warrant your jeers.

Over the years, legions of secretaries have typed and retyped the many drafts of the manuscript. In particular, Jo Ann Fuller, Janet Haynes, Marilyn Hogge, Deborah Holleman, Betty Johnson, Vera Lewis, Laurita Melton, Cathy Owens, Sandra Strauss, Cheryl Thompson, Angelika von Ramm, and many others devoted countless hours to this project. We hope they all realize how grateful we are for their work.

As for the scenery, the forest of decision trees that burgeon throughout this book were drawn by the green thumb of Mayre M. Loomis. For her long hours in the hot greenhouse, we thank her.

Truly, the book has been years in the making. Our original contract called for us to deliver the manuscript June 1, 1975. We were six years, one month and twenty-two days late. During that time Martin Kessler, our publisher, continually and gently prodded us—calling every year or so to remind us that not only were we supposed to be working on a book, we were supposed to finish one. For his patience and confidence, we thank him. Indeed, we appreciate the fine work of all those at Basic Books—particularly Maureen T. Bischoff, Brenda Bowen, and Bart De Castro.

We also thank Richard and Sadie Howe, who provided a quiet place during the summer to write some of those early drafts. Our wives, too, were an integral part of the project: Judith H. Behn offered her editorial assistance while we rewrote, and Bodil Vaupel periodically reminded us that we might want to use some quick analysis in our own personal decisions. But it is for their loving support, for their belief that we could—and would—finish the book, that we are most grateful. Cecil B. deMille never had it so good.

Quick Analysis for Busy Decision Makers

Preface

FACED with an important and puzzling decision, how can *you* organize your thinking to make an intelligent choice? With little time to ponder over the dilemma, let alone collect information, how can *you* think analytically about a decision? This book answers these questions. It explains how to use the ideas of *quick analysis* to help make personal, business, and governmental decisions when you do not have much time or information. When you do face a decision, you must—most often—act quickly. Moreover, you are not apt to possess a large statistical data base from which to draw either information or comfort. In such situations, the traditional analytical techniques are of little value. The fundamentals of quick analysis can, however, be quite helpful.

Researched Analysis

All analysis may be divided into two kinds: researched analysis and quick analysis. Researched analysis comprises all those analytical tools that are designed to help researchers structure complex phenomena and probe extensive data bases, and includes operations research, mathematical modeling, computer simulation, regression analysis, optimization, experimental design, linear and nonlinear programming, dynamic programming, the analysis of

3

variance, Markov processes, queuing theory, cost/benefit analysis, and game theory. These methods of analysis require time, data, and usually a computer. Most people—and most analysts—consider such tools to comprise the universe of analytical methods; most of the research energies of analytical "methodologists" are devoted to further developing and refining such methods, and most courses on analysis deal exclusively with these methods. Clearly, these techniques of researched analysis are important and useful. But there is also quick analysis, and in many situations it is even more valuable.

This book has evolved from our efforts to teach an introductory course in analysis at Duke University's Institute of Policy Sciences and Public Affairs. Beginning with an emphasis on researched analysis, this course passed through three distinct stages. Originally, like so many other introductory courses, it was a smorgasbord of tools, techniques, and tricks. We introduced the students to decision analysis, gave them a sample of probability theory, a taste of modeling, a quick swallow of game theory, and a sip of computer simulation. The results, however, were not very satisfying; the students found the new ideas appetizing, but they never had an opportunity to digest any one set of ideas sufficiently to be able to appreciate and use them. And the course lacked a unifying theme. All it served the students was a collection of savory intellectual memories.

Consequently, we replaced the traditional smorgasbord with a single analytical approach. We wanted to give the students sufficient experience with one collection of analytical tools so that they would understand its theoretical base, could apply it to resolve real problems, and would recognize its limitations. For a variety of reasons, we selected decision analysis. After all, everyone makes decisions.

The results still were not completely satisfactory. There was a mismatch between the traditional, research-oriented techniques of decision analysis and the types of decisions our students actually made and would make—indeed, the types of decisions everyone makes most frequently. Researched decision analysis requires much time to design a complicated decision tree and much information to satisfy the traditional demands of this analytical form. Rarely are they available.

Thus, we continued to experiment in our research with analytical approaches to decision making that could and would be used by practicing decision makers. And we continued to modify our course. In the third (and current) stage of its evolution, the researched analysis aspects of decision analysis have been replaced with our quick analysis approach to decision making.

Preface

Quick Analysis

This book does introduce the fundamentals of decision analysis, but only the quick analysis fundamentals. Indeed, it will barely be recognized by those who have taken other courses under the "decision analysis" label, for it contains none of the specialized techniques presented in most books on the subject. We do not explain how to update a beta prior using binomial sampling. In fact, we do not use a single formal probability model. For, unfortunately, when a decision must be made without very much time or data, the specialized techniques of decision analysis are not very helpful. On the other hand, the ideas of quick analysis, which require a sharp pencil or perhaps a pocket calculator rather than the latest-generation computer, are designed to help resolve decision dilemmas when time is short and data are sparse.

If you must make a decision quickly, what can you do? You can follow your intuition. You can apply some rules of thumb. You can select the option that minimizes regret (that is, follow a "max-min" decision rule). Or you can do some quick analysis.

Problems characterized by the absence of both adequate time and ample data occur more frequently than those that can be subjected to researched analysis, yet they are largely ignored in the analytical literature and in analytical courses. Moreover, quick analysis is also valuable for undertaking a "first-cut" analysis (an initial examination of the problem). In many situations, the problem must be resolved quickly and the first cut is also the last. In other circumstances, quick analysis can help develop a perspective on a complex problem, determine and organize its basic elements, reach a preliminary decision, and determine what aspects of the problem require more extensive, researched analysis.

As we have developed it, quick analysis is derived from decision analysis. Most of the research in decision analysis is devoted to expanding the theoretical scope of the field to encompass increasing levels of complexity. Yet little of even fundamental decision analysis is used by practicing decision makers in either government or business.[1] Consequently, our work has been in the opposite direction; we have attempted to develop general ideas and concepts that can help decision makers to think systematically about decisions they must make when the absence of adequate time and data precludes the application of the techniques of (researched) decision analysis.

There is a clear need for simple ideas that real decision makers can use in real time. With respect to budgetary decisions, for example, Aaron Wildavsky, former president of the Russell Sage Foundation, has emphasized the decision maker's need for simple rather than sophisticated decision aids.

Instead of prestige attaching to the spurious claim to have considered everything, men might vie with one another to see whether they could not develop shorter cuts and better approximations to lessen the burden of calculation. As it is now, there is virtually no discussion of the rules of thumb currently in use because the practitioners know how rough their tools are and rightly fear that the necessity for using some such methods will not be appreciated.[2]

The methods of quick analysis *are* those analytical methods especially designed to help busy decision makers. Quick analysis uses decision "saplings" (simple decision trees with only a few branches, as described in chapter 2, which capture the essence of the decision dilemma), judgmental probabilities, and preferences. Quick analysis also involves a collection of very elementary techniques for thinking about some of the decomposed elements of the decision —ideal probability generators, reference gambles, sequential trade-offs— which are valuable tools not only for making decisions but for making forecasts, evaluating outcomes, and analyzing conflicting consequences. The ideas of quick analysis may be crude in their lack of mathematical sophistication, but they are useful to managerial and professional decision makers in any field.

In an article on understanding and improving decisions, Paul Slovic of Decision Research divides the types of decisions people must make into repetitive decisions (such as selecting or rejecting job applicants) and unique, one-time decisions. For unique decisions, Slovic writes, "If the leadtime is long and the decision is important enough, then decision analysis is the relevant aiding technology. If the leadtime is short, I see no recourse other than to rely on educated intuition."[3] We disagree. We believe that a decision analysis—though admittedly a quick analysis—can help even when the leadtime is very short. Intuition still plays an important role, as it does in any decision, but it can be aided and focused by using a simple decision sapling to concentrate one's analytical and intuitive energies on the essence of the dilemma.

For decisions that must be made quickly, analysis does not mean collecting and processing information but thinking analytically. And, significantly, the ideas of quick analysis flow directly from the fundamental *concepts of analytical thinking* (which are discussed in chapter 1). These five concepts provide the basis for both researched and quick analysis. Because quick analysis involves few complicated techniques and because the dynamics of quick analysis are not so much a function of cookbook procedures as of creative thinking, the underlying significance of the concepts of analytical thinking is much more apparent when doing (and studying) quick analysis.

In fact, quick analysis may be the best way to develop that problem-analysis gestalt required to think analytically. When confronted with a dilemma, the first question should be: "What is the problem, and how can I best think analytically about it?" Quick analysis provides a framework for concentrating all one's analytical energies on work that will contribute specifically and most directly to the resolution of the dilemma.

Preface

Unfortunately, many analysts, in academia, business, and government, are afflicted with the "data-technique" syndrome. Having been taught how to use a variety of analytical techniques to massage various types of data sets, they begin with the question: "What data do I have, and what techniques do I know to manipulate those data?" The results of such "analysis" may be only peripherally related to the real problem, but if the "analyst" has used the most sophisticated technique in his analytical bag of tricks, he then believes he has done his part. This data-technique syndrome has given analysis a bad name. It results in much "sophisticated" but quite useless analysis. The resolution of any meaningful problem involves not only mathematical objectivity but also intelligent subjectivity. Real dilemmas never come with all the necessary data, and it is best to make that clear from the beginning. The problems confronting busy decision makers cannot be resolved without making explicit subjective judgments; quick analysis dramatizes how essential the intelligent blend of subjective and objective thinking is.

Most decision makers simply do not have the advanced mathematical background necessary to undertake (or even consume) researched analysis. But they have a clear need to analyze problems. Quick analysis, because it uses only high school algebra, is specifically designed to fulfill this need. Anyone confronted with a decision can use it to resolve the dilemma quickly (or, if time permits, to determine what aspects of the problem could be directly illuminated by some researched analysis by professionals).

When Richard Zeckhauser, now Professor of Political Economy at Harvard, started his first day on the job as an analyst in the Defense Department, his boss, Alain Enthoven (now a professor at Stanford University), chatted with him for a while about Zeckhauser's highly mathematical college thesis. As Zeckhauser recalls it, the conversation then went something like this:

> "That was good fun. Let's talk about your work here in the Defense Department. Do you know how to add, subtract, multiply, and divide?"
> "Yes."
> "Do you understand what marginal analysis is?"
> "Yes."
> "Good, that and common sense is what you will need."[4]

For this book, even an understanding of marginal analysis (thinking about the additional benefits and additional costs that result from some incremental, or marginal, change in policy) is not necessary. What is required is a willingness to do a little arithmetic and think systematically.

Three Audiences

In writing this book, we had three audiences in mind. The first consists of practicing decision makers. The mayor of Indianapolis, the president of Honeywell, the public interest lawyer in Washington, and the chief heart surgeon at Duke Hospital are constantly making decisions like those described in the following chapters. This book is consciously written to be accessible to such decision makers and is designed to help them improve the quality of their decisions.

The second intended audience consists of students preparing for a career in one of the decision-making professions: business, public policy, medicine, education, law, journalism, architecture, and so forth. Because decision makers in the various professions constantly encounter dilemmas similar—if not identical—to the ones analyzed in this book, we feel that the ideas of quick analysis and the concepts of analytical thinking should be a part of any professional curriculum. (And students who learn quick analysis should be well prepared and well motivated to learn researched analysis.)

The third intended audience for this book consists of those individuals who want to improve the quality of their personal decisions. Many of the examples used in the book are drawn from our personal experiences and those of our friends. One of the main reasons we believe that the ideas of decision analysis are useful is that we have personally found them so.

Many individuals in each of these three audiences are skeptical about the usefulness of analytical methods, and for good reasons. Too often, analysts devote their efforts to developing complex mathematical techniques; they then try to justify their work by fabricating obscure problems to which the techniques might be applied. Such analysts frequently worry more about their mathematical models, the structure of their analysis, than about the problems they are purportedly tackling.

To avoid such pitfalls, we have carefully illustrated this book with a number of real decision problems. We always begin with the decision rather than with an analytical idea; in each chapter we describe a decision dilemma, analyze it, explain the general principle employed to resolve it, and outline a variety of other decisions for which the principle would be helpful.

This book is written for decision makers, not analysts. Quick analysis is not the impenetrable sorcery of some clique of professional analysts; it can be understood and done by decision makers themselves. Quick analysis provides a framework for analyzing a decision completely; none of its parts are obscured behind some complicated computer print-out, delegated to an analyst, or usurped by some other professional. Our goal has been to make the ideas of decision analysis accessible, so that a decision maker can use them without consulting a specialist.

Preface

To make this book exoteric (rather than esoteric), we have avoided the complex notation, such as $\bar{v}\,''(e,z,a_2^\circ)$ and $k[\hat{y}\,(z)/\theta]$, found in many books on decision analysis. Furthermore, as those familiar with the language of decision analysis will note, we have modified the jargon to make it less formidable by using the most descriptive and meaningful words and phrases available. We write about "preference-probabilities" rather than "utils" or "BRLTs," about "gambles" rather than "lotteries," and about "uncertain quantities" rather than "random variables." "I never used a logarithm in my life," George Bernard Shaw once lamented, "and could not undertake to extract the square root of four without misgiving."[5] But Shaw could have understood this book.

Contributions

In addition to making decision analysis available to a much wider audience, we attempt in this book to make some contributions to the field of decision theory. In reality, there are two such fields, and thus two such theories. The prescriptive theory of the mathematical field concerns how people might make *better* decisions. The descriptive theory of the psychological field concerns how people actually *do* make their decisions. In this book, we have attempted to reformulate the basic principles of mathematical decision theory and the methods for applying it in ways that mesh with what psychological decision theory tells us about human cognitive processes.

This book also attempts to define the most fundamental models of decision theory—the basic building blocks from which all the other, more complex models used in decision theory are constructed. The usual research in decision analysis has concentrated on defining more complex problems and developing new techniques (or expanding old ones) to solve such decision problems. We have attempted to move in the opposite direction—to define what features of a decision problem make it a dilemma and to codify the key steps necessary to resolve each of these basic prototypes.

Finally, this book attempts to apply decision theory to a new set of problems. Usually, the applications of decision theory have concerned problems for which it was necessary to make complex calculations from large data sets and for which there was adequate time to make such calculations. We have devoted our attention to an entirely different class of problems—ones for which either the necessary data do not exist or there is not enough time to make the requisite calculations or both. Although this class of problems contains most of the important decisions faced by executives in business and government, it has been virtually ignored in the decision analysis literature.

We believe that the prospects for better decision making depend not so much on the refinement of complex analytical techniques as on the extension of analysis to real life decision problems. That is why we have devoted our research, thinking, and writing to the quick analysis branch of decision analysis. Our objective has been to develop and explain some ideas that will be helpful to practicing decision makers and, at the same time, stimulate the thinking of decision theorists.

This book won't help you master the clarinet, skate backwards, or write poetry. We do believe, however, that it will help you make better decisions.

PART I

The Fundamentals of Quick Analysis

Chapter 1

The Concepts of Analytical Thinking

MOST decision makers are busy. They have to make their decisions in a short time and with limited information. As Walter D. Scott, formerly an associate director of the Office of Management and Budget, remarked, "You have to be able to make big decisions by 3 o'clock the same afternoon even if you haven't had a chance to do all the homework you want."[1] If you "spend two years studying something," Oregon's former governor Tom McCall observed, "by the time you conclude it's a good thing to do, the best time for doing it may have passed."[2] This problem does not afflict only the executive branch of government. University of Rochester professor Richard F. Fenno, Jr., has written about the U.S. House of Representatives:

> Individually and collectively, House members are called upon to make decisions, sometimes within the space of a few hours, on matters ranging from national security to constituency service. In short, a body of 435 men must process a work load that is enormous, enormously complicated, and enormously consequential. And they must do so under conditions in which their most precious resources, time and information, are in chronically short supply.[3]

How should a busy mayor, an overworked corporate executive, or a harried consumer organize his or her thinking about puzzling decisions to make the most of the limited time and data available? This book presents some ideas to help busy decision makers resolve their decision dilemmas. Our hope is that *you* will find these ideas useful in organizing your own thinking about the decisions you have to make.

Quick Analysis for Important, Puzzling Decisions

The ideas of quick analysis will prove most helpful when you are confronted with an important and puzzling decision but have only a few minutes or hours to think about it. If a decision is not particularly important or puzzling, or if you are willing to devote weeks or months to the decision, other approaches may be more appropriate.

Unimportant decisions, for example, are made by snap judgments or habit. When shopping for a can of tomato soup you may decide between Campbell's soup and the house brand by making a snap judgment; it isn't worth your time to weigh the benefits of the superior (or, at least, consistent and well-known) taste of Campbell's soup against its cost premium of two cents. Wrote William James, "Few men can tell off-hand which sock, shoe, or trousers-leg they put on first."[4] Yet, through habit, such repetitive decisions are made. Other kinds of unimportant decisions are made on the basis of simple decision rules. For example: Carry an umbrella if the probability of rain is greater than 20 percent.

Even when a decision is important, you may not need to think about it very carefully. The decision has to be puzzling—a real dilemma. Many decisions are not. For example, if you need to decide between several job offers, one of which is preferable to all the others in terms of type of work, salary, location, and so forth, your choice is obvious.

Further, when a great deal of time and information is available, the sophisticated techniques of researched analysis may be appropriate. But when it is necessary to think systematically about important and puzzling decisions even though time is short and data are sparse, the ideas of quick analysis can prove invaluable.

Decisions as Dilemmas

What makes a decision problem puzzling? When you have to choose between two or more courses of action, what makes it difficult to see immediately which choice is best? There are three major complications that can turn a decision into a dilemma.

The Concepts of Analytical Thinking

First, you may not know the precise consequences of your alternatives. The future is uncertain, and that uncertainty may influence the outcome of your decision. A corporate executive may need to decide whether to continue or terminate construction of a plant in another country without knowing whether the plant can be completed. A patient may have to decide whether to undergo an eye operation that might improve his vision or leave him blind. A governor may have to decide whether to veto a bill without knowing if his veto will be overridden or sustained. In other cases, the consequences of a decision may be uncertain because they depend upon future decisions that you have not yet made. For example, a business executive's immediate decision about whether to test market a new product may depend upon how the results of the market test will affect the future decision about whether to drop the product or produce and distribute it nationwide.

The next nine chapters of this book focus on decision dilemmas where the decision is puzzling because the consequences of the alternatives are unknown. Chapters 2 through 9 present a cluster of powerful concepts for structuring problems where the outcome of the decision depends upon future uncertain events. Chapter 10 concerns current decisions whose outcomes will be influenced by the decision maker's future choices.

The second major factor that can make a decision problem puzzling is a clash between conflicting consequences. A U.S. representative may have trouble deciding how to vote on a bill that he thinks will help reduce inflation but increase unemployment. A consumer may be perplexed over whether to buy an expensive car with special safety and comfort features instead of a less costly model. A corporate executive may wonder whether the loss in short-term earnings resulting from a major capital investment is compensated for by the long-term increase in productivity. Chapter 11 describes some concepts that can be helpful when the essence of the dilemma is a trade-off between conflicting consequences.

The third reason a decision may be a dilemma is "complexity." Some decision problems are so complicated that they are hard to pin down and define precisely; there are too many alternatives, too many uncertainties, too many possible consequences. A corporate executive deciding where to locate a new plant may be bewildered by the countless decision possibilities and considerations. Throughout this book, we stress how systematically to cut a decision dilemma of mind-boggling complexity down to manageable size.[5]

The Five Concepts of Analytical Thinking

How can you best think about an important and puzzling decision dilemma? What should you do when faced with a decision that you believe is worth some serious, systematic thought? Using a few basic concepts and some methods based on these concepts, a decision maker can think analytically about a decision problem to make the best use of the limited time and information available. The essence of these concepts is contained in the five basic imperatives for intelligent analysis:

1. Think!
2. Decompose!
3. Simplify!
4. Specify!
5. Rethink!

1. Think!

The time you spend on a decision problem is divided between two basic tasks: (1) thinking, and (2) gathering and processing information. Most people devote 99 percent of their decision-making time to gathering and processing information—talking to people about the problem, reading relevant material, developing complex models or theories, or carrying out elaborate chains of calculations. Although these activities may be useful, you can usually reach a more intelligent decision if you spend a greater proportion of your time thinking hard, trying to pin down the essence of the dilemma you face. In most cases, it makes sense to devote at least half the time available to thinking.

"Model simple; think complex," admonishes Garry D. Brewer of the Yale School of Organization and Management.[6] The difficulty with much analysis, especially analysis done by "quantitative types," is that the analysis is so complex that its relationship to the problem to be solved is obscure—even to the analyst. The model itself (that is, the structure of the analysis) becomes the driving force. A great deal of time is devoted to developing an elaborate model and to carrying out lengthy calculations, and relatively little time is devoted to thinking intelligently about the problem at hand.[7] Complex models often prevent complex thinking.

Professor Donald C. Eteson of Worcester Polytechnic Institute has characterized the use of complex calculations without appropriate thinking as the "brute force and ignorance technique." Eteson often used this phrase to ridicule students who had developed silly, complicated solutions to his electrical engineering problems. Reliance on "brute force and ignorance" often leads to the wrong answer—or to the right answer to the wrong question. In analyzing a decision, you should continually think about the appropriateness of your analysis in terms of your actual dilemma, the resolution of which, after all, is the purpose of all your work.

Often, such thinking requires the ability to use simple numbers, to add a few together and understand their implications. Today, most Americans are "literate." But how many are "numerate"? How many can make simple calculations and interpret simple numbers? How many corporate executives can read and understand the tables and charts prepared by their planning staffs? How many U.S. senators can make useful back-of-the-envelope calculations to check the statistical arguments made by lobbyists? How many are in the habit of doing so? Observes Steven Muller, the former president of Johns Hopkins University, "In the 20th Century anyone who is mathematically illiterate is as bad off as someone who can't read."[8]

Professor Richard Zeckhauser of Harvard argues that "one of the best tools of policy analysis is long division." Why? Because it is the simplest method for answering the question: "How much did I accomplish for how much?"[9] Thinking analytically about most decisions requires an ability to handle simple numbers—a fluency in the elementary language of mathematics.

2. Decompose!

"Analysis" is usually associated with the sophisticated mathematical manipulation of complex data sets. The word "analysis," however, is derived from the Greek αναλυω, one meaning of which is "to resolve into its elements." Thus, analysis is a mode of thinking. To analyze a problem is to decompose it, to break it down into its component parts. This is a key to resolving any puzzling decision: Decompose it into its most important components, work individually with those components, and then recombine the results to make the decision.

This process of decomposition is what most people—at least those who've misplaced their pocket calculators—employ to multiply multidigit numbers. Few people can multiply 7,467 by 9,883 in their heads. So to solve this problem, most people write it down on a piece of paper, decompose it into its parts (7 times 3, 7 times 8, and so on), and then add these parts together to get the final answer. If they were to multiply four-digit numbers in their heads, few of them would expect to get the right result; consequently, they are willing to do the simple work of systematically decomposing the problem, using pencil and paper, to be sure of getting the correct answer.

A decision maker should also be willing to organize his thinking about a decision dilemma by writing each of its components down on a piece of paper in a systematic way. This book describes some methods for such decomposition of decisions—ideas that are to decision making as the methods of multiplication and long division are to arithmetic.

Unfortunately, most people are reluctant to decompose, consciously and systematically, their own problems. Maybe they believe that decision making is a natural talent that does not require structure. Or perhaps they feel a little silly and self-conscious about organizing their thinking on paper. Apparently, they are confident that their own minds—in some mysterious yet wonderful way—can make consistent, intelligent choices every time.

Unfortunately, research in cognitive psychology is proving just the opposite.[10] Ever since George A. Miller of Harvard University discovered "the magical number of seven, plus or minus two"—that is, the inability of the human mind to hold more than five to nine bits of information in short-term memory[11]—there has developed an increasing recognition of the human mind's limitations for processing information. There are, writes Herbert A. Simon of Carnegie-Mellon University, "limits to human rationality." To emphasize these limits, Simon developed his "principle of bounded rationality":

> The capacity of the human mind for formulating and solving complex problems is very small compared with the size of the problems whose solution is required for objectively rational behavior in the real world—or even for a reasonable approximation to such objective rationality.[12]

It is, in part, for his work on uncovering and describing the limits to human cognitive abilities that Simon was awarded the Nobel Prize in Economics.

When making a decision, these limitations can produce biases, inconsistencies, and distortions.[13] Intellectual self-discipline is required to avoid ignoring important alternatives, uncertainties, decisions, or trade-offs. For this, the analytical framework of quick analysis is most valuable. It helps the decision maker identify the most important components of the decision—the ones that create the dilemma—and concentrates attention on them. Then, with the further assistance of those wonderful tools of man, pencil and paper, it is possible to work with each component individually, while keeping track of the others.[14]

But you need not take our word on faith. A simple experiment can demonstrate the efficacy of analysis. The next time you confront a puzzling decision problem, make the decision "in your head." Then sit down with pencil in hand and do a quick analysis of the decision, using the ideas of systematic decomposition described in this book. In most cases, we believe, a quick analysis will yield a decision in which you are more confident.

3. Simplify!

Most important decision puzzles are so complicated that it is impossible to analyze them completely. To undertake a complete analysis, the decision maker would be required to:

1. specify all possible decision alternatives
2. predict all possible consequences of every alternative
3. estimate the probability of every consequence
4. appraise the desirability of every consequence
5. calculate which decision alternative yields the most desirable set of consequences

As Simon's principle of bounded rationality makes clear, however, such an ideal rationality can never be attained because of the limits of time, information, and intellectual capacity. For example, to decide how much money to place in the federal budget for cancer research, a complete analysis would have to include, among other things, consideration of all the other possible ways this money might be used (such as kidney research, food stamps, military salaries, and tax credits for energy conservation), and all the possible implications of these alternatives (including the future of the papacy, the profitability of uranium mining, the prospects for interplanetary travel, and the popularity of serial music).

If any decision problem is to be resolved in a limited amount of time, it is impossible to take into account all of the possibly relevant factors. You must simplify—indeed, you must simplify *drastically*. You must decide what is really important and what is inconsequential; you must decide which few factors to include in your first-cut analysis, and which additional factors to include in your second-cut analysis—if there is time for a second cut. The objective is to isolate the most critical factors and describe their essential relationships.

The "logic of simplification" is, for most people, a difficult concept. All of us feel uncomfortable leaving things out. Moreover, the idea of simplification carries some unfortunate connotations; to do a simplified analysis implies that our thinking is simplistic—unworthy of the true talents of our mind. Consequently, we try to consider as many factors as possible in the time we have available. Even if a decision maker attempts to think about a hundred different factors influencing a decision, however, the choice will inevitably be based on very few, perhaps only one or two. Along with other psychologists, Herbert Simon has devoted much of his work to identifying how people go about "simplifying the choice problem to bring it within the power of human computation."[15]

Analytical simplification works for several reasons. First, the human mind is only capable of doing simplified analysis. The limitations to our cognitive talents prevent us (no matter what we would like to believe) from swiftly performing a comprehensive analysis. Since people can consider only a limited number of factors anyway, it only makes sense to select explicitly and carefully those few on which to concentrate.

Indeed, this is the second reason why simplification works: A structured yet simplified analysis can be based on the decision maker's conscious judgments about which factors are important and which are not. Once it has been decided that certain factors are peripheral—that they do not create the dilemma or affect its essence—they can be safely ignored, at least until the results of the first-cut analysis suggest that one or two of them may, in fact, be important.

Finally, simplification works because it encourages the decision maker to use intuition to its best advantage. Indeed, an analytical decision maker must exploit his intuition at every point in the analysis: in deciding why the decision is a dilemma; in determining what factors are most important and breaking the problem down into these components; in specifying his beliefs about uncertainties and his preferences for outcomes; and in rethinking the results to see if they make sense or warrant further analysis. Simplification provides a clear structure for making intuitive but explicit judgments about each of the important factors, concentrating the decision maker's intuition where it will make a difference.

The question is not whether to simplify. Any decision maker must—and will. The only question is whether this process of simplification will be unconscious or conscious, disorganized or analytical.

4. Specify!

Decisions depend upon judgments—judgments about the nature of the dilemma, the probabilities of events, and the desirabilities of consequences. Decision making is inherently subjective, but that does not mean it must be vague. The more specific the judgments made while thinking about a decision, the more helpful they will be.

Consider the case of probability judgments. For many important, puzzling decisions, the decision maker is uncertain about the future consequences of

The Concepts of Analytical Thinking

some or all of the alternatives. Often, this uncertainty is so important that the decision maker will want to consider explicitly what the chances are for realizing the most significant outcomes of each alternative. In certain circumstances a decision maker may have some statistical data available that can be used to calculate these probabilities. For example, previous experience may indicate that the probability of a spare part being defective is 0.005. In such a case, it clearly makes sense to work with this statistical probability.

For most decision problems, however, relevant statistical data will not be available. Here, the decision maker must rely on *judgmental probability* assessments. Such assessments are based on data, although not on statistical data that can be processed by formal mathematical methods. Rather, the data consist of relevant bits and pieces of information the decision maker has in his head or can look up.

Most people state such probability assessments with words or phrases like "probably," "unlikely," or "almost certainly." Unfortunately, such words and phrases are ambiguous. Most people use the word "probably" to describe a wide range of uncertainties. Various studies have shown that some people use "probably" to mean something like a 50-to-60-percent chance, while other people interpret "probably" as meaning at least a 90-percent chance. (More on this in chapter 4.) Numerical—though still judgmental—probabilities have the advantage over such probability phrases, for they are much more specific and unambiguous. Furthermore, numerical probability assessments permit a decision maker to perform certain arithmetic calculations that may help determine the preferable decision.

Two classes of people tend to be particularly reluctant to use judgmental probabilities. The first group includes scientists, engineers, and others who have been rigorously trained in the use of objective statistical data. Although available objective statistical data certainly should be utilized in making a decision, in many cases people must still determine their own judgmental probabilities.

The second class of people includes students of literature, history, languages, or the fine arts who have had little exposure to mathematics. These people are not bothered by the subjective nature of such probability assessments but rather by their numerical expression. "A ninety-five-percent chance" is, however, just as good an English phrase as "extremely likely." Indeed, when clarity is important, it is better.

In *The Elements of Style,* William Strunk, Jr. and E. B. White write:

> If those who have studied the art of writing are in accord on any one point, it is on this: the surest way to arouse and hold the attention of the reader is by being specific, definite, and concrete. The greatest writers—Homer, Dante, Shakespeare—are effective largely because they deal in particulars and report the details that matter. Their words call up pictures.[16]

The purpose of language is the communication of ideas, of images. But then, of what value is the statement "It will probably rain tomorrow," if the speaker means there is a 60-percent chance while the listener can conclude that the probability of rain is anything between 50 and 100 percent? Writes White, "since writing is communication, clarity can only be a virtue."[17]

Significantly, words like "probably" or "unlikely" may reflect more than imprecise communication. They may reflect imprecise thought. The speaker who says "It will probably rain tomorrow" never really bothered to determine exactly how likely it is to rain. He uses the word "probably" to mask his unwillingness to think carefully about this uncertainty. In his classic essay, "Politics and the English Language," George Orwell wrote that our language "becomes ugly and inaccurate because our thoughts are foolish, but the slovenliness of our language makes it easier for us to have foolish thoughts."[18] One of the advantages of specific statements like "The probability of rain is ten percent" is that before we can use them we are required to think.

In addition to making judgments about uncertainties, a decision maker must evaluate his preferences for the possible outcomes of the various decision alternatives. A decision maker might initially describe his preference for each outcome by writing a few sentences or paragraphs about it. To make a decision, however, it is necessary to determine the *relative* desirability of the outcomes and, to do so, lengthy appraisals are often summarized by short descriptions. But, again, phrases like "not so bad" or "highly desirable" are ambiguous. By using specific *preference-probabilities* (as described in the next chapter) you can improve your ability to think analytically about your relative preferences for the consequences you face.

Although those who are unable or unwilling to use numbers may lose themselves in a maze of imprecise thought, those who insist on basing a decision upon only those factors that can be measured bias their analyses in a futile search for the grail of objectivity. By ignoring those factors that cannot be measured, "quantitative" decision makers let their technical capabilities be a substitute for their own judgments. Decisions should be based upon those factors that the decision maker believes to be most important, not upon ones about which it is easiest to find data. That is why we discuss the imperative of simplification before the imperative of specification. You cannot specify your judgments about the important elements of a decision until you simplify your problem so that you are dealing only with its most important features.

To undertake a quick analysis, a decision maker begins by deciding what is important: Why is this decision a dilemma? What are the key factors that create the dilemma? Once you have identified the important uncertainties, you will find it difficult to ignore those for which there exist no data. When you have identified the important consequences, you cannot disregard those that are intangible. Quick analysis is a way to avoid the measurement trap because it focuses attention on the important components of a decision rather than the easily quantifiable ones.

To use quick analysis, you must decide what uncertainties and what outcomes will most directly influence your decision, and then you must make explicit, to yourself if not to others, what your predictions and preferences are. Obviously, when specifying probabilities for future, uncertain events and preferences for possible consequences, you will have to make subjective, intuitive judgments. We do not deny this; indeed, we stress it. For if the decision is yours to make, it is your judgments that are important. The purpose of specifying these judgments with a few numbers (as described in chapter 2) is to force yourself to think carefully about your own values and beliefs.

This book emphasizes decision problems where measurable data are not available. In such situations, it is frequently useful to specify your subjective judgments by using numbers, though these numbers should not be the product of arbitrary quantification. You should exploit numbers, when it makes sense to do so, to specify your understanding of your decision problem as completely and precisely as possible. Do not let the numbers push you around. Push the numbers around.

5. Rethink!

The "Catch-22" of decision making is this: decision problems worth solving do not have a solution. As we emphasized in the discussion of simplification, all decision analyses are incomplete. Time, information, and cognitive capabilities limit the scope and detail of any analysis. Thus, it is impossible to obtain "the correct solution" to any real life decision dilemma.

From this catch follows an important corollary: No real life decision can be made objectively. Because no analysis can ever be made complete, the subdecisions about what to include and what to ignore depend upon a number of personal, subjective judgments. Thus, the overall decision ultimately depends upon these judgments, too.[19]

Because all analyses are incomplete and are ultimately based on subjective judgments, decision making is best viewed as a creative process of discovery. The first stage in this process is to think about your decision dilemma, decompose it into its basic elements, simplify these elements so the problem is manageable, specify your judgments concerning the likelihood and desirability of the most important possible outcomes of the few decision alternatives you have considered, and then work with this structure and these judgments to reach a first-cut decision.

The second stage in this creative process is to rethink your problem and your analysis of it. Your first cut, based on your original judgments, does not provide the ultimate answer to your decision problem. If you have more time —and if the decision warrants more analysis—you will want to think more carefully about your assumptions and your judgments, change them as you see fit, and, perhaps, perform some side calculations and collect some additional information.

If you have more time available and are still puzzled about the decision, you can rethink the problem again by doing a third-cut analysis and perhaps even a fourth cut. At no point will you ever reach *the* best decision, because you will never be able to analyze your problem completely. The more you work on the problem, though, the more you will discover and the better your decision will be.

This does not mean that you should keep on rethinking about a decision indefinitely. The general rule, as stated by Professor John Rawls of Harvard, is that "we should deliberate up to the point where the likely benefits from improving our plan are just worth the time and effort of reflection."[20] A decision maker should continue to analyze a decision only as long as the expected costs of further analysis are less than the expected benefits. Throughout this book, and especially in the last chapter, on the dynamics of analysis, we suggest ways to help determine when an analysis—and the decision resulting from it—is satisfactory, and when and how to think further about it.

A dilemma, by definition, can never be solved. There is no objective answer, no correct solution. Rather, within the limits of time and information, a dilemma is "resolved" to the degree warranted by its importance. Consequently, analysis is a search for an acceptable resolution—a dynamic process, not a mechanical procedure. A decision maker must constantly rethink his definition of the problem, his judgments about its components, and his assessment of their relationships until he is satisfied with his decision.

Quick Analysis as a Decision-Making Tool

With their physical limitations constantly dramatized by the power and speed of other animals, humans have long sought to develop tools that exploit the strengths they do have and to overcome their weaknesses. In contrast, our intellectual capabilities have been so clearly superior to those of other species that we have come to believe that our minds need little assistance. As we noted earlier, research in cognitive psychology suggests otherwise. In a review of "Behavioral Decision Theory," Paul Slovic, Baruch Fischhoff, and Sarah

The Concepts of Analytical Thinking

Lichtenstein of Decision Research observe that "a decade or more of research has abundantly documented that humans are quite bad at making complex, unaided decisions."[21] The human mind needs tools, too.

Quick analysis is a decision-making tool designed to exploit the intellectual strengths we do have and to overcome our cognitive handicaps. Moreover, quick analysis is designed specifically to aid in making those decisions that people most frequently confront.

Though the quality of a decision will always depend upon the decision maker's wisdom and experience, anyone can improve his own decision-making skills through the thoughtful use of systematic analysis. This is true even when there is little time or information. Analytical thinking can help even the busiest decision maker.

Chapter 2

The Basic Decision Dilemma: The Angina/Bypass Surgery Decision

OLLERTON WATT, a manufacturing executive, must make one of the most important decisions of his life. The decision does not involve his responsibilities as head of his firm's Chicago plant. Nor does it concern the uncompleted biography of Cyrus H. McCormick, the inventor and industrialist, on which he has been working for a decade. Rather, Watt's decision concerns his own life and future and that of his family, too.

For over a year, Watt has been suffering from angina pectoris—chest pains caused by coronary heart disease. (Arteriosclerosis, or hardening of the arteries, blocks the flow of blood in the three major coronary arteries that provide blood, and thus oxygen, to the heart muscles. When, because of excitement or exercise, the heart needs extra blood, the result can be angina pains.) Last week, Watt had a complete cardiac work-up, including an angiogram, and now his physician, Dr. Roberta Dwightson, has told him that although two of his three coronary arteries are clear, the third is 90-percent blocked. This explains why Watt has chest pains whenever he walks up two flights of stairs or takes a half-mile stroll through Lake Shore Park, near his Chicago apartment.

Medical therapy has proven, for Watt, to be a completely inadequate remedy, and so Dr. Dwightson has told him that he can elect to have surgery to bypass the blocked blood vessels and relieve the pain. Such bypass surgery involves the removal of a section of the saphenous vein from the patient's leg;

this vein is then used to bypass the blocked coronary artery. All indications are that, upon successful completion of the operation, Watt's angina will be completely relieved and he will be able to engage in moderate exercise without suffering from chest pain. There is, however, little evidence to indicate that the operation will prolong Watt's life. In fact there is a considerable ongoing debate within the medical profession about the impact of coronary bypass surgery on life expectancy.

Watt's problem is not unique—approximately two million Americans have angina, and over one hundred thousand bypass operations are performed each year in the United States—but that does not make Watt's decision any easier. For there is no guarantee that the operation will be a success. Indeed, Dr. Dwightson has told Watt that, given his age of fifty-five, his medical history, and his physical condition, there is a 10-percent chance that he will die on the operating table.[1]

Watt is clearly worried as he explains his problem to his wife and daughter. How significant, really, is the 10-percent chance of dying? Are the angina pains really crippling, or are they more a mere discomfort? Should he ask Dr. Dwightson any more questions? Should he ask for more tests? Should he worry about finishing his book, or is that too unimportant to influence his decision? Indeed, what factors are important for him to consider—and how should he consider them? How, Watt wonders, should he determine if the potential benefits of the operation are worth the risk?[2]

Analyzing the Dilemma: Structuring the Decision

Ollerton Watt's problem is truly a dilemma. There is no right or wrong decision; different people will—and do—make different choices. Consequently, the purpose of undertaking an analysis of the angina decision dilemma is not to determine what is the correct answer, but to determine how a decision maker could organize his thinking about this problem so that his choice truly reflects his beliefs about how likely each uncertain outcome is, and his preferences for those various outcomes.

Although this decision dilemma can be described in a few brief paragraphs, it involves almost all of the features that complicate even the most intricate decision problem. As with any other decision dilemma, the alternative selected depends upon how the decision maker structures his thinking and upon his predictions and preferences. Indeed, the purpose of organizing your thinking about a decision problem is to focus your attention on your key predictions (your assessments of the probabilities of the most important uncertain events) and on your critical preferences (your appraisals of the relative desirabilities of the most important outcomes).

How should Ollerton Watt think about his decision? The first step is to describe the essential features of the problem. This can be done in several ways; one is a simple prose paragraph.

> Mr. Watt has two alternatives. One alternative is not to have bypass surgery. The result of this choice is certain; Mr. Watt will continue to live but will also continue to have angina attacks. The second alternative is to have bypass surgery. There are two possible outcomes of this choice. There is a 90-percent chance that the operation will be a success; Mr. Watt will live and will have no chest pains. There is, however, a 10-percent chance that Mr. Watt will die during surgery.

This describes the essential features of the decision dilemma. Since there is no evidence that the operation will prolong life expectancy, this factor does not influence the decision and is thus ignored. Other factors, such as Mr. Watt's chances of completing the book on which he is working, have also been ignored; they might be included in a more elaborate, second-cut analysis.

The short preceding paragraph is not the only way to describe this decision problem. It is also possible to use a diagram called, in the idiom of decision analysis, a *decision tree.* A decision tree is a road map for a decision problem. It lays out in schematic form the decision alternatives, the uncertain events, the possible outcomes of such events, and the consequences of each outcome, all in the order that the decision maker will face them.

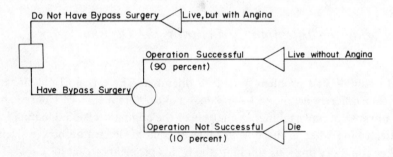

Figure 2–1. A Decision Tree for the Angina Decision Dilemma.

A decision tree is read from left to right. The first component on a decision tree is a square *decision node,* which indicates the (initial) decision facing the decision maker. For Mr. Watt's problem (figure 2–1), there are two choices ("Have Bypass Surgery" and "Do Not Have Bypass Surgery"), indicated by two *decision* (or alternative) *branches* attached to this decision node. The upper decision alternative, "Do Not Have Bypass Surgery," has a known, certain outcome; thus, this decision branch leads directly to a triangular *terminal node* to which is attached a *consequence branch* labeled "Live, but with Angina." For the lower decision alternative, "Have Bypass Surgery," the outcome is uncertain; thus, the lower decision branch leads to a circular *uncertainty* (or chance or event) *node* to which are attached two *outcome* (or chance or event) *branches.* The upper outcome branch is labeled "Operation Successful" and the probability of this outcome occurring is given underneath in parentheses. (The lower outcome branch is similarly labeled.) To each outcome branch is attached a terminal node and a consequence branch. For example, the consequence of a successful operation is to "Live without Angina."

The decision-tree description of the problem provides exactly the same information—no more, no less—as does the one-paragraph description. But, as with a road map, once you learn the basic symbols, a schematic presentation is more helpful than an expository one. If you want to get to Devonshire Street in downtown Boston, would you rather have a road map or a set of written instructions?

A decision tree has several other advantages. First, drawing a decision tree forces you to decompose your decision problem into its more manageable component parts. The decisions to be made, the uncertain events to be faced, the possible outcomes for each uncertainty, and the consequences of each final outcome are the basic components of any decision problem.

Second, drawing a decision tree forces you to be explicit in simplifying your problem. You must decide what factors to include in your analysis (to draw on your tree) and what factors to ignore. For example, Mr. Watt has ignored the question of whether he will finish his book because the book is not central to the reason why this decision is a dilemma. Mr. Watt's dilemma is a question of life and death, and the quality of life, and thus he decides to ignore that factor. He has also ignored the possibility that surgery will not cure his angina; it is possible that he would survive the operation but still suffer from chest pains, but the chances of this happening in Watt's particular case are one-half of 1 percent. Consequently, he can ignore this complication, at least for a first-cut analysis. These and other complications can be added in a second cut.

Third, drawing a decision tree requires you to specify your beliefs about uncertainty and your preferences for the outcomes. There is, for example, a specific place under each outcome branch to indicate the probability that that outcome will occur. Also (as will be explained shortly), there is a specific place to note your preferences for the terminal outcomes.

Finally, a decision tree presents the various factors in their proper relationship with each other. Reading the decision tree from left to right, the decision

maker confronts the various sequences of decisions, uncertain events, outcomes, and consequences just as he may confront them in real life.

Analyzing the Dilemma: Uncertainty and Probabilities

There is no magic formula for resolving the angina/bypass surgery dilemma.
But with the problem decomposed into its essential features, the fundamental
nature of the dilemma is clear: Does Mr. Watt prefer (1) the riskless alternative
of living with angina, or (2) the risky alternative with a 90-percent chance of
living without angina, and a 10-percent chance of dying? To answer this
question, Watt must think carefully about the uncertainties he faces and his
relative preferences for the possible outcomes.

First, Watt must examine the uncertainties. He has been told by his doctor
that, if he has bypass surgery, he faces a 10-percent chance of dying. What does
this mean? It does not mean that ten out of every one hundred people who have
bypass surgery die; the overall death rate is about 4 percent.[3] Watt is not an
average patient; he has particular problems that complicate his case and make
his chances of survival less than average. By comparing him with men with
similar complications and health characteristics, Dr. Dwightson has decided
that Watt's chances of surviving surgery are 90 percent.

Still, exactly what does it mean that Watt has a 90-percent chance of living
and a 10-percent chance of dying? The decision tree in figure 2–2 provides an
interpretation. Here there is a choice between two gambles: having bypass
surgery or drawing a ball from an urn that contains 90 green balls and 10 white
balls. The possible outcomes for both gambles are the same: Watt can either
live without angina or die. When Dr. Dwightson tells Watt that she believes
there is a 90-percent chance of his surviving bypass surgery, she is really
making the judgment that his chances of living (and dying) are identical for
both gambles in figure 2–2. If there were 99 green balls and only 1 white ball
in the urn, Dwightson would quickly recommend gambling on the urn. If,
however, there were 80 green balls and 20 white ones in the urn, she would
tell Watt that his chances of living were better with surgery. The 90 percent
is thus a *judgmental probability;* it specifies Dr. Dwightson's best judgment
about how likely each outcome of bypass surgery is for Watt.

The decision in figure 2–2 is strictly a hypothetical one. The decision node
on this decision tree is drawn as a diamond (rather than as a square) to
emphasize the hypothetical nature of the choice. Neither Watt nor Dwightson
actually faces this decision, yet thinking about it helps to analyze the real
decision that confronts Watt. The hypothetical decision provides a means of

The Basic Decision Dilemma

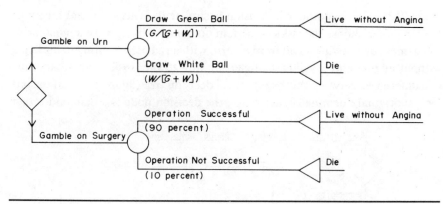

Figure 2-2. An Objective Interpretation of a Judgmental Probability.

specifying, in a clear and unambiguous way, exactly what Dr. Dwightson thinks the chances are for the uncertain outcomes in Watt's original dilemma. The advantage of the hypothetical decision in figure 2-2 is that there are only two possible outcomes, live or die; the interjacent outcome of the original decision does not complicate this choice. Thus, this hypothetical decision concentrates the attention of Watt and Dwightson on the uncertainty Watt faces, and provides an unambiguous interpretation of Watt's probability assessment: If Watt agrees that the probability of his surviving bypass surgery is 90 percent, this is the same as saying he is indifferent about choosing between the two alternatives in figure 2-2 (with this indifference denoted on the decision tree by the arrow pointing up each alternative branch). (More on probabilities in chapter 4.)

Analyzing the Dilemma: Outcomes and Preferences

The next step in analyzing Ollerton Watt's dilemma is to make some judgments about the relative merits of the three different outcomes. Obviously, living without angina is the best outcome, and dying is the worst. The difficult question is how the third, interjacent outcome—living, but with angina—compares with the other two. Is it almost as good as living without angina? Or is it so bad that it is only slightly better than dying? How can Watt specify his relative preferences for these three outcomes in a manner that will help him resolve his original dilemma?

Decision analysis provides an answer: another hypothetical decision (see figure 2–3). This hypothetical decision is similar to Watt's original dilemma: He can either choose the riskless, certain outcome of living with angina, or he can gamble by drawing a ball from an urn, with a red ball resulting in his living without angina and a yellow ball causing him to die. In fact, there are only two differences between this hypothetical decision tree (figure 2–3) and the one for the original dilemma (figure 2–1)—the decision node is a diamond rather

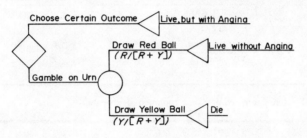

Figure 2–3. Using a Hypothetical Decision to Think about Relative Preferences for Three Outcomes.

than a square, and the uncertain outcome is determined by drawing a ball from an urn rather than by the success or failure of surgery. The latter difference is helpful, for it eliminates the subjective nature of the chances that surgery will be a success. For the hypothetical decision in figure 2–3, there is no ambiguity about the chances of living without angina or dying; these chances are specified by the proportions of red and yellow balls in the urn.

If the urn contains 50 red balls and 50 yellow balls, which hypothetical alternative should Watt choose: living with angina, or a 50-50 chance of living without it versus dying? Unless the angina pain were extremely intense, frequent, and crippling, most people would not choose the gamble if it meant only a 50-percent chance of living. Watt decides that in this situation he prefers the riskless alternative.

Suppose, however, the urn contains 99 red balls and 1 yellow one. Now what should Watt choose? Most people with serious angina problems would be willing to risk a 1-percent chance of dying for a 99-percent chance of living without angina. Watt decides that in this case he prefers the risky alternative.

Watt has now made two specific statements about his relative preferences for the three outcomes. If the probability of living is great enough (99 percent) he prefers the risky alternative; if the probability of living is too low (50 percent) he prefers the riskless alternative. The only difference between these two hypothetical decisions is the probability of drawing a red ball (and thus the probability of living without angina), yet the increase in this probability from 50 percent to 99 percent causes Watt to switch his preference from the riskless to the risky alternative.

The Basic Decision Dilemma

As the number of red balls in the urn increases from 50 to 99 (while the number of yellow balls decreases from 50 to 1), the risky alternative gets better and better. Indeed, as the number of red balls increases, there comes a point at which Watt switches from preferring the riskless alternative to preferring the risky one. This is called the *switch point* or *switch probability,* and shall be denoted by the letter V. If the probability of drawing a red ball is less than V, Watt prefers the riskless alternative. If the probability of drawing a red ball is greater than V, Watt prefers the risky alternative. As the probability of drawing a red ball increases from just below V to just above it, Watt switches his (hypothetical) decision from the riskless to the risky alternative.

The probability V can also be called an *indifference probability,* since it is the probability that makes Watt indifferent between the riskless and risky alternatives of his hypothetical dilemma. If the proportion of red balls in the urn is V (so that the proportion of yellow balls is $1 - V$), Watt is indifferent between the two choices. The interjacent outcome (living, but with angina) is just as good as a gamble that gives a V chance of the best outcome (living without angina) combined with a $1 - V$ chance of the worst outcome (dying). To specify his relative preferences for the three possible outcomes of his original dilemma, Watt needs to determine his indifference probability, V.

Clearly, V is somewhere between 50 and 99 percent. Determining these lower and upper bounds for V, however, was easier than determining V itself. Indeed, the two bounds were chosen precisely because they were easy. The best way to assess an indifference probability is to start with a large range and narrow it down.

For example, suppose there are 60 red and 40 yellow balls in the urn for the hypothetical decision. Which alternative will Watt choose? He decides that he prefers living with angina to a gamble that has a 40-percent chance of dying combined with a 60-percent chance of living without angina. Consequently, the lower bound for V moves up to 60 percent.

Now suppose there are 95 red and 5 yellow balls in the urn. Here Watt decides that he would take the gamble, even though it involves a 5-percent chance of dying. Thus, the upper bound for V moves down to 95 percent. Further, Watt decides that if the urn contained 75 red and 25 yellow balls, he would still take the riskless alternative, but if it contained 85 red and 15 yellow balls, he would prefer the risky choice. Consequently, the lower and upper bounds for V are moved closer: to 75 and 85 percent, respectively.

Clearly, V is somewhere between 75 and 85 percent, but exactly where is difficult to say. Should V be 78 percent or 83 percent? As would be expected, Watt has a hard time deciding. Tentatively, he decides that his V should be 80 percent, while making a mental note to go back and rethink this hypothetical decision if his real life choice is at all affected by a small change in V.

Resolving the Dilemma: Recombining the Components

By specifying V, his indifference, or switch, probability, to be 80 percent, Watt has resolved—indirectly but unequivocally—his dilemma. For the hypothetical decision of figure 2–3, Watt has decided that if the probability of living without angina is greater than 80 percent he prefers the risky alternative, but if the probability is less than 80 percent he prefers the riskless one. For his original dilemma—which is structurally identical to his hypothetical decision —the probability of living without angina is 90 percent. Since this probability is better than the indifference probability of 80 percent, Watt should decide to have surgery.

This reasoning is quite straightforward. It is based on a fundamental idea that can be used to help resolve all sorts of decisions. This is the *substitution principle:*[4] If a decision maker is indifferent between two outcomes, he can replace one outcome on his decision tree with the other without affecting his preferences for the alternatives in the decision he faces. For example, suppose you face a decision for which one possible outcome, in addition to a number of different monetary outcomes, is a two-week paid vacation in Bermuda. Then, if you are indifferent about choosing between such a vacation and $5,000 in cash, you could ease the task of thinking about that decision by replacing the outcome of a trip to Bermuda with a $5,000 outcome. Your choice between the original alternatives would not be affected by such a substitution, and you might find it easier to think about your dilemma if the consequences of all the outcomes were monetary.

The substitution principle can be applied to uncertainties as well as outcomes. That is, if a decision maker is indifferent between an uncertain event (with specified outcomes and probabilities) and a particular outcome, he can substitute one for the other, again without affecting his preferences for the alternatives in the decision he faces. For example, Ollerton Watt has decided that he is indifferent between living with angina and drawing a ball from an urn containing 80 red and 20 yellow balls, with a red ball meaning that he will live without angina and a yellow ball meaning that he will die. Consequently, he can substitute the gamble for the certain outcome on his original decision tree without affecting his preferences for that decision. The original decision tree is reproduced as figure 2–4a. Then, in figure 2–4b, the substitution principle is employed—the live,-but-with-angina outcome is replaced with a gamble that gives an 80-percent chance of living without angina and a 20-percent chance of dying. To indicate that the substitution principle has been applied, and that something has been replaced by an equivalent gamble, the no-surgery alternative branch is broken and an equals sign inserted (———— = ————). The important concept behind the substitution principle is that if Watt prefers the lower alternative in figure 2–4a, he should also prefer it in figure 2–4b and vice versa; substituting for an outcome a gamble that, in Watt's mind, is equivalent to that outcome should not change his preferences for the two original alternatives.

The substitution principle is also applied to the uncertain outcome of the have-bypass-surgery alternative. Here the interpretation of judgmental probability is employed. Watt and his doctor agree that his chances of surviving surgery are 90 percent. This, as was stated in figure 2–2, means that Watt is indifferent between the uncertainty of bypass surgery and the uncertainty of an urn with 90 green and 10 white balls (when the outcomes of the two uncertainties are the same). Because of this indifference, Watt can replace the

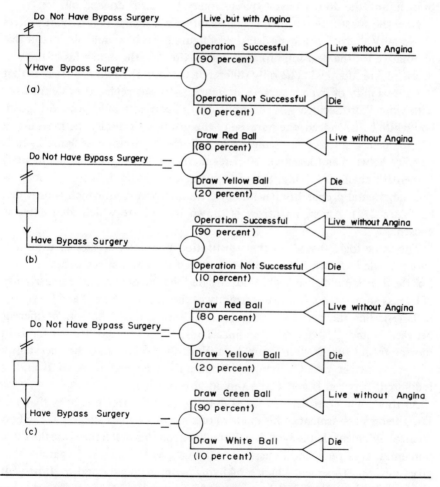

Figure 2–4. The Logic of Using the Substitution Principle to Resolve Ollerton Watt's Angina/Bypass Surgery Decision Dilemma.

first (real) uncertainty on his decision tree with the second (hypothetical) one, again without affecting his choice for the two alternatives. This is done in figure 2–4c.

The choice between the alternatives in figure 2–4c is obvious. The outcomes of the two alternatives are identical. Consequently, the choice can be made simply by comparing the probabilities of getting the best (live-without-angina) outcome. Watt (or anyone) prefers gambling on drawing a green ball from an urn with 90 percent green balls to gambling on drawing a red ball from an urn with only 80 percent red balls. Thus, for the hypothetical dilemma of figure 2–4c, at least, Watt prefers to have bypass surgery. Accordingly, on this decision tree, an arrow is drawn down the have-bypass-surgery alternative branch, and the do-not-have-bypass-surgery branch is crossed off.

Now the substitution principle comes into play. It says that if Watt prefers the surgery alternative for the decision of figure 2–4c, he should also prefer this alternative for the decision of figure 2–4b. After all, the outcomes of the two decisions are identical. The only difference between the two decisions is that the uncertainty of bypass surgery in figure 2–4b was replaced in figure 2–4c with what Watt decided was the equivalent uncertainty of an urn with green and white balls. Indeed, the purpose of the urn was to specify the meaning of a 90-percent chance of surviving surgery. Since the decision of figure 2–4b is a choice between an (objective) 80-percent chance of living and a (judgmental) 90-percent chance of living, the greater chance of living is better (as long as this judgmental probability has an objective interpretation, which is provided by figure 2–2). Again, an arrow is drawn to indicate which alternative is chosen.

The same logic (based on the substitution principle) applies in using the choice made in figure 2–4b to decide between the alternatives in figure 2–4a. For the decision in figure 2–4b, Watt decided that he preferred the uncertainty of bypass surgery (A), to the uncertainty of the urn with 80 red and 20 yellow balls (B). For the decision in figure 2–3, Watt decided he was indifferent between B and C, living with angina. Thus, when C is substituted for B in moving from figure 2–4b to figure 2–4a, Watt should prefer A, the uncertainty of bypass surgery, to C, living with angina. If he prefers A to B and is indifferent between B and C, he should also prefer A to C.

At this point Watt decides to rethink his analysis. He concludes that Dr. Dwightson's assessment of his chances of surviving bypass surgery is the best medical judgment that is available. But what about his preferences for the three outcomes? Is he really indifferent between living with angina and a gamble that gives him an 80-percent chance of living without angina and a 20-percent chance of dying? Should V be perhaps 83 percent or 78?

It does not make any difference! The decision is the same whether V is 80 or 83 or 78 percent. In fact, as long as Watt is convinced that V is less than

90 percent, then he prefers to have the surgery. Thus, when rethinking his analysis, Watt decides to concentrate his attention on V, his indifference probability. And although Watt is not sure exactly where, between 75 and 85 percent, V ought to be, he is satisfied that V is indeed less than 90 percent. Thus, Watt is satisfied with his decision to have bypass surgery.[5]

Decisions and Uncertainty

No decision maker can perfectly predict the future. Yet, for any decision you must make, your choice depends upon what you believe will be the future consequences of your current actions. If you are a manufacturing executive attempting to plan next year's production schedule, you cannot know for sure whether the price of a raw material will rise or fall, whether a competitor will introduce a new product, or what the level of consumer demand will be. You can make an educated guess, but you cannot know for sure. As Professor Robert O. Schlaifer of the Harvard Business School has written, "Virtually all important business decisions are made under uncertainty."[6]

When faced with uncertainty, it is difficult to make good predictions. In 1966, the Boeing Company decided to market the 747 based on its engineers' estimates of the costs of manufacturing the airplane. These estimates proved to be too low by nearly a half. Consequently, by mid-1975, although the company had received almost 300 orders for the plane, it had yet to recover its nearly $1 billion in start-up costs. Explained William McPherson Allen, the retired chairman of Boeing:

> I have the greatest confidence in the ability of Boeing to design good, sound airplanes and—along with this—its ability to produce them efficiently. I don't have much confidence in our ability to prophesy the costs.[7]

For public policy decisions, predictions are also important. Recognizing this, Congress has given the Congressional Budget Office the responsibility of predicting the cost of every piece of legislation reported out of the various committees of the Senate and House of Representatives. And financial costs of new policies are not the only consequences that need to be predicted. When Congress was deciding whether to establish the U.S. Postal Service, it had to predict not only how much the new, quasi-public corporation would cost to operate, but how well it would deliver the mail.

In government, as in business, accurate predictions are difficult to obtain. In their book on the implementation of public programs, Jeffrey L. Pressman and Aaron B. Wildavsky observe, "Our assumptions about new public programs are far removed from reality. We assume that the people ostensibly in charge can predict the consequences of their actions and that often is not the case."[8]

The problem of uncertainty complicates personal decisions as well. Selecting a new job, purchasing a car or life insurance, and deciding whether to undergo open heart surgery all require that you make predictions about which you cannot be certain. Consequently, if your decision—be it personal, business, or governmental—is sufficiently important to warrant some analysis, you will definitely want to think systematically about the uncertainties involved. The predictions you make—the probabilities you assess for the various possible outcomes—can significantly influence your decision.

How probabilities can affect a decision is illustrated by an explanation suggested by syndicated columnist Joseph Alsop for the differences in French and American policies toward the Middle East in October 1974.

> If you want to understand some of the more nasty recent developments, there is a simple place to start. It can be said on very high authority that the French government of President Valery Giscard D'Estaing thinks there is close to a 100 percent chance of renewed war in the Mideast.
>
> If you think that there is a 50 percent chance of the dam breaking, and the countryside therefore being drowned, your natural impulse is to try desperately to strengthen the dam. That has been, and is, the policy of Secretary of State Henry A. Kissinger.
>
> In contrast, if you think the dam is absolutely sure to break, you snatch up what you can and head for the high ground. That is the French policy. . . .[9]

But how do you react when you think there is a 75-percent chance of the dam breaking? Or a 90-percent chance? The probability of an event occurring can be anywhere from 0 to 100 percent; at what point do you switch from attempting to strengthen the dam to heading for the high ground?

How the decision maker assesses the probabilities is not the only factor affecting a choice complicated by uncertainty. How the decision maker values the various outcomes is also important. The third special prosecutor in the Watergate investigations, Henry S. Ruth, Jr., has suggested how different preferences for outcomes can result in different decisions about whether to prosecute a criminal case, even when there is agreement about the probabilities: "Some people say that if a prosecutor has a one percent chance of success he should proceed. I don't happen to share that."[10] Different decisions about whether to prosecute could result from different evaluations of the pluses of a conviction and the minuses of an acquittal when compared with the certain consequence of not prosecuting at all.

The Basic Decision Dilemma

The Prosecutor's Dilemma

When given a criminal case, a public prosecutor (or district attorney) has two alternatives: one that is risky, and one that is riskless. The riskless alternative is not to prosecute, for the outcome is certain: no decision. The risky alternative is to prosecute, for this can result in one of two possible outcomes: conviction, which is the best possible outcome, or acquittal, which is the worst. The basic features of the prosecutor's decision dilemma are quite simple, even if making the decision is not.

Indeed, a decision tree for the prosecutor's dilemma (figure 2–5) is identical to the one used to analyze the angina/bypass surgery dilemma. For both decisions there are two alternatives. One of these alternatives is riskless; it results in a certain outcome. The other alternative is risky; it can result in an outcome that is better or in one that is worse than the interjacent outcome of the riskless alternative. (In figure 2–5 and in other decision trees throughout this book, we place some descriptive information in square brackets under a branch. For example, [Risky] alternative and [Best Consequence].)

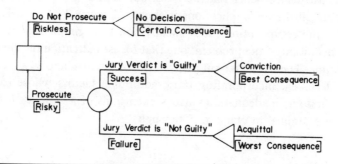

Figure 2–5. The Prosecutor's Decision Dilemma.

Obviously, the prosecutor's decision will depend upon his assessment of the probability of conviction and his preference for the three consequences. Watergate prosecutor Henry Ruth looked at it one way. In Dashiell Hammett's *The Maltese Falcon*, Sam Spade explained to Casper Gutman how other prosecutors view this same decision:

Bryan is like most district attorneys. He's more interested in how his record will look on paper than in anything else. He'd rather drop a doubtful case than try it and have it go against him.[11]

Ruth might prosecute if the probability of success was 40 percent; Bryan might not do so even if that probability was 90 percent. Of course, the prosecutor's decision problem could be more complex. For example, for the risky alternative, prosecute, the prosecutor might want to consider a third possible outcome: a hung jury or a mistrial. There might be another decision alternative: plea bargain. Also, it might not be possible to consider the case in isolation from others; after winning the current case, the prosecutor might have to decide whether or not to prosecute an accomplice.

Similarly, the angina/bypass surgery dilemma involved many more factors than were incorporated into the original decision tree. In his first-cut analysis, Ollerton Watt ignored his concern for finishing his book and the possibility that the bypass operation might not cure his angina. If Watt had considered it important, he could have attached another consequence branch to each terminal node to indicate whether he would complete his book. Also, he could have considered another alternative: delay surgery until his book was finished. Indeed, he might have wanted to consider the uncertainty about whether he would ever be able to complete it. Finally, he could also have added another outcome branch to the uncertainty node that results from electing surgery, in order to incorporate the possibility that the operation neither succeeds nor fails, the consequence being that he lives, but with angina. A decision tree incorporating all these complications is shown in figure 2–6.

Whatever the complications, it is usually best to begin an analysis with a simplified definition of the problem, one that focuses attention on the essence of the dilemma. Then, if a first-cut analysis proves unsatisfactory, a second cut can be undertaken, incorporating those additional factors whose exclusion makes the first cut inadequate. (Various extensions of a simplified, first-cut analysis are examined in chapters 5 through 12.)

The Basic Decision Dilemma

Like the prosecutor's and bypass surgery dilemmas, many decisions involve a choice between a riskless alternative on the one hand and a risky alternative with only two possible outcomes on the other. This is the simplest of all decisions involving uncertainty, yet it captures the fundamental reason many important decisions are dilemmas. Moreover, this simple, basic dilemma is a component of every more-complicated decision that involves uncertainty; consequently, it is called *the basic decision dilemma*. Similarly, of all the possible decision trees involving uncertainty, the one for the basic dilemma is the simplest; it has the least number of branches and thus is called *the basic decision sapling* (see figure 2–7).

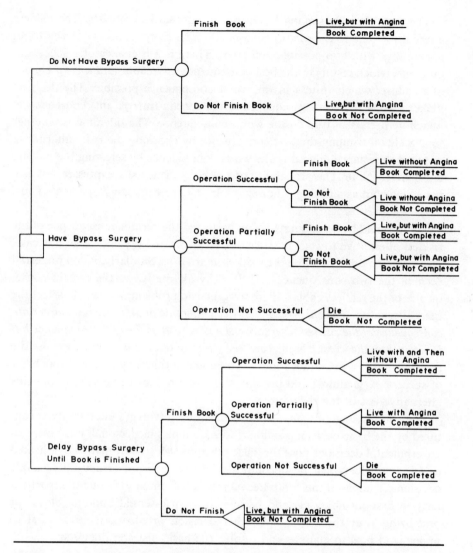

Figure 2–6. A Possible Second-Cut Decision Tree for Ollerton Watt's Angina/Bypass Surgery Decision Dilemma.

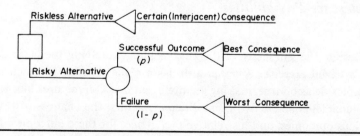

Figure 2–7. The Basic Decision Sapling.

The basic decision sapling has only two alternative branches. The riskless alternative leads to a certain consequence. The risky alternative leads to an uncertainty with two possible outcomes. There is a p chance of a successful outcome, which results in the best consequence attainable, and a $1-p$ chance of a failure, which results in the worst consequence possible. The decision maker prefers the best consequence to the certain (interjacent) consequence, which he prefers in turn to the worst consequence. The dilemma is whether to gamble on winning the best consequence by choosing the risky alternative or avoid the chance of getting the worst consequence by selecting the riskless alternative. (Note: The probability of success, p, is usually expressed not as a percentage but as a decimal. For example, 0.75 rather than 75 percent. Thus, $1-p$ becomes 0.25.)

There would be no dilemma if you preferred the certain consequence of the riskless alternative to *both* possible outcomes of the risky choice; in this case, you would obviously choose the riskless alternative. Similarly, if you preferred *each* of the two consequences of the risky alternative to the certain consequence of the riskless choice, there would be no problem; you would select the risky alternative. *The only reason there is a dilemma at all is because the certain consequence of the riskless alternative is not as good as the best consequence but is better than the worst.* (Note: the "risky alternative" is so named because the decision maker is uncertain about the outcome of this choice. If the probability of success, p, is almost 100 percent, the risk may not be very high, but this alternative is still the risky one.)

The quintessence of many decision dilemmas involving uncertainty is captured by the basic decision sapling. Indeed, numerous personal, business, and governmental decisions pose the basic dilemma. Moreover, many complicated decision problems can be decomposed into a series of structurally simple decision dilemmas of this kind. Because it is confronted so frequently (particularly in first-cut analyses) and because it is an essential building block for organizing your thinking about other decision problems, it is essential to understand how to analyze and resolve the basic decision dilemma.

Preference-Probabilities

Despite the simplicity of the basic sapling, resolving the basic dilemma is not a trivial exercise. Whether a decision maker is using a basic sapling or a complex decision tree, making an intelligent decision requires him to integrate his judgments about two quite different factors: the chances of realizing the various outcomes, and his relative preferences for these outcomes. No matter how simple or complicated the decision tree, the same judgments about uncertainties and preferences must be made. Both these tasks are demanding, in part because humans are simply not in the habit of clearly specifying their predictions and preferences. When confronted with decisions involving uncertainty, the human mind attempts to cope with the entanglement by focusing on one or maybe two characteristics of the alternatives while ignoring the others.[12] After all, even if some scheme could be developed to specify probabilities and another to specify preferences, how could these two rather different devices then be combined to make a decision? Making specific judgments hardly seems worth it if they lead you nowhere.

The beauty of using probabilities to specify preferences is that they lead you somewhere. If probabilities can provide a means to assess preferences, the results can easily be integrated with the probabilities used to assess uncertainties. Since both are probabilities, with unambiguous interpretations, whether they reflect judgments about uncertainties or preference is unimportant. The various probabilities can be combined (as described in chapters 5 and 6) and compared to help make the decision.

When analyzing a decision dilemma, it is necessary to specify one's relative preferences only for those outcomes that can possibly result from the decision. There is no need to compare these outcomes, such as "acquittal" or "live without angina," with the disaster of nuclear war or the blessings of eradicating cancer. To resolve the bypass surgery dilemma, the prosecutor's dilemma, or any other basic decision dilemma, a decision maker need only specify his relative preferences for the three possible outcomes. Indeed, it is really only necessary to make a single judgment about preferences: to decide how good the interjacent outcome is, compared with the best and the worst outcomes.

To do this, decision analysts define a hypothetical *reference gamble*.[13] Such a gamble has two *reference outcomes:* the *Best* reference outcome, which is often the best outcome that can possibly result from the actual decision, and the *Worst* reference outcome, which is usually the worst outcome that can result from the actual decision. (Hereafter, *Best* and *Worst* will be used to mean the best and worst reference outcomes of the reference gamble that is being used to help analyze the original decision.) The outcome of this reference

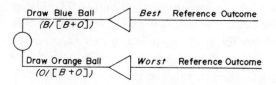

Figure 2–8. A Reference Gamble.

gamble is determined by drawing a ball from an urn. The urn might contain blue and orange balls, where drawing a blue ball would result in the *Best* outcome and drawing an orange ball would result in the *Worst* (see figure 2–8).

To specify a preference for any outcome that is interjacent to the *Best* and the *Worst,* the decision maker needs to decide what probability of drawing a blue ball from the urn makes him indifferent between the certainty of the interjacent outcome and the uncertainty of the reference gamble (see the hypothetical decision in figure 2–9). If the probability of drawing a blue ball is too low, the decision maker will prefer the interjacent outcome; if this probability is too high, he will prefer the reference gamble. Somewhere in between is his indifference probability.

We have chosen to call this indifference probability a *preference-probability,* for it is not only used to specify preferences but is also a probability.[14] Since the letter p has come to be standard notation for a probability, we have chosen the letter V to denote a preference-probability, for it indicates the *value* of a particular outcome to the decision maker.

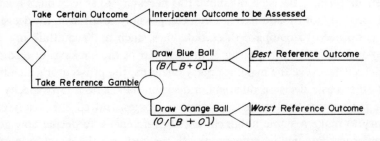

Figure 2–9. Using a Reference Gamble to Assess a Preference-Probability for an Interjacent Outcome.

A preference-probability provides a measure of a decision maker's preference for a particular outcome—an unambiguous statement about how the decision maker evaluates that outcome compared with the *Best* and the *Worst* reference outcomes. The scale for preference-probabilities goes from 0 to 1.0 (just as does the scale for any other probability). The higher a preference-probability is, the better the decision maker thinks that outcome is. If the preference-probability for an outcome is 1.0, that outcome is just as good as the *Best* reference outcome; if the preference-probability for an outcome is 0, that outcome is equivalent in value to the *Worst* outcome.

To see this, note what happens if the interjacent outcome of the hypothetical decision in figure 2–9 is replaced with the *Best* reference outcome. In this situation, what is the decision maker's indifference probability? Exactly 1.0. The only way that anyone can be indifferent between these two choices is if

The Basic Decision Dilemma

there are only blue balls and no orange balls in the urn; that is, if the probability of drawing a blue ball is 1.0. (Similar logic indicates that the preference-probability for the *Worst* reference outcome must be 0.) Thus, any outcome the decision maker thinks is equivalent to his *Best* reference outcome also has a preference-probability of 1.0.

The virtue of preference-probabilities is that a decision maker can assess one for any outcome that is interjacent to the *Best* and the *Worst* reference outcome. Then the substitution principle applies: If a decision maker has assessed a preference-probability, V, for a particular outcome, he is indifferent between that outcome for certain and a reference gamble with a V chance of the *Best* and a $1 - V$ chance of the *Worst;* consequently, this outcome can be replaced with the equivalent reference gamble. In fact, all the interjacent outcomes of a decision can be replaced with their equivalent reference gambles. The result of this use of the substitution principle is that the decision has been converted into one for which the only possible outcomes are the *Best* reference outcome and the *Worst* reference outcome. The decision can thus be made easily by selecting the alternative that gives the highest chance of getting the *Best* outcome.

This is what was done to resolve Ollerton Watt's bypass surgery dilemma. The interjacent outcome, living with angina, was replaced with what Watt decided was his equivalent reference gamble: an 80-percent chance of living without angina (the *Best*) and a 20-percent chance of dying (the *Worst*). Watt then decided that he preferred having bypass surgery, since that alternative actually led to a (real) reference gamble with a 90-percent chance of the *Best*, while not having surgery was equivalent (in his mind, at least) to a reference gamble with only an 80-percent chance of the *Best*. (In later chapters, we will discuss how this logic can be used to resolve dilemmas with uncertainties of even greater complexity.)

In a sense, Watt made his decision by comparing preference-probabilities for his two alternatives. His preference-probability for the riskless, no-surgery alternative (which guarantees him the interjacent outcome) is 80 percent; he assessed this using the reference gamble. Determining the preference-probability for the risky, surgery alternative is even easier; this alternative leads directly to a (nonhypothetical) reference gamble with a 90-percent chance of the *Best* and a 10-percent chance of the *Worst*. Thus, the preference-probability for the risky alternative is 90 percent, which is better than the 80-percent preference-probability for the riskless alternative. Using the best and worst outcomes of a basic dilemma as the *Best* and *Worst* outcomes for the reference gamble facilitates the analysis; for then the risky alternative leads directly to a reference gamble, and thus the only remaining task is to assess (1) the probability of getting the best from the risky alternative, and (2) the preference-probability for the riskless choice.

Actually, to resolve his dilemma satisfactorily, Watt did not have to specify that p, his probability of surviving surgery, was 90 percent and that V, his preference-probability for the interjacent outcome, was 80 percent. All he really needed to do was determine which was greater. If Watt is convinced that $p > V$, then the risky alternative with a p chance of the *Best* is better than the riskless alternative. If, on the other hand, he decides that $V > p$, he prefers the riskless choice, since it is equivalent to a reference gamble with a V chance of the *Best*. As long as Watt can specify which probability is greater, he need not specify each separately.

To resolve decisions that are more complex than the basic dilemma, however, it is necessary to specify probabilities and preference-probabilities. Consequently, there is real value in learning to be as specific as possible about indifference points, even when analyzing a basic dilemma. Most people are not in the habit of thinking about indifference probabilities. Indeed, thinking about uncertainty in terms of specific probabilities is difficult. What really is the difference between an 85-percent chance and one of 90 percent? To be able to decide what probability makes you indifferent between a sure outcome and a reference gamble takes practice.

No one would really want to start off using decision analysis to make a life-and-death decision such as whether to have bypass surgery. People need to experiment personally with the principles of decision analysis, to develop their own analytical skills, to test and evolve their own decision-making style. Only after practice in thinking analytically about numerous minor and simple decisions will people develop the confidence necessary to use quick analysis to help make the truly significant decisions they face.

Basic Decision Dilemmas in Business

Numerous decisions made by business executives are basic dilemmas. Whether a corporation should make a bid to take over another firm is one good example. In 1968, Chris-Craft Industries was considering an attempt to take over control of Piper Aircraft Corporation. To be successful, Chris-Craft would have to purchase 51 percent of the 1.64 million shares of outstanding stock in Piper. If, however, the takeover bid were unsuccessful, that is, if Chris-Craft were unable to obtain control of Piper, then it would be stuck with a significant amount of cash (it raised $40 million for the tender offer) tied up in Piper stock, which it could not sell without lowering the price of the stock and suffering a large loss.

This corporate takeover decision can be described by a basic sapling (see

The Basic Decision Dilemma

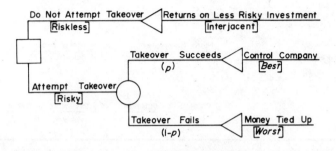

Figure 2–10. The Corporate Takeover Decision Dilmma.

figure 2–10). As with any other basic dilemma, the choice will depend upon how the firm assesses the probability of successfully completing the takeover, and upon how it appraises its relative preferences for the profits to be made from controlling the other company (the best outcome), the losses to be incurred if its money is tied up because the takeover bid fails (the worst outcome) and the returns that could be earned from an alternative, less-risky investment (the certain, interjacent consequence). Obviously, the profits to be made from controlling the target company must be larger than those available through other investments; otherwise, there would be no dilemma.

In 1969, Chris-Craft launched an effort to take over Piper. Piper, however, resisted and eventually organized a friendly or "white knight" takeover by Bangor Punta Corporation. Chris-Craft ended up with 45 percent of Piper's stock—not enough to control the firm—and over $40 million tied up in the enterprise.[15]

In 1980, a consortium of Japanese firms, led by one of the nation's biggest trading companies, Mitsui & Company, faced a basic dilemma concerning a $3.5 billion petrochemical plant it was building in Iran. Construction of the plant was begun in the mid-1970s but was delayed, first by the Iranian revolution and then by that nation's war with Iraq, during which the plant was bombed five times. Consequently, the Mitsui group, which had already invested $1.4 billion in the plant, faced the decision of whether to attempt to complete the project (which had been 85-percent finished when the war broke out and could have been completed within six months). (See the basic sapling in figure 2–11.) The risky alternative, to invest still more funds in the plant, had two possible outcomes: The project is finished, the consequence being a profit (the best); or it is not finished, the consequence being a loss of several billion dollars (the worst). The riskless alternative, to cancel the project, had as a consequence a $1.4 billion loss, which was interjacent to the other two. One executive commented: "If we continue the construction, we'll fall into hell. If we withdraw, we'll fall into hell."[16] (One of the complications that can

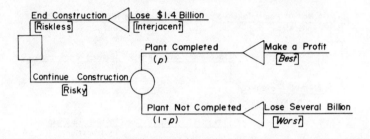

Figure 2–11. Mitsui's Iranian Petrochemical Plant Dilemma.

distort an analysis of this dilemma is the $1.4 billion already sunk into the project. For a discussion of why "sunk costs don't count," see the appendix to chapter 8.)

A final example of a basic dilemma in business concerns the choice a number of book publishers faced in the late winter and early spring of 1976. Several journalists and writers were interested in preparing a campaign biography of Jimmy Carter, and numerous publishers were approached with proposals. It was clear that sales of a Carter biography would be high only if Carter won the Democratic presidential nomination, though in that case sales would be *very* high.

To resolve this basic dilemma (see the sapling in figure 2–12), each publishing house needed to appraise its relative preferences for three outcomes: the large profit to be earned from a biography of Carter the presidential nominee; the loss to be incurred from a biography if he were not nominated; and the normal profit that would be earned by publishing a less risky book. Further, because of the leadtime required to write and publish the biography, each publisher needed to assess the probability that Carter would win the Democratic nomination long before the results of the state conventions and primaries were in.

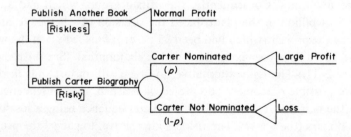

Figure 2–12. The Book Publisher's Dilemma.

The Basic Decision Dilemma

All the major publishing houses reached the same conclusion: The chance of Carter capturing the nomination was too small to risk the investment. One writer started looking for a publisher in March 1976 and in mid-May was still being told that Carter did not have a good enough chance. One observer concluded, "The publishing industry was pretty much asleep about Carter."[17] (More on the book publisher's dilemma in chapters 6, 7, and 9.)

Basic Decision Dilemmas in Government

Public officials, too, are frequently confronted with basic decision dilemmas. There is, for example, the problem that Mount Baker in northwest Washington posed for the U.S. Forest Service in the spring of 1975. Mount Baker, a dormant volcano, was showing signs that it might act up again. Snow was melting, ice was shifting, and clay, ash, and sulfur were shooting into the air. Officials feared that, even if the volcano did not erupt, part of the Sherman Crater's rim might collapse, causing a massive mud slide. A University of Washington geophysicist observed: "This phenomenal increase in thermal activity on Mount Baker is all so very unusual. We have nothing in the historical record to compare it with. We have no way of knowing what will happen."[18] A spokesman for the U.S. Geological Survey provided a more useful assessment for Forest Service decision makers: "Geological Survey scientists have concluded there is a one-in-100 probability in 1975 that a mudflow will be generated on the slopes of Mt. Baker that will be capable of traveling the eight miles to Baker Lake."[19]

Despite the uncertainty, officials had to decide whether to close for the summer the recreation and resort areas surrounding Baker Lake. Again, the basic sapling is applicable (see figure 2–13). Structuring the decision as a basic

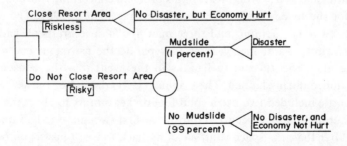

Figure 2–13. The Mount Baker Decision Dilemma.

decision dilemma could have helped Forest Service officials think analytically about whether to close the resort area. (They eventually did close it.) (More on the Mount Baker dilemma in chapter 5.)

When the Bay Area Rapid Transit (BART) system was being constructed in the early 1970s, public officials faced a basic dilemma of a different sort. Gophers in the San Francisco-Oakland area have a habit of eating electrical cables. BART officials needed to decide whether to encase their control signals in metal or in plastic sheathing. Metal was more expensive, but it was also known to be gopher-proof. And, of course, if the gophers ate through the plastic, all the cables would have to be replaced with the more expensive, metal casing (see figure 2–14).

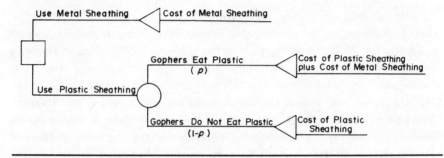

Figure 2–14. BART's Cable Sheathing Decision Dilemma.

BART officials gambled on the plastic sheathing—and lost. The gophers ate through it, and eight miles of cables had to be replaced at an additional cost of $700,000. Thus, for this uncomplicated decision, the difference between the best and the worst outcome was $700,000. Though the structure of the decision problem was simple, the outcome was not inconsequential.[20]

Another example of a basic dilemma in government is the National Aeronautics and Space Administration's problem concerning the launch-abort system for the space shuttle, which took its first flight in 1981. The one-man *Mercury,* two-man *Gemini,* and three-man *Apollo* spacecrafts all had special rocket or ejection-seat mechanisms to separate the astronaut compartment from the main rockets and fuel tanks in the event that the booster rocket malfunctioned during launch. The original (1971) design for the seven-person space shuttle included two extra solid-fuel rocket motors to abort the mission if a booster malfunction occurred during the first two-and-one-half minutes of flight. (After that, the space shuttle can fly back to earth just as on one of its returns.) But in 1973, NASA made a controversial decision to abort the space shuttle's launch-abort system.[21]

Clearly, this is a basic dilemma (see figure 2–15). The riskless alternative is

The Basic Decision Dilemma

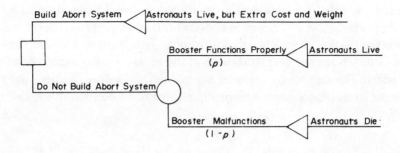

Figure 2–15. NASA's Shuttle Abort-System Decision Dilemma.

to build the abort system; this results in the certain (or at least almost certain) outcome that the astronauts will survive the launch, though there are additional expenses involved. This is why the interjacent outcome is not as good as the booster-functions-properly outcome, which results from the risky, do-not-build-abort-system alternative. Still, the certain outcome of the riskless decision is better than the worst, astronauts-die outcome of the risky alternative.

The probability of booster malfunction is quite low; of the first fifty-eight manned space flights launched by the United States and the USSR, none was aborted during launch, though each nation did have one near miss. Further, the additional cost, in weight and dollars, of building the launch-abort system is significant; the original abort system weighed 96,000 pounds compared with the 190,000 pounds that the shuttle, occupants, and equipment weigh (without the abort system). The decision is thus not obvious. It is impossible to build a perfectly fail-safe space shuttle. There are a lot of design decisions about what risks to take and what ones to avoid. Clearly, for this decision, the less the weight of the launch-abort system and the greater the probability of booster malfunction, the more apt people are to select the riskless alternative.

Other consequences of the various outcomes (such as the loss of the spacecraft and the failure of the mission if the booster malfunctions) could be noted but these do not influence the decision regarding whether to build the launch-abort system. There is another complication, however, that can influence the decision: If a booster malfunctions, will a launch-abort system work properly and save the astronauts' lives? Including this factor in the analysis requires more than a basic sapling; a second-cut analysis of this problem will be discussed in chapter 5.

Presidents and governors must resolve basic decision dilemmas when they decide whether to sign or veto a bill—the riskless alternative is to sign it; the risky choice is the veto, with the outcome being the best or the worst, depending upon whether the veto is sustained or overridden. Similarly, a representative from a "safe" congressional district must resolve a basic dilemma when deciding whether to seek reelection or run for the Senate—running for reelection is the riskless alternative; the risky choice is to campaign for the Senate, with victory being the best outcome, and losing (and thus being out of office) the worst. Throughout government and politics, as well as business and our personal lives, people must continually resolve basic decision dilemmas.

Applying the Concepts of Analytical Thinking

If you are familiar with any of these specific decision dilemmas, you may be distressed because one or several factors that you consider important have been ignored. In some cases, complicating considerations have been consciously omitted from an initial analysis of the problem and will be introduced in later chapters. But this is the way that an analysis should proceed. To think analytically about any decision dilemma it is helpful to consider first only the essential features of the problem. Once the most significant aspects of the decision puzzle are understood, additional complexity can be introduced—but only if the additional insight gained is worth the time and resources that further analysis will consume. The initial process of simplification is crucial. As the quick analysis for the angina/bypass surgery dilemma illustrates, it is important to prune from the decision tree all the extraneous branches, which conceal the essential character of the dilemma, and then to undertake a complete, first-cut analysis, using only this simplified formulation of the problem.

The approach taken to resolve the structurally simple but perplexing angina/bypass surgery dilemma dramatizes how the five concepts of analytical thinking can be applied to help make decisions:

- Thinking means identifying why the decision is a dilemma—determining that, at its most fundamental level, the choice is between an essentially riskless alternative and a risky one with two possible outcomes.
- Decomposing means separating the decision into its alternatives, uncertainties, outcomes, and consequences—using a decision tree to break the dilemma down into its basic components.
- Simplifying means determining which factors are most important—concentrating attention on those few, key uncertainties, outcomes, and consequences that create the dilemma.
- Specifying means making unambiguous judgments about the values of the key factors—assessing judgmental probabilities for the uncertainties and preference-probabilities for the outcomes.
- Rethinking means considering whether your first-cut analysis was sensible—determining if you are satisfied with the judgments to which your decision is most sensitive.

The Basic Decision Dilemma

These concepts provide the intellectual framework for thinking analytically about a wide variety of decision dilemmas. The application of these concepts to the bypass surgery dilemma has already introduced the fundamental ideas of decision analysis; this chapter has outlined all the principles necessary to analyze any dilemma created by uncertainty.

Much of this book is devoted to extending these simple ideas to decisions for which multiple uncertainties or multiple consequences create a dilemma that is structurally more complex than the basic dilemma. Still, the basic decision dilemma remains the core problem. It is useful for thinking about every decision presented in this chapter and for many more to come. After all, thinking analytically about decision dilemmas is a skill. It requires practice. Clearly, it is best to learn to sail a small dinghy with a single sail before you undertake to sail a ketch with a mainsail, mizzen, spinnaker, and two jibs. It is important to learn how to set a single sail under a variety of conditions— in light air or in a heavy breeze, when close-hauled or reaching and running —before attempting to adjust a number of different sails at the same time. Similarly, it makes sense to develop the ability to resolve basic decision dilemmas that require the determination of only a single preference-probability before attempting to evaluate the numerous preference-probabilities required to resolve more-complex dilemmas.

Chapter 3

Resolving the Basic Dilemma: Mayor Willis's Decision

PAYNE WILLIS had to make the decision by noon. The application was due at the Department of Transportation (DOT) at the end of the day and if it was not on the 1:00 plane to Washington, Zenith City would get neither traffic safety project and his reelection campaign would be in real trouble. The mayor had on his desk the two completed applications and a memo from the traffic department concerning both proposals. But the memo was really not much help. The traffic commissioner had recommended the Street Improvement Plan because he was certain that DOT would make the grant for that project. The commissioner, Willis knew, did not want to recommend the Experimental Safety Program and have Washington reject it. His traffic chief did not like to take risks. "When it comes to making decisions," Willis would often complain, "O'Conahue is simply too conservative."

Willis understood the large risk in submitting the Experimental Safety Program to DOT. The memo from the traffic department explained it well. If, however, DOT accepted the city's application for this new and innovative proposal, which involved not only street improvements but also a special seat-belt effort and a major alcohol-and-driving campaign, it would be a real plus for the city—and for the mayor's own reelection campaign. But if he submitted the application and DOT rejected it—and the mayor thought this was more likely—the city would be without any traffic safety program and the jobs, both public and private, that it would provide. And then Willis would be in a really tough reelection fight against Joe "Flash" Mann, the hero of Zenith University's only national football championship team and the nephew of the state's junior senator, who was already passing out bumper stickers with the slogan, HE CAN DO MORE FOR ZENITH CITY.

The mayor's initial gut feeling was to submit the Street Improvement Plan. After a little thought, he changed his mind to the Experimental Safety Program. Still, as he reviewed the two applications once more, Willis was worried that submitting the Street Improvement Plan was really the safest, and perhaps the best, choice. He decided to submit it and started to move on to other business, when he had an inspiration.

Willis called Chris Rocke into his office. A recent graduate of a leading business school, Rocke had specialized in public management and policy analysis and had been hired by the mayor as a policy aide only a few weeks before. At a cocktail party the previous Saturday, Rocke had outlined the basic ideas of decision analysis to Willis, and the mayor was curious to see if this new-fangled approach could help him with his decision.

ROCKE: Well, what do you think you should do?
WILLIS: I think I probably ought to accept O'Conahue's advice. The Experimental Safety Plan would be really great for the city, but I don't think that it is worth the risk. There's a pretty good chance we could end up with nothing and that would be terrible. And, after all, the Street Improvement Plan is not so bad.
ROCKE: What you're saying is that you think "not so bad" is better than a "not very likely" chance of "really great" when this is combined with a "pretty good chance" of "terrible."
WILLIS: I guess that is what I mean, but that makes it sound so muddled. No one would call that type of reasoning "analytical."
ROCKE: Okay then, let's try to organize your thinking. What are the important features of your decision?

The mayor reviewed his problem for Rocke, and the aide listed the essential details and assessments as follows:

1. DOT will certainly approve the Street Improvement Plan if it is submitted.
2. It is "not very likely" that DOT will approve the Experimental Safety Program.
3. There is a "pretty good chance" that DOT will reject the Experimental Safety Program.
4. The mayor can submit only one proposal and if it is rejected the city must wait until next year to submit another.
5. If approved, the Experimental Safety Program would be "really great" and clearly superior to the Street Improvement Plan.
6. The Street Improvement Plan is "not so bad" and certainly better than nothing.
7. To submit the Experimental Safety Program and have it rejected would be "terrible."

8. Thus, when the three possible consequences are ranked, the order of the mayor's preferences is:
   1. Experimental Safety Program, "really great" (best);
   2. Street Improvement Plan, "not so bad" (interjacent);
   3. No safety program, "terrible" (worst).
9. The dilemma is that, though the Experimental Safety Program is best, it is not certain that the city will get it; it is, however, certain that the Street Improvement Plan will be approved.

Rocke then summarized all this information in a decision sapling describing all the essential features of the mayor's decision dilemma.

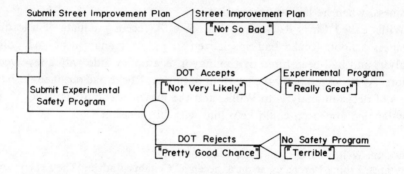

Figure 3–1. Mayor Willis's Traffic Safety Dilemma.

The Dynamics of Analysis

As usually presented, analysis (no matter what the approach or technique) appears to be linearly deductive rather than dynamically iterative. The analytical tool is introduced as a recipe—clear, sequential, and mechanical—with the assumptions necessary to use the tool provided in a convenient, checklist form. Even the concepts of analytical thinking, because they are presented in a list, can be misinterpreted as "the five *consecutive* steps of analytical thinking." But these concepts need to be applied simultaneously and iteratively, as the last imperative, rethink, clearly implies.

Too often analysis appears to be no more creative than adding up a column of numbers: "Just follow the formula." You may want to check each of the steps to make sure of the addition, or even to add up the columns backwards as a double-check. But once you are convinced that your arithmetic is correct, your problem is solved.

Resolving the Basic Dilemma

Real dilemmas do not have a "solution." They may be "resolved"—given the limits of information, time, the state-of-the-analytical-art, and the importance of the problem itself—to the satisfaction of the decision maker. But dilemmas cannot, by definition, be "solved" in the sense that there is, or can be, one universally accepted result. Indeed, from the beginning—from the very definition of the problem—any analytical thinking involves so many subtle subdecisions that no formula can capture the necessary creativity. Analysis is not a mechanical procedure but a dynamic process.

The dynamics of analysis are difficult to communicate, particularly in a book, article, or lecture. Such formal presentations are just too neat, too clean. There are no mistakes, no backtracking, no discoveries while walking home, no changing one's mind. The fifty-minute lecture or the editor's page limit permits nothing but the sanitized version of a completed (but originally messy) analysis. Yet even if an analytical tool is easy to understand in the abstract, it may be difficult to apply in practice. Indeed, if the mechanics are simple, it may be impossible to convince people that the dynamics can be quite complex.

This chapter is devoted to analyzing and resolving the basic decision dilemma confronting Mayor Willis. To dramatize the dynamic process of analysis, we have consciously chosen a dialogue format, for it illustrates the evolutionary thought process involved in working through such a problem. Discovering something about one part of the problem may cause you to go back and rethink other parts. For example, in the process of assessing one probability, you may think of something that makes you return and reassess some other probability, or even revise your decision tree.

Many readers will be tempted to skip to the next chapter. *Please do not ignore the ideas presented here.* The dialogue between the mayor and his policy aide illustrates the careful, iterative process of analytical thinking. It explains not only what needs to be done, but how it can be done.

Decision making is as much an art as a science, but that does not mean it should be unsystematic. To resolve a decision dilemma, you must make a number of relatively simple subdecisions.[1] Decision analysis involves decomposing the problem into the relevant subdecisions, thinking about these simpler decisions, and then recombining the results of these subdecisions to resolve the dilemma. But the process is not as mechanical as this one-two-three-step description would suggest. Which subdecisions should be made? Which subdecisions are more critical and thus deserve more thought? Are there different ways of thinking about these subdecisions—would thinking about some other, hypothetical decisions help sharpen your judgments about the actual problem? Are your subdecisions consistent—are there other questions that could be asked to help determine if your judgments truly reflect your beliefs about uncertainty and your preferences for outcomes? Any analysis involves a lot of rethinking—a lot of analysis of the analysis.

In this chapter, while the mayor thinks about how to make the various judgments that are necessary to resolve his decisions, his policy aide thinks about exactly what judgments need to be made—and remade. Even those with experience in thinking analytically about decisions will find it valuable to have a colleague help work through the resolution of a dilemma.[2] Indeed, this chapter illustrates how we (the two authors) often sit down together to work out each other's decision dilemmas.

Specifying the Mayor's Uncertainty

ROCKE: You said before that you thought it was "not very likely" that DOT would approve the Experimental Safety Program. What do you mean? Is the chance of approval 49, 35, 20, or only 5 percent?

WILLIS: I mean that the chances are quite a bit less than fifty-fifty. But I can't tell you if they are 35 or 20 percent or whatever. After all, all I can do is give you a rough guess. There is no way to know whether the chance is exactly 35 percent or not.

ROCKE: I understand that, but if we are to analyze this decision systematically, we need to be as specific as possible. Does the memo from O'Conahue give you any help in making a more intelligent guess?

WILLIS: Be serious. I know more about Washington—and DOT—than he does.

ROCKE: Okay then, let's make the best use of your admittedly limited knowledge of what's going on in Washington. Imagine a bag with ten tennis balls in it. Five are white and five are green. You can't see inside the bag and you are going to draw, blindly, one ball from it. Which do you think is greater: the chance that DOT will approve your Experimental Safety Program or the chance that you will draw a white ball from this bag?

WILLIS: There is a better chance of drawing the white ball—but so what? It sounds a bit flaky to me.

ROCKE: Bear with me for just a few minutes. I'm trying to get you to make an educated guess about the probability that DOT will approve the Experimental Safety Program.

WILLIS: Okay.

ROCKE: What you said means that you think there is less than a 50-percent chance that DOT will approve the application. Now think about another bag with only one white ball and nine green ones. Which do you think is greater: the chance that DOT will approve your Experimental Safety Program or the chance that you will draw a white ball from this bag?

WILLIS: Now I'd bet on DOT.

ROCKE: Good, that means you think there is something between a 10- and a 50-percent chance that DOT will approve the Experimental Safety Program.

WILLIS: Sure—that's what *I* think. But that doesn't mean that's what it is. There might be a 70-percent chance for all I know.

Resolving the Basic Dilemma

ROCKE: Yes, in fact, come July, when DOT makes its announcements, you will either have it or you won't, and if you submit the experimental plan and don't get it some wise guy can say, "Look, you were wrong. The chance wasn't between 10 and 50 percent at all. It was zero." But *you* have to make your decision this morning, and to do that you should attempt to make use of your best judgments even if the information you have isn't perfect.

WILLIS: Okay, I'll stop kibitzing and play along. I do understand what you're trying to do. You want me to say how many white balls are in the bag when I think the chance of DOT approving the Experimental Safety Program is the same as the chance of drawing a white ball. I think, if the bag had—three white balls and seven green ones I would have a hard time deciding which gave me the better chance. I guess that means I think there is a 30-percent chance that DOT will approve the Experimental Safety Program application.

ROCKE: Correct. But it's usually best not to jump to conclusions too quickly. It often helps to narrow down the range of possibilities first. What if the bag had four white balls and six green ones?

WILLIS: I'd have a better chance trying to draw a white ball.

ROCKE: And if the bag had two white balls and eight green ones?

WILLIS: Now I'm not so sure. It looks pretty close. Washington hasn't been too good to us lately, and I don't see why things should improve. In fact, I'd like to change my mind. Is that okay?

ROCKE: Absolutely. If thinking about your decision a little more helps improve your judgments, you ought to make use of this revision.

WILLIS: Then I want to say that I think the chance of DOT approving the experimental program's application is 20 percent. It seems to me that if the bag has one white ball and nine green ones, the chance is greater that DOT will approve the application. But if the bag has three white balls and seven green ones, I would stand a better chance of drawing a white ball. Consequently, I must think there is something between a 10- and 30-percent chance that DOT will approve the Experimental Safety Program.

ROCKE: Right.

WILLIS: Okay, then I must think it is about 20 percent. But don't try to get me to say whether the chance is 15 or 25 percent. I'm stretching it just to be as specific as 20 percent.

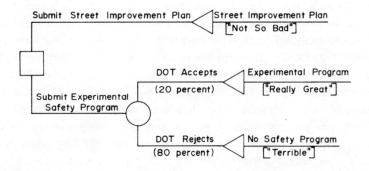

Figure 3–2. Mayor Willis's Decision Tree with Specific Probabilities.

ROCKE: Fine. If we put one hundred balls in the bag, you might be able to make a more refined judgment, but if you're comfortable with the 20 percent figure we might as well work with it. Anyway, it may not matter in the end whether we use 20 percent or 15 or 25 percent or even 10 or 30 percent. If we have to, we can think through this probability again, but we can leave that until we see if it's important. Right now, we want to put this probability on the decision tree.

WILLIS: Wait a minute. Don't we also have to worry about the chance that DOT will reject the application? But—of course—if I think there is a 20-percent chance that DOT will accept, I must think that there is an 80-percent chance that it will reject the application. And that number sounds reasonable.

Thinking with Probabilities

This dialogue illustrates the initial steps in analyzing a decision. First, you must simplify the problem and decompose it into its relevant parts. For this task, a decision tree is helpful.

Next you must make specific statements about the probabilities associated with each uncertain event. Most decision problems that are worth the time for even a simple analysis are complicated by uncertainty. Consequently, in most cases, you will find it helpful to indicate on your decision tree the important uncertain events that can result from each of your alternative choices, and the relevant outcomes for each uncertain event. Then you need to specify the probability that each outcome will occur.

In special situations, you may have available some statistical data from which these probabilities can be calculated. For example, in chapter 2, Ollerton Watt's doctor was able to assess, using medical data, that Watt had a 10-percent chance of dying during bypass surgery.

More often, however, relevant statistical information will not exist or, if it does, you will be required to make a decision before all the data can be collected and analyzed. Such is the case with Mayor Willis's assessment of the probability that DOT will accept the application for the Experimental Safety Program. This uncertain event will occur only once; it is not possible to collect data on similar events. In such situations, a busy decision maker will have to "guesstimate" the probability of each uncertain outcome occurring.

Though they are guesstimates, judgmental probability assessments should be specific. Saying that an event is "unlikely" or "possible" or "almost certain" may suffice for casual conversation, but such phrases are too vague to be of much help in analyzing a decision problem. Further, although a probability assessment may not be calculated from statistical data, it is not a random guess. You undoubtedly have some understanding of how likely the relevant, uncertain outcomes are, and you may be able to collect a little more information quickly. By thinking carefully about each uncertainty, you can assess your personal judgmental probability that each outcome will occur. Chris Rocke's tennis-balls-in-a-bag system may sound strange at first, but, as will be discussed in the next chapter, it is based on a profound and powerful definition of judgmental probability.

There are two ways to express a probability assessment. It can be given either as some percentage between 0 and 100 percent, or as a decimal number between 0 and 1.0. In everyday conversation we might speak of a "20-percent chance," but mathematicians, using p for probability, would write this as "$p = 0.20$." The probability assessment for each outcome is placed in parentheses under the appropriate event branch, and you can use either system of notation when labeling your decision diagram. When doing the simple calculations described later in this book, however, you are less likely to make a mistake in locating the decimal point if you use the probability numbers between 0 and 1.0.

The third step in analyzing a decision is for the decision maker to evaluate his preferences for the various possible final outcomes.

Specifying the Mayor's Preferences

ROCKE: Now we have to appraise the relative merits of the three possible results. For many decision problems, the consequences can be evaluated by putting a dollar value on each, but I don't think that would be appropriate here.

WILLIS: I agree. Why can't we just assign some index value to each outcome? We might use a scale from -10 to $+10$, or from 0 to 10, or 0 to 100. Isn't that the usual way people make appraisals when dollar values don't work?

ROCKE: Yes, but that's trickier and more complicated than it may seem at first glance. Suppose, for instance, you used the -10 to $+10$ scale.

WILLIS: Well, then I would say that getting the Experimental Safety Program is worth $+10$, since that's the best possible result. And since getting nothing is the worst, I would make it worth -10. And—

ROCKE: And what value would you assign to getting the Street Improvement Plan?

WILLIS: Oh, I don't know. I guess something like -1, or -2, or -3. I really don't know.

ROCKE: That's the point. You don't know for two reasons. One: It's just plain difficult to evaluate how you feel about the merits of one outcome as compared to the other possibilities. It isn't too difficult to rank the outcomes from best to worst, but making your subjective feelings more specific is usually difficult. Two: It's hard to know what -1, or -2, or $+8$ means on a scale from -10 to $+10$. Your preferences are very subjective. Nothing we can do about that. But we can attempt to use a meaningful scale that will permit you to think systematically about your preferences, and that will produce some results that can help you make the final decision.

WILLIS: Something like the white and green balls in the bag, I suppose. Okay, what is it?

ROCKE: Let's use a scale from zero to one.

WILLIS: Okay, then getting the Experimental Safety Program gets a value of 1.0 and getting nothing gets a value of 0. But that doesn't solve the problem of how I should evaluate the Street Improvement Plan. What value should I give it?

ROCKE: That's up to you. But I can tell you how to go about making a meaningful appraisal. Suppose you have the Street Improvement Plan for sure—which you do. Now, rather than Washington, let the bag with ten white and green balls decide whether or not you get the experimental program. If you draw a white ball from the bag, you get the experimental program; if you draw a green ball, you get nothing.

If most of the balls are white, you would obviously be quite willing to trade in the Street Improvement Plan for the gamble, and if most of the balls are green, you wouldn't. The question is what is the specific combination of white and green balls that makes you not care whether you stick with the Street Improvement Plan or take the gamble.

WILLIS: I probably ought to narrow down the range again, rather than jump to a quick conclusion.

ROCKE: Right.

WILLIS: Okay. If the bag has five white and five green balls—that would give me a fifty-fifty shot at winning the experimental program—I would certainly take the gamble. Getting that project is so much better than nothing or the Street Improvement Plan that it is well worth the risk. But if the bag contains only one white ball, I would certainly stick with the standard street program.

ROCKE: Given that, let's narrow the range further. What about if the bag has two white balls and eight green ones?

WILLIS: Then—no, I'd still have to stay with the Street Improvement Plan. That chance at the experimental program isn't good enough.

ROCKE: What if the bag has four white balls and six green ones?

WILLIS: That's almost fifty-fifty. Well, not quite. Still, I think I'd take that gamble. So it looks like a combination of three white and seven green balls makes me indifferent between the gamble and the Street Improvement Plan. That means if I have a 30-percent chance of winning approval for the Experimental Safety Program and a 70-percent chance of nothing, I don't care whether I take that gamble or the Street Improvement Plan for sure. Now that I have decided that, what do I do?

ROCKE: We assign a preference-probability of 0.3 to the outcome "Street Improvement Plan."

WILLIS: And I guess I have already assigned a preference-probability of 1.0 to "Experimental Safety Program" and a preference-probability of 0 to "No Safety Program." That makes sense, given the way I got the 0.3 for the Street Improvement Plan. If I have a choice between the Experimental Safety Program for sure on the one hand and the gamble between the experimental program and nothing on the other, the bag would have to contain all white balls before I would be indifferent between the gamble and the experimental program for sure; thus, the Experimental Safety Program should get a preference-probability of 1.0.

Resolving the Basic Dilemma

ROCKE: You've got it. Preference-probability is a probability, so its scale from 0 to 1.0 gives an appraisal of any outcome in terms of a hypothetical "reference gamble" between the *Best* and the *Worst* reference outcomes. If you assign an outcome a preference-probability of *V*, that means you think that this outcome is worth the same as a gamble that gives you a *V* chance of the *Best* outcome and a $1 - V$ chance of the *Worst* outcome. Now let's put your preference-probabilities on your decision tree.

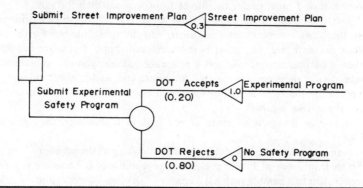

Figure 3–3. Mayor Willis's Decision Tree with Specific Probabilities and Preference-Probabilities.

Preference-Probabilities

On a decision tree, there is a space inside each terminal node to put the preference-probability assessed for that outcome. In figure 3–3, this has been done for the three outcomes of Mayor Willis's dilemma.

The preference-probability assessed by a decision maker for an outcome is clearly a subjective number. It does, however, have a specific, unambiguous meaning. A preference-probability is a clear statement about how the decision maker evaluates an outcome. It is a probabilistic statement that compares the outcome with a reference gamble on the *Best* and the *Worst* reference outcomes. Individuals can disagree about what preference-probability to assess for a particular outcome, but that is because people have different preferences. Once, however, the reference gamble is defined—that is, once the two reference outcomes are determined—the meaning of a preference-probability assigned to any interjacent outcome is clear.

And now, back to our story.

Putting the Pieces Back Together

WILLIS: Wait a minute! I see it. I should submit the Street Improvement Plan. I knew it all along. If I'm indifferent between the Street Improvement Plan and a 30-percent gamble on the Experimental Safety Program, and if I think if I submit the Experimental Safety Plan I have only a 20-percent chance of having it approved, then I must prefer the Street Improvement Plan for sure.

ROCKE: Exactly. You are making use of what is called the "substitution principle." If you think two outcomes are equivalent, you can substitute one for the other on your decision tree. Or, what is more relevant here, if you are indifferent between a particular outcome and a reference gamble, you can substitute the gamble in your decision tree for that final outcome, and it won't change your preference for that alternative or for anything else. We can do this on your decision tree. (See figure 3–4.)

WILLIS: Sure—that makes it all clear. If you look at it that way, the decision is obvious.

ROCKE: There is another, slightly different way of looking at the problem. You gave the Street Improvement Plan a preference-probability of 0.3 because you felt it was equivalent to a gamble with a 0.3 chance of the *Best* outcome and, of course, a corresponding 0.7 chance of the *Worst*. What preference-probability would you give to submitting the Experimental Safety Program?

WILLIS: A value of 0.2, I suppose, since it leads directly to a reference gamble with a 0.2 chance of the *Best* outcome.

ROCKE: Precisely. So you can put this preference-probability on your original decision tree. (See figure 3–5.)

WILLIS: Of course—that makes it clear. I obviously prefer the alternative with the higher preference-probability, since that implies a greater chance of the *Best* outcome and thus a smaller chance of getting the *Worst*. It's intriguing how preference and probability are related in this way. But I'm not sure how often I'll be able to use these ideas.

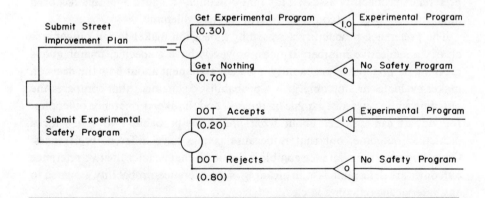

Figure 3–4. Mayor Willis's Decision Tree with the Reference Gamble Substituted for the Street Improvement Plan Consequence.

Resolving the Basic Dilemma

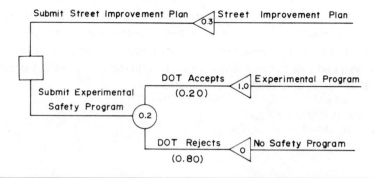

Figure 3–5. Mayor Willis's Resolved Decision Tree with the Preference-Probability for the Uncertain Event.

ROCKE: When we get to work through some other problems, especially ones with a more complicated structure, you'll see the basic logic and usefulness of preference-probabilities. The idea is both simple and profound.

The Fundamentals of Quick Analysis: A Summary

The process of thinking analytically about a decision dilemma can be summarized as follows.

1. Simplify the decision problem and decompose it into its component parts by using a decision tree.

2. Assess your judgmental probability for each uncertain event. For a basic dilemma, there is only one uncertain event, so only one probability assessment is needed. (More on probability assessments in the next chapter.)

3. Determine your subjective evaluation of the relative merits of each of the possible final outcomes by assigning a preference-probability for each. For a basic dilemma, there are only three possible outcomes. If the best and worst outcomes of the dilemma are selected as the *Best* and *Worst* outcomes of the reference gamble, then they get preference-probabilities of 1.0 and 0 (respectively). Then there is only one outcome for which a preference-probability must be carefully assessed.

4. Determine the preference-probability for each possible alternative and select the alternative with the largest preference-probability. For a basic dilemma, this step is straightforward. For decisions complicated by multiple uncertainties, the substitution principle and a few probability calculations provide a means of assessing, indirectly, a preference-probability for each alternative. (This process is explained in chapters 5 and 6.)

65

5. Reconsider your assumptions, your simplifications, your probability assessments, and your preference-probabilities to determine if your decision is so sensitive to any of this initial work that it is worth your time to do some more analysis and collect more information. It is this final stage of any decision analysis that Willis and Rocke are now discussing.

Sensitivity Analysis

WILLIS: I'm still troubled. There isn't much difference between a preference-probability of 0.2 and one of 0.3. It's not as if the numbers came out 0.1 and 0.8. And, after all, the 0.2 and 0.3 really came out of my head. They're just based on my own feelings.

ROCKE: Sure. If you're concerned about your analysis, let's determine if any part needs more work. What particularly troubles you?

WILLIS: Well, I'm pretty confident about the preference-probabilities I assigned. They reflect my best judgment, and since I'm the mayor—the one who's responsible for making the decision and who gets held accountable for the consequences—the decision has to be based on the preference-probabilities I develop for the city.

But in my probability assessments, I'm attempting to predict what will happen in Washington, and I just can't know for sure. Not that I'm really all that disturbed about saying there's a 20-percent chance that DOT will accept the Experimental Safety Program. That's what I think. But suppose the probability is 40 percent. Then the preference-probability of submitting the Experimental Safety Program would be 0.4 and that would be the best decision. There isn't much difference between a 20-percent chance and a 40-percent chance, but for this decision it makes all the difference in the world. What I decide depends upon what I think is the probability DOT will accept the Experimental Safety Program.

ROCKE: That's a pretty good explanation of what's called "sensitivity analysis." Since your final decision is really sensitive to this probability assessment, it is worth your time to do a little more thinking about your chances with the application for the experimental program.

WILLIS: But I only have until noon. Then we have to get this thing on the plane. There's not much I can do in an hour and a half.

ROCKE: Okay, but is there something you can do? Is there some way you can get some more information to help you decide if you think the probability of DOT approving the Experimental Safety Program is greater or less than 30 percent? For your purposes that's all you have to know. With your first-cut analysis completed, you know where to focus your remaining attention. All you need to work out is whether you think this chance is more or less than 30 percent.

WILLIS: Right. If I think it's less than 30, I shouldn't take the risk—then the probability of getting the experimental program would be less than my indifference probability. But if I conclude the chances are better than 30 percent, then, given my preference, I should decide the gamble is worth it.

Resolving the Basic Dilemma

ROCKE: So, is there some way you can help improve your judgment about this probability?

WILLIS: I could call Senator Gregory. His colleague there in Washington has never been much help to me—and he certainly isn't going to give me any worthwhile assistance in this election year. But "Fish" Gregory has always given me valuable advice. I'll see if my secretary can track him down.

Later—

ROCKE: What did the senator say?

WILLIS: It looks like I should submit the Experimental Safety Program. Fish reports that everyone in Washington knows that Zenith City hasn't gotten its fair share of federal assistance during the past year, and the word has gone out to the agencies that we deserve a little more help. And Fish says that he'll have one of his staffers follow the papers through the bureaucracy.

He didn't guarantee anything, but when I asked him what the chances were, he thought they were fifty-fifty. I didn't ask the senator about the balls in the bag—he'd probably think I was nutty—but on the basis of this new information I'd certainly have to say that the chances are better than 30 percent for getting DOT to accept the Experimental Safety Program.

ROCKE: Okay then, we ought to get that application off.

WILLIS: You're right. And I certainly feel more comfortable with this decision than I did a few hours ago. But let me get something clear.

This problem boils down to two probabilities: the probability that DOT will accept the Experimental Safety Program, and the indifference probability of the reference gamble I substitute for the Street Improvement Plan. But I don't even have to specify the two probabilities. All I really need to decide is which is greater. If I think the probability of getting the Experimental Safety Program is greater than my indifference probability for the Street Improvement Plan, I prefer to gamble on the experimental program. But if the probability of DOT approving the experimental program is the lower one, I want to choose the certain Street Improvement Plan.

ROCKE: Correct—but only theoretically. How do you think about these two probabilities unless you specify them? Your analysis will be very fuzzy unless you actually attempt to specify your judgments.

Further, this problem is a relatively easy one to think about. It has only a few components. All you really need to worry about are two probabilities—that of success for the risky alternative, and your indifference probability for the riskless alternative. It is easy to keep these two straight and to compare them in your head. But what happens when your problem is complicated by many uncertainties and possible outcomes? How do you keep everything straight then? The only way I know is to specify all the probabilities and preference-probabilities as best you can—and write them down. At that point you will discover that the experience you developed working with a simple problem will be very valuable.

WILLIS: Okay. Let's get this Experimental Safety Program's application on the plane.

Practicing Quick Analysis

How much thinking and rethinking a decision dilemma deserves depends upon the importance of the decision and upon the difference one can expect more analysis will make. As they are developing their analytical decision-making skills, however, some people may want to suspend this rule. Many decisions are, themselves, worth no analysis at all. But learning how to assess probabilities and appraise preferences requires practice and this is best done on simple problems.

And now, to learn what resulted from Mayor Willis's analysis, we return to Zenith City, where the mayor has again summoned his assistant.

Intelligent Decisions and Fortunate Outcomes

WILLIS: Well, we really blew it. It looks like your decision analysis doesn't work too well. DOT rejected the application for the Experimental Safety Program and our football knucklehead has already held a press conference to say that if he had been mayor he would have submitted the Street Improvement Plan, and if *he* had submitted the experimental program it would have been approved. What does your decision analysis tell us we should do now?

ROCKE: Wait a minute. There was no guarantee that the Experimental Safety Program would get accepted. Even Senator Gregory said there was only a fifty-fifty chance. That's like flipping a coin and gambling that it will come up heads. Well, it came up tails and you knew that could happen. But you decided, on the basis of your preferences for the various possible outcomes, that it was worth the gamble. Decision analysis helps you make your best judgments when confronted with uncertainties. But it doesn't eliminate the risk.

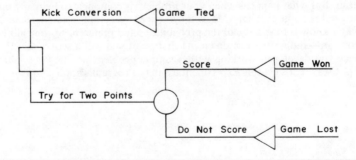

Figure 3–6. The Extra-Point Decision Dilemma.

Resolving the Basic Dilemma

WILLIS: Yeah, I understand. I'm just mad because of Mann. At Zenith U., "Flash" may have been a big hero, but now he's just a Monday-morning quarterback.

ROCKE: An excellent analogy. Remember the 1975 Rose Bowl game? USC scored with less than two minutes to go, making the score 16 to 17 for Ohio State. Then they had to decide whether to kick the conversion or try for two points. That decision problem is similar to the one you had. Even the decision tree is the same. (See figure 3-6.)

WILLIS: So? What happened?

ROCKE: USC tried for the two points and got them—and won the game, 18 to 17. But if they hadn't made it, a lot of Monday-morning quarterbacks would have complained about that decision.[3]

WILLIS: Of course, the decision wasn't precisely the same. They could have kicked and missed—and lost. Shouldn't there be another uncertainty node on the decision tree? (See figure 3–7.)

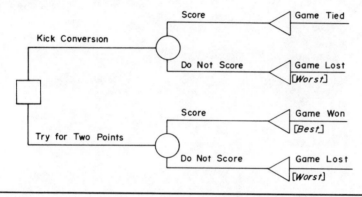

Figure 3–7. A More Complex Decision Tree for the Extra-Point Decision Dilemma.

ROCKE: Yes, but *your* decision diagram could have looked like that too. After all, it was possible that DOT would reject the Street Improvement Plan. (See figure 3–8.)

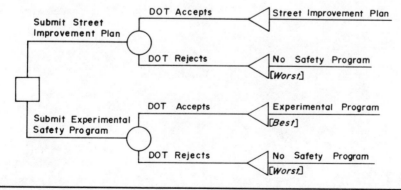

Figure 3–8. A More Complex Decision Tree for Mayor Willis's Traffic Safety Dilemma.

WILLIS: I guess you're right. I just made the assumption that the Street Improvement Plan would have been approved, but I suppose there was a one- or two-percent chance that it would have been rejected.

ROCKE: And I bet you made a lot of other simplifying assumptions to resolve your decision. You assumed that Congress wasn't going to cut the funds for traffic safety, and that DOT wasn't going to delay the announcements of experimental grants until after the election. We could have attempted to include these complications in your analysis, but don't forget that we only had a few hours.

WILLIS: Yeah, we didn't have much time, and we didn't have much information. I guess what quick analysis does is help you make the best decision based on what you've got. Okay—let's try it again soon. We'll just have to deal with "Flash" as best we can.

Mayor Payne Willis returned to his desk and Chris Rocke, smiling, walked back to her office.

Chapter 4

Thinking About Uncertainty

"ALL public policy presupposes a forecast," Alan Greenspan, the chairman of President Ford's Council of Economic Advisers, once observed.[1] The debate in August 1975 over whether the price of petroleum from domestic wells should be decontrolled focused, for example, on different forecasts of the effects of decontrol.

- To help reduce dependence on imports and stem the out-flow of American dollars and jobs, I will veto the six-month extension [of price controls]. Painful as they are, higher prices do promote conservation, and higher prices do promote increased efficiency in the use of petroleum products. (President Gerald R. Ford)[2]
- Immediate decontrol will cost the United States consumer 6 cents a gallon for the fuel he burns and roughly twice that much again in food, clothing and other produce he buys to sustain his family. (U.S. Representative John D. Dingell)[3]
- The net effect of decontrol and removal of the import fees will be no more than 3 cents per gallon by the end of 1975 on refined petroleum products and could be 2 cents or less. (Eric R. Zausner, deputy administrator of the Federal Energy Administration)[4]
- We're very concerned that decontrol will drive us out of business. (Henry A. Rosenberg, Jr., chairman of Crown Central Petroleum Co., an independent refining firm in Baltimore)[5]
- The return of competition to the petroleum marketplace will be the best thing that ever happened to the American fuel consumer. (R. S. Ilacqua, a petroleum analyst with the investment banking firm of L. F. Rothschild & Co)[6]

71

The dependency of decisions upon predictions is obviously not limited to public policy questions. Standard business decisions—whether to introduce a new product, raise prices, increase inventory, or expand production—are all dependent upon forecasts.

- This car [the Pacer] will pull us out of the slump ahead of the industry. (Roy D. Chapin, Jr., chairman of American Motors, when the Pacer was introduced in February 1975)[7]
- Ultimately, it's [the compact car is] the kind of car that will be the standard-sized car in this country. (Richard D. McLaughlin, vice president for sales of Chrysler Corporation, introducing its 1977 models with emphasis on the compact car)[8]
- We still think that more [farm] acreage will be planted this year and more fertilizer applied. (Garvin C. Matthiesen, president of Allied Chemical's agriculture division, commenting on the demand for fertilizer)[9]
- Anyone who raises [fiber] prices now is crazy. When business is soft and people are reacting to prices, well, that's certainly not the time to raise prices. Our customers are certainly not going to pay for it. (David Caplan, president of Concord Fabrics, Inc., in September 1976)[10]
- By the end of this decade, we will see digital watches with five or more functions [month, day of month, hour, minute, second] retailing at $9.95 to $12.95. (Benjamin M. Rosen, a partner in Coleman & Co., a New York investment banking firm, in July 1975)[11]

Also, when making personal decisions about where to live or what job to take, predictions can be very important.

- Another major earthquake [along the San Andreas Fault] is inevitable. It could happen in 100 years, in 10 years, or one minute from now. (Dr. Peter Ward, geophysicist and head of the U.S. Geological Survey's earthquake mechanics and prediction branch in Menlo Park, California)[12]
- "The job [of Secretary of State] is a blind alley . . . I don't think it would ever be offered to me, but if it were, I'd refuse it. Where does it lead?" (Senator Frank Church, commenting in the summer of 1976 on the possibility that he might be appointed Secretary of State in a Carter administration)[13]

Probabilistic Predictions

These predictions were offered with much confidence, although there was little guarantee that they would come true. There is always uncertainty, that annoying specter that haunts every prediction. It is impossible to be absolutely sure that a new job will be a blind alley, or that decontrolling petroleum will raise the price at the gas pump by precisely six cents, or that a new product, be it a compact car or a cheap digital watch, will be a success. We may have some vague vision of coming events, but we can never be sure until time lifts the murky curtain that obscures the future.

This uncertainty inevitably complicates major decisions. Indeed, that is why they are major decisions. As Arthur M. Schlesinger, Jr., wrote, "All major presidential decisions are taken in conditions of what General Marshall, speaking of battle, used to call 'chronic obscurity'—that is, on the basis of incomplete and probably inaccurate intelligence."[14] Decisions—presidential, corporate, or personal—become dilemmas because of our uncertainty about important future events. We cannot select the best alternative until we know the consequences of each, and if the consequences are uncertain, then the best choice becomes uncertain too.

Still, decisions must be made—and they must be based on predictions. Such predictions should reflect the uncertainty about the future. Rather than assert that a forecast is infallible, it is necessary to hedge—to make a probabilistic prediction.

The most common hedge is to predict that something "probably" will happen. (The emphasis has been added in all of the following quotations.)

- We'll *probably* cross over from being an industry with excess capacity to one with a deficiency of capacity, maybe in 1978 or 1979. (C. Edward Meyer, Jr., president of TWA, in August 1976)[15]
- The USSR will *probably* achieve a significant ICBM delivery capability with megaton warheads by 1959. U.S. will *probably* not have achieved such a capability. (The "Gaither Report" of 1957, which predicted what became known as "the missile gap")[16]
- At anticipated production and consumption rates, we [the U.S.] *probably* will be importing half the oil we consume by the end of the decade. (Howard W. Blauvelt, chairman of Continental Oil Co., in March 1976)[17]

But there are numerous other words and phrases that can be used to hedge a prediction.

- I think we have *a better than even shot* at a safe opening of schools. (Boston Mayor Kevin H. White, in September 1975, before the first day of school under the Phase II desegregation order)[18]
- There is *probably* both oil and gas down there [in the Baltimore Canyon Trough off the New Jersey coast]. But I've been saying this for five years—that there is *a greater chance* for gas than oil—and I still believe it. (J. R. Jackson, a member of Exxon Corporation's exploration department, in August 1976)[19]
- I now believe confidently that there is *much better than an even chance* that there will be no need for gas rationing in the United States. (President Nixon, at a press conference on February 25, 1974)[20]
- There is a *possibility* of using almost all the winter wheat we have before June, leaving us with little reserve. But I think it will be *impossible* to run clear out.

(Jim Jordan, Kansas City Board of Trade representative for Union Equity Cooperative Elevators, commenting on U.S. wheat reserves, January 1974)[21]

- I think that there is *a high likelihood* that there will be an increase in the level of hostilities, and I think that *the probabilities* of a full all-out invasion by the North are *relatively constrained*. I think in part because North Vietnam will not discount *the probability* of the reintroduction of U.S. air. I think that we can expect increased hostilities. I hope that it does not take place. I would not put *the probability* of an all-out invasion *very high*. (Secretary of Defense James R. Schlesinger, January 10, 1974, responding to a question on the likelihood of the resumption of "general hostilities" in Vietnam)[22]

- It's *very unlikely* that King Faisal and any of the others will be prepared to withdraw the embargo until there's been another round of negotiations, and until at least that initial step of disengaging the Israeli-Syrian forces has been achieved. (George W. Ball, former undersecretary of state, February 6, 1974, discussing the Middle East and the Oil Embargo)[23]

- There is *a possibility* of a fire due to impact of burning propellant pieces, but steps have been taken to reduce this to *a minimum*. . . . There would be *a slight chance* of a fire occurring or a person being struck by an object. . . . *The possibility* of having to destroy the missile during the time it overflies the United States is *low* due to missile reliability. (Draft Environmental Statement, February 1974, prepared by the Department of the Air Force, concerning Operation Giant Patriot, which involved test firing eight Minuteman II missiles from Malmstrom Air Force Base in Montana into the Pacific Ocean)[24]

What does it mean, however, to say "There is a possibility"? How likely is it if "It's very unlikely"? And how small is "a slight chance," or a possibility that is "low" or another that is "minimum"? Certainly these are not predictions that can be used to analyze a decision. To resolve a decision dilemma, specific probabilistic predictions about the most important uncertainties are needed. These phrases are simply too ambiguous.

Not that there is no value in ambiguity. After all, the people who made these predictions were not only using these statements for decision-making purposes. They were also attempting to explain to the public what future events might happen, or attempting to convince the public that the future would be okay. If President Nixon had said "There is an 80-percent chance that there will be no need for gas rationing," he would have been immediately criticized for (1) overestimating the probability—"The chances are probably closer to even," the commentators would have asserted—and (2) ignoring what would happen if the other outcome (to which he assigned only a 20-percent chance) occurred. Similarly, the Air Force avoided additional controversy over Operation Giant Patriot by not specifying whether the "slight chance of a fire occurring or a person being struck by an object" meant 5 percent or 0.5 percent. Thus, for assuaging the general public (the purpose of many public predictions), such phrases may have some utility.

The use of these phrases, however, should not be made a virtue. They communicate very little information. Consider, for example, a report in the

Thinking About Uncertainty

New York Times in early 1974 concerning the uncertainty over a strike by National Football League players: "Will there be a strike in pro football this summer? The way the two parties, owners and players, are marching to the negotiating table, the answer has to be probably."[25] Aren't you glad you asked?

Another example of how such words muddle the message is provided in an exchange between the former attorney general, Elliot L. Richardson, and a reporter at a Justice Department press conference on the Wednesday (October 23, 1973) following the "Saturday Night Massacre" (emphasis added).

> *Reporter:* Mr. Richardson, the White House sources have said that the President was *confident* that the Supreme Court would uphold his position [with respect to the confidentiality of the Watergate tapes]. Are you aware of that confidence, and if it is true, why didn't he wait for the Supreme Court to act?
>
> *Richardson:* His lawyers told him, certainly, I think from the beginning, that his chances were *good.* I understood them to tell him that they were *better than even.* As of Thursday of this week, Mr. Charles Alan Wright told me he thought that the President had *a 50-50 chance* of winning in the Supreme Court of the United States.[26]

"Better than even" cannot be equivalent to "a 50-50 chance" and, for the President, a 50-percent chance of winning in the Supreme Court certainly could not be described as "good" nor make him very "confident."

Ambiguous Probability Phrases

As Donald H. Woods has written in *The Harvard Business Review,* "judgments about uncertainty are difficult to transmit."[27] To test the communicative content of some common probability phrases, we asked a group of our students for their specific, numerical interpretation of twenty-one different probabilistic expressions, many of which were mentioned earlier. The students were permitted to choose any of 101 numbers—the integers between 0 percent and 100 percent—to interpret the phrases.

The result (see table 4–1) was a collection of quite divergent interpretations of these verbal predictions. Even for statements that suggest very high or very low probabilities, the range of interpretations was quite large. For example, interpretations of the phrase "There is a much better than even chance that . . ." ranged from 55 to 92 percent. Some people thought that "There is a slight chance that . . ." meant less than 5 percent, while others interpreted this to be a probability greater than 50 percent. Certainly, if your objective is to communicate a specific understanding of how possible a future event is, such phrases are not very useful; they create quite different images in different people's minds.[28]

Table 4-1

Interpreting Probability Phrases

Probability Phrases	Specific Interpretation (in Percent)				
	Lowest	Lower Quartile	Median	Upper Quartile	Highest
There is a much better than even chance that...	55	70	74	78	92
There is a possibility that...	5	25	35	45	70
There is a high likelihood that...	60	80	85	90	97
The probability of... is relatively constrained.	5	20	27	35	65
The probability of... is very high.	71	85	90	95	100
It is very unlikely that...	1	5	10	12	30
There is a slight chance that...	2	10	15	20	54
The possibility is low that...	3	15	20	24	45
The chances are better than even that...	51	57	60	60	87
There is no probability, no serious probability that...	0	1	3	5	40
There is little chance that...	2	10	12	20	49
It is probable that...	20	61	73	80	98
It is unlikely that...	4	18	20	29	45
There is a good chance that...	30	65	71	75	90
It is quite unlikely that...	1	7	10	15	35
It is improbable that...	4	12	22	30	82
There is a high probability that...	40	80	85	90	98
There is a chance that...	1	26	35	50	70
It is very improbable that...	1	5	9	10	80*
It is likely that...	40	65	70	79	95
They will probably...	50	65	75	78	95

The median is the "middle" response—the number that divides all the responses into two equal groups, half above and half below this point. For example, half the students interpreted the phrase "There is much better than an even chance that. . ." to mean that the chance was 74 percent or greater. The other half thought it meant the chance was 74 percent or less.

The lower quartile is the 25th percentile; one quarter of the responses were below the lower quartile and three quarters were above it. For example, 25 percent of the students interpreted the phrase "There is much better than an even chance that. . ." to mean that the chance was 70 percent or less. The other 75 percent of the students thought it was 70 percent or greater.

The upper quartile is the 75th percentile.

N = 163, except for the last phrase for which N = 81.

* Eighty percent may seem like an absurd interpretation of "It is very improbable that. . ." This phrase, however, seems to be particularly ambiguous. Responses included 80, 70, 55, and 35 percent.

Thinking About Uncertainty

It may be argued that if these statements had not been abstract but had referred to specific events, the range of numerical probabilities would have been narrower. For example, if people had been asked to interpret the statement "It is very improbable that there will be a nuclear war next year," no one would have thought that "very improbable" meant an 80-percent chance, or a 55-percent chance, or even a 35-percent chance (though these responses *were* found in our survey). In such a case, however, the responses would have reflected not only interpretations of the probability phrase, but also personal judgments about the true probability of nuclear war. If a phrase itself has any specific meaning, that meaning should be independent of the type of event to which it is applied.

In another test of this kind, a group of national security analysts were asked to interpret the statement "The cease-fire is holding but it could be broken within the next week." The analyst who wrote that sentence intended it to mean that there was a 30-percent chance of the cease-fire being broken. But most of the other analysts interpreted this to mean that the probability was 50 percent—or greater. Another analyst, who helped prepare the original assessment, believed the probability was 80 percent, though she and the author of the sentence originally thought they were agreed on the chance that the cease-fire would be broken.[29]

Unfortunately, this "laboratory experiment" has been replicated in the real world. In early 1961, President Kennedy ordered the Joint Chiefs of Staff to study the Central Intelligence Agency's plan for an invasion of Cuba by expatriates. The general in charge of the evaluation concluded that its chances of overall success were "fair," by which he meant that they were 30 percent. Yet, when the Joint Chiefs sent their report to the president, no probabilities were included; instead the report stated, "This plan has a fair chance of ultimate success." The rest is history. Years later the general felt that the misinterpretation of the word "fair" had been one of the central misunderstandings of the Bay of Pigs fiasco, and he was still unhappy with himself for not insisting that a specific, numerical assessment be used. Recalled the general, "We thought other people would think that 'a fair chance' would mean 'not too good.' "[30]

Ambiguous probability phrases also plague legal communications. For example, there is much confusion over the commonly used statement that, for a conviction, "a reasonable man" must believe that the evidence indicates a person to be guilty "beyond a reasonable doubt." A survey of 347 judges found that some thought this meant that there had to be a 70-percent chance that the defendant was guilty (one judge even thought this meant only a 50-percent chance) and nearly a third of the judges thought it meant 100 percent. A group of 69 jurors gave similarly divergent responses.

To convict an individual of negligence in a civil action, the judge or jury must find the defendant guilty "by preponderance of the evidence." More than half of the judges in this survey thought this meant the probability here was 55 percent that the defendant was guilty, with other interpretations ranging from below 50 percent to 100 percent. But the median of the jurors' interpretations was a 75-percent chance of being guilty. (Again, the range of jurors' responses was from below 50 percent to 100 percent.)[31] Obviously, despite the common use of the phrase *by preponderance of the evidence* for a very specific purpose, there exist quite different interpretations of how probable a defendant's guilt must be to convict him.

Incredibly, some segments of American society explicitly prefer probability phrases rather than specific probability statements. For example, when a doctor testified in a civil trial that there was a 90-percent chance that a particular accident had caused the plaintiff's hernia, the Missouri Court of Appeals said this was "speculation and conjecture" and remanded the case for a new trial. This time, the doctor testified that it was "within reasonable medical certainty" that the accident had caused the hernia and the state's court of appeals accepted this as a "definite affirmance."[32]

In a letter to the editor of the *New England Journal of Medicine,* one doctor suggested (apparently seriously) a ranking of probability phrases to help in "the deciphering of statements regarding the frequency of certain physical and laboratory findings."[33]

1. Always	7. Not Unusual	13. Infrequent
2. Usual	8. Not Uncommon	14. Seldom
3. Common	9. Not Infrequent	15. Unusual
4. Frequent	10. Not Rare	16. Rare
5. Often	11. Not Usual	17. Unheard of
6. Occasional	12. Uncommon	18. Never

Why should anyone need to learn the ordering of these eighteen words and phrases, when they already have committed to memory the digits from 0 to 100?

The Two Interpretations of Probability[34]

For a decision maker, ambiguous probability statements are useless. They simply do not provide the information necessary to analyze a decision. The chief executive officer of a firm, deciding whether to file a patent-infringement suit, needs to know from his lawyers not that he has "a good chance" or "a pretty good chance" of winning the case in court, but whether the probability of winning is 55 percent, 65 percent, or 95 percent. A governor who must decide whether to propose a controversial program needs to know from his legislative liaison staff not that the chances of passage are "poor" or "slight," but whether the probability is 15 percent, 25 percent, or 3 percent. Many decision makers have specialized staff assistance to help make predictions, but to be helpful, such forecasts must be specific, numerical statements about the probability that an event will or will not occur.

How should people make probabilistic predictions? How can you organize your thinking to develop a specific forecast that is truly consistent with your beliefs about uncertainty? You may argue that a phrase such as "there is a slightly better than even chance" summarizes your thinking—particularly your uncertainty—better than "there is a 60-percent chance," which sounds so precise, so confident. How do you know there is not a 55-percent chance, or a two-thirds chance? Certainly people should not pretend to be more confident about their predictions than their information warrants. To clarify why it is helpful in decision making to use specific, numerical probability estimates, and to explain how to make them, it is necessary to distinguish two interpretations of probability.

When empirical data are available, it is quite easy to make a probabilistic prediction. If baseball fans are asked the chance that George Brett, who is currently batting .333, will get a hit on his next at-bat, they will answer, "The probability is one-third." They will not say, "There is a pretty good chance"; unless they have some more information about how well Brett feels today or hits against this particular pitcher, they will make a specific numerical prediction based on average past performance. Similarly, if people know that for every 100,000 students who take the Scholastic Aptitude Test, 16,000 of them earn a score of 600 or greater, then when asked to predict the probability that any student will score 600 or better, they will respond, "There is a 16-percent chance." They will not say, "the probability is low," for even though they do not know the particular student, they have some very specific information about students in general.

When probabilities are derived from past observations, they are called "objective," "empirical," "relative-frequency," or "long-run frequency" probabilities. This is the first interpretation of probability, which evolved from the need to make probabilistic predictions for games of chance. The probability that a flipped coin will turn up heads is one-half. The probability that a rolled die will turn up "four" is one-sixth. Since the uncertain event occurs (or can occur) many times, it is easy to determine, from a long series of trials, how frequently any particular outcome will occur. A relative-frequency probability is simply the ratio of the number of occurrences of the outcome in question (hits, scores of 600 or greater, heads, fours) to the total number of uncertain events (at-bats, students taking the test, flips, rolls). It is not difficult to make this type of very specific probability statement.

Weather forecasters do it all the time. When they say, "There is a 40-percent chance of rain tomorrow," they are making a relative-frequency probability statement. What they are really saying is "On those days in the past, when the meteorological conditions were very similar to those we have today, it rained on the following day 40 percent of the time." The weather forecaster is not guaranteeing that it will or will not rain tomorrow; he is simply giving you the relative-frequency chance that it will.

You can use relative-frequency probabilities to make your personal decisions. The decision may be a simple one: "Should I carry an umbrella today?" And you may have your standard decision rule: "I will take an umbrella if the probability of rain is 30 percent or greater." The decision question may also be more complicated and not one you confront frequently. For example, you might want to decide among

1. picnicking on the beach (which would be ruined by rain)
2. sailing your boat (which would be made unpleasant by rain)
3. planting your garden (which would be interrupted by rain)
4. reading a book (which would be unaffected by rain)

If you want to think analytically about this decision, you need the weather forecast in the form of a specific probability statement.

Other decisions, more worthy of analysis, will depend upon relative-frequency probabilities. For example, when attempting to decide what to do about crime (either in a personal or public policy sense), relative-frequency predictions can be helpful. When Joseph D. McNamara was the police chief of Kansas City, Missouri, he explained the value of such predictions.

> The first priority should be to devise methods of determining the average citizen's probability of being victimized by a stranger in a serious crime—murder, robbery, aggravated assault, forcible rape or burglary. This information would allow mayors, police chiefs and heads of other criminal justice agencies to make informed decisions on how best to fulfill their fundamental duty to provide for the safety of those they serve. For the citizen, the same information on his vulnerability would permit him to make rational judgments on how well he is being protected by his government.[35]

There are, of course, many uncertain events that will never repeat themselves. How can a decision maker systematically assess the probability that the state legislature will sustain a gubernatorial veto, or that the public will buy ten million electric toothbrushes in their first year on the market? These are one-shot events, and the relative-frequency interpretation of probability is simply not appropriate.

In such situations, probabilistic predictions must be subjective or *judgmen-*

tal. Under this second interpretation, probabilities reflect an individual's *degree of belief* or *degree of confidence* that a particular event will occur.[36] Since these probabilities are based on the predictor's judgment, different individuals can—quite legitimately, given their different knowledge and evaluation of that information—make different probabilistic predictions. Still, the interpretation of a judgmental probability, such as "There is a 10-percent chance that the Red Sox will win the pennant,"[37] is completely unambiguous.

A judgmental probability is assessed using an *ideal probability generator.* To think about how likely it is that the legislature will sustain a gubernatorial veto, it is helpful to compare this uncertain event with an easily comprehended but uncertain process that produces truly random outcomes. For example, if you think it is exactly as likely that the legislature will sustain a veto as it is that a flipped coin will end up heads, then your judgmental probability of a veto being sustained is 0.5. It is possible to argue about what this judgmental probability should be, but its meaning is perfectly clear.

There are a number of different ideal probability generators. One is a hypothetical coin that does indeed have an equal chance of landing heads or tails; a real coin would only approximate this ideal since all real coins are slightly imbalanced and consequently slightly favor heads or tails. Or the ideal probability generator could be a perfectly fair die that is rolled or a perfectly fair roulette wheel (and how many of these exist?) that is spun. It is customary in decision analysis to use an urn (or a bowl) filled with a number of balls of different colors, randomly mixed up.

Assessing Judgmental Probabilities

Governor Peter Timtree must decide whether or not to veto a new tax bill that he thinks is very regressive and contains no incentives for economic growth. Consequently, Timtree asks his legislative aide, Barry Ternett, to assess the probability that the legislature will sustain a veto. Ternett has made these assessments before and, although he has the governor's confidence about legislative affairs, Ternett knows he has usually been too optimistic in predicting that the governor's position will prevail in the legislature.

Not that this would be unexpected. Ternett is responsible not only for predicting whether the legislature will support the governor's position, but for convincing the legislative leadership and individual representatives and senators to vote with the governor. Consequently, Ternett knows that, when he makes a prediction about the probability of legislative support, he often confuses his desire to convince the governor that he is a good lobbyist with his need to make unbiased predictions. He also knows that he has a general tendency to be too optimistic in his predictions about uncertain outcomes that he hopes will occur.

Ternett wants to think systematically about the probability that a gubernatorial veto will be sustained. To do this, he knows he has to concentrate his thinking on the probability that this uncertain outcome will occur, and eliminate the influence of the consequences of the different possible outcomes—some of which he likes and some of which he does not. Therefore, Ternett attempts to compare the probability of sustaining the veto with the probability of drawing a green ball from an urn containing 100 balls, some of them green, some white.

There is a problem, however, in comparing the uncertain outcome of drawing a ball from this urn with the uncertain outcome of the legislative vote—the consequences are different. To concentrate his thinking on the probabilities, Ternett creates a new, hypothetical decision (see figure 4–1) and asks

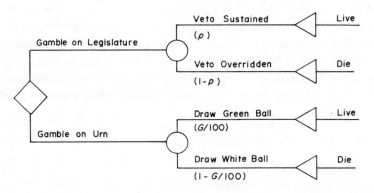

Figure 4–1. Using an Ideal Probability Generator to Decide on a Judgmental Probability for an Uncertain Outcome.

himself: If my life depended upon it, would I gamble on the urn or the legislature? Does Ternett have a better chance of living if he gambles on the legislature overriding the governor's veto or if he gambles on the urn? By thinking about these two hypothetical gambles, with identical consequences, Ternett can separate his assessment of probabilities from his preferences for the outcomes. The only difference between the two hypothetical alternatives (gambling on the legislature and gambling on the urn) is the probability of living, and this hypothetical decision thus focuses Ternett's attention on the uncertainty involved in the governor's original dilemma.

If a hypothetical gamble between life and death seems too macabre, you can use other hypothetical consequences: winning $100,000 versus nothing, or a two-week, all-expenses-paid vacation in Tahiti versus nothing. The purpose is to eliminate the influence that different consequences of the two alternatives might have on the choice and thus to concentrate your thinking on the probabilities. "When a man knows he is to be hanged," Samuel Johnson observed, "it concentrates his mind wonderfully."[38]

Of course, which gamble Ternett prefers depends upon the number of green balls in the urn. The idea (as first described in chapter 3) is to adjust the number of green and white balls in the urn until Ternett is indifferent between the two alternatives. Then Ternett can conclude, so far as he is concerned, the probability that the legislature will sustain the governor's veto is $G/100$, where G is the number of green balls in the urn.

It is important, however, not to make a specific probability judgment immediately. Thinking about uncertainty is difficult, as Amos Tversky of Stanford University and Daniel Kahneman of the University of British Columbia dramatize in their classic article, "Judgment Under Uncertainty: Heuristics and Biases." From substantial research into how the mind copes with uncertainty, these two psychologists have concluded that "people rely on a limited number of heuristic principles which reduce the complex tasks of assessing probabilities and predicting values to simpler judgmental operations." These simple, unconscious rules of thumb "are quite useful, but sometimes they lead to severe and systematic errors." One of the best-documented heuristics is "anchoring and adjustment": When required to make an estimate, people begin with some initial value—perhaps just a wild guess—and then make adjustments to obtain a final number. Unfortunately, report Tversky and Kahneman, such "adjustments are typically insufficient." The initial "anchor" is just too strong.[39]

To avoid the flawed adjustment process altogether, when deciding upon a judgmental probability it is best not to begin with an assessment that will become a burdensome anchor to future thinking. Rather, it makes more sense to start by determining upper and lower bounds for the probability—numbers that are clearly outside the range of possibility—and then begin, slowly, to narrow the range. Thus, Ternett first determines that if the urn contains 50 green and 50 white balls, there is no doubt that he has a much better chance of living by gambling on the urn (see figure 4–2). On the other hand, Ternett concludes, if the urn has only 10 green balls (and 90 white ones), he would certainly bet his life on the legislature. Having thus first determined that the probability of sustaining a gubernatorial veto is somewhere between 0.1 and 0.5, Ternett continues to narrow the range down until he is convinced the probability is somewhere between 0.25 and 0.35. That is, if the urn contains 25 green balls and 75 white ones, Ternett thinks he has a better chance of living by gambling that the legislature will sustain a gubernatorial veto. But if the urn has 35 green balls and 65 white ones, he would rather gamble on drawing a green ball from the urn.

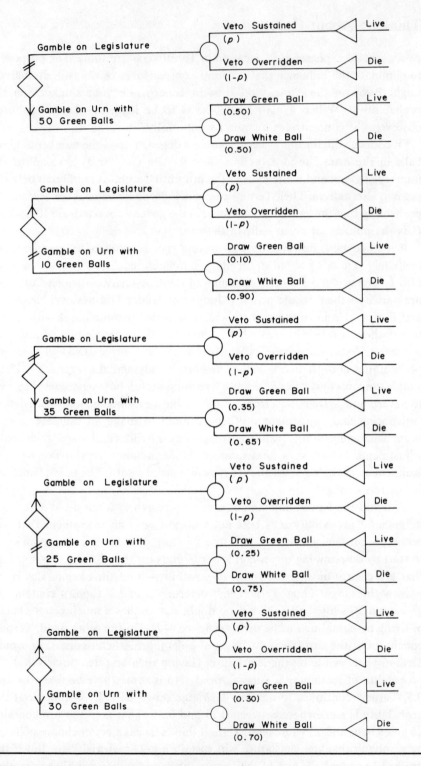

Figure 4–2. Barry Ternett's Thought Process for Deciding that the Probability a Veto Will Be Sustained is 0.3.

Thinking About Uncertainty

At this point, Ternett decides that there is a 30-percent chance that the legislature will sustain a veto. He recognizes, nevertheless, that the purpose of this probability assessment is to help the governor make his own decision about whether to veto the tax bill, and that if this decision is sensitive to his judgmental probability Ternett may need to rethink his assessment. Still, he decides, a probability of 0.3 reflects his best judgment about the uncertain chances of sustaining a veto.

Note that we say Ternett *decides* that the probability is 0.3. As the decision trees in figures 4–1 and 4–2 emphasize, making a probability assessment is, in fact, a decision—one of the many subdecisions that must be made to resolve this or any other decision dilemma. Ternett has not merely estimated some unknown, but nevertheless true, probability. Rather, by comparing this uncertain event with an ideal probability generator, he has decided exactly what, in his best judgment, are the chances of the legislature sustaining a veto.[40]

Naturally, you may be skeptical that this approach will help you make better predictions and thus better decisions. If so, the next time you need to predict the probability that some desirable event will occur, make a specific probability judgment in your usual way. Then remake the probability assessment using the ideal model—with life and death as the consequences. Did the second approach change (that is, lower) your prediction that the favorable outcome would occur? If so, you can see how this method of thinking about uncertainty helped direct your attention to the probability of the desired outcome, rather than your preference for it.

Probabilities, Data, and Judgment

Comparing an uncertain event with an ideal probability generator—for which there exists an objective, relative-frequency interpretation—does not eliminate the subjective nature of a judgmental probability. Someone else could follow the same procedure and reach a quite different conclusion. An ideal probability generator helps organize your thinking, but it does not convert the final probability assessment into an objective number.

Even the use of relative-frequency probabilities to make predictions about the future is subjective. To use such information, you must assume that the future will be very similar to the past. The weatherman must decide what meteorological indicators are most relevant, collect data on them, and then, based on similarities between the past and the present, predict the future. To use data on the incidence of crime, public policy makers must assume that past patterns of crime will continue into the future—or that the trends that alter such patterns are predictable. And if you want to use the data to decide whether to go out at night, you will have to assume that "the average citizen's probability of being victimized by a stranger in a serious crime" is the same as your own probability of being victimized, or else you will have to assess a judgmental probability that reflects your own, rather than the average citizen's, vulnerability to crime. Using relative-frequency data to make probabilistic predictions is not a purely objective process.

Of course, even for one-time-only events, some relative-frequency information might be helpful. In the past year, for example, Governor Timtree might have vetoed ten bills and had eight vetoes sustained. Consequently, someone might assert that the probability of sustaining a veto of the tax bill would be 0.8. But that is quite superficial reasoning. The other ten bills first passed the legislature by different majorities, and there were different coalitions of interest groups supporting each of the two sides of each bill. In fact, none of the ten previously vetoed bills was similar to the pending tax legislation.

Moreover, the anchoring and adjustment heuristic creates some real hazards for anyone who attempts to begin assessing a judgmental probability by using some dubiously relevant, relative-frequency information. If Barry Ternett begins his task by noting the governor's 80-percent success rate for the year, he might ignore some important, specific characteristics of this bill, and the forces supporting it, that make the probability of sustaining a veto much less than 50 percent.

Any probabilistic prediction requires judgment. Using an ideal probability generator is a useful way to think about uncertainty. Not jumping to a quick conclusion, but slowly narrowing down the range of possibilities can help you make an intelligent decision about a judgmental probability.

Uncertainty and Knowledge

To get in the habit of making judgmental, but specific, probabilistic predictions, assess the probability that the following uncertain outcomes will occur:

- When you awake tomorrow, it will be raining.
- Tomorrow's late-city edition of the *New York Times* will have a six-column banner headline.
- The Dow Jones Average will go up tomorrow.
- The Republican nominee will win the next U.S. presidential election.
- The Chase Manhattan Bank will raise its prime rate during the next month.
- The next session of Congress will adjourn before October 31.
- The number of people riding the New York City subway system will increase this year.

Thinking About Uncertainty

Making these and other probability judgments will help you practice your predictive skills. Like any other aspect of analytical decision making, the ability to think systematically about uncertainty can only be developed with experience.

Clearly, you will know more about some of these uncertain events than others. You may have just heard the weather report on the radio, or you may work for the Chase Manhattan Bank. In such cases, you may be quite confident of your predictions, and the probabilities you assign to the uncertain outcomes will be close to either 0 or 1. On the other hand, you may never have heard of Dow Jones, let alone how well he is hitting this season. In such situations, you would have to assign a probability closer to 0.5 to indicate your greater uncertainty.

One hundred and fifty years ago, the French mathematician Laplace wrote in his *Essai philosophique sur les probabilités:*

> Strictly speaking it may even be said that nearly all our knowledge is problematical; and in the small number of things which we are able to know with certainty, even the mathematical sciences themselves, the principal means for ascertaining truth—induction and analogy—are based on probabilities.[41]

Laplace argued that probabilities were merely an expression of our ignorance. "Probability is relative, in part to this ignorance, in part to our knowledge."[42]

The more information you have about what an uncertain outcome will be, the closer you will place the probability to 1 or to 0. "Perfect information" means that you know that the event will occur or that it will not occur, and that you can assign a probability of 1 or of 0 without any fear of being proven wrong.

In contrast, assigning the probability 0.5 to a possible outcome is to confess complete ignorance about what the uncertain event even is—whether it concerns the stock market or baseball—let alone about whether that outcome will occur. You simply have no idea whether it is more likely that the outcome of a particular event will be A than B, left than right, yes than no, red than green. Clearly, anyone who says the probability of nuclear war occurring next year is 50 percent must be absolutely ignorant of what the event, nuclear war, really is. To say that the probability of nuclear war is 4 percent or 0.4 percent is to indicate some knowledge about what it will take to produce such an outcome.

Often, we have some general information about the nature of an uncertain event, and this information can be used to help make a probability assessment different from 0.5. For example, suppose you were asked to assess the probability that Dow Jones would get a hit on his next at-bat. If you knew that Jones played baseball in the major leagues but had no idea how well he played or even what team he played for, you might want to assess this probability to be the average batting average of all the players in the major leagues—about .250. You do have some information about this uncertainty. Even though you have never heard of Jones, you know (1) that he plays major league baseball, and (2) that no major league baseball player gets a hit 50 percent of the time. Consequently, the knowledge you do have can be used to assess a probability different from 0.5.

We would, of course, like to be able to assign a probability as close to 0 or to 1 as possible. That would make our decision much easier; it would reduce the uncertainty. The weatherman would like to be able to tell us, with complete assurance, that the probability of rain tomorrow is 0, or that the probability of rain is 1. That makes it easy for us to decide whether to go to the beach. When he is forced to say the probability of rain is 0.5, he is hedging, confessing ignorance about whether it will rain—and he is not giving us very much help with our decision.

The Meaning of Probabilistic Accuracy

What does it mean to say that a probabilistic prediction is accurate? If Governor Timtree concluded that the probability of his veto being sustained was 0.45 and his aide Ternett said it was 0.3, and the legislature did in fact sustain the veto, who can say whether Ternett or Timtree was "correct"? Were you "wrong" to predict that the chance a coin would come up heads was 0.5, when it in fact came up heads? The probability you assign to any particular outcome is obviously based on personal judgment and, after the event, when the outcome has either occurred or not, it is impossible to determine if your probabilistic assessment was too high, too low, or just right. Because any specific uncertain event will only occur once, it is impossible to judge the "accuracy" of any single prediction.

You are not "right" or "wrong" on any single prediction, but as a predictor you may be very accurate or quite inaccurate over a period of time. Suppose you made one hundred predictions in which you said, "The probability of this happening is one-sixth." Suppose of the one hundred events you predicted, only eight actually occurred. You would be a rather poor predictor, at least concerning those events for which you said there existed a one-in-six chance, and if someone was familiar with you and your predictions he would want to convert any one-in-six prediction you made into an 8-percent chance.

Of course, it is possible that you were indeed making a good prediction each time you said the probability was one-sixth, and it was fate that made you look bad. The chances of that happening, however, are very small; a few calculations can show they are less than one in a hundred.[43] Thus, if you discover that your predictions are biased in one direction or another, you should begin to adjust the probabilities you assign so that, in the long run, your predictions are "correct"—in the relative-frequency sense. If for every 600 times that you predict an event will occur with probability of one-sixth, 100 of these events do indeed occur, then you are making "accurate" predictions.

Just as you need to check your own predictions (and those of people on whose judgment you rely) to be sure that they are accurate in the long run, so you need to be as discriminating as possible when you make forecasts. Predictions may be consistently too confident—too close to 0 and 1. Conversely, some people may hedge too much, by making predictions closer to 0.5 (or some long-run frequency trend) than need be. The closer to 0 or 1 a prediction is, the more value it has to a decision maker. Thus, there is the need to take into account all the available information to make the most discriminating and helpful prediction.

In Jackson, Mississippi, from 1964 through 1978, it rained, on the average, 111 days per year. Consequently, a weather forecaster in Jackson could go on the radio every morning and say, "The probability of rain today is 30 percent." Over the long run he would certainly be accurate; on almost exactly 30 percent of the days it would rain. But the citizens of Jackson would soon discover that he was giving almost no information. After all, the data also indicate that the probability of precipitation is 39 percent in January but only 16 percent in October.[44] Further, this weather forecaster would not be using all the available data about temperature, cloud formations, and winds to help him discriminate between the different days of the year and thus to make more valuable predictions of the probability of rain.

Long-run accuracy is not the only goal when making predictions. Discrimination is important too.

Overconfidence

Unfortunately, most people attempt to discriminate more than their knowledge warrants. This is one of the fundamental conclusions of the psychological research on uncertainty.[45] People are overconfident. For example, suppose that an individual is asked to make a large number of different probabilistic predictions and that for some of these uncertain events he decides that there is a 90-percent chance that a particular outcome (call it A) will occur. When these uncertain events take place, however, it invariably turns out that outcome A actually occurs less than the predicted 90 percent of the time. The results will be below 90 percent (say 75 percent) rather than above it, indicating that the individual was more confident in his predictions than was warranted by his own knowledge of the uncertain events. Furthermore, research shows, when the significance of the consequences to the decision maker increases, so does overconfidence.[46]

A Duke colleague, Phillip J. Cook, suggests that such overconfidence might be called the "Sherlock Holmes Phenomenon": We all believe that, if we are only clever enough, we should be able to make some elementary yet invariably accurate deductions from very meager evidence. In an attempt to demonstrate to ourselves—if not to others—our superior mental capabilities, we make unwarranted, overconfident predictions. Moreover, when we examine a historical event (whether it be the Japanese attack on Pearl Harbor or the results of last year's World Series), we search for reasons why it was entirely predictable, even though before the event itself the evidence was very confusing and mixed and some very intelligent people made some very confident (but very poor) predictions. Our unfailing ability to create some sort of post hoc logic further reenforces our self-image as cerebral equals of the great Holmes.

"Creeping determinism" is what Baruch Fischhoff of Decision Research calls the "tendency to perceive reported outcomes as having been relatively inevitable."[47] Fischhoff's research indicates that people's judgments about how they would have predicted future events is significantly influenced by hindsight knowledge. For example, he presented people with an obscure historical situation and asked them to assign probabilities to various possible outcomes; these predictions were significantly biased towards whichever of the outcomes they were told actually happened. Moreover, if after an uncertain event occurs, people are asked to replicate their original, before-the-event prediction, their response will be significantly biased towards what they now know happened.[48] These people, reports Fischhoff, "perceive a past which held too few surprises for them."[49] Little wonder that we predict a future with little appreciation for the many surprises that it, too, holds.

To counteract the tendency towards overconfidence, it helps to consider explicit reasons why you might be wrong. If you initially think there is an 85-percent chance that the Republican presidential candidate will win the next election, carefully draw up a list of all the possible reasons why that might not happen: The leading GOP candidate may become involved in a scandal; war may break out in the Middle East; the Democratic ticket may be particularly attractive; and so forth. None of these possible reasons may, in itself, be overwhelming, but together they can serve to deflate overconfidence. Explicitly developing reasons why past events might not have happened has been found to reduce hindsight bias, and specific attempts to consider why you might be wrong have worked to reduce overconfidence about the future.[50]

Thinking About Uncertainty

Calibrating Yourself

Despite these difficulties, it is possible to become a good probabilistic predictor. Weather forecasters provide the best example. They are quite well calibrated; that is, it does indeed rain on approximately 70 percent of the days for which they predict that the probability of rain is 70 percent.[51] Of course, weather forecasters do have a number of advantages. All the predictions they make are of a similar type; they are trained to make probabilistic predictions; they have current information on important meteorological conditions plus an extensive data base on past events and relationships; and they get instant feedback.[52]

Not all of these conditions can be replicated, but it is possible to design your own probabilistic predictions for which you receive quick feedback.[53] Moreover, the ideas discussed above, particularly the creation of reasons why a prediction might be wrong, can be consciously used to help overcome overconfidence. Finally, the use of an ideal probability generator can provide a concrete interpretation of the probabilities being assessed.

Consequently, making a series of short-term probabilistic predictions, drawing upon immediate events in your own life, can provide you with some helpful information about the quality of your own probabilistic judgments. How likely is it that I will finish this project by the end of the day? How likely is it that sales will top $10,000 this week? How likely is it that the committee will approve the bill at this afternoon's session? Next, after an initial series of predictions, calibrate yourself. Were you overconfident? Underconfident? Then, design a second series of predictions and see if you can reduce your own biases. To be able to think intelligently about uncertainty, people need to train themselves to make accurate—well calibrated—probabilistic predictions.

The Inevitability of Uncertainty

Uncertainty is frustrating. "There is nothing the stockmarket loathes more than uncertainties," wrote Leonard Silk in the *New York Times*.[54] Uncertainty complicates decision making because it leaves you—well—uncertain.

Even when the future is most unpredictable, however, many people attempt to ignore the uncertainty. In the winter of 1973–74, during the Arab oil embargo that followed the Yom Kippur War, the *Wall Street Journal* carried this front page headline:

Unknown Evil

FUEL SHORTAGE FAILS
TO CHANGE '74 BUDGETS
AT MANY CORPORATIONS

Impact Is So Uncertain That
Firms Hew to Old Plans;
Good News for Economy

Airlines, Autos Do Cut Back

The accompanying article reported:

> The impact of energy shortages has added myriad uncertainties to next year's budget assumptions, but few of the effects can be measured. As a consequence, corporations for the most part are sticking with their old budgets just as if nothing had happened.[55]

But things had happened. The future was going to be different—quite different —from the past. The "unknown evil" could not be measured, that is, predicted exactly, but corporate decision makers could have attempted to assess the probability of the most likely and significant outcomes of the embargo. For example, an increase in petroleum prices was easily predictable; the only real uncertainty was the size of the increase. Yet, by "sticking with their old budgets," these executives were making the absurd assumption that the consequences of the decisions they had made were unaffected by the coming inflation in fuel costs. American automobile manufacturers made a major error when they failed to predict how the dramatic increases in the price of fuel would alter consumer decisions.

Those who must defend their decisions publicly or argue their proposals before a group have a motive for ignoring uncertainty: their need to make a confident prediction of the benefits of their decision or proposal. Graham T. Allison, dean of the Kennedy School of Government at Harvard University, has called this "The 51–49 Principle."

> The law of the game [of bureaucratic politics]—he who hesitates loses his chance to play at that point and he who is uncertain about his recommendation is overpowered by others who are sure—pressures players to come down on one side of a 51 to 49 issue. . . . Because he must compete with others, the reasonable player is forced to argue much more confidently than he would if he were a detached judge.[56]

Uncertainty makes us personally uncomfortable. An uncertain world is a confused world, and in our search for security we yearn for that perfect prediction—a guiding star by which we can chart our future decisions. Decision makers thus search for certainty. Paul Slovic of Decision Research reports, "Examination of business decisions and government policy making suggests that, whenever possible, decision makers avoid uncertainty and the necessity of weighting and combining information."[57] So does the public. Wrote H. L. Mencken: "The public . . . demands certainties; it must be told definitely and a bit raucously that this is true and that is false. But there *are* no certainties."[58]

A common tactic for eliminating uncertainty is to employ a historical analogy. If important characteristics of the present can be found to have distinct similarities with the past, then we can confidently predict that the future too will follow as the past. Ernest R. May, professor of history at Harvard, has explained in his book *"Lessons" of the Past*[59] how foreign policy decision makers, when faced with uncertainty, use simplistic historical analogies to predict the future. Indeed, in the quest for the certain world, decision makers in all fields seek that perfect historical parallel. For example, Donald Woods reports that corporate managers pursue the same grail.

> In estimating the value to their company of a potential investment, the managers in the organizations studied are preoccupied with searching for a comparable prior investment rather than identifying the relevant variables and forecasting the underlying uncertainty. Uncertainty is avoided like the plague, while the certainty of historical information is accorded such a premium that it dominates the managers' mental process completely.[60]

The generals, in business as well as government, all insist on fighting the last war. As Arthur Schlesinger has written, "[George] Santayana's aphorism must be reversed: too often it is those who *can* remember the past who are condemned to repeat it."[61]

To make intelligent decisions in a world of uncertainty requires that we make probabilistic predictions that do not underestimate the obscurity of the future. An analytical decision maker must be able to confess that he cannot perfectly predict the future but also must be able to make intelligent probabilistic guesses. This is what is required to chart a sensible course through what Shakespeare called "Life's uncertain voyage."[62]

Appendix: Working with Probabilities

To think analytically about a decision dilemma complicated by uncertainty, it is necessary to assess the probability that the various outcomes will occur. Sometimes this can be done directly—wholistically. Sometimes it makes sense to decompose an uncertainty—the uncertainty of primary concern—into two or more related uncertainties, assess these related probabilities directly (as was done in this chapter to assess the probability that a state legislature would override a gubernatorial veto) and then combine these related probabilities to obtain the one in question. Such an indirect (analytical) approach can be helpful if the uncertainty in question is sufficiently complex to distort one's intuitive grasp of probability—and the uncertainty does not have to be very complex to do that.

The analytical task of indirectly assessing a probability can be made easier by using a probability tree. Such a probability tree can organize one's thinking and clarify the relationships among the various probabilities—between (1) the probability to be assessed indirectly and (2) the probabilities that are assessed directly and then used to help obtain the one of primary concern.

A probability tree can make clear the mathematical relationship among these probabilities. To recombine the directly assessed probabilities to get the one of primary concern, it will be necessary to do a few calculations. There are, of course, formulas for making these calculations, but they can get complex, and it is always difficult to remember which formula is the proper one —when one can remember any formula at all. It is usually a straightforward task, however, to construct the appropriate probability tree for indirectly assessing a specific probability. The probability tree makes it clear what the necessary calculations are.

To construct and use a probability tree, some simple standard notation about probabilities is helpful.

- A is a particular outcome. $\overline{A}$ is read "Not A" and means the reverse of A. For example, A could be the outcome that the legislature sustains the governor's veto, and $\overline{A}$ could be the outcome that the legislature overrides the veto.
- Prob(A) is the probability that A occurs, and Prob($\overline{A}$) is the probability that A does not occur (or, alternatively, the probability that Not A does occur).
- A vertical line or slash in a probability statement means "given" or "conditional on." Thus "Prob($B|A$)" is the probability that outcome B will occur given that A occurs, and "Prob($B|\overline{A}$)" is the probability that outcome B will occur conditional on A not occurring. Such probabilities are called *conditional probabilities*, since they indicate the probability that one event will occur conditional on some other event occurring. Prob(B) is the *unconditional probability* that B will occur —the probability that B will happen independently of whether A or $\overline{A}$ occurs. Prob($B|A$), on the other hand, is the number to which the probability of B would

Thinking About Uncertainty

change if you were told that *A* had occurred. For example, if *B* stands for the House overriding the governor's veto and *A* for the Senate doing so, Prob(*B*) is the probability that the House will override regardless of what the Senate does, but Prob(*B*|*A*) is the probability that the House will override given that you know the Senate has overridden.

- The comma in a probability statement means "and." Prob(*A,B*), which is the same as Prob(*A* and *B*), is the probability that *both A* and *B* will occur. This is often called the *joint probability*—the probability that *A* and *B* jointly occur. Thus, Prob(*A,B*) would mean the probability that *both* the Senate and the House vote to override the governor's veto.

The probability tree in figure 4–3 uses this notation. On this probability tree, every branch has two labels. An outcome branch for an uncertain event has the outcome listed above the branch and the probability of getting that outcome listed below it. A consequence branch for a terminal outcome has the consequence(s) of that terminal outcome listed above it, and the probability of getting that terminal outcome below it. Note that although a decision tree begins with a (square) decision node, a probability tree begins with a (round) uncertainty node, since a probability tree describes only a series of uncertain events; no decision is involved.

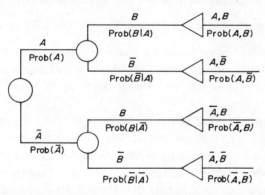

Figure 4–3. A Probability Tree.

Referring to this probability tree, the four basic probability rules can easily be defined and explained.

1. The Probabilities-Have-To-Add-to-One Rule, Part I: The probabilities for all the outcome branches coming from a single uncertainty node must sum to 1.0. That is,

$$\text{Prob}(A) + \text{Prob}(\bar{A}) = 1.0;$$
$$\text{Prob}(B|A) + \text{Prob}(\bar{B}|A) = 1.0; \text{ and}$$
$$\text{Prob}(B|\bar{A}) + \text{Prob}(\bar{B}|\bar{A}) = 1.0.$$

This rule should be obvious. Since the outcome branches coming from a single uncertainty node represent all the (mutually exclusive) possible outcomes, one of them must occur. Thus, the probability that one of these events will happen is 1.0.

2. The Multiplication Rule: To obtain the probability for any terminal outcome, multiply together the probabilities for the different outcome branches along the path from the initial uncertainty node to that terminal outcome.

$$\text{Prob}(A,B) = \text{Prob}(A) \times \text{Prob}(B|A);$$
$$\text{Prob}(A,\bar{B}) = \text{Prob}(A) \times \text{Prob}(\bar{B}|A);$$
$$\text{Prob}(\bar{A},B) = \text{Prob}(\bar{A}) \times \text{Prob}(B|\bar{A}); \text{ and}$$
$$\text{Prob}(\bar{A},\bar{B}) = \text{Prob}(\bar{A}) \times \text{Prob}(\bar{B}|\bar{A}).$$

Again, this should be intuitively reasonable. The probability that both the Senate and the House will override the governor's veto is the probability that the Senate will vote to override, $\text{Prob}(A)$, times the probability that the House will vote to override given that the Senate does, $\text{Prob}(B|A)$.

3. The Probabilities-Have-To-Add-to-One Rule, Part II: The probabilities for all the terminal outcomes on a probability tree must sum to 1.0.

$$\text{Prob}(A,B) + \text{Prob}(A,\bar{B}) + \text{Prob}(\bar{A},B) + \text{Prob}(\bar{A},\bar{B}) = 1.0.$$

The reasoning is similar to that for rule 1. Since the terminal nodes represent all the different (and mutually exclusive) possible final outcomes, one of these outcomes must occur. Thus, the probability that one of these events will happen is 1.0.

Actually, this third rule is derived from the first two. Take the probabilities for the four different terminal outcomes (line 1), and substitute for each terminal probability the corresponding product of probabilities from rule 2 (to give line 2). Then combine the two terms with $\text{Prob}(A)$ and the two terms with $\text{Prob}(\bar{A})$ (line 3). Then use rule 1 to note that $\text{Prob}(B|A) + \text{Prob}(\bar{B}|A) = 1.0$, and $\text{Prob}(B|\bar{A}) + \text{Prob}(\bar{B}|\bar{A}) = 1.0$ (line 4). But, of course, also by rule 1, $\text{Prob}(A) + \text{Prob}(\bar{A}) = 1.0$.

(line 1) $\text{Prob}(A,B) + \text{Prob}(A,\bar{B}) + \text{Prob}(\bar{A},B) + \text{Prob}(\bar{A},\bar{B}) =$

(line 2) $[\text{Prob}(A) \times \text{Prob}(B|A)] + [\text{Prob}(A) \times \text{Prob}(\bar{B}|A)] + [\text{Prob}(\bar{A}) \times \text{Prob}(B|\bar{A})] + [\text{Prob}(\bar{A}) \times \text{Prob}(\bar{B}|\bar{A})] =$

(line 3) $\text{Prob}(A) \times [\text{Prob}(B|A) + \text{Prob}(\bar{B}|A)] + \text{Prob}(\bar{A}) \times [\text{Prob}(B|\bar{A}) + \text{Prob}(\bar{B}|\bar{A})] =$

(line 4) $\text{Prob}(A) + \text{Prob}(\bar{A}) = 1.0.$

4. The Addition Rule: Finally, to get the probability for any particular consequence, add up the probabilities of all the terminal outcomes having that consequence. For instance,

96

Thinking About Uncertainty

$$\text{Prob}(B) = \text{Prob}(A,B) + \text{Prob}(\bar{A},B).$$

The first and third terminal nodes on the probability tree (figure 4–3) represent outcomes for which B occurs; thus the probability of B occurring is the sum of the probabilities for these two terminal outcomes. Similarly, for Not B (or $\bar{B}$):

$$\text{Prob}(\bar{B}) = \text{Prob}(A,\bar{B}) + \text{Prob}(\bar{A},\bar{B}).$$

This is merely the summation of the probabilities for the second and fourth terminal nodes in figure 4–3, the only terminal outcomes for which $\bar{B}$ is a consequence. Finally, using this rule to determine $\text{Prob}(A)$ can provide a consistency check with the other rules:

$$
\begin{aligned}
\text{Prob}(A) &= \text{Prob}(A,B) + \text{Prob}(A,\bar{B}). &\text{rule 4}\\
&= [\text{Prob}(A) \times \text{Prob}(B|A)] + [\text{Prob}(A) \times \text{Prob}(\bar{B}|A)]. &\text{rule 2}\\
&= \text{Prob}(A) \times [\text{Prob}(B|A) + \text{Prob}(\bar{B}|A)]. &\text{rearranging terms}\\
&= \text{Prob}(A) \times [1]. &\text{rule 1}
\end{aligned}
$$

The following example illustrates how these four rules can help a decision maker assess a probability indirectly. A governor needs to decide whether to submit a particular bill to the state legislature. One of the factors that will influence his decision is how likely he thinks it is that the House of Representatives will actually pass the bill. This probability can, of course, be assessed directly by comparing this uncertain event with an ideal probability generator. But it may be difficult to think carefully about this uncertainty without decomposing it into the various uncertain outcomes that lead to passage. In this case, taking these related uncertainties explicitly into account may be the best way to assess this probability.

The probability tree in figure 4–4 is just one way of decomposing the uncertainty about whether the House will pass the bill. It is a rather complex decomposition and might represent a third or fourth cut in this analysis. (For a discussion of multicut analysis, see chapter 9.) The tree specifies the different ways that the bill can pass. The normal sequential process is for the bill to be (1) approved by the appropriate subcommittee, (2) approved by the full committee, (3) placed on the House calendar by the Rules Committee, and then (4) passed by the entire House. This process is depicted by the four top most branches on the decision tree.

Of course, the House can approve the bill by attaching it to another bill as an amendment. It can do this (1) even if the bill is not approved by the subcommittee, (2) if the bill is approved by the subcommittee but not by the full committee, or (3) even if the bill is approved by the subcommittee and the full committee but is not placed on the House calendar by the Rules Committee. Actually, this could also be done after the bill had gone all the way to the

House floor (that is, was placed on the calendar by the Rules Committee) but had been rejected by the full House. To the governor, however, this possibility seems so unlikely that it is not included on his probability tree. Thus, the probability tree is a simplification; it does not include all the possible sequences of uncertain events that could lead to passage (or rejection) of the bill.

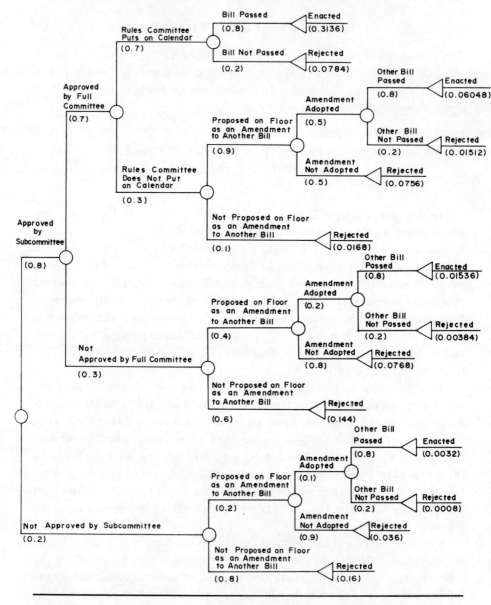

Figure 4–4. A Probability Tree for Assessing the Probability That a House of Representatives Will Pass a Particular Bill.

Thinking About Uncertainty

The four different ways given on the probability tree for passing the bill (the four "Enacted" consequence branches denote these terminal outcomes) are the ones that the governor considers the most likely means of passage and thus the ones that he wants to include in his analysis.

The probabilities given on the probability tree for each of the outcome branches are assessed directly by the governor (or his staff) by comparing the uncertain event with an ideal probability generator. Note, for example, that the probability that the bill is adopted as an amendment to another bill is clearly dependent upon how far the bill made it through the regular legislative process. If the bill was rejected by the subcommittee, this probability is 0.1:

Prob(Amendment Adopted|Not Approved by Subcommittee) = 0.1.

If the bill was approved by the subcommittee but rejected by the full committee, this probability is 0.2:

Prob(Amendment Adopted|Approved by Subcommittee but Not by Full Committee) = 0.2.

If the bill was approved by both the subcommittee and the full committee, but not placed on the House calendar by the Rules Committee, this probability is 0.5:

Prob(Amendment Adopted|Approved by Subcommittee and Full Committee but Not by Rules Committee) = 0.5.

Clearly, the probability that the bill is adopted as an amendment to another bill is conditional on the outcomes of other uncertain events.

Now, note that the four probability rules are illustrated by this probability tree:

1. The probabilities for all of the outcome branches attached to each of the uncertainty nodes sum to 1.0.
2. The probabilities for the terminal outcomes are obtained by multiplying the outcome branch probabilities along the path leading from the initial uncertainty node to that terminal outcome. For example, the probability for the top most terminal outcome is $(0.8) \times (0.7) \times (0.7) \times (0.8) = 0.3136$.
3. The probabilities for all the terminal outcomes sum to 1.0:
   $0.3136 + 0.0784 + 0.06048 + 0.01512 + 0.0756 + 0.0168 + 0.01536 + 0.00384 + 0.0768 + 0.144 + 0.0032 + 0.0008 + 0.036 + 0.16 = 1.0$.
4. The probability that the bill will be approved (somehow) by the House is obtained by summing up the probabilities of the terminal outcomes with this consequence (in other words, by summing the probabilities of those terminal nodes with a consequence branch labeled "Enacted").
   Prob(Bill Approved) $= 0.3136 + 0.06048 + 0.01536 + 0.0032$
   $= 0.39264$
   $\cong 0.39$ or 0.4

Note, it does not make sense to claim that the probability that the bill will pass is 0.39264. This number was obtained from a series of calculations based on a collection of probabilities that were assessed to only one significant figure. How can the probability of any event derived from these assessments be known to five significant figures? Thus, the probability that the bill will pass has been assessed, indirectly, to be 0.39 or 0.4. If using such a number when analyzing the decision about whether to submit the bill makes it difficult to decide between the alternatives, the most appropriate way to resolve the dilemma is with a sensitivity analysis.

Also note that it is not worth adding any additional paths for passage of the bill to the probability tree unless they will make a significant contribution to the total probability of passage. In figure 4-4, one terminal outcome with the "Enacted" consequence has a probability of only 0.0032, which contributes virtually nothing to the overall probability. Unless an additional path with the "Enacted" consequence has a higher probability than this, it can be safely ignored.

The four probability rules discussed here are easy to understand. They are quite intuitive because they concern simple combinations of uncertain events. But intuition about probability can quickly mislead once the problem gets slightly complex. In such situations, a little quick analysis—a little decomposition of the problem—can be very helpful. By decomposing a complex uncertainty into a number of simpler uncertainties (for which the probability-assessment task is more intuitive) and then using the probability rules, a decision maker can easily overcome his intuitive handicap.

Chapter 5

Double-Risk Dilemmas: Candidate Moynihan's Decision

ON September 14, 1976, Daniel Patrick Moynihan narrowly won the Democratic senatorial nomination in New York, and faced a tough campaign against the incumbent, James L. Buckley. Among the decisions that Moynihan had to make—and make quickly—was what to do about his teaching responsibilities at Harvard University. Moynihan had tenure at Harvard, but given the leave he had taken to be ambassador to the United Nations in 1975–76, he could not keep that tenure without teaching two courses during the fall semester. Moynihan would have liked, of course, to maintain his Harvard tenure as insurance, just in case he lost to Buckley. But this would require him to teach a one-hour class on Mondays and Wednesdays and a two-hour seminar on Tuesdays, severely reducing the time he could spend campaigning in New York. Thus candidate Moynihan's dilemma: Although teaching at Harvard during the fall semester would mitigate the consequences of losing the Senate race, it would also reduce his chances of winning.[1]

Both of Moynihan's alternatives were gambles; regardless of whether he decided to teach at Harvard, he could win or lose his Senate campaign. Consequently, the basic decision dilemma and the decision sapling of chapters 2 and 3 are not directly helpful in analyzing this decision. Moynihan's dilemma was not whether to select the risky or the riskless alternative, but which risky alternative to take. Both of his choices were gambles with the same best

101

outcome. The difference between them was that if he chose not to teach but to campaign full time, his chances of winning were better, but if he elected to teach and campaign part time, the consequences of losing were not as bad. Thus, candidate Moynihan faced a *double-risk decision dilemma.*

The double-risk decision dilemma can be illustrated with the simple decision tree in figure 5–1. The problem is decomposed into two alternatives, each of

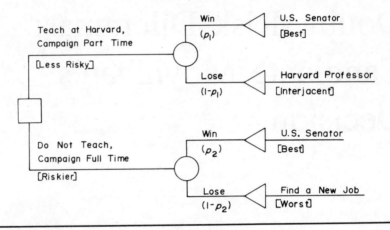

Figure 5–1. Candidate Moynihan's Double-Risk Decision Dilemma.

which leads to an uncertain event with two possible outcomes. To analyze this type of dilemma, it is necessary—as with every other decision analysis—to specify probabilities and preferences. For Moynihan's problem, this means specifying the probabilities for two uncertain outcomes (winning, given full-time campaigning; and winning, given part-time campaigning) and preferences for the three different final outcomes (U.S.-Senator, Harvard-Professor, Find-a-New-Job). Once these probabilities and preferences have been specified, the resolution of the dilemma may not be as immediately obvious as it was in the case of the basic decision dilemma, but it can be easily determined.

Specifying Probabilities

The process for making subjective but analytical judgments about probabilities has been described in detail in chapters 3 and 4 and will not be repeated here. The basic idea is to compare the one-time uncertain event in question (here, winning or losing the Senate race) with an ideal probability generator

Double-Risk Dilemmas

—such as an urn with 100 balls, each either white or green—that is easily understood and has a clear relative-frequency interpretation.

Moynihan was favored to defeat Senator Buckley, so the chances of his winning were greater than 50 percent regardless of whether he campaigned full time or part time. Assume that an analysis of these two uncertainties leads to the conclusion that the probability of winning by campaigning full time is 70 percent and the probability of winning by campaigning part time is two percentage points less. This difference might seem quite small, but there were a large number of factors (not just the amount of time that Moynihan spent campaigning) that would influence the outcome of this election: the simultaneous presidential contest between Ford and Carter, international events, the cleverness of the two candidates' media and advertising advisors, local party organization and enthusiasm, and so forth. Both candidates were well known in the state—Moynihan had received much publicity as U.N. ambassador and from his summer primary campaign against Bella Abzug—so the additional campaigning that he might do would not influence too many voters. Thus, let $p_1 = 0.68$, and $p_2 = 0.70$. (Note that if p_1 is greater than p_2 there is no dilemma, for if part-time campaigning results in both a greater chance of winning and a better consequence of losing, this alternative is clearly preferred.)

Specifying Preferences

The first step in thinking about preferences for the various possible outcomes of a decision is to determine which outcome is the best and which is the worst. Usually, this part is quite easy. For candidate Moynihan, the best outcome is to be elected to the Senate—otherwise there would be no reason to run. And the worst outcome is to have to look for another job—otherwise there would be no dilemma. If the Harvard-Professor outcome rather than the Find-a-New-Job outcome was the worst, then the campaign-full-time alternative would clearly be the better choice; campaigning full time would not only result in the greater chance of winning (0.7 rather than 0.68), but it would also result in the better outcome (Find-a-New-Job) if the campaign was lost. Thus, the U.S.-Senator outcome is assessed a preference-probability of 1.0, and the Find-a-New-Job outcome a preference-probability of 0.

Of course, the two final outcomes labeled "U.S. Senator" are not precisely identical, since the ways Moynihan gets to these two outcomes are different. He might prefer to win while spending part of the fall teaching, or he might prefer to win without the bother of having to commute between Cambridge and New York. For the purpose of making this decision, however, these two outcomes are virtually indistinguishable and should be given the same preference-probability: 1.0.

This illustrates one of the subtle but fundamental benefits of explicit, systematic analysis: Merely drawing a decision tree can elicit an important insight. In this case, drawing the decision tree makes it obvious that the best outcome of either alternative is essentially the same. "Well, that's obvious," someone might say. Sure it is. But it may not be so "obvious" until you draw the decision tree; before that, one of the alternatives might somehow appear to be better.

For example, consider the medical dilemma of whether to operate on a patient. In this double-risk dilemma (which is discussed in more detail later in this chapter), death can result from either alternative, and if that is the outcome it makes no difference—to the patient, the doctor, or the family—what alternative was chosen. The consequence, death, is the same. Yet, that is not the way it always appears. In a discussion of one of the chief complaints about the use of decision analysis in medicine ("I'm not going to let my patient die of a curable disease") William B. Schwartz, M.D., of the Tufts University School of Medicine, examines a common but fallacious attitude:

> Letting a patient die without operation, to take an example, seems worse to many practitioners than losing him during a valiant surgical effort. "Never mind the odds," goes the argument, "How would you feel if a treatable lesion were discovered at autopsy, and you had failed to use a lifesaving procedure?" Even when the potential value of operation is outweighed by the risk, fear of a lost opportunity for dramatic cure may dominate the decision. Patients and their families often share this attitude. We are rarely criticized for actions leading to a bad outcome as long as there was some hope of a good result. Thus, it's easier to go against the odds and to operate than to face the possibly unpleasant consequence of inaction. "At least I tried," is almost always a good defense.[2]

But, of course, the outcome is the same whether the physician chose to operate —a life has been lost. Drawing a simple decision tree can make that not-so-obvious fact very obvious.

For candidate Moynihan's dilemma, the difficult part of thinking about preferences is to evaluate the outcome of being a Harvard professor. All that is required, however, is an evaluation of the *relative* merits of this interjacent outcome—relative to the other two possible outcomes involved in the decision: being a U.S. senator, and having to find a new job. Thus, the simple concept for specifying relative preference—the preference-probability—and the simple process for thinking about it—the reference gamble—can be used to specify a preference-probability for the interjacent outcome of this decision.

Since the senator outcome has been given a preference-probability of 1.0 and the new-job outcome has been assigned a preference-probability of 0, these are the two reference outcomes for the reference gamble, which will be used to

Double-Risk Dilemmas

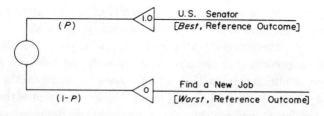

Figure 5–2. Reference Gamble.

assess preference-probabilities for all other, interjacent outcomes. Since for this decision there is only one interjacent outcome, there is only one other preference-probability to assess.

This is done by comparing the interjacent outcome, Harvard-Professor, with the reference gamble having a P chance of the *Best* (senator) and a $1 - P$ chance of the *Worst* (find a new job). Here P is not the probability of some uncertain event involved in the actual decision but a relative-frequency probability produced by some ideal probability generator. For example, P could be the probability of drawing a green ball from an urn with 100 balls; then P would be the proportion of green balls in the urn, or $P = G/100$. And $1 - P$ would equal $(100 - G)/100$.

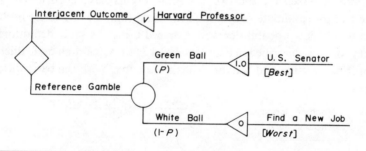

Figure 5–3. Using the Reference Gamble to Assess the Preference-Probability for the Interjacent Outcome.

To assess the preference-probability for the professor outcome, it is necessary to adjust the number of green balls in the urn. If $G = 98$, the probability of getting the *Best* is 0.98, and the candidate would prefer the risk of the reference gamble to the interjacent outcome of being a Harvard professor. If $G = 10$, so that the probability of getting the *Best* equals 0.10, the candidate would choose the interjacent outcome over the reference gamble. The question is: What is the candidate's indifference probability? Starting with 10 green balls and 90 white balls in the urn and replacing white balls with green ones, the reference gamble becomes better and better. As this process takes place—as the probability, *P,* of getting the *Best* increases—at what point does the candidate switch from preferring the interjacent outcome to the reference gamble? This switch probability is the candidate's preference-probability for the interjacent outcome. That is because P_{switch} is the probability that makes the candidate exactly indifferent between the reference gamble and the interjacent outcome.

Assume, for example, that candidate Moynihan's switch probability is 0.30. Moynihan thinks that being a U.S. senator is much better than being a Harvard professor or finding another job. And, although finding another job would not be that difficult, he definitely prefers teaching his courses at Harvard (and living in his home right off Harvard Square) to working and living somewhere else.

Resolving the Double-Risk Decision Dilemma

The preference-probabilities assessed for the three possible outcomes and the probabilities assessed for the two uncertain events have been noted on the decision tree for candidate Moynihan's dilemma (figure 5–4.) These probabilities and preference-probabilities were assessed using the same definitions and thought processes described in chapters 2 and 3 to resolve such basic dilemmas as the angina decision and Mayor Willis's dilemma. With the basic dilemma,

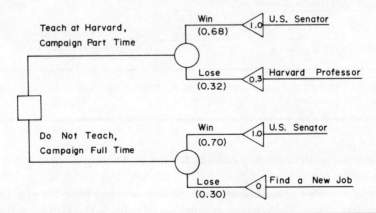

Figure 5–4. The Decision Tree for Candidate Moynihan's Dilemma, with All Probabilities and Preference-Probabilities Specified.

Double-Risk Dilemmas

all that is required is to determine whether the preference-probability for the interjacent consequence of the riskless alternative is greater than or less than the probability of getting the *Best* outcome on the actual decision sapling. But candidate Moynihan is not faced with a basic dilemma. There are still only three different possible outcomes (and thus only one interjacent outcome between the *Best* and the *Worst*), but the choice is not between a risky and a riskless alternative. Both alternatives are risky, and the implications of the foregoing analysis are not immediately obvious.

Nevertheless, by using the fundamental concept that was the key to the logical resolution of the basic dilemma—the substitution principle—this double-risk decision can also be resolved. The trick is to substitute for the interjacent outcome the reference gamble for which the candidate has exactly the same preference. He is indifferent between being a Harvard professor for sure and a reference gamble with a 30-percent chance of being in the Senate and a 70-percent chance of having to look for a new job. Consequently, this reference gamble can be substituted on the decision tree for its equivalent interjacent outcome (figure 5–5).

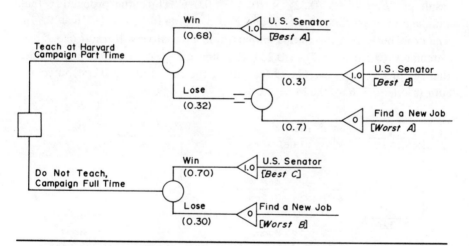

Figure 5–5. Using the Substitution Principle.

Still, the resolution of the dilemma is not clear. In fact, this decision tree looks more complicated. Whereas before there were two uncertainties and four outcomes, there are now three uncertainties and five outcomes. How can this more complex-looking decision tree help resolve the dilemma?

The answer is that although the number of uncertainties and outcomes has indeed increased, the number of *different* possible final outcomes has been reduced to two. There are now five final outcomes, but each one is either

U.S.-Senator (the *Best*) or Find-a-New-Job (the *Worst*). The decision tree in figure 5–4 contained three *different* outcomes and thus was complicated by the existence of three different preference-probabilities: 1.0, 0.3, and 0. But the decision tree that resulted from the use of the substitution principle (figure 5–5) has outcomes with only two preference-probabilities: 1.0 and 0. Thus, it is possible to make this decision by deciding which alternative gives the better chance of getting a *Best* outcome. This is the rationale for converting the decision tree in figure 5–4 into the one in figure 5–5.

Clearly, the probability that the campaign-full-time alternative will produce the *Best* outcome is 0.70. The more complicated question is what is the probability that the campaign-part-time alternative will result in the *Best*. There are two *Best* outcomes that can result from this decision, *"Best A"* and *"Best B,"* and it is necessary to combine these two into a single *"Best"* outcome.

This can be done by making some probability calculations (as described in the appendix to chapter 4). The probability that the campaign-part-time alternative will result in *"Best A"* is 0.68. The probability that this alternative will result in *"Best B"* is $(0.32) \times (0.3) = 0.096$. Thus, the probability that campaigning part time results in any *Best* outcome is $0.68 + 0.096 = 0.776$. The probability that the campaign-part-time alternative will result in a *Worst* outcome is $(0.32) \times (0.7) = 0.224$. (See figure 5–6. As a double-check, note that the probabilities calculated for getting the *Best* and the *Worst* outcomes sum to one: $0.776 + 0.224 = 1.0$.)

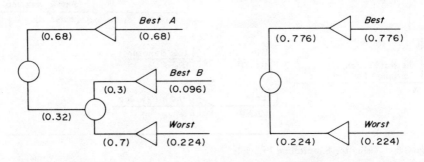

Figure 5–6. Using Probability Rules to Determine the Total Probability of a *Best* Outcome.

These probability calculations reduce the set of uncertainty nodes and outcome branches that emanates from the campaign-part-time decision branch in figure 5–5 to a single reference gamble with a 77.6-percent chance of the *Best* and a 22.4-percent chance of the *Worst*. And since the two *Best* outcomes that can result from this decision branch are identical, this new representation of the uncertainty is equivalent to the original one. All that has been done is to determine the overall probabilities for getting the *Best* and the *Worst*. Consequently, this new diagram of the uncertainty can be substituted for the one in figure 5–5 (see figure 5–7).

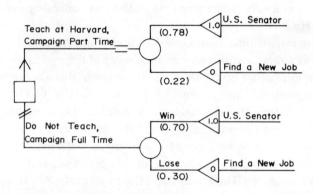

Figure 5–7. Candidate Moynihan's Decision as a Choice between Two Reference Gambles.

The probabilities that have been used are 0.78 and 0.22, however, not 0.776 and 0.224. These probabilities were obtained from the rather rough assessments of the probability of winning while campaigning part time (0.68) and the indifference probability for the interjacent outcome of being a Harvard professor (0.3). These original probabilities were not assessed to three significant figures, and there should be no pretense that numbers calculated from them could be that "accurate" either. As M. J. Moroney, Fellow of the Royal Statistical Society, observed: "It is an easy and fatal step to think that the accuracy of our arithmetic is equivalent to the accuracy of our knowledge about the problem at hand. We suffer from 'delusions of accuracy.' "[3] Accordingly, the calculated probabilities have been rounded-off to two digits.

These probabilities could have been rounded-off to a single digit—to 0.8 and 0.2—without affecting the decision, for the implications of the analysis are now quite clear. The decision, as presented in figure 5–7, is a choice between two reference gambles. Each decision branch leads to an uncertainty node with two possible outcomes, U.S.-Senator (the *Best*) and Find-a-New-Job (the *Worst*). The only difference is the probability of getting the *Best*. For the campaign-full-time alternative, this probability is 0.7. For campaigning part time, it is 0.78 (or 0.8—it does not make any difference). For the double-risk dilemma described in figure 5–7, the campaign-part-time alternative is clearly superior, for it leads to a greater chance of the *Best* outcome.

This is the same as saying that the preference-probability for the campaign-full-time alternative is 0.7 and the preference-probability for the campaign-part-time alternative is 0.78. The first preference-probability (0.7) follows directly from the original specification of the problem in figure 5–4. The candidate is indifferent between campaigning full time and a reference gamble with a 70-percent chance of the *Best* and a 30-percent chance of the *Worst* because this is precisely the gamble that results from choosing the campaign-full-time alternative.

The campaign-part-time alternative does not, however, result in a reference gamble, but in a gamble with a 68-percent chance of the *Best* and a 32-percent chance at an interjacent outcome. Thus, to compare this alternative directly with the campaign-full-time alternative, it is necessary to find an equivalent reference gamble such that the candidate is indifferent between the uncertain consequences of campaigning part time and the uncertain consequences of this reference gamble. This can be done by assessing a preference-probability for the interjacent outcome, using the substitution principle, and making a few probability calculations. The conclusion of such an analysis is that the candidate is indifferent between the risk incurred by campaigning part time and the risk involved in the reference gamble with a 78-percent chance of becoming a U.S. senator and a 22-percent chance of having to find a new job.

It may be, of course, that the implications of such an analysis are completely unsatisfactory; the candidate may be convinced that the indifference probability simply cannot be as high as 0.78, and thus that one has not thought carefully enough about some critical step in the analysis. In such a case more thinking is required. But if the candidate is satisfied, if the analysis is indeed convincing, then his preference-probability for the campaign-part-time alternative is 0.78.

The interpretation of a preference-probability for a decision alternative is the same as its interpretation for a final outcome. If someone assesses a preference-probability for a terminal node to be V, he is indifferent between the (certain) consequences that result from that final outcome and a reference gamble with a V chance of the *Best* and a $1 - V$ chance of the *Worst*. Similarly, if someone assesses a preference-probability for a decision branch (either directly or indirectly through some analysis) to be V', he is indifferent between the (uncertain) consequences that result from selecting that decision and a reference gamble with a V' chance of the *Best* and a $1 - V'$ chance of the *Worst*. Consequently, just as one indicates the preference-probability for a final outcome by displaying it inside that terminal node, so one indicates the preference-probability for a decision alternative by displaying it inside the node at the end of that decision branch (figure 5–8).

All this explains the relationship between the original decision tree (figure 5–4), the decision tree that resulted from the analysis (figure 5–7), and the decision tree that displays the final conclusions (figure 5–8, which is just figure 5–4 with preference-probabilities indicated for the two alternatives). Only two steps were taken to convert figure 5–4 into figure 5–7. First, the substitution principle was used to replace the interjacent outcome with a reference gamble in which the probability of getting the *Best* was precisely that probability that made the candidate indifferent between the interjacent outcome and that reference gamble. (This is exactly what must be done to resolve the basic dilemma.) Second, some probability calculations were made to determine the overall probability of getting the *Best* outcome. (This is necessary because the probability of getting the *Best* is obscured by multiple uncertainties.) Consequently, if the decisi⌐n maker prefers the campaign-part-time alternative in figure 5–7, he should also prefer it in figure 5–4. Indeed, if the candidate agrees that

1. the probability of winning given part-time campaigning is 0.68,
2. the probability of winning given full-time campaigning is 0.7, and
3. the probability that makes him indifferent between being a Harvard professor for sure and taking a reference gamble with a U.S. senator as the *Best* outcome and Find-a-New-Job as the *Worst* is 0.3,

then the above analysis indicates that he also prefers to teach during the fall semester and campaign part time.

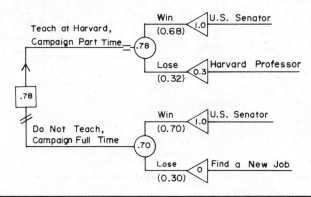

Figure 5–8. The Decision Tree for Candidate Moynihan's Dilemma, with Preference-Probabilities Specified for the Two Alternatives.

Sensitivity Analysis

Still, this simple statement may not be completely convincing. After all, each of these three probabilities was a rough assessment—a subjective judgment. Perhaps the probability of winning given a full-time campaign should be specified as 0.75, or the probability of winning with a part-time campaign assessed as 0.65. Or perhaps, after some more thinking, it is concluded that the indifference probability (preference-probability) for the interjacent outcome is not 0.3 but 0.4, or maybe 0.2. If so, this type of reanalysis might lead to a different decision. Consequently, there is a need for some sensitivity analysis—a check to determine if the conclusion reached is too "sensitive" to the probability assessments made or if it holds even if these assessments are modified somewhat.

A general calculation is helpful. Let p be the probability of winning given a part-time campaign. Let $p + d$ be the probability of winning given a full-time campaign, so that d is the marginal increase in the probability of winning that results from switching from a part-time to a full-time campaign strategy. And let V be the indifference probability of the reference gamble for the interjacent outcome. Then the decision tree of figure 5–5 can be relabeled with these variables (figure 5–9).

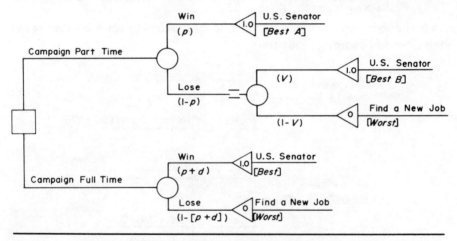

Figure 5–9. Sensitivity Analysis: Using the Substitution Principle.

The same type of probability calculation can now be made to determine the probability of getting the *Best* outcome from each alternative. For full-time campaigning, the probability is obviously $p + d$. For part-time campaigning, however, there are two *Best* outcomes. The probability of getting *"Best A"* is p. The probability of getting *"Best B"* is $(1 - p) \cdot V$. Adding these two probabilities gives the total probability that the campaign-part-time alternative will result in a *Best* outcome: $p + [(1 - p) \cdot V]$. Thus, as figure 5–10 shows, the campaign-part-time alternative is still preferred as long as $p + [(1 - p) \cdot V]$ exceeds $p + d$, that is, as long as $p + [(1 - p) \cdot V] > p + d$. Subtracting p from both sides, this inequality becomes $(1 - p) \cdot V > d$; and now dividing

Double-Risk Dilemmas

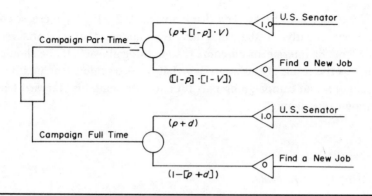

Figure 5–10. Sensitivity Analysis: A Choice between Two Reference Gambles.

both sides by $(1 - p)$ yields $V > d/(1 - p)$. If V exceeds $d/(1 - p)$, the probability of getting the *Best* outcome is higher for part-time than for full-time campaigning. (See figure 5–10.)

Assessing a few specific values for these three variables (p, d, and V) completes the sensitivity analysis. For example, suppose that $p = 0.68$ and $d = 0.02$ (the original assessments for these two probabilities). Then the inequality $V > d/(1 - p)$ becomes $V > 0.0625$ (since $0.02/0.32 = 0.0625$). If V is assessed to be greater than 0.0625, part-time campaigning is preferred; if V is less than 0.0625, a full-time campaign is best. Thus, $V = 0.0625$ is the *switch point*, the point at which the candidate switches from preferring full-time to part-time campaigning. (More generally, $V_{switch} = d/(1 - p)$.) If $p = 0.68$ and $d = 0.02$, the campaign-part-time alternative is the best even if the preference-probability for the interjacent outcome is as low as 0.07—and, as the original description of the problem indicates, it is certainly greater than this.

But of course p and d might be different. To check out the implications of other assessments of these probabilities, suppose that $p = 0.75$ and $d = 0.05$. That is, assume that the probability of winning with a part-time campaign is 75 percent, and that campaigning full time would increase the probability of winning, to 80 percent. Both of these assessments are unrealistically high (*Congressional Quarterly* only assessed the race as "Leans Democratic,"[4] and a 5-percentage-point benefit from three more days of campaigning per week is quite large), but both of these shifts will raise the switch point for the preference-probability for the interjacent outcome. They only increase V_{switch} to 0.20, however. In other words, the campaign-part-time alternative is still preferred as long as the indifference probability for the interjacent outcome, Harvard-Professor, is greater than 0.2.

Even if p is increased to 0.8 (and d remains at 0.05), V_{switch} increases only to 0.25. Consequently, if the candidate is confident that his preference-probability for the interjacent outcome is something above 0.25, he should be confident—as the result of this analysis—that he also prefers teaching during the fall semester and campaigning part time to sacrificing his Harvard tenure for full-time campaigning.

Rethinking the Analysis

This sensitivity analysis provides some extra insight into the fundamental conflict that makes this decision a dilemma, for it focuses attention on how the consequence of losing and the probability of losing are affected by switching from full-time to part-time campaigning. This switch increases the probability of losing, from $1 - (p + d)$ to $(1 - p)$, but it also makes the consequence of losing better by increasing the preference-probability of losing from 0 to V. Thus, the decision is a dilemma because it is not clear whether the "unemployment insurance" obtained by campaigning part-time—insurance that will pay off only if the campaign is lost—is worth its cost, which is the increased chance of losing that a part-time campaign entails.

Which is the dominant consideration: the better consequence of losing or the increased probability of doing so? As this sensitivity analysis indicates, the value of the probability, p, affects the answer. The larger p is, the smaller is the chance of losing (with either alternative), and thus the less effect that the differential in preference-probability between the two different consequences of losing will have on the preference-probability differential for the two alternatives. Or, to put this another way, the larger p is, the smaller is $(1 - p)$, and thus the larger is $V_{switch} = d/(1 - p)$; the larger V_{switch}, the greater must be the preference-probability differential for losing (which is $V - 0$) in order for the campaign-part-time alternative to be best. The variable d is important, too. The larger d is, the less likely it is that the campaign-full-time alternative will result in a loss, and thus the less important will be the preference-probability differential between losing with this strategy and losing with a part-time campaign. The larger d is, in other words, the larger is V_{switch}, and thus the larger V must be for the campaign-part-time alternative to be best.

Consequently, if these two probabilities, p and d, are given unreasonably large values, the analysis is biased against the campaign-part-time alternative. Since $V_{switch} = d/(1 - p)$, as p and d become greater, so does V_{switch}. Yet, even under such conditions, if it is clear that V exceeds V_{switch}, then it is also clear that the best decision is to campaign part time. This type of thinking is often called *worst case analysis*—even when making the "worst case" for the campaign-part-time option, simple analysis demonstrates that it is still superior.

This sensitivity analysis also illustrates an important feature of intelligent, creative, and careful analysis. The purpose of decision analysis is not to calculate a single, simple preference-probability for each alternative and then mechanically select the largest. If one alternative has a preference-probability of 0.43 and a second has a preference-probability of 0.42, is this sufficient evidence that the first alternative is better? Obviously not. A variety of judgments, simplifications, and assumptions produced these two preference-probabilities. A small change in any one of them could reverse the ranking of these two preference-probabilities. Nevertheless, it may be possible to conclude—after sensitivity analysis—that the preference-probability of the first alternative is greater than 0.43 and that of the second less than 0.42. (Or more analysis might again result in overlapping preference-probabilities, in which case neither alternative would be clearly better and either could be selected without fear of making a major mistake.) It is not the difference between two exact, single-number preference-probabilities that is most convincing, but the conclusion that the plausible ranges for the two preference-probabilities do (or do not) overlap.

Alain C. Enthoven of the Stanford University Graduate School of Business has proposed "ten practical principles for policy and program analysis," the first of which is "Good analysis is the servant of judgment, not a substitute for it." Enthoven thus emphasizes the importance of sensitivity analysis—determining how the conclusions of an analysis depend upon the judgments that went into it.

> A good analysis should help the decision maker by telling him how the choice depends upon key judgments, rather than trying to tell him what the answer is. A good analysis will search out and highlight the key questions of value, the uncertainties and the intangibles, and not bury them . . . . So much of the literature on decision theory describes how to find the best answer, given certain input data and assumptions rather than emphasizing finding out how answers depend upon assumptions . . . . A good analysis will include sensitivity tests . . . that tell the decision maker which assumptions really matter and which don't.[5]

Sensitivity analysis is clearly essential when analyzing a decision such as candidate Moynihan's dilemma, in which the decision maker has little information and for which little more can be obtained. It might have been possible to obtain some "hard" input data by taking a post-primary poll, but it would still have been necessary to translate that polling information into the required probabilities. Thus, although some professionals are obviously better at interpreting polling results than others, any assessment of the probability of winning the election would necessarily be based on assumptions and judgments.

Even without much data, a quick sensitivity analysis can nevertheless result in an unambiguous resolution of a decision dilemma. Using the concepts of analytical thinking—simplifying the decision down to its most important factors and then decomposing these factors into probabilities and preferences so that each can be specified—it is possible to generate some very useful insight into the fundamental nature of the dilemma and to resolve it.

Medical Double-Risk Decision Dilemmas

The double-risk dilemma provides a useful perspective for analyzing a variety of decision problems, including those faced by the physician who must decide whether to treat a patient for a particular illness. Even after all the relevant diagnostic tests have been performed, a physician may still be uncertain about whether a patient has a serious disease that warrants a particular treatment or merely has some temporary symptoms for which the treatment would provide no benefit and might actually be harmful to the patient.

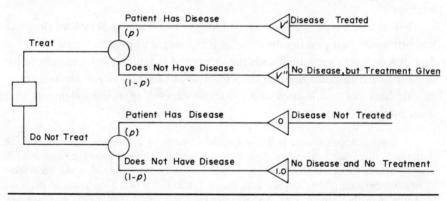

Figure 5–11. The Physician's Double-Risk Decision Dilemma.

For many medical double-risk dilemmas, the best outcome is to have neither the disease nor the treatment, while the worst is for the disease to go untreated. In these situations, it is often convenient to assign these two outcomes preference-probabilities of 1.0 and 0, respectively. An analysis of this dilemma is simplified by the need to assess only one probability, p, since the chance of having the disease is the same whether treatment is given. The analysis is complicated, however, by the existence of two interjacent outcomes (Disease-Treated and No-Disease,-but-Treatment-Given) and thus the need to assess two preference-probabilities, V' and V''.

Double-Risk Dilemmas

Because the probability of having the disease is the same for both alternatives, there cannot be a dilemma unless V' is greater than zero and V'' is less than 1.0. For example, $V' = 0$ means that if the patient has the disease the treatment accomplishes nothing; the consequence is the same (the *Worst*), which is why $V' = 0$. And since treating a patient who does not have the disease has some undesirable side effects (which is why $V'' < 1.0$), the obvious decision in this case (when $V' = 0$) is do not treat. On the other hand, $V'' = 1.0$ means that if the patient does not have the disease, it makes no difference whether the treatment is applied; there are no potentially harmful side effects to treating a patient who does not have the disease. In this case (when $V'' = 1.0$), however, because treating a patient who has the disease does have some benefits ($V' > 0$), the obvious decision is to treat.

An illustrative example of this generic dilemma is the one faced by a physician whose patient has several of the symptoms of acute appendicitis. Should the physician perform an appendectomy? If the patient does have appendicitis, there is a 1-percent chance that, without an operation, he will die from a perforated appendix. But if an appendectomy is performed, there is still a 0.1-percent chance of death from complications of surgery (figure 5–12).[6]

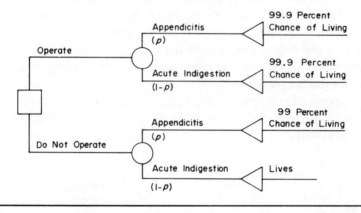

Figure 5–12. The Appendectomy Decision Dilemma.

For a first-cut analysis of this dilemma, the problem can be simplified by assuming that the only relevant consequence of the decision is whether the patient lives or dies. For a second cut, considerations about the overall health of a living patient can be considered. But for this analysis, a preference-probability of 1.0 will be given to the outcome "Lives" (the *Best*) and one of 0 to the outcome "Dies" (the *Worst*) (figure 5–13). The result is a reference gamble that can be used to assess preference-probabilities for all outcomes of the decision. The preference-probability for each outcome becomes simply the

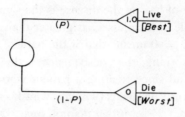

Figure 5–13. Reference Gamble for the Appendectomy Dilemma.

probability of the patient living, and these preference-probabilities can be noted in the terminal nodes of the decision tree (figure 5–14).

None of the "outcomes" on this decision tree has been assigned a preference-probability of 0. But that is not required. Nor is it required that the two reference outcomes used in the reference gamble be two of the actual outcomes on the original decision tree. All that is essential is that (1) the *Best* reference outcome for the reference gamble be as good as or better than all of the possible outcomes of the actual decision and (2) the *Worst* reference outcome be as bad as or worse than all of the possible outcomes. If these two conditions are satisfied, the resulting reference gamble can be used to assess preference-probabilities for the various outcomes of the actual decision, all of which are then interjacent to the two reference outcomes. (More about appropriate reference outcomes in chapter 6.)

For the appendectomy decision dilemma, the important consequence for each outcome is specified as the probability of the patient living (figure 5–14). But, using the substitution principle, it is possible to obtain a decision tree for

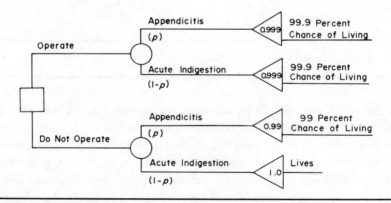

Figure 5–14. The Appendectomy Dilemma with Preference-Probabilities.

Double-Risk Dilemmas

which all outcomes are either patient-lives (the *Best*) or patient-dies (the *Worst*) (figure 5–15).

This new decision tree involves more uncertainty, but only two different possible outcomes, patient-lives and patient-dies. As in candidate Moynihan's dilemma, a few probability calculations can reduce this decision tree to a choice between two reference gambles. For the operate decision, the probability of dying is $[p \times (0.001)] + [(1 - p) \times (0.001)] = 0.001$. (This is clear from figure 5–16.) For the do-not-operate decision, the probability of dying is $p \times (0.01)$. (Consequently, the preference-probability for the operate decision is 0.999, and for the do-not-operate decision it is $1.0 - [(0.01) \times p]$.)

What should the physician do? The answer is to choose the alternative with the lowest chance of death.[7] But that chance depends upon the probability that the patient actually has acute appendicitis. It is helpful, therefore, to calculate a switch point for p. To do this, set the two probabilities of dying equal to each other: $0.001 = (0.01) \times p_{switch}$, or $p_{switch} = 0.1$. If p is less than p_{switch} ($p < 0.1$), the probability of dying is less for the do-not-operate decision. If p exceeds p_{switch} ($p > 0.1$), the probability of dying is less if the physician operates. If $p = 0.1$, the probabilities of dying are exactly the same for the two alternatives, and it makes no difference which is selected. (For a switch-point

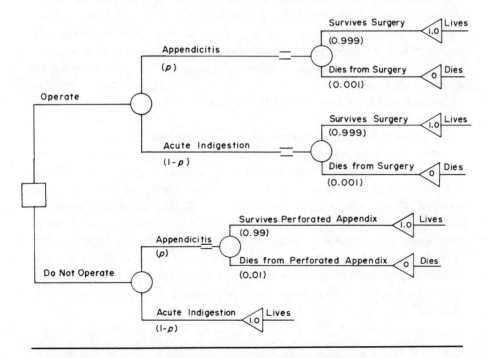

Figure 5–15. Using the Substitution Principle to Resolve the Appendectomy Dilemma.

119

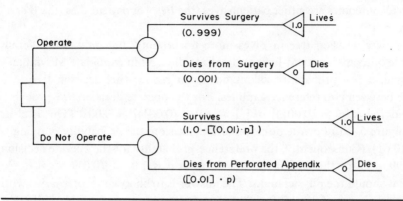

Figure 5–16. The Appendectomy Dilemma as a Choice between Two Reference Gambles.

analysis of the general physician's dilemma of figure 5–11, see the appendix to this chapter.)

This quick analysis[8] reveals the essential character of this double-risk dilemma and highlights the central role of the switch probability. For any individual patient, a first-cut analysis of the decision requires two basic assessments: (1) the probability that the patient has acute appendicitis and (2) the switch probability. The second is, in turn, dependent upon the physician's assessment of two more probabilities: this patient's chances of dying from a perforated appendix, and from surgical complications. The probabilities used in this analysis were for the population as a whole and, to make a specific decision, a physician would need to reassess them to reflect the individual patient's health.

Once these latter two probabilities have been assessed, the switch point can be determined and compared with the patient's probability of having appendicitis. If, for example, the probability assessments produced $p_{switch} = 0.15$ and $p = 0.5$, the decision would be obvious and no further analysis would be required. If, however, $p_{switch} = 0.22$ and $p = 0.25$, a second cut would be needed. Such a second cut could involve indirectly reassessing (using a probability tree such as those described in the appendix to chapter 4) the probability of death from a perforated appendix and from surgical complications. It could involve a more detailed breakdown of the outcomes resulting from each alternative. Or it could involve specifying in more detail the health consequences of living.[9]

Double-Risk Dilemmas

Other Double-Risk Dilemmas

The threat of a natural disaster—flood, hurricane, epidemic—can pose a double-risk dilemma for public officials. In August 1976, when the long-smoldering Grand-Soufrière volcano on Guadeloupe Island in the Caribbean threatened to erupt, French officials had to decide whether to evacuate the area. As with all double-risk dilemmas, both alternatives were risky. The riskier alternative was not to evacuate. The less risky one was to do so, and the French did evacuate 72,000 local residents—two weeks before Grand-Soufrière erupted.[10]

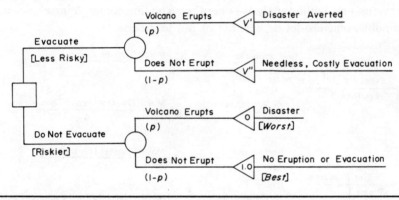

Figure 5–17. A Volcano/Natural Disaster Decision Dilemma.

This decision seems to have been clear. The probability of the volcano erupting may have been so high, say 0.9, and the consequence of an eruption without an evacuation so bad, that V' and V'' were nearly 1.0. For other potential disasters, however, the choice may not be obvious.

For example, what should be done in the face of a potential earthquake? Even with the latest equipment, such a disaster cannot be predicted with certainty. Nevertheless, future scientific advances may mean that some day public officials will be given a probabilistic prediction that a major earthquake will occur in the next month. As the *Washington Post* noted in an editorial, such predictions will

create enormous problems for individual citizens, as well as public officials. What do you do, for instance, if the prediction says—as weather forecasts now do—that there is a 50 percent chance of an earthquake today? Or, what do you do if an earthquake is said to be highly likely within the next two weeks?[11]

Indeed, one scientist already predicts that the chance is "pretty good—about

50-50"—that an earthquake registering 5.0 or 6.0 on the Richter scale will occur in New England in the next fifty years,[12] and another scientist says there is a 50-50 chance that a "large earthquake" will strike somewhere in California in the next ten years.[13]

When should public officials call for an evacuation? The decision depends —as always—upon the probabilities and the consequences. How likely is the earthquake? Even a probability of 20 percent seems large. But the consequences of an evacuation are not all benign—merely calling for an evacuation might create a public panic.[14] The final outcome of an evacuate decision and a no-earthquake outcome might have to be assessed a preference-probability (V'' in figure 5–18) as "low" as 0.75. In such a situation, the decision may not be obvious, and a quick analysis—there being no time for anything else—could help public officials decide whether or not to evacuate.[15]

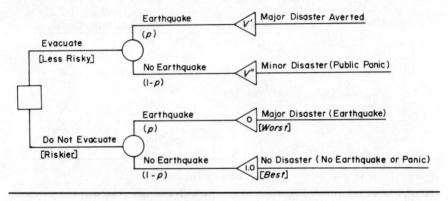

Figure 5–18. An Earthquake/Natural Disaster Decision Dilemma.

In the United States, there exist a number of potential natural disasters, such as earthquakes in California or the eruption of Mauna Loa, the Hawaiian volcano. The sleeper of a disaster, however, is the one presented by Mt. Baker in Washington.[16] In chapter 2, a dilemma created by Mt. Baker—whether to close a nearby resort area—was examined as a basic decision dilemma. It might also be helpful to analyze it as a double-risk problem (see figure 5–19), since the mudslide that threatens the resort area surrounding Baker Lake can occur whether or not U.S. Forest Service officials order an evacuation, and the two possible (uncertain) outcomes of the decision to close the resort area may have different consequences. To evaluate the decision to close the resort—to assess a preference-probability for this decision branch—it may help to decompose the outcome of this alternative in order to take explicitly into account the uncertainty about the occurrence of a mudslide. For this description of the dilemma, three different consequences have been specified for each outcome

Double-Risk Dilemmas

—the size of the disaster, the extent to which the economy is hurt, and the amount of criticism of the Forest Service—and thus three separate consequence branches have been attached to each final-outcome node. As a first cut, the two possible outcomes of the close decision can be evaluated directly (preference-probabilities V' and V'' can be assessed directly) using a reference gamble. If more careful thinking about the three conflicting consequences is warranted, the trade-offs between them can be explicitly analyzed. (Trade-off analysis is the subject of chapter 11.)

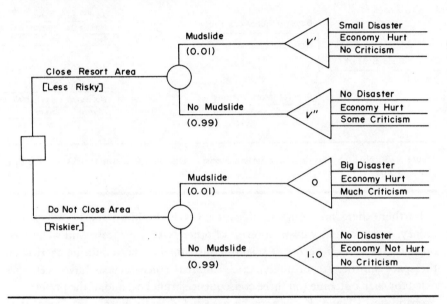

Figure 5–19. The Mount Baker Decision Dilemma Reconsidered: A Double-Risk Decision Tree.

Similarly, NASA's dilemma about whether to build a launch-abort system for the space shuttle (figure 2–15) can also be analyzed as a double-risk dilemma (see figure 5–20). The booster rocket can malfunction whether or not the abort system is built. Regardless of whether this decision is analyzed as a basic or double-risk dilemma, the preference-probability for the no-abort-system alternative is p, the probability that the booster functions properly. This is because this alternative (the risky one in the basic dilemma and the riskier one for the double-risk approach) results in either the *Best* or the *Worst* outcome. The decision depends upon an evaluation of the other alternative: Is the preference-probability for the abort-system alternative greater or less than p? To assess a preference-probability for this alternative, it is helpful to consider the uncertainty concerning the functioning of the booster rocket. In this situation, the double-risk approach would prove useful.

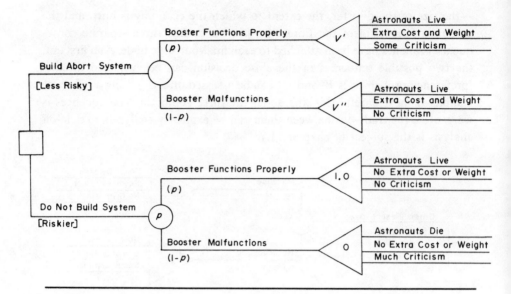

Figure 5–20. NASA's Shuttle Abort-System Decision Dilemma Reconsidered: A Double-Risk Decision Tree.

Further, there are some significant costs in building the abort system: money, or opportunity costs in terms of other NASA projects; and weight, or opportunity costs in terms of scientific instruments that could be carried on the space shuttle. Accordingly, three different consequences have been specified for each outcome (on three consequence branches) and, if the preference-probabilities V' and V'' cannot be assessed directly with confidence, it is possible to take the trade-offs among these consequences into account.

Explicitly including public criticism as a consequence of the outcomes of these two dilemmas points up an important feature of all double-risk decision dilemmas: There is no safe choice. Which of the two decisions is best depends upon which of the two uncertain outcomes will occur. For one outcome, one alternative is clearly best; for the other, the second is preferred. For many basic dilemmas (such as the angina decision, the prosecutor's decision, the corporate takeover decision, and Mayor Willis's decision) the uncertain event cannot occur unless the risky decision is selected. For the double-risk decision, however, both alternatives are risky. Whether it is a physician grappling with how to treat a patient who may or may not have a disease, or a public official attempting to decide how to cope with an epidemic that may or may not occur, there is a chance of being wrong.

Double-Risk Dilemmas

The Value of Quick Analysis

A story about an analytical friend of ours, Jens, dramatizes how quick analysis can resolve what initially appears to be an intractable dilemma. It was 6:00 on a cold and rainy winter night when a friend, Greg, dropped by Jens's office to offer him a ride home. Jens wanted to accept the ride—a walk home that night would be most unpleasant—but he could not remember whether his wife Karen had agreed that morning to pick him up after work (approximately 6:30). Jens could remember, however, that if his wife did stop by to pick him up and he was not there, she would become a bit grumpy. A call to his wife's office revealed only that she had already left. What should Jens have done?

Fortunately, Jens was well acquainted with the ideas of quick analysis and immediately drew a double-risk decision tree (see figure 5–21). As this diagram

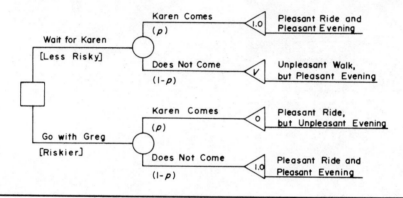

Figure 5–21. Jens's Quick Analysis Double-Risk Decision Tree.

indicates, there are two *Best* outcomes: (1) a ride home with Karen and (2) a ride home with Greg, provided that Karen does not come. There is one *Worst* outcome: taking the ride with Greg only to have Karen show up at Jens's office. Two outcomes thus get a preference-probability of 1.0, and another gets a preference-probability of 0. This leaves just two factors for Jens to assess: the preference-probability for the interjacent outcome—the cold, damp walk home; and the probability that Karen would come to pick Jens up.

All Jens could conclude about the last preference-probability, V, was that it should be much greater than 0 but also much less than 1.0. He decided to focus his analytical attention on the probability p. He simply could not remember his morning's conversation with Karen—or even what they had discussed. Still, Jens was confident that the probability was greater than 50 percent—at least 60 or 70 percent.

Eureka! The dilemma is resolved. For if $p > 0.5$, then the preference-probability for accepting Greg's ride, which is simply $(1 - p)$ (the probability that the go-with-Greg alternative will result in the *Best* outcome) must be less than 0.5. At the same time, the preference-probability for waiting, which is $p + [(1 - p) \times V]$, must be greater than 0.5. Even without assessing a precise number for the probability p, or any number for the preference-probability V, it is possible—by deciding that p is greater than 0.5—to determine which alternative is preferred.

So Jens made his decision—even though he did not have much time or much data—with the help of a little quick analysis. He waited, Karen came, and they spent a pleasant evening together, in part discussing how Jens decided to wait.

"That's some analysis, that quick analysis," Karen observed.

"It's the best there is," Jens agreed.[17]

Double-Risk Dilemmas

Appendix: Sensitivity Analysis for Double-Risk Dilemmas

A number of double-risk dilemmas can be described by the general decision tree of figure 5–22. Alternative B is the riskier alternative because, although it can result in the *Best* outcome, it can also result in the *Worst*. The preference-probability for at least one of the two outcomes of alternative A is between 0 and 1.0 (otherwise there would be no dilemma); consequently, alternative A is less risky, since its range of possible outcomes is less extreme. This is the form of the physician's dilemma (figure 5–11), the natural disaster dilemma (figure 5–17), and NASA's shuttle abort-system dilemma (figure 5–20). Candidate Moynihan's dilemma is just a special case of this general problem, with $V' = 1.0$.

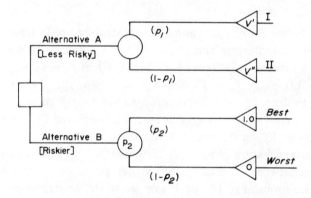

Figure 5–22. A General Double-Risk Dilemma.

For this general double-risk dilemma, sensitivity analysis can be quite helpful. It reveals that if p_2 is less than both V' and V'', the decision maker prefers the less risky alternative A, regardless of the specific values of p_1, p_2, V', and V''. On the other hand, if p_2 is greater than both V' and V'', the decision maker prefers the riskier alternative B, again regardless of the specific values of the four factors.

To see this, let V_a be the preference-probability for alternative A and V_b be the preference-probability for alternative B. Then, applying the substitution principle, V_a and V_b can be assessed indirectly in terms of the four factors that create the dilemma, p_1, p_2, V' and V'':

$$V_a = [(p_1) \times (V')] + [(1 - p_1) \times (V'')]; \text{ and}$$
$$V_b = p_2.$$

Setting $V_a = V_b$, the switch point for p_2 can be determined in terms of the other three factors:

$$p_{2(\text{switch})} = [(p_1) \times (V')] + [(1 - p_1) \times (V'')].$$

Now note that the higher p_2 is, the better the riskier alternative is. Thus, if p_2 is higher than $p_{2(\text{switch})}$, the decision maker prefers the riskier alternative B; if p_2 is less than $p_{2(\text{switch})}$, the decision maker prefers the less risky alternative A.

Also note that $p_{2(\text{switch})}$ is simply the probabilistic average of V' and V''. If p_1 is close to 1.0, $p_{2(\text{switch})}$ is close to V'. If p_1 is close to 0, so that $(1 - p_1)$ is close to 1.0, $p_{2(\text{switch})}$ is close to V''. If $p_1 = 0.5$, $p_{2(\text{switch})} = (V' + V'')/2$. Thus, $p_{2(\text{switch})}$ is some number between V' and V''.

Another way to see this is to rearrange the equation for $p_{2(\text{switch})}$:

$$p_{2(\text{switch})} = V'' + [(V' - V'') \times (p_1)].$$

This is an equation for $p_{2(\text{switch})}$ as a linear or straight-line function of p_1 (with V'' as the vertical intercept and $(V' - V'')$ as the slope). To see this, graph $p_{2(\text{switch})}$ as a function of p_1 (see figure 5–23). When $p_1 = 0$, $p_{2(\text{switch})} = V''$. When $p_1 = 1.0$, $p_{2(\text{switch})} = V'$. When $p_1 = 0.5$, $p_{2(\text{switch})} = (V' + V'')/2$. (Note that, to draw figure 5–23, it was assumed that V' is greater than V''. This is not necessary. If V'' is greater than V', the straight line merely slopes downward from V'' on the left to V' on the right.)

The important feature of figure 5–23 is that $p_{2(\text{switch})}$ must lie somewhere in the region between V'' and V'. The switch point for p_2 can *not* be below the preference-probability V'' (or V') or above the preference-probability V' (or V'').

To see the significance of this, suppose that p_2 is less than both V' and V''. Then it is not possible (regardless of the value of p_1) for p_2 to be greater than

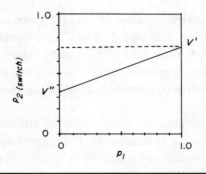

Figure 5–23. Sensitivity Analysis for a General Double-Risk Dilemma: The Switch Point for p_2 as a Linear Function of p_1

Double-Risk Dilemmas

$p_{2(\text{switch})}$; consequently, the less risky alternative A must be preferred. If, on the other hand, p_2 is larger than both V' and V'', then it is not possible (again, regardless of the value of p_1) for p_2 to be less than $p_{2(\text{switch})}$. Consequently, if p_2 is larger than both V' and V'', the risky alternative B must be preferred.

This sensitivity analysis means that, for a double-risk dilemma of the form of figure 5–22, if the initial assessments produce a value for p_2 that is less than V' and V'', the next question is: Am I convinced that p_2 is indeed less than both V' and V''? If so, no further analysis is necessary; simply choose alternative A. For in this situation, the probability of getting the *Best* from the riskier alternative is less than the preference-probabilities for the two outcomes of the less risky alternative and, consequently, the preference-probability for the riskier alternative can *not* be greater than the preference-probability for the less risky one. (A similar thought process would be followed if the initial assessment for p_2 was greater than both V' and V''.)

For candidate Moynihan's dilemma, this analysis is not very helpful. For his problem, p_2 is about 0.7, $V' = 1.0$, and V'' is about 0.25. Consequently, p_2 is neither clearly greater nor less than V' and V''.

On the other hand, this is the general type of analysis that Jens used to resolve his dilemma. Jens's dilemma is another special case of this general double-risk dilemma, with $p_1 = p_2 = (1 - p)$, $V' = V$, and $V'' = 1.0$. For Jens's problem, the switch point for p is determined by assessing (indirectly with the help of the substitution principle) the preference-probabilities for the two alternatives and setting them equal to each other:

$$p_{\text{switch}} + [(1 - p_{\text{switch}}) \times (V)] = (1 - p_{\text{switch}}).$$

Solving this equation for p_{switch} gives it as a function of V:

$$p_{\text{switch}} = (1 - V)/(2 - V).$$

Using this last equation to calculate p_{switch} for a few different values of V can be quite revealing:

V	0	0.25	0.5	0.75	1.0
p_{switch}	0.5	0.43	0.33	0.2	0

Regardless of the value of V, p_{switch} can not be greater than 0.5. If Jens is convinced that the probability that Karen will pick him up is greater than 0.5, his dilemma is resolved; he should wait for Karen.

PART II

Range-of-Risk

Dilemmas

Chapter 6

Analyzing Range-of-Risk Dilemmas: The Out-of-Court Settlement Decision

ON Tuesday, March 25, 1975, Gail Kalmowitz faced the most important decision of her life. Born two months prematurely in 1953 at Brookdale Hospital in Brooklyn, Kalmowitz grew up nearly blind. Later, she sued the hospital and two doctors for administering "uncontrolled amounts of oxygen," treatment that, she claimed, resulted in eye damage. In March 1975, while the jury was deliberating in a Brooklyn courtroom, Kalmowitz was offered a $165,000 out-of-court settlement. She had to decide whether to accept this certain amount or gamble that the jury would make an even greater award.[1]

On July 29, 1976, the parents of Edward J. Farrell, IV had to make a similar decision. Their son was blinded shortly after he was born two weeks prematurely in October 1969 at the Holy Cross Hospital in Silver Springs, Maryland. Suing for $3.5 million, the parents asserted that excessive oxygen had been administered. As the jury announced that it had reached a verdict, the lawyers for the two sides reached an out-of-court settlement of $500,000.[2]

Another example is the decision faced by Thomas Zarcone in July of 1977. Two years earlier, Zarcone had been selling coffee from his truck outside the traffic court in Hauppauge, Long Island, when a deputy sheriff handcuffed him and took him into the chambers of a judge who was "irritated by the quality of the coffee" that Zarcone was selling. Zarcone sued, and while the jury was deliberating, he was offered a $205,000 settlement.[3] Again, the choice was between two alternatives, one of which was much more risky than the other.

Out-of-court settlement decisions are common in civil suits. People involved in insurance cases, corporate and personal liability cases, and patent-infringement cases—both as plaintiffs and defendants—must often decide whether to accept an out-of-court settlement. Many criminal cases present an analytically similar problem: the plea-bargain dilemma. Here a defendant must decide whether to accept a plea bargain arranged by his attorney (the riskless alternative) or gamble on a trial (the risky alternative) that could result in either acquittal (the best consequence) or conviction and a more severe sentence (the worst consequence). The analytical characteristics of the out-of-court settlement problem are common to other decision dilemmas, particularly those faced by business executives. (A number of such business decisions are discussed at the end of this chapter.)

All these decision dilemmas involve a range of possible outcomes. The out-of-court settlement problem, for example, involves a choice between a riskless alternative (accept the settlement) and a risky one (reject the settlement), but uncertainty about whether the jury's verdict will be favorable or not is compounded by uncertainty about the *size* of the jury's award. A decision tree used to describe such a *range-of-risk decision dilemma* would explicitly indicate that range of risk. The decision tree in figure 6–1 presents the out-of-court settlement problem as a range-of-risk dilemma. The three dots, or "ellipsis," between the outcome branches labeled "Highest Possible Award" and "Lowest Possible Award" indicate that something has been omitted—namely, the very large number of other possible outcomes between these two extremes.

Range-of-risk dilemmas are the subject of part II of this book. How can the

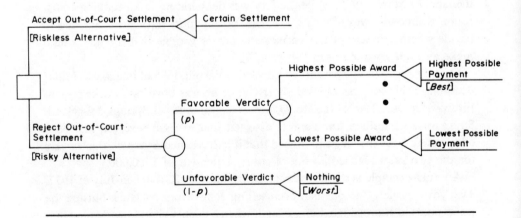

Figure 6–1. A Range-of-Risk Decision Tree for the Out-of-Court Settlement Dilemma.

Analyzing Range-of-Risk Dilemmas

additional complexity of a range of risk be handled analytically? What simplifications are appropriate? Necessary? What are the components into which the problem should be decomposed? What subdecisions need to be made? How can these judgments be recombined to reach a resolution of the dilemma? If the original analysis is not completely persuasive, how can additional complications be added in a second-cut analysis? Finally, how can the dynamics of analytical thinking contribute to an understanding of the essential nature of the dilemma and its quick yet satisfactory resolution?

A First-Cut Analysis

J. C. "Cookie" Phillips is injured in an automobile accident with a car driven by Dirk Peters. Phillips brings suit for $1.5 million for pain and suffering—and for his injuries, too. Peters's insurance company offers to settle out of court for $400,000. What should Phillips do?

As the decision tree in figure 6–2 indicates, this is a range-of-risk dilemma. If the jury reaches a favorable verdict, it could award Phillips anything from nothing up to $1.6 million. Phillips's lawyer thinks that the jury could reach a favorable but financially inconsequential verdict, it could award Phillips a hundred thousand dollars more than he requests, or its judgment could be somewhere in between. Note, however, that Phillips will not get all of the award, for his lawyer has taken the case on a contingent-fee basis and will receive 25 percent of any settlement (whether it is awarded by the jury or

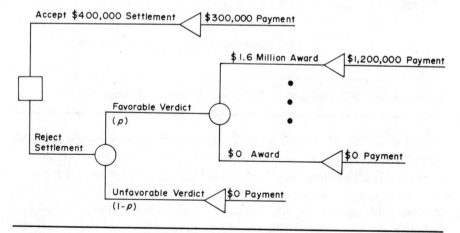

Figure 6–2. J. C. Phillips's Out-of-Court Settlement Dilemma.

agreed to out of court). Consequently, on all of the following decision trees, the actual payments to Phillips (the terminal consequences) are only 75 percent of the award paid by Peter's insurance company.

Since Phillips's out-of-court settlement dilemma presents a choice between a riskless alternative (accept the settlement) and a risky one (reject the settlement), it can be analyzed as a basic decision dilemma. This requires a simplification, but so does any analysis. The essential question is not whether the analysis is based on a simplified description of the problem, but whether that simplification is adequate for reaching a satisfactory decision. Thus, Phillips can use a decision sapling for a first-cut analysis of his dilemma, and if he is uncomfortable with the implications of this analysis, he can undertake a second cut based on a less simplified description of the problem.

The major simplification required to analyze Phillip's dilemma with a decision sapling is to use a single terminal outcome—a point estimate—to approximate the entire range of risk involved in the uncertain amount of any jury award (figure 6–3). The mathematical sign, $\approx$, meaning "approximately equal," is used to indicate that the range of risk of a favorable verdict has been approximated by this terminal outcome. The $\approx$ notation is used to emphasize that an approximation has been made and that a favorable verdict will not necessarily result in that specific payment.

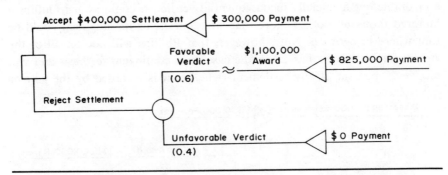

Figure 6–3. A Decision Sapling for J. C. Phillips's Out-of-Court Settlement Dilemma.

Now it is necessary to specify two key factors: the probability of a favorable verdict and the size of the (assumed certain) jury award that would result from such a verdict. Phillips's lawyer thinks that the chance of winning a favorable verdict is somewhat better than 50-50—60 percent he says—and that if there is a favorable verdict the jury's award will be over a million dollars—$1.1 million is his "best guess." This would give Phillips (after his lawyer takes his cut) a payment of $825,000.

The next step is for Phillips to think carefully about his relative preferences

Analyzing Range-of-Risk Dilemmas

for the three possible outcomes. As before, using a reference gamble to assess preference-probabilities provides an unambiguous standard for specifying the relative desirability of the outcomes. In chapters 2 and 3, this was done by making the best and worst outcomes on the decision sapling the *Best* and *Worst* reference outcomes of the reference gamble. But this is not a rule, just a matter of convenience; it makes the task of assessing relative preferences easier, for the decision maker need only think about one preference-probability.*

This approach would be simple enough here, too, but it could lead to some future complications. Note that the best outcome on the decision sapling in figure 6–3 is not really the best possible outcome. This sapling is a simplification, and it is possible (says Phillips's lawyer) that Phillips could actually end up with $1.2 million (or 75 percent of the maximum possible award of $1.6 million). Thus, it might make more sense for the analysis of *this* decision to make $1.2 million the *Best* reference outcome of the reference gamble (figure 6–4). If Phillips decides to undertake a second-cut analysis—with a more sophisticated simplification of the dilemma—his decision tree may include a payment greater than $825,000. If so, he would have to start all over again and

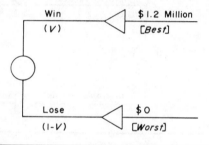

Figure 6–4. The Reference Gamble for Assessing Preference-Probabilities for J. C. Phillips's Dilemma.

Any two outcomes can be used as reference outcomes for a reference gamble provided that (1) the *Best* reference outcome is as good as or better than every outcome of the decision being analyzed and (2) the *Worst* reference outcome is as bad as or worse than all of the outcomes of the actual decision. If these two conditions are met, all of the actual outcomes involved in the decision will be interjacent to the two reference outcomes. Then, for every possible outcome of the dilemma, it is possible to specify a preference-probability (V), some number between 0 and 1.0 such that the decision maker is indifferent between that outcome for sure and the reference gamble with a V chance of getting the *Best* reference outcome and a 1 − V chance of getting the *Worst*. If the outcome being evaluated is, however, better than the *Best* reference outcome, it is impossible to assess a meaningful preference-probability. If you had a choice between $100 for sure and a reference gamble that gave you a V chance at $50 and a 1 − V chance at $0, what value of V would make you indifferent between these two alternatives? None, of course; you would always prefer the certain $100. You can only assess a preference-probability for $100 if the *Best* reference outcome is equivalent to or better than $100. Within the constraints provided by the two conditions above, you can use *any* pair of reference outcomes. Then, using the substitution principle, *all* alternatives can be evaluated in terms of the probability of getting the *same Best* reference outcome.

create a completely new reference gamble. Thus, if a second-cut analysis is a possibility, it might make more sense to prepare for that contingency from the beginning.

To use the decision sapling of figure 6–3 and the reference gamble in figure 6–4, two preference-probabilities must be determined. The preference-probability for the outcome of the unfavorable verdict, $0, is defined by the reference gamble to be 0. But Phillips needs to assess preference-probabilities for $300,-000 and $825,000. He concludes that his preference-probability for $300,000 is 0.55; that is, he is indifferent between $300,000 for sure and a 55-45 chance at $1.2 million or nothing. He thinks that $825,000 is such a large sum that he would only prefer the reference gamble to this amount for sure if the probability of getting the *Best* outcome of $1.2 million were greater than 90 percent. His preference-probability for the $825,000 is thus 0.90. The preference-probabilities are displayed on the decision sapling in figure 6–5.

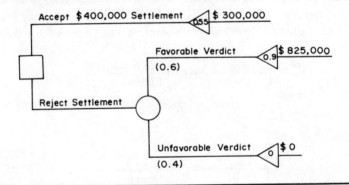

Figure 6–5. A Decision Sapling for Phillips's Dilemma, with Preference-Probabilities for Terminal Outcomes.

Resolving the First-Cut Dilemma

Having specified all the necessary probabilities and preferences, the process of resolving the dilemma is straightforward—use the substitution principle and the rules of probability (see figure 6–6). Since Phillips's preference-probability for $300,000 is 0.55, a reference gamble with a $V = 0.55$ chance of getting the *Best* can be substituted for this outcome. Similarly, a reference gamble with $V = 0.90$ can be substituted for the $825,000 outcome. These substitutions are shown in figure 6–6a. Then, the rules of probability (described in the appendix of chapter 4) are used to determine the probability of getting the *Best* outcome for each alternative. The results of these calculations are shown in figure 6–6b.

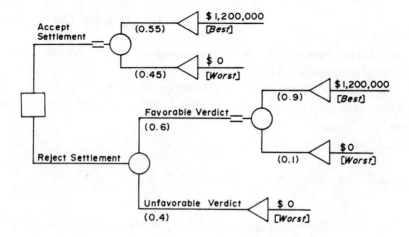

(a) Using the Substitution Principle.

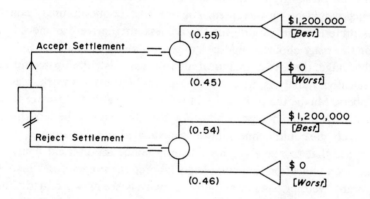

(b) Using the Probability Rules.

Figure 6–6. Resolving the First-Cut Analysis of J. C. Phillips's Out-of-Court Settlement Dilemma.

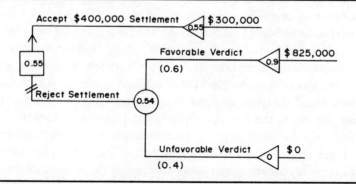

Figure 6–7. Resolution of Phillips's Out-of-Court Settlement Dilemma, Based on a First-Cut Analysis.

This analysis suggests that the preference-probability for the riskless accept-settlement alternative is 0.55 and for the risky reject-settlement alternative is 0.54. These preference-probabilities are shown on the decision sapling in figure 6–7, which indicates the resolution of Phillips's dilemma based on a first-cut analysis.

A Second-Cut Analysis

As John Chancellor would say on election night, "It looks too close to call." Could a decision be comfortably made when the difference in preference-probabilities is only 0.01? Given that these preference-probabilities were derived from rather gross simplifications of the nature of the dilemma, such confidence would be unwarranted. Anyone who unquestioningly concluded that his preference-probability for the riskless alternative was indeed higher than for the risky choice would be guilty of phoney precision.

At this stage, then, two analytical alternatives exist. Phillips could undertake a sensitivity analysis; he could go back and rethink his work, reassessing his numbers. Maybe the probability of a favorable verdict is greater than 0.6; or perhaps his preference-probability for $300,000 should be less than 0.55. Alternatively, he could define a more sophisticated simplification of the problem and use that to reanalyze his dilemma. Since the first-cut analysis was based on a simplification that completely ignored the range-of-risk involved in the favorable verdict, such a second-cut analysis seems warranted. But this choice is a matter of judgment. It takes some experience with quick analysis to develop a sense of whether more detail should be incorporated into the analysis or whether enough factors have been introduced and an investigation into the sensitivity of a decision to changes in these factors is more appropriate.

In this case, it seems reasonable to analyze explicitly the quite substantial uncertainty that exists over the amount of money that the jury could award Phillips. The out-of-court settlement decision is a dilemma not only because it is difficult to decide whether to gamble on getting the desirable outcome from a favorable verdict or accept the certain, known settlement. It is also a dilemma because the desirable outcome—the exact size of the jury award—is itself unknown. There are two important uncertainties and both influence Phillips's decision; indeed, in the first-cut analysis, the preference-probability assessed (indirectly) for the reject-settlement alternative obviously depended upon the single, point estimate used to approximate the size of the jury award.

To incorporate his uncertainty about the size of the jury award directly into his analysis, Phillips adds two more branches to his decision tree, to represent the possibility of two equally probable awards, one high and one low (figure 6–8). He concludes, after consulting again with his lawyer, that there is a

Analyzing Range-of-Risk Dilemmas

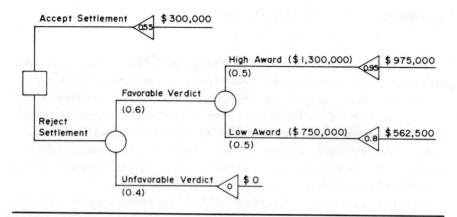

Figure 6–8. A Decision Tree for a Second-Cut Analysis of Phillips's Dilemma.

50-percent chance that the award will be $1,300,000 and a 50-percent chance that the award will be $750,000. Of course the award could range anywhere between a small, nominal sum (or maybe even nothing) and $1.6 million (or $100,000 more than Phillips requested). The $1.3 million and the $750,000 are merely representative numbers. The $1.3 million figure is a good guess of what a high award might be, and represents all the awards between $1.1 million (Phillips's original point estimate, used in his first-cut analysis) and $1.6 million. The $750,000 award represents all possible awards less than $1.1 million. Phillips and his lawyer think that these are reasonable numbers—that it is equally likely that an award would be near $750,000 or $1.3 million.

Though more complicated than a decision sapling, the decision tree for the second-cut analysis is still a simplification. There are an infinite number of possible jury awards, and it is impossible to display them all on a decision tree —or to include them all in any type of analysis. The decision tree for the second-cut analysis is not a description of reality; rather it is an attempt to develop a useful tool for analyzing the dilemma. If, after this analysis is completed, it is unsatisfactory, additional complications can be added.

The next step in the second-cut analysis is to assess preference-probabilities for the two new outcomes: the $975,000 payment that Phillips would get from the $1.3 million award (don't forget the lawyer's fee) and the $562,500 he would receive from the $750,000 award. Using the same reference gamble as before, since the preference-probabilities for the other outcomes are based on this reference gamble (figure 6–4), Phillips concludes that his preference-probabilities are 0.95 for $975,000 and 0.8 for $562,500. (This means that Phillips is indifferent between $562,500 for sure and a reference gamble with an 80-percent chance of winning $1.2 million and a 20-percent chance of winning nothing.) These preference-probabilities are displayed on the decision tree in figure 6–8.

Resolving the Second-Cut Dilemma

What must Phillips do now to resolve his dilemma? His second-cut decision tree (figure 6–8) is neither the basic sapling of chapters 2 and 3 nor the double-risk tree of chapter 5. Still the next step is to use the same fundamental concepts that helped resolve those two types of decision dilemma. The substitution principle and the rules of probability provide the means for obtaining a basis of comparison between the two alternatives in terms of reference gambles with identical reference outcomes. This process is described by the sequence of four decision trees in figure 6–9 (see pages 143–44).

Since Phillips is indifferent between $975,000 for sure and a reference gamble with a 0.95 chance of winning the *Best* reference outcome, he can replace that $975,000 outcome on his decision tree with this reference gamble. Similarly, he can replace the $300,000 and $562,500 outcomes with their equivalent reference gambles. The resulting decision tree (figure 6–9a) appears, however, to be excessively complicated. There are more uncertainty nodes, outcome branches, and outcome nodes than in the original second-cut decision tree (figure 6–8). How can this more complex-looking tree help resolve the dilemma? As before, the reason is that although the number of uncertainties has, indeed, increased, the number of different possible final consequences has been reduced. The original decision tree contained four different payments, requiring four different preference-probabilities. The new decision tree contains only two: the *Best* and *Worst* reference outcomes of $1,200,000 and $0, respectively.

Although there are five different uncertain events on this decision tree, it is possible, with a little arithmetic, to reduce this complicated collection of uncertainties to a choice between two reference gambles. This is the rationale for converting the tree of figure 6–8 into the tree of figure 6–9a. Since Phillips does not care how he gets $1.2 million (or $0), the dilemma described in figure 6–9a can be resolved by determining which alternative gives the greatest chance of getting this *Best* outcome. For the accept-settlement alternative, this probability is 0.55. Thus, the only question remaining is: What is the probability that the reject-settlement alternative will result in a *Best* outcome?

That question can be answered (as a similar one was in chapter 5 for the double-risk dilemma) by using the multiplication and addition rules of probability described in the appendix to chapter 4. To do this, it is helpful to work backwards on the decision tree, successively simplifying it as shown in figures 6–9a through 6–9d. (A simple way to make these calculations is shown in the appendix to this chapter.)

The chain of calculations summarized in figure 6–9 reduces the entire dilemma to a choice between two reference gambles. As indicated in figure 6–9d, the reject-settlement alternative leads to a reference gamble with a 0.53 chance

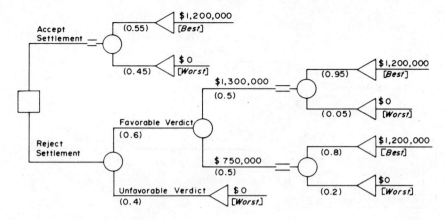

(a) Using the Substitution Principle.

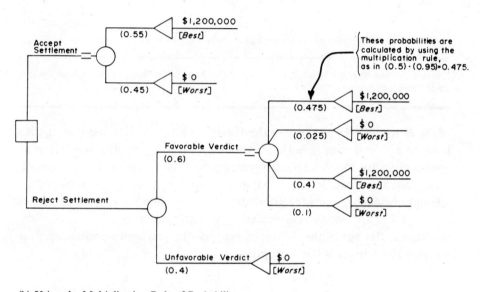

(b) Using the Multiplication Rule of Probability.

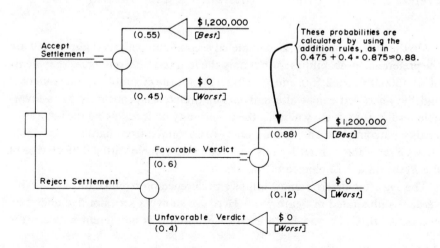

(c) Using the Addition Rule of Probability.

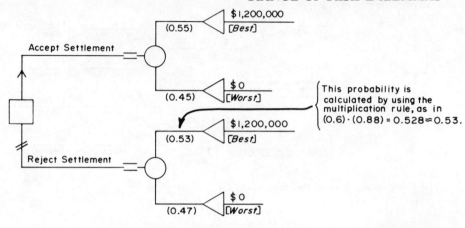

(d) The Out-of-Court Settlement Dilemma Reduced to a Choice between Two Reference Gambles.

Figure 6–9. Four Steps for Resolving the Second-Cut Analysis of Phillips's Out-of-Court Settlement Dilemma.

of the *Best* and a 0.47 chance of the *Worst*. The accept-settlement alternative leads to a reference gamble that was obtained directly by assessing a preference-probability for the $300,000 consequence of accepting the settlement. And since these two reference gambles have the same reference outcomes, Phillips obviously prefers the alternative that gives him the greatest chance of the *Best*. For this second-cut analysis, the better alternative is to accept the settlement. But again, the difference between the preference-probabilities for the two alternatives is not very great.

Preference-Probabilities for Alternatives and Uncertain Events

On the decision tree for the completed second-cut analysis (figure 6–10) are the preference-probabilities for not only the four terminal outcomes (payments of $0, $300,000, $562,500, and $975,000) but for the favorable-verdict outcome and the reject-settlement alternative. The preference-probability for a favorable verdict, 0.88, is shown inside the uncertainty node following the favorable-verdict outcome branch. This number was obtained from figure 6–9c, which shows a favorable verdict leading to a reference gamble with a 0.88 chance of the *Best* and a 0.12 chance of the *Worst*.

The logic for determining Phillips's preference-probability for a favorable verdict is illustrated in figure 6–11. Here are shown a series of five uncertain events: A, B, C, D, and E. In each case, Phillips is indifferent between the

144

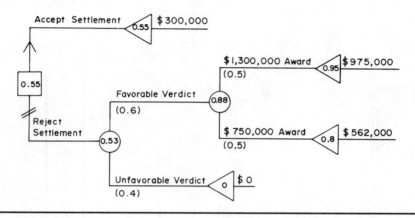

Figure 6–10. Resolution of J. C. Phillips's Out-of-Court Settlement Dilemma, Based on a Second-Cut Analysis.

uncertain event and the one that follows it (for instance, he is indifferent between B and C). Accordingly, he is indifferent between the actual range of risk that results from a favorable verdict (on the left) and the 0.88 reference gamble (on the right). There are four steps in determining this indifference.

(1) *A to B*. This is the initial simplification. Phillips approximates the entire range of risk by a two-branch outcome fork with a 50-50 chance of $975,000 versus $562,500. In a sense, Phillips is making a substitution. He is saying that he is indifferent between the actual range of risk that would result from a favorable verdict and a 50-50 gamble on $975,000 versus $562,500. If so, he can substitute one uncertainty for the other on his decision tree without affecting his preference for the favorable-verdict outcome.

(2) *B to C*. This involves the use of the substitution principle. The two simplified outcomes, $975,000 and $562,500, are replaced with their equivalent reference gambles. If Phillips is indifferent between $975,000 and a 0.95 reference gamble and also between $562,500 and a 0.8 reference gamble, he should be indifferent between B and C.

(3) *C to D*. Here the multiplication probability rule is applied. Phillips is indifferent between C and D because the probability of winning $1.2 million is the same for both.

(4) *D to E*. Now the addition probability rule is used. Phillips is indifferent between D and E because, again, both of these uncertainties give the same chance of winning $1.2 million.

Now if Phillips is indifferent between A and B, and between B and C, then he should also be indifferent between A and C. Continuing this logic, he should also be indifferent between A and D, and, finally, between A and E.

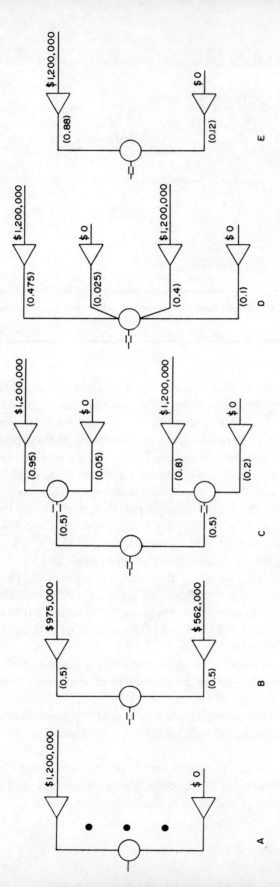

Figure 6-11. The Logic for Indirectly Assessing the Preference-Probability for the Uncertain Outcome of a Favorable Verdict.

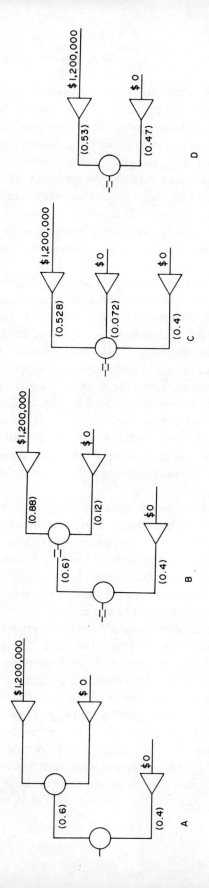

Figure 6-12. The Logic for Indirectly Assessing the Preference-Probability for the Uncertain Outcome of the Reject-Settlement Alternative.

If, however, Phillips is indifferent between A and E—if he is indifferent between taking his chances with the range of risk that results from a favorable verdict and taking his chances with a 0.88 reference gamble—then his preference-probability for a favorable verdict is, by definition, 0.88. That is, if Phillips knew that the jury had reached a favorable verdict but did not yet know what amount it had decided to award, this analysis suggests that Phillips would be willing to trade in his rights to that uncertain award for a gamble that gave him an 88-percent chance at $1.2 million (the *Best*) and a 12-percent chance at $0 (the *Worst*). But this is nothing more than the definition of a preference-probability—this time applied to an uncertain event rather than to a known outcome.

Recall that the rationale for undertaking the second-cut analysis of Phillips's dilemma was to get a better handle on his preference for the outcome of a favorable verdict. The only difference between the decision sapling used in the first cut and the decision tree used in the second was that Phillips replaced the single, point estimate for the jury award with a two-branch outcome fork. The first-cut simplification, Phillips concluded, was too drastic; it ignored an important factor—the uncertainty about the amount of a jury award. To think more systematically about his preference for this risky outcome, Phillips explicitly incorporated into his analysis some of the uncertainty involved. The sole purpose of replacing the point estimate used for the jury award with a two-branch outcome fork was to provide a better assessment of Phillips's preference for the favorable-verdict outcome and thus for the reject-settlement alternative.

There is nothing sacred, however, about the 0.88 preference-probability obtained from this analysis. Phillips might want to double-check to see if this indirectly assessed preference-probability makes sense to him. If he knew that the jury had reached a favorable verdict but had yet to be told the size of the award, would he indeed be indifferent between the risk inherent in accepting the jury's judgment and the risk involved in a reference gamble that gives him a 0.88 chance at $1.2 million and a 0.12 chance at $0? If Phillips thinks he prefers the 0.88 reference gamble, he should lower the preference-probability for a favorable verdict below 0.88. On the other hand, if he prefers the jury-award gamble, he should raise the preference-probability for that uncertain event above 0.88. The analysis—the decomposition, simplifications, assessments, and recombinations—that produced the 0.88 is not a mechanical procedure that calculates a single correct number for the preference-probability. It is a quite subjective process; its sole purpose is to provide the decision maker with some insight into his own preference for the favorable verdict. If the decision maker thinks that the preference-probability he obtained from his analysis is completely unreasonable, he should reject it. If he is unsure of the preference-probability, he can adjust it or undertake a more detailed analysis.

Analyzing Range-of-Risk Dilemmas

Similar logic was used to obtain Phillips's preference-probability for the reject-settlement alternative (see figure 6–12). Outcomes or uncertainties between which Phillips is indifferent are substituted for each other, until every one of the outcomes is either a *Best* or *Worst* reference outcome. Then, the probability rules are used to combine the resulting, complex uncertainty into a single reference gamble. (In figure 6–12, the 0.88 reference gamble was substituted directly for the range of risk involved in a favorable verdict, but the longer, indirect substitution of figure 6–11 would have produced the same result.) From this analysis, Phillips concludes that he is indifferent between the reject-settlement alternative (and all the risk that it entails) and a reference gamble with a 53-percent chance of the *Best* and a 47-percent chance of the *Worst.* In other words, he concludes that his preference-probability for the reject-settlement alternative is 0.53.

The entire purpose of this indirect assessment was to give Phillips a better way of thinking about his preference for the reject-settlement alternative. If he is unhappy with the resulting preference-probability—if he thinks that he is not at all indifferent between the 0.53 reference gamble and rejecting the settlement—then he should develop a more satisfactory one. The purpose of the analysis is not to make the decision but to *help* make the decision as the line on the jacket indicates. The analysis should not take on a life of its own. The analyst is the master and should use his analytical tools to help him better understand the dilemma he faces.

Reference Gambles as Yardsticks

The second-cut analysis produced the same conclusion—accept the proposed settlement—as did the first cut. But there are some differences, which illustrate the purpose of taking an additional cut at the problem. To see these differences, compare the decision sapling for the completed first-cut analysis (figure 6–7) with the decision tree for the completed second cut (figure 6–10). The preference-probability of 0.88 obtained for the favorable-verdict outcome in the second-cut analysis is slightly lower than the one of 0.9 obtained for this same outcome in the first cut. Thus, Phillips's second, more sophisticated approach suggests that he does not value the (uncertain) outcome of a favorable verdict quite as highly as he first thought.

It is possible to make this comparison between the preference-probabilities obtained in the two different analyses *only because* the same reference gamble was used to assess preference-probabilities in both cases. In the first cut, the preference-probability of 0.9 was obtained directly, by making a drastic simplification so that a favorable verdict results in an award of $1.1 million and then directly assessing Phillips's preference-probability for the resulting payment of $825,000. For the second cut, the preference-probability of 0.88 was obtained indirectly from the still quite drastic simplification of approximating all possible jury awards with just two, a high one of $1.3 million and a low one of $750,000. Then, the preference-probabilities for the consequences of these two outcomes ($975,000 and $562,500) were obtained directly—using the *same* reference gamble, with the *same* reference outcomes—and combined, using the probability rules to obtain a preference-probability for a favorable verdict.

Comparing preference-probabilities to determine the relative desirability of outcomes, uncertain events, or alternatives is possible because of the definition of a preference-probability: It is that probability of winning a reference gamble that makes the decision maker indifferent between that gamble and some other outcome, uncertainty, or alternative. The 0.9 preference-probability assessed in the first cut for a favorable verdict indicates that Phillips is indifferent between that uncertainty and a (reference) gamble that gives him a 90-percent chance of winning $1.2 million and a 10-percent chance of winning $0. The preference-probability assessed in the second cut indicates that he is indifferent between the consequence of a favorable verdict and a (reference) gamble that gives him an 88-percent chance at winning $1.2 million and a 12-percent chance at winning $0. Clearly, an 88-percent chance of winning is not as good as a 90-percent chance (as long as the stakes are the same).

Thus, introducing the uncertainty about the amount of the jury award appears to lower its desirability to Phillips. He prefers having $825,000 for sure to gambling on a 50-50 chance of getting $975,000 versus $562,500. And since these are the approximations used for the amount of the jury award in the first and second cuts, they suggest a slight downward adjustment in Phillips's preference for the consequence of a favorable verdict.

Also note that the preference-probability of 0.53 obtained for the reject-settlement alternative in the second cut is slightly lower than the 0.54 preference-probability obtained initially. This suggests that Phillips does not think as highly of the consequences of rejecting the settlement as he first did. And that, of course, has been the real purpose of all this analysis—to help Phillips evaluate his (relative) preferences for the two choices he has.

The second-cut analysis was designed to help Phillips think more carefully—more systematically—about his preference-probability for the risky alternative. Since the outcome of the accept-settlement alternative is known, once the reference outcomes of the reference gamble are chosen, the preference-probability for this riskless alternative can be assessed directly; this preference-probability is merely a statement of the decision maker's relative preference for the certain outcome of the riskless alternative—relative to the outcomes of the reference gamble. Assessing a preference-probability for the reject-settlement alternative is complicated, however, by the quite numerous and very uncertain outcomes of this risky choice. This preference-probability could also be assessed directly. But Phillips decided to undertake some analysis to help him determine just what his relative preference was for this collection of uncertain outcomes—relative, again, to the outcomes of the same reference gamble.

After analyzing any decision problem, a decision maker can choose among alternatives by selecting the alternative with the highest preference-probability. But one should not forget why this makes sense. Preference-probabilities are nothing more than indifference probabilities. They indicate what the probability of winning the *Best* in a reference gamble must be to make the decision maker indifferent about choosing between that reference gamble on the one hand and either a certain outcome or another real-life gamble on the other. All the alternatives involved in a decision dilemma can be compared to the outcomes of the same reference gamble. The higher the probability of winning the *Best,* the better the reference gamble is. Therefore, the higher the indifference probability for an alternative is, the more the decision maker should like it. By choosing the alternative with the highest indifference probability (preference-probability) the decision maker is automatically choosing the alternative he likes the most.

The reference gamble is a simple, convenient yardstick that any decision maker can use to measure his relative preference for the various possible outcomes and alternatives involved in his dilemma. Sometimes, particularly when he wishes to determine his preference for a final outcome, he uses this yardstick to measure his preference directly. But when he wants to think about his preference for a collection of uncertain outcomes, he may choose to measure this indirectly. He can do this by using the reference-gamble yardstick to measure his preferences for the different possible outcomes and then combining all these preferences, taking into account the likelihood that each possible outcome will be the actual one.

A decision becomes a dilemma when it is difficult to compare the two (or more) available alternatives with each other directly—when there appears to be no sensible or meaningful way to lay them side by side to determine directly which one is truly best. Deciding between certain outcomes (such as two weeks vacation and three, or a $50 million profit and an $80 million profit, or ten thousand lives saved and twenty-five thousand) is easy. There exists a common, simple scale of comparison. But when uncertainty is involved, that scale disappears. By using the yardstick of a reference gamble, a measure of the desirability of each alternative, its preference-probability, can be obtained. Then, the two alternatives can be compared directly by comparing their respective preference-probabilities.

From his second-cut analysis, Phillips concludes that he is indifferent between the complex gamble involved in rejecting the out-of-court settlement and the simple reference gamble with a 0.53 chance of winning $1.2 million and a 0.47 chance of winning nothing. He previously determined that he is indifferent between the $300,000 certain consequence of the out-of-court settlement and a reference gamble with a 0.55 chance of winning the *Best* and a 0.45 chance of winning the *Worst* (the same reference outcomes). Thus, his second-cut analysis reenforces his original conclusion.

The difference between the preference-probabilities for the two alternatives is still small, however. Originally, the preference-probability for accepting the settlement was 0.55 and for rejecting it 0.54. Now these preference-probabilities are 0.55 and 0.53—hardly a big change. So what should Phillips do next? Should he undertake another cut, with a more sophisticated (less drastic) simplification for the range of risk? Or is now the right time to do some sensitivity analysis? These questions are addressed in chapter 9, where the analysis of J. C. Phillips's out-of-court settlement problem is continued.

Other Range-of-Risk Dilemmas: Business Investment Decisions

The basic decision dilemma (of chapters 2 and 3) involved a choice between a riskless alternative and a risky alternative for which there were only two possible outcomes, one better and one worse than the certain outcome of the riskless alternative. Building upon this basic dilemma, this chapter has examined a decision that is also between a riskless and a risky alternative, but in which the uncertainty of the risky alternative involves a large number of possible outcomes, some of which are better and some of which are worse than the certain outcome of the riskless alternative. This general type of decision problem—the range-of-risk dilemma—occurs frequently, particularly in business. When a firm must decide whether to make a particularly risky investment —one with a large number of uncertain profits and losses—a quick analysis similar to the one presented in this chapter may help the firm's executives make the decision or at least understand the key features of their dilemma so that they know which factors warrant more detailed and researched analysis. Since every firm always has some form of essentially riskless investment (bank notes, government securities, and the like), any risky investment opportunity presents a range-of-risk dilemma, the essence of which can be captured by one of the two range-of-risk decision trees of figure 6–13.

Whether to invest in the development of a new product is a common business decision that can be analyzed as a range-of-risk dilemma.[4] In 1981,

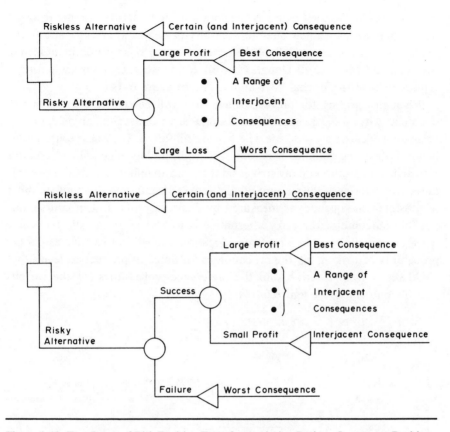

Figure 6–13. Two Range-of-Risk Decision Trees for Analyzing Business Investment Decisions.

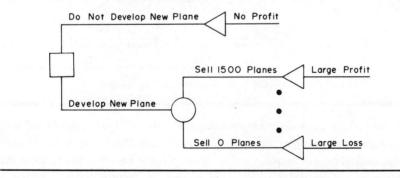

Figure 6–14. McDonnell Douglas's New-Product Range-of-Risk Dilemma.

for example, McDonnell Douglas Corporation had to decide whether to spend $2 billion to develop a new one-hundred-fifty-passenger aircraft for short- and medium-range commercial flights. Boeing Company was the dominant firm in the field, and McDonnell Douglas had to decide whether to compete for the replacement of the Boeing 727s and 737s (see figure 6–14).[5]

When prospecting for oil, a business firm will encounter a range-of-risk dilemma. After some geological studies of a particular region, an oil company or an oil wildcatter must decide whether to drill for oil. The riskless alternative is not to drill; the outcome is certain: no profit, no loss. The risky alternative is to drill, and if the company strikes oil there are an infinite number of possible outcomes in terms of the amount of oil discovered, and thus an infinite number of possible consequences as measured by financial profit. But of course, one possible outcome of the risky alternative is to find no oil at all. To decide whether to drill for oil in a particular location, the wildcatter must assess the probability of striking oil, the probabilities for different production levels that could result from a strike, and the preference-probabilities for the various possible outcomes (see figure 6–15).

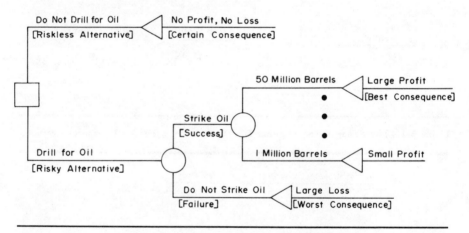

Figure 6–15. A Range-of-Risk Decision Tree for an Oil-Drilling Decision.

For many business investment decisions, a firm will have ample time and data to analyze the problem quite thoroughly. Before deciding whether to drill for oil, a wildcatter will want to collect a lot of data; he will want to examine the history of nearby wells and of similar regions, determine the geological layers where petroleum might be trapped, and perhaps make some seismic tests.[6] But there are many business decisions for which such information is simply not available.

Back in the late 1950s, Ventron Corporation (then Metal Hydrides Inc.) was considering whether to buy a government-built plant that produced sodium

Analyzing Range-of-Risk Dilemmas

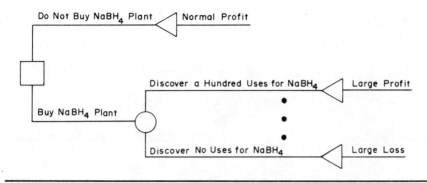

Figure 6–16. A Decision Tree for the Ventron Corporation's Decision Concerning the Sodium Borohydride Plant.

borohydride ($NaBH_4$). The output of the plant was fifty times greater than the market demand for the chemical, so such a venture would be profitable only if the company's chemists could develop some new uses for the compound. Deciding whether to invest in this sodium borohydride plant was a dilemma that had to be resolved without much data (figure 6–16). Ventron Corporation did buy the sodium borohydride plant, and its scientists developed a variety of uses for the chemical in the pharmaceutical, textile, chemical pulpwood, and pollution control industries. Today, the company makes 90 percent of the sodium borohydride consumed in the world, and the chemical accounted for half of the company's 1976 sales of $25 million.[7]

Other Range-of Risk Decisions: Legal Decisions

Not all decision dilemmas that can be analyzed with the help of the range-of-risk decision trees in figure 6–13 have money as the most important consequence. For example, there is the dilemma faced by the defendant who is accused of a crime and whose attorney has arranged a plea bargain with the prosecutor. Should the defendant accept a plea bargain or should he demand a trial? Accepting the plea bargain would require him to spend one year in prison. Rejecting it would lead to a trial for a more serious offense, which might result in acquittal and thus no time in prison. But a trial could also result in conviction, with a chance of a much longer sentence. For this type of decision problem, the important consequence is not money but time—time spent in prison.

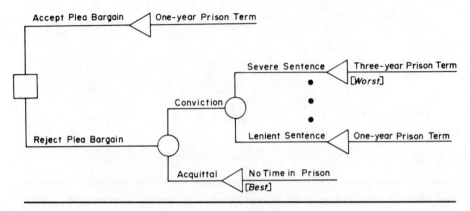

Figure 6–17. A Decision Tree for a Defendant's Plea-Bargain Dilemma.

Although the defendant's dilemma might be best analyzed with the help of a range-of-risk decision tree, the prosecutor may be able to analyze his own decision quite satisfactorily by using a decision sapling (see figure 2–5). Why? Because the defendant is concerned about how many years in prison will result from conviction, while the prosecutor is not. For the prosecutor, conviction is the best possible outcome and the length of the sentence does not affect his preference for this outcome very much. For the defendant, however, the number of years spent in prison might be quite important; if so, he would want to use the more complicated, range-of-risk decision tree in his analysis.

A defendant might, however, be more concerned about how conviction, acquittal, or a plea bargain would affect his reputation than in the time spent in prison. If so, the key consequence of conviction, a damaged reputation, would be the same regardless of the length of the sentence, and a decision sapling would be the appropriate analytical aid.

A decision tree is merely a tool to help analyze a decision. Exactly how sophisticated a tree should be used depends upon the needs of the decision maker. Not all business investment decisions, not even all those involving an infinite number of possible financial outcomes, warrant an analysis any more complicated than one based on the basic decision dilemma. The book publisher's dilemma discussed in chapter 2 (figure 2–12) is just such a problem.

Describing this problem with a basic decision sapling ignores the uncertainty involved in the number of books that will be sold *if* Carter wins the Democratic presidential nomination. Consequently, it is possible to draw a decision tree (figure 6–18) similar to the ones used in this chapter that takes into account the uncertainty over the number of Carter biographies that will be sold if he is nominated. But it is not obvious that this additional complication adds much to a publisher's understanding of his decision.

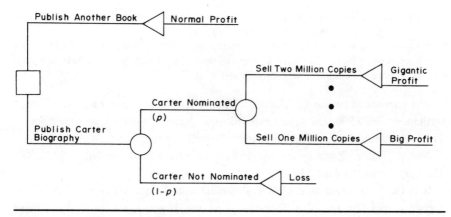

Figure 6–18. A Range-of-Risk Decision Tree for the Book Publisher's Dilemma.

In the out-of-court settlement problem, the possible final consequences of a favorable verdict are quite disparate. A favorable verdict could even result in a jury award that is less than the out-of-court settlement. For the Carter biography, however, the range of risk was not this large. Rather, the key uncertainty was whether Carter would win the nomination. If he did, it was obvious that the profit on a Carter biography would be significantly larger than normal. There would exist some uncertainty about the total sales (and thus profit) of the book, but this uncertainty was not all that great. It is possible to analyze this dilemma quite satisfactorily by using a decision sapling and approximating the consequence of a Carter nomination with the profits on the sale of, say, 1.5 million copies.

This should have been the approach for any first-cut analysis. Only after completing an analysis using the basic decision sapling and concluding that more analysis was required to resolve the dilemma satisfactorily should a publisher have undertaken a second-cut analysis using a range-of-risk decision tree.

Intelligent Decisions and Fortunate Outcomes

In that Brooklyn courtroom in March 1975, Gail Kalmowitz decided to accept the $165,000 out-of-court settlement. A few minutes later, she learned that the jury had reached a favorable verdict and would have awarded her $900,000. "You shouldn't have done it," one juror told her.[8]

But before the jury's verdict was known, the best decision was not all that evident. There was much uncertainty, as Kalmowitz herself noted.

- I felt they [the jurors] were coming back too fast and I was afraid that they had ruled against me and I'd lose everything . . . [9]
- I think I made a wise decision. Everybody said, "You've got it won." But I wasn't sure. They [the lawyers for the hospital] said they definitely would have appealed and there's a chance I would have lost it all.[10]

The parents of Edward J. Farrell, IV, also decided to accept an out-of-court settlement, for $500,000. And again, minutes later, the verdict became known. The jury would have awarded Jimmy Farrell nothing.

As for Thomas Zarcone, he rejected an out-of-court settlement of $205,000. The jury awarded him $141,000.

It is far from clear that Gail Kalmowitz and Thomas Zarcone made bad decisions and Mr. and Mrs. Farrell a good one. If you knew more about these three dilemmas—about the uncertainties involved and the decision makers' preferences—you might, in fact, reach the opposite conclusion. There is an important distinction between the decision made, which can be intelligent or foolish, and the final outcome, which can be fortunate or disastrous.

After the settlement, Kalmowitz said she was happy with her decision, although several months later she was not so sure. "If I had known then what I know now, I would have waited," she said.[11] But, of course, she did not know. She had only limited information and limited time in which to make the decision. A decision can be judged only on the basis of the information available at the time the decision is made—not on what is learned later.

Judging a decision—not the outcome—requires determining whether the decision is consistent with the decision maker's preferences for outcomes and beliefs about uncertainty. As William B. Schwartz, M.D., of the Tufts University School of Medicine wrote about the resistance of physicians to the use of decision analysis:

> Good decisions inevitably lead to some bad outcomes, just as bad decisions sometimes lead to good ones. The quality of a decision must therefore be evaluated on the basis of what is known when it is made, not ex post facto.[12]

Did the decision maker think analytically about all the uncertainties involved? Was all the information available used to assess the necessary probabilities? Did the decision maker incorporate his true preferences into his assessment of preference-probabilities for the possible consequences of his decision, and thus into his evaluation of the alternatives?

Suppose you were offered a choice between $10,000 for sure and $20,000 if Edward M. Kennedy wins the next presidential election (but nothing if he loses). Would you not select the certain $10,000 (even if it would not be paid until after the election)? Suppose Kennedy then won. Would you have made a bad decision? Certainly not—not unless you had possessed some special information clearly indicating that Kennedy's chances were significantly greater than 50 percent. Your decision could have been quite intelligent, even though the outcome left you disappointed.

We all tend to focus on what might have been. When the *New York Times* reported the story of Gail Kalmowitz on its front page, the headline was "Nearly Blind Student Accepts $165,000, Forfeiting $900,000 Award From Jury." And when the *Washington Post* reported the story about Edward Farrell's out-of-court settlement, its headline emphasized the loss to the hospital: "Jury Verdict: $500,000 Too Late." Indeed, for the out-of-court settlement decision, the outcome will always be unfortunate for one of the two parties, either the plaintiff or the defendant. If the two parties to the suit agree to a settlement, one of them will be disappointed if the jury's verdict is learned. And if they do not settle, the same is true. Yet, nevertheless, it is possible that *both* the plaintiff and the defendant made intelligent decisions.

Certainly both Gail Kalmowitz and Mr. and Mrs. Farrell could have made good decisions. Neither the Kalmowitz nor Farrell family was wealthy and thus both of these plaintiffs were probably reluctant to take big gambles. For example, suppose each family was given a choice between (1) a reference gamble with a 50-50 chance at $1 million or nothing and (2) $300,000 for sure. Undoubtedly, both families—if they thought very much about the decision— would have selected the $300,000 riskless alternative. Wouldn't you? For both families there had to be *some* out-of-court settlement that they would have preferred to the uncertainties of the jury's decision. The real question is: How large must the out-of-court settlement be for the decision maker to prefer this riskless alternative to the risky choice of gambling on the jury? (This question of risk aversion for monetary uncertainties is discussed in chapter 8.)

Most important decisions are complicated by uncertainty. Reducing or eliminating the uncertainty can help. But in many cases, such as the uncertainty concerning the jury's verdict, this is impossible. For other decisions, it will cost more to obtain the necessary information than eliminating the uncertainty is worth. And for many other decisions, there simply is not enough time to collect more data; the decision must be made with the limited information available. In such situations, it is helpful to organize your thinking about the dilemma, ascertain the key uncertainties, assess their likelihood, and determine the best alternative. Even the most intelligent analysis, does not, however, always result in a fortunate outcome.

Appendix: Determining Preference-Probabilities for Uncertain Outcomes

For the out-of-court settlement problem, and certainly for more complex decisions, it is quite cumbersome to resolve the dilemma by repeatedly using the substitution principle and making the necessary calculations based on the probability rules to obtain the preference-probability for each uncertain event. Fortunately, a little arithmetic can produce the same result.

By definition, the preference-probability of any reference gamble is the chance of getting the *Best* outcome. But this preference-probability can also be obtained by multiplying the probability of each outcome by its preference-probability and then adding the result. For example, the reference gamble that Cookie Phillips thinks is equivalent to accepting the $400,000 out-of-court settlement gives a 0.55 chance of a $1,200,000 payment with a preference-probability of 1.0, and a 0.45 chance of $0 with a preference-probability of 0 (see figure 6–6a). Thus, the preference-probability of this uncertain event is

$$V = (0.55 \times 1.0) + (0.45 \times 0) = 0.55.$$

This result is not surprising, but it illustrates how to determine preference-probabilities for more-complex uncertain events.

Consider, for example, the task in the second-cut analysis (figure 6–8) of determining the preference-probability of the uncertain event that results from a favorable verdict (and thus for the favorable-verdict outcome itself). A favorable verdict leads to a 0.5 chance at a $975,000 payment, which has a preference-probability of 0.95, plus a 0.5 chance at a $562,000 payment, which has a preference-probability of 0.8. Now there are two steps to determine the preference-probability for this uncertain event: (1) multiply the preference-probability of each outcome by the probability of getting that outcome and (2) add up these products.

$$V = (0.5 \times 0.95) + (0.5 \times 0.8) = 0.475 + 0.4 = 0.875 \approx 0.88.$$

This 0.88 preference-probability for a favorable verdict is identical to the one obtained in figure 6–9 by using the substitution principle and making the appropriate probability calculations.

Similarly, it is easy to obtain the preference-probability for the reject-settlement alternative by calculating the preference-probability for the uncertain event that results directly from it.

$$V = (0.6 \times 0.88) + (0.4 \times 0) = 0.528 + 0 = 0.528 \approx 0.53.$$

Note that in making this calculation the 0.88 preference-probability obtained above for a favorable verdict is multiplied by the 0.6 probability of obtaining a favorable verdict, while the preference-probability of 0 for an unfavorable verdict is multiplied by the 0.4 probability of getting an unfavorable verdict. The result, a 0.53 preference-probability for the reject-settlement alternative, is the same as the one obtained in figure 6–9.

This simple arithmetic process does not apply solely to uncertain events with only two possible outcomes. It can be generalized to apply to any uncertain event. If an uncertain event can result in ten different outcomes, then the preference-probability of that uncertain event (and the alternative or outcome that leads to it) is

$$V = p_1 V_1 + p_2 V_2 + p_3 V_3 + p_4 V_4 + p_5 V_5 + p_6 V_6 + p_7 V_7 \\ + p_8 V_8 + p_9 V_9 + p_{10} V_{10},$$

where p_3 is the probability that the uncertain event will result in the third outcome and V_3 is the preference-probability of this outcome.

This process applies whether the outcome branch of the uncertain event leads to an outcome node, another uncertain event, or even a decision node. The reason lies in the definition of a preference-probability. The preference-probability of any outcome of an uncertain event is merely the decision maker's indifference probability for the reference gamble. And, given the substitution principle, whatever is attached to this outcome branch can be replaced with its equivalent reference gamble. For example consider the generalized uncertainty of figure 6–19; if the third outcome branch (with probability p_3) leads to a node with a preference-probability of V_3, that node and whatever follows (no matter how complicated) can be replaced with a simple reference gamble with a V_3 chance of the *Best* and a $(1 - V_3)$ chance of the *Worst*.

The probability that the uncertain event will result in a best outcome from the third outcome branch (*Best 3*) is $p_3 \times V_3$. And this, of course, applies to all the other outcome branches. Thus, to obtain the probability that the uncertain event will result in a *Best* outcome (any *Best* outcome), it is only necessary to add up the probabilities that it will result in each of the individual *Best* outcomes (*Best 1, Best 2, Best 3, . . . Best 10*): $p_1 V_1 + p_2 V_2 + p_3 V_3 + \ldots + p_{10} V_{10}$. This simple arithmetic process for determining the preference-probability for uncertain events is mathematically identical to the application of the substitution principle and the appropriate probability rules. Only it is much easier.

But do not forget what the resulting number means. This preference-probability—like any other preference-probability for a final outcome, uncertain event, or decision alternative—is an indifference probability. It is the probability of obtaining the *Best* outcome in a reference gamble that makes the decision maker indifferent between the uncertain event and this reference gamble.

This preference-probability could always be assessed directly. But sometimes, when thinking about such a preference-probability, it is helpful to de-

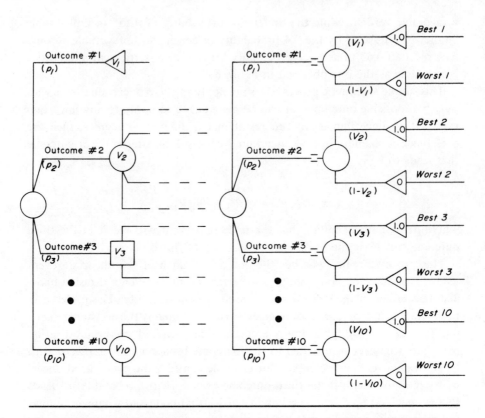

Figure 6–19 Using Simple Arithmetic to Obtain the Preference-Probability for a Complex Uncertain Event.

compose the uncertain event into its component outcomes, assess preference-probabilities for these outcomes directly (or even indirectly) and then recombine the results of such an analysis to obtain the preference-probability for the original uncertain event. Still, the resulting preference-probability is nothing more than an indifference probability. Just because it has been obtained from other numbers using the rules of arithmetic does not mean that this number is any more correct—any more accurate—than a preference-probability assessed directly. (For this reason, it usually makes sense to round off all preference-probabilities that are obtained indirectly to two significant figures.)

Preference-probabilities, whether obtained directly or indirectly, are nothing more than subjective judgments about indifference probabilities. An analytical decision maker should be careful always to view them as such. After indirectly obtaining a preference-probability for an uncertain event, a decision maker should always ask "Is this preference-probability reasonable? Has my analysis helped me to think more intelligently about my indifference probability for this uncertain event?" Asking questions like these can help a decision maker avoid any "delusions of accuracy."

Chapter 7

Assessing Your Ignorance: Lessons from the Spending Shortfall

IN January 1976, the Office of Management and Budget published the *Federal Budget* for fiscal year 1977. That budget also contained estimates of federal outlays for the fiscal year then in progress, FY 76 (July 1, 1975 to June 30, 1976). Because the federal government was switching from a July–June fiscal year to an October–September one, the budget document also contained estimates for the "transition quarter" (July 1, 1976 to September 30, 1976). These spending estimates were $373.5 billion for FY 76 and $98.0 billion for the transition quarter.[1]

Six months later, on July 16, 1976, the Office of Management and Budget (OMB) released some revised spending estimates: $369.1 billion for FY 76, then just completed, and $102.1 billion for the then-in-progress transition quarter.[2]

Two weeks after that, OMB released the final data for FY 76, showing actual outlays of $365.6 billion.[3] And on October 27, 1976, the final figures for the transition quarter revealed actual expenditures of $94.5 billion.[4] (See table 7–1.)

That was the beginning of the now-infamous "spending shortfall," or, as Paul H. O'Neill, deputy director of OMB, described it, the "outlay underrun."[5] Over a fifteen-month period, federal outlays were $11 billion less than had been budgeted. This inability to spend what had been planned—what Representative Jim Wright, the House majority leader, called "the simple musclebound-

TABLE 7–1

The Spending Shortfall for FY 76 and the Transition Quarter[6]

		FY 76	Transition Quarter	15-Month Total
Actual Outlays		365.6	94.5	460.1
January 1976	Estimate	373.5	98.0	471.5
	Shortfall (Actual Minus Estimate)	−7.9	−3.5	−11.4
July 1976	Estimate	369.1	102.1	471.2
	Shortfall (Actual Minus Estimate)	−3.5	−7.6	−11.1

All figures in billions of dollars.

ness of the Federal Government"[7]—is a phenomenon usually associated only with developing nations. It called for a congressional investigation.

Hearings held by the House Budget Committee in November 1976 focused on four specific questions about the spending shortfall:

1. Why did the executive branch not spend the money specified in the congressional budget resolutions? The second budget resolution for FY 76, adopted on December 12, 1975, set a ceiling on outlays of $374.9 billion; the second budget resolution for the transition quarter, adopted on May 13, 1976, set a ceiling of $102.2 billion.
2. To what extent had the federal government's failure to spend at the levels planned contributed to the pause in the recovery of the U.S. economy from the 1974–75 recession? As an economic stimulus, Congress had authorized a $90.3 billion deficit during this fifteen-month period, but the actual deficit had been only $78.3 billion—$12 billion less than Congress planned.
3. How much of the $11 billion not spent in FY 76 and the transition quarter would spill over into the next fiscal year? The expenditures of these funds could require a third congressional budget resolution to raise the outlay ceiling for FY 77, and might result in a larger federal deficit than was planned or desired.
4. Why could OMB not produce better estimates of federal expenditures? The July 1976 estimate for FY 76 expenditures, which was off by $7.9 billion even though that fiscal year had already ended, was the most troubling.

The debate over these issues reflected, in part, the partisan struggle between a Republican president, uncomfortable with large federal budget deficits, and a Democratic congress, which had legislated those deficits to stimulate the economy. Everyone wanted to know what effect the spending shortfall had on GNP growth, unemployment, and inflation. O'Neill's testimony implied that the pause in economic expansion had not been caused by the spending short-fall.[8] He also reported that "in the absence of the Federal spending shortfall

. . . the current unemployment rate would be no more than 0.1 lower and the number of jobs would be 100,000 higher. . . . The inflation rate would probably be raised by 0.1 percent."[9] The Congressional Budget Office (CBO) provided different data. Testified CBO director Alice M. Rivlin, "It seems likely that the shortfalls were a major cause of the current economic lull, lowering the growth of real GNP by roughly 1.0 percentage points (annual rate) during the second and third quarters of 1976."[10] CBO also estimated that, because of the shortfall, unemployment was "currently about 100,000 to 150,000 higher" and "about 125,000 to 185,000 jobs" had not been created, and that "inflation rates would have been 0.1 to 0.2 higher had the shortfall . . . not taken place."[11]

The hearings also provided everyone with the opportunity to make a political point. Representative Wright intoned:

> Mr. Chairman, this is somewhat alarming. There has been some disparity shown in past years but never anything like 7.4 [the percentage error of the estimate for the transition quarter]. The miscalculations in the past appeared to have been well below 1 percent, more like in the range of one-half percent. Then all of a sudden, in fiscal 1976, we discover almost a full percent disparity [for FY 76].[12]

Naturally, OMB's O'Neill viewed the shortfall from a different perspective.

> I must admit to some degree of amazement that so many people seem to be dismayed that Federal spending and the Federal deficit for fiscal year 1976 and the transition quarter turned out to be lower than originally estimated last January. Usually, it is cost overruns that arouse the wrath of the public, and ourselves, I might add, but in this instance, we are under attack for not having spent enough . . . . I hope that you will permit me to take some pleasure in the good news implicit in the shortfall. It is hard to be dismayed when interest rates are lower than predicted, [when] we receive more for selling oil leases than was anticipated, and [when] the requirements of income maintenance programs are less than we thought that they would be.[13]

Representative Delbert L. Latta was even more amazed: "The complaint appears to be that the American taxpayers may have been saved about $15 billion by the Administration."[14]

Forecasting Techniques and Inherent Uncertainties

In FY 77, federal outlays were again below estimates, and, as the president was now a Democrat, the political debate turned into a less partisan discussion of the real difficulties in estimating federal outlays. Even at the November 1976 hearings, O'Neill had used historical data to argue that "the estimating problem . . . is a bipartisan one."[15] He emphasized that "one percent of $400 billion [the size of the federal budget for FY 77] is $4 billion. While we may not like to be off in our estimates by $4 billion, we may have great difficulty in avoiding a 1-percent or even a 2-percent error."[16] But it was the bias in the error that troubled many at OMB and CBO. Why was there always a shortfall? Why were the estimates of expenditures consistently too high?

Errors in budget estimates can come from two general sources: (1) mistakes in forecasting techniques and (2) inherent uncertainties in the factors employed when using those techniques.[17] For example, the econometric models used to forecast expenditures for unemployment compensation can be improved (perhaps perfected), but there will always be uncertainty about the numbers used as inputs for those models (such as the unemployment rate over the coming year). Thus, it is possible to eliminate the consistent bias in spending estimates. CBO concluded that "the 1978 shortfall in outlays . . . can be attributed primarily to the tendency of federal agencies to overestimate what they can accomplish [and thus spend] each year."[18] But all the uncertainty will not go away. Even if all the forecasting models are working perfectly—that is, without any bias—there still exists significant residual uncertainty.

Indeed, anyone attending the congressional hearings on the spending shortfall should have been impressed with the inherent uncertainties involved in making budget estimates. Part of the uncertainty comes from the "entitlement" nature of many federal programs, including social security, medicare and medicaid, veterans' benefits, unemployment compensation, farm price supports, Aid to Families with Dependent Children, Food Stamps, and Civil Service and railroad retirement. Congress does not set expenditure levels for these programs. Rather, it and the individual states establish benefit formulas that determine who is eligible and how much those who are eligible shall receive. Consequently, actual expenditures for entitlement programs, which account for approximately one-half of federal outlays, depend upon the number of people who apply and qualify for benefits. Estimates of such expenditures are derived from related economic, demographic, and meteorological predictions, which are themselves inherently uncertain.

Additional uncertainty in outlay estimates arises from the large number of agencies, bureaus, and regional and field offices of the federal government, each of which makes independent decisions about when to spend appropriated funds. The spending pattern of any individual federal office or agency fluctuates, and the sum of their actions is thus also uncertain. Further, state and local governments are responsible for spending the funds for various federal programs, and the cumulative impact of their behavior in any given fiscal year is difficult to predict.[19] OMB found twenty-seven different budget accounts for which spending for FY 76 and the transition quarter differed (plus or minus) by more than $300 million from January 1976 estimates.[20]

Assessing Your Ignorance

Yet, few congressmen appeared willing to accept that uncertainty might be inherent in budget estimates. Rep. Brock Adams, chairman of the Budget Committee, asked:

> Isn't it possible, since the [appropriations] bills are in place [at the beginning of the fiscal year] and we are looking at a very limited number of congressional actions outstanding, to determine more accurately the outlay figures for purposes of applying a ceiling or for knowing whether fiscal policy is being carried out more effectively. Everything for fiscal 1977 is in place with the exception of the spring supplemental. Why don't we know more?[21]

In her response, CBO director Rivlin felt compelled to say: "It should not be forgotten that outlay estimates will never be perfect." Still, Representative Robert N. Giaimo asked: "Can you [CBO] develop a greater independence from OMB in obtaining the precise information necessary to reduce or eliminate the 1-percent margin of error? . . . Can we get better estimating than 1-percent margin of error in a $400 billion budget?"[22] CBO and others may be able to develop their own more refined statistical techniques for predicting future outlays from current data, and such techniques may even be able to reduce the estimation errors to less than 1 percent.[23] Given, however, that CBO, just like OMB or anyone else, will have to obtain the data from which those predictions are derived from the individual spending agencies, it ought to be clear that "greater independence from OMB" will not produce "the precise information" that Rep. Giaimo hoped would eliminate the estimation error.

Of all the members of the House Budget Committee who attended the hearings, only one, Rep. Robert L. Leggett, seemed to accept uncertainty as inherent in all budget estimates and to be more concerned about the implications of this uncertainty than in a futile quest for infallible numbers. Leggett questioned OMB's O'Neill.

> You indicate . . . how difficult it is to explain a 2- to 4-percent error. You are talking about outlays; and you have indicated that traditionally that has been where the error is. . . .
>
> If that is true, then it raises a question with respect to our procedure. Last year, for example, the task force [of the Budget Committee, on economic projections], after rigorous review of the Defense budget, indicated that defense spending was accelerating a little too fast with respect to purchases. We recommended a reduction of approximately $4 billion. The Department of Defense seemed to come apart at the seams. They literally invaded Capitol Hill. We were subjected to all sorts of innuendo from Pennsylvania Avenue, to the effect that pseudo-Americans were making slashing curtailments, and jeopardizing the posture of the United States all over the world.
>
> As a result Mr. Giaimo had a compromise amendment where he suggested we cut the budget authority $2 billion and spending on the order of a half billion dollars. Even that was too much for Mr. [Sam] Gibbons to accept because he apparently felt

from his vantage point there was a critical problem as to our Nation's defense and we should not decrease budget authority by more than a billion and should not decrease spending by more than $100 million. What you are saying here is that the estimating errors inherent in these calculations approximate the amounts recommended for reduction by the task force in the first instance . . . .

If you admit the error is 1 percent of the overall $400 billion plus program, how can you get into a serious debate with this committee if we reduce the program by, say $1 billion or $2 billion . . . ?[24]

Leggett also commented on the charade of pretending that budget estimates are more accurate than they are.

This brings up, of course, a whole series of queries when we go into conference with the Senate. Many times we spend long, tough hours and days worrying about whether or not it ought to be $50 million or $70 million or $30 million. The Senate adopts the theory of rounding off to the nearest $100 million. Many of us in the House have felt that was not really a very expert way of handling things.

What you are telling us is there are probably 200 items which are actually different because of poor estimates. Perhaps when we round off, maybe that would be a more accurate way of doing things.[25]

Yet, Congress continues to devote an inordinate amount of time to symbolic dickering over whether $100 billion appropriations should be increased or decreased by less than a billion. In the spring of 1980, for example, the House of Representatives voted down a budget resolution for FY 81 because it contained too much for guns and not enough for butter. But, as the *Washington Post* explained in an editorial: "The amounts of money now in dispute are too small. The defeated resolution called for $153.7 billion in defense outlays. The rebellion among the Democrats was led by people who would have settled for $153.0 billion. That's a difference of less than half a percentage point."[26] That difference was not only less than half of 1 percent of the $153 billion in defense outlays, but also only about a tenth of 1 percent of the total outlays for FY 81 of over $600 billion.

That difference was also smaller than the potential impact on the budget of small shifts in unemployment, inflation, and interest rates. Rudolph G. Penner, former assistant director of OMB for economic policy, explained at the time the effect of changes in such factors.

A 1 percentage point error in forecasting the unemployment rate will cause a $5 billion to $7 billion error in forecasting outlays and about a $20 billion error in forecasting receipts. A 1 percentage point error in forecasting inflation leads to a $1 billion to $2 billion error in estimating outlays on indexed programs [programs whose benefit levels change with the inflation rate] and a $6 billion to $8 billion error in the receipts estimate. A 1 percentage point error in forecasting interest rates can mean a $1 billion to $3 billion difference in the cost of interest payments on the national debt.[27]

Still, Congress behaves as if it can predict the federal budget to the penny.

Assessing Your Ignorance

Suggesting Uncertainty: Scenarios and Ranges

One way to convey uncertainty is not to give a single number—a point estimate—but to provide several estimates, each one dependent upon a different scenario of the future. For example, in November 1976, when OMB prepared its *Current Services Estimates For Fiscal Year 1978*, it first developed four different sets of economic assumptions based on the possible combinations of high or low inflation, with high or low unemployment. Then OMB provided estimates of receipts, outlays, and the deficit for each of these four different "economic paths."[28] For example, table 7–2 contains OMB's estimates of "current services" outlays—that is, outlays assuming no policy changes—for FY 78.

TABLE 7–2

Current Services Estimates of Federal Outlays for FY 78 Based on Alternative Economic Assumptions[29]

		Inflation	
		Higher (6.5%)	Lower (5.0%)
Unemployment	Higher (6.5%)	453.2	452.2
	Lower (5.5%)	448.0	447.1

All figures in billions of dollars.

Similarly, a month later, when the Congressional Budget Office published corresponding figures in its *Five-Year Budget Projections: Fiscal Year 1978–1982*, CBO noted that "considerable uncertainty exists concerning the economic outlook in the period 1978 through 1982"[30] and thus provided three sets of economic assumptions. CBO labeled these alternative scenarios (1) "Baseline Assumptions," (2) "Less Vigorous Economic Expansion," and (3) "More Rapid Economic Expansion."[31] Providing alternative estimates based on "optimistic" and "pessimistic" scenarios is a common method for indicating uncertainty.

Estimating a range of possible outcomes is another means for indicating uncertainty. Alternative scenarios imply such a range. For example, CBO's scenarios for economic expansion suggested that the actual path would lie somewhere in the range between "more rapid" and "less vigorous" expansion. Similarly, current services estimates that OMB obtained from its four alternative economic paths implied the ranges shown in table 7–3.

These figures make it clear that in November 1976 there was greater uncertainty about the budget projections for FY 78 than for FY 77, which had actually begun six weeks earlier. This is only reasonable. The further into the

TABLE 7-3

Ranges of Alternative Federal Receipts, Outlays, and Deficits from OMB's Current Services Estimates for November 1976[32]

| | FY 77 | | | FY 78 | | |
	High	Low	Width of Range	High	Low	Width of Range
Receipts	357.8	353.6	4.2	415.5	396.0	19.5
Outlays	412.9	412.0	0.9	453.2	447.1	6.1
Deficit	59.3	54.2	5.1	56.2	32.6	23.6

All figures in billions of dollars.

future one attempts to project, the less certain one will be, and thus the wider should be the range of estimates.

The numbers also give the impression, however, that the actual figures will not fall outside the range given—that, for example, federal outlays for FY 77 will not be less than $412 billion nor greater than $412.9 billion. Moreover, Paul O'Neill, when discussing these estimates with the press, gave that impression explicitly: "Outlays in Fiscal Year 1977 we believe are now going to come in between $412 billion and $412.9 billion. So the range there is quite small. But for Fiscal Year 1978, the range we believe is between $447.1 billion and $453.2 billion."[33]

Admittedly, these were *current services* estimates; they assumed the continuation of the services provided by current federal programs with *no* policy changes. Since, in November 1976, the president was already proposing policy changes and it was obvious that Congress would make some before the first day of FY 78 (October 1, 1977), the current services estimates should not be viewed as predictions for FY 78. The OMB document emphasized that "the current services estimates are neither recommended amounts nor estimates as to what the figures for 1978 will actually turn out to be."[34] Rather, they are made to provide a planning base for the executive and legislative branches and thus merely suggest what would happen under the assumption—which everyone recognizes as unrealistic—that there would be no change in federal policy.

The same caveat cannot be made for the FY 77 current services estimates. That fiscal year had begun and all the appropriations bills had been passed. Only the supplemental appropriations bills remained to be considered, and there was really little that Congress (or another president) could or would do to change federal policy during the early months of the 1977 session that would have any effect on receipts, expenditures, or the deficit for that year. Yet, when FY 77 was over, the results were as shown in table 7-4. Receipts fell within the range of the current services estimates, but outlays were well below the

TABLE 7–4

November 1976 Current Services
Estimates for FY 77 and Actual Results

	Actual[35]	Estimated Range
Receipts	356.9	353.6–357.8
Outlays	401.9	412.0–412.9
Deficit	45.0	54.2– 59.3

All figures in billions of dollars

range and consequently so was the deficit. Federal outlays were $11 billion, or 2.7 percent, below the bottom of OMB's estimated range.

Despite the hand wringing over the FY 76 spending shortfall, despite O'Neill's testimony that "we may have great difficulty avoiding a 1-percent or even a 2-percent error,"[36] and despite his stressing that "1 percent of $400 billion is $4 billion,"[37] OMB estimated a range of federal outlays of only $900 million—less than one-quarter of 1 percent. That range simply did not suggest the real dimensions of the intrinsic uncertainty about federal outlays, which O'Neill so carefully explained to the House Budget Committee that very same month.

Thus, although a range may be better than a point estimate in that it suggests some uncertainty, it is inadequate unless accompanied by some indication of how likely it is that the actual number will fall outside that range. In practice, this is rarely done. Either it is specifically stated—as O'Neill did at his press conference—that the number will be within that range, or this is the intended implication. But, of course, as the FY 77 experience indicates, there is certainly some chance that the number will fall outside the given range. Speaking of budgetary and economic predictions, Denis Healey, the British Chancellor of the Exchequer, complained, "The numbers contained in the forecasts—specific to one-half percent, in every case—give a spurious impression of certainty."[38] Edgar R. Fiedler, of the Conference Board, has developed a number of rules of forecasting, including "Economists state their GNP projections to the nearest tenth of a percentage point to prove they have a sense of humor."[39]

Unfortunately, when OMB published its current services estimates in January 1978, it provided only one set of economic assumptions and only a point estimate for outlays: $460.4 billion for FY 78; $492.4 billion for FY 79.[40] Not $460.3 billion or $460.5 billion; for FY 78, OMB estimated that outlays would be $460.4 billion—correct to four significant figures.

What had happened to O'Neill's 1- or 2-percent possible error? Two months later it reemerged. In March 1978, noting that "most Federal agencies are again falling below their spending plans for 1978," OMB revised its current services estimates for outlays for FY 78 downward by 7 billion to $453.5 billion. Reported OMB, "The general tendency to overestimate spending for the current year, which caused shortfalls in all but one year since 1970, continues to be a major problem."[41] Indeed, when the fiscal year ended on September 30, 1978, outlays proved to be even lower: $450.8 billion.

Garry D. Brewer of Yale's School of Organization and Management calls the use of multidigit point estimates "phoney precision."[42] Aaron Wildavsky, former president of the Russell Sage Foundation, calls it "spurious specificity."[43] Whatever you want to call it, it should be clear that point estimates, particularly when given to four significant figures (or even with narrow ranges), convey a false sense of confidence of our knowledge of the future. And, when it is obvious that the quantities being estimated are quite uncertain, it is difficult to base a decision on those estimates unless they are also accompanied by some statement that adequately specifies that uncertainty.

Specifying Uncertainty: Medians and Quartiles

When making decisions about agency requests for funds for specific projects or programs, legislators need to account for the uncertainty in the proposed budgets. They need to ask, "How good is this estimate?" This is illustrated by the following exchange, in 1971, between Rep. Julia Butler Hansen, chairman of a House appropriations subcommittee, and George B. Hartzog, director of the National Park Service:

> *Mrs. Hansen:* Are the amounts being requested . . . merely estimates or are they based on actual engineering evaluations?
> *Mr. Hartzog:* These are what we would call class A estimates. They are not the result of construction drawings, but they are the result of on-the-site surveys by professional personnel. They are not just horse-back guesses.[44]

Unfortunately, distinguishing between "class A estimates" and "horse-back guesses" hardly specifies the uncertainty.

One way to indicate uncertainty when estimating an uncertain quantity is with a *confidence interval.* For example, a "90-percent confidence interval" means that there is a 90-percent chance that the actual value will fall within the given range and a 10-percent chance that it will fall outside of it. If OMB's $412.0–$412.9 range for federal outlays in FY 77 had been its 90-percent confidence interval, OMB would have believed that there was a 5-percent chance that actual outlays would be less than $412 billion and another 5-percent chance that outlays would be more than $412.9 billion. Or, if this range had been OMB's 50-percent confidence interval, they would have believed that there was a 25-percent chance that actual outlays would be less than $412 billion, a 50-percent chance that outlays would be between $412 and $412.9 billion, and a 25-percent chance that outlays would be greater than $412.9 billion.

When an estimate is expressed as a range, the uncertainty in that estimate is specified only when a probability is assigned to that range. Bracketing a range with "optimistic" and "pessimistic" estimates is not very helpful; like the probability words discussed in chapter 4 (table 4–1), these descriptions of uncertain quantities are very ambiguous. What exactly is the probability that an uncertain quantity will fall within an optimistic-to-pessimistic range?[45] If, however, a range is defined with a given probability (or confidence level), it is clear that the wider the range the more uncertain is the estimate of the quantity.

In addition to the appropriation of government funds, there are a variety of decisions, such as those range-of-risk dilemmas discussed in chapter 6, that involve uncertain quantities. The amount of an out-of-court settlement, the size of corporate sales or profit, the number of years spent in jail, the amount of oil discovered, the number of books sold—these are all uncertain quantities which can influence a decision. To resolve dilemmas complicated by uncertain quantities, it is necessary to think carefully about the extent of that uncertainty.

When undertaking first-cut and second-cut analyses of range-of-risk dilemmas, a median estimate and a 50-percent confidence interval can be very helpful. The *median estimate* of an uncertain quantity is the number that divides the entire spectrum of possible outcomes into two, equally probable ranges. This number is also called the *50th-percentile estimate*, since there is a 50-percent chance that the uncertain quantity will be below it (and a 50-percent chance that it will be above it). The median estimate is thus chosen so that, as economist Paul A. Samuelson writes, "if you had to risk most of your eating money on one side or the other, you honestly wouldn't know on which side of your estimate to bet."[46]

Often, it is useful to think of the point estimate of an uncertain quantity as just such a median estimate; this specifies the meaning of a point estimate or "best guess." There may well be differences about what this number *should be,* but there can be no differences about the *interpretation* of anyone's median estimate: It is equally likely that the actual value will turn out to be above as below this estimate. Thus, if OMB and CBO eliminate the bias in their point estimates for annual outlays, they would discover that actual outlays were below their estimate for half the years and above it for the other half.

In chapter 6, the first-cut analysis of J. C. Phillips's out-of-court settlement dilemma was undertaken using a decision sapling (see figure 7–1). Although

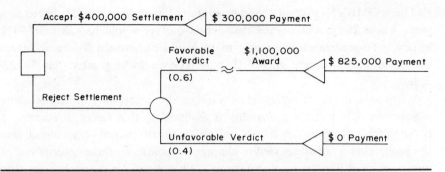

Figure 7–1. A Decision Sapling for J. C. Phillips's Out-of-Court Settlement Dilemma.

it was explicitly stated that a favorable verdict would result in an infinite number of possible jury awards, the entire range for this uncertain quantity was simplified down to a single point estimate: $1.1 million. This number was Phillips's median estimate of the size of the jury award. That is, Phillips decided that if the jury reached a favorable verdict, the award was equally likely to be above $1.1 million as below it.

To specify a 50-percent confidence interval, two numbers are required. The first is the *25th-percentile estimate,* the number that divides the entire spectrum of possible outcomes into two ranges such that there is a 25-percent chance that the actual value of the uncertain quantity will be below this estimate (and thus a 75-percent chance that the actual value will be above it). The second number necessary to define the 50-percent confidence interval is the *75th-percentile estimate*, the number that divides the spectrum of possible outcomes into two ranges, with a 75-percent chance that the actual value will be below this number. Thus, there is a 50-percent chance that the actual value will fall between the 25th- and 75th-percentile estimates.

The 25th-, 50th-, and 75th-percentile estimates divide the spectrum of possible outcomes into four equally probable ranges. There is a 25-percent chance that the actual value of the uncertain quantity will be:

1. less than the 25th-percentile estimate,
2. between the 25th-percentile and median estimates,
3. between the median and 75th-percentile estimates, and
4. above the 75th-percentile estimate.

Consequently, these three estimates are often called the *quartiles,* with the 25th percentile being the *lower quartile* and the 75th percentile the *upper quartile.* The 50-percent confidence interval, or the region between the upper and lower quartiles, is often called the *interquartile range.*

Figure 7–2 illustrates how the three estimates J. C. Phillips made (in chapter

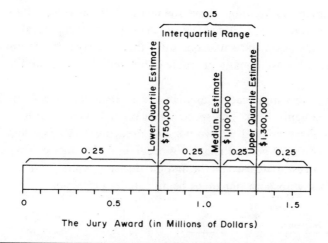

Figure 7–2. Four Equally Probable Ranges and the Interquartile Range Created by Phillips's Lower-Quartile, Median, and Upper-Quartile Estimates.

6) divide the entire range of possible jury awards into four intervals of equal probability. The lower quartile estimate was $750,000; the upper quartile estimate was $1.3 million. And, of course, the median estimate was $1.1 million. That means that Phillips thinks there is a 25-percent chance that an award will be below $750,000. He also thinks that there is a 25-percent chance that it will be between $750,000 and $1.1 million, a 25-percent chance for it to be in the range between $1.1 million and $1.3 million, and a 25-percent chance of it being above $1.3 million. And he thinks that there is a 50-percent chance that it will fall between $750,000 and $1.3 million; this implies that he also thinks there is a 50-percent chance that the actual value will fall outside (above or below) this interquartile range.

Often, when attempting to resolve a decision dilemma complicated by an uncertain quantity, using a single, median estimate is unsatisfactory. In such situations, the lower- and upper-quartile estimates can be used in a second-cut analysis to indicate the extent of the uncertainty involved. Rather than let the median estimate approximate the entire spectrum of possible outcomes, the lower quartile can be used to stand for the lower half of the spectrum and the upper quartile for the upper half. Because there is a 50-percent chance that the actual value will fall below the median, and the lower quartile is at the probabilistic midpoint of this range, the lower quartile can be used to represent the range of possible outcomes below the median. And since there is a 50-percent chance that the actual value will be below the median, this representative (lower-quartile) outcome is given a probability of 0.5. Using similar logic, the upper quartile is used to approximate the upper half of the spectrum of possible outcomes (the range above the median) and is assigned a probability of 0.5. Thus, rather than let a single (median) point estimate stand for all the possible values of an uncertain quantity, the spectrum of outcomes can be approximated by two equally probable outcomes, the upper and lower quartiles.

This was the simplification used in the second-cut analysis of Phillips's decision (see figure 7–3). The spectrum of possible jury awards—$0 to $1.6 million—was represented by two possible outcomes, $750,000 and $1.3 million, each with a 50-percent chance of occurring. This required replacing the single, median estimate used on the first-cut decision sapling with a two-branch outcome fork with both outcomes being equally probable.

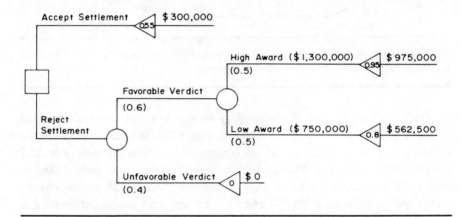

Figure 7–3. A Decision Tree for a Second-Cut Analysis of Phillips's Dilemma.

The $750,000 is Phillips's lower-quartile estimate for the size of the jury award, and the $1.3 million is his upper-quartile estimate. Using this two-outcome simplification for the spectrum of possible awards, Phillips assigns a probability of 0.5 to the $750,000 outcome, for this lower-quartile estimate has been selected to represent the range of possible awards below the median estimate of $1.1 million. Similarly, he assigns a probability of 0.5 to the $1.3 million outcome, since this upper-quartile estimate has been selected to stand for the range of possible awards above the median.

A measure of the uncertainty in the median or best-guess estimate of the jury award is provided by the distance between the upper and lower quartiles—by the width of the interquartile range. Assessing the upper and lower quartiles to be $900,000 and $1.2 million would have suggested much more confidence in the median estimate (of $1.1 million). Conversely, if the upper and lower quartiles were $500,000 and $1,400,000, this would have reflected even greater uncertainty about the size of the jury award.

Assessing Your Ignorance

Assessing Medians and Quartiles

Median and upper- and lower-quartile estimates provide a way to specify one's ignorance about the size, or value, of an uncertain quantity. A wide variety of methods, both direct and indirect, have been developed to help people assess these estimates.[47] Unfortunately, comparative experiments with these various assessment techniques have not revealed any single one as clearly superior to the others.[48] As Robin M. Hogarth of the Center for Decision Research at the University of Chicago's Graduate School of Business observes, "There is no reason why one kind of assessment procedure should be *the* most effective in *all* situations."[49] Consequently, it is not possible to prescribe the one, optimal procedure for specifying one's uncertainty about an uncertain quantity.

To undertake a quick analysis of a decision dilemma, however, a straightforward approach is usually the best. To determine how an uncertain quantity affects a decision, often all that is needed is a few particular estimates—the median and the upper and lower quartiles. It would appear most reasonable to assess these estimates directly.[50]

When a decision is a dilemma because of the uncertainty in the value of some quantity, begin by assessing a median estimate. Select this number so that, even if you had "to risk most of your eating money," you could not decide on which side of this estimate to bet that the actual value would fall.

Next, assess upper- and lower-quartile estimates. To obtain the lower quartile, assume that you have been told that the actual value is below your median estimate. Then determine the number such that you cannot decide whether to bet that the actual value will be below this number or above it (but, of course, less than the median). This number is your lower-quartile estimate. Similarly, assess the upper quartile by determining that number that divides the range above the median into two equally probable subranges.[51]

Now comes the rub. Because assessing such estimates is a difficult cognitive task, the human mind employs "heuristics" to simplify the chore. Unfortunately, as we noted in chapter 4, Amos Tversky and Daniel Kahneman have found that using these mental conveniences can bias any estimate.[52]

For the task of assessing estimates for uncertain quantities, one important heuristic identified by Tversky and Kahneman is *anchoring and adjustment.*[53] To assess various estimates of an uncertain quantity, people begin with a point estimate for the median and then make adjustments above and below this estimate to obtain their upper and lower quartiles. Unfortunately, the original point estimate is, psychologically, such a heavy "anchor" that these adjustments are much too small. Consequently, the upper- and lower-quartile estimates tend to be too close to the median estimate. This appears to be true even if the individual's knowledge about the uncertain quantity is very limited and even if the initial point estimate is strictly a guess or comes from the suggestion of someone else equally ignorant about the uncertain quantity.

The anchoring and adjustment heuristic is well known.[54] The practical implications of its use—interquartile ranges that are much, much too small—have been repeatedly demonstrated by cognitive psychologists. One survey of the literature reported, "The overwhelming evidence from research on uncertain quantities is that people's probability distributions tend to be too tight."[55] Thus far, no practical and universally applicable procedure for eliminating this bias has been developed and tested.[56]

Kahneman and Tversky also note that, when people assess their median estimate of an uncertain quantity, they tend to focus their thinking on the unique situational features of the particular case facing them, and tend to ignore the information contained in the actual outcomes of similar cases.[57] For example, when J. C. Phillips and his lawyers thought about the size of the uncertain jury award, they would tend to base their median estimate (according to this heuristic) upon the unique features of the accident with Dirk Peters (and perhaps upon the lawyer's unique courtroom rapport with a jury). They would tend to ignore the similarities that the case of *Phillips* v. *Peters* had with a large number of other automobile accident claims cases; that is, they would pay little if any attention to the large amount of information contained in the distribution of jury awards in other, similar automobile accident cases.

By focusing on the "singular information or case data" that Phillips had about his law suit and ignoring the "distributional information or base-rate data" from similar suits,[58] he would tend to produce a median estimate for the jury award that was too high (or too low). For example, suppose that in cases similar to Phillips's 90 percent of the jury awards were between $200,000 and $2 million (with 5 percent below $200,000 and 5 percent above 2 million). Phillips might still decide that his median estimate for the award in his—very unique—case should be $3 million. (One reason he might do this is because he did not even think of the possibility of obtaining such background data.) But obviously the distribution of awards in similar cases contains information that is directly relevant to Phillips's decision. He knows that the accident was clearly Peters's fault and believes that the jury will recognize this, too. But all those past juries that have made the awards between $200,000 and $2 million also thought that the defendant was at fault—and in only a very few cases did these juries make awards greater than $2 million. How can Phillips's *median* estimate be $3 million? Does he really think that there is a 50-percent chance that his award will be much higher than 95 percent of other, similar awards? Is Phillips's case *that* unique?

As Kahneman and Tversky write, "The tendency to neglect distributional information and to reply mainly on singular information is enhanced by any factor which increases the perceived uniqueness of the problem."[59] Each of us likes to believe that his own situation is unique. And, of course, it is. But we are all connected to the larger world, too. To pretend that one's own situation is so unique that it has no relationship to the experience of others is foolish.

Thus, as Kahneman and Tversky suggest, it makes sense to begin the process of thinking about one's median estimate by selecting a reference class of similar uncertain quantities. In some situations, such a class may not exist. But for many range-of-risk dilemmas, such as those discussed in chapter 6, there is a natural reference class.

- For the oil-drilling decision (figure 6–15), the oil wildcatter will have drilled a large number of other wells and can use the distribution of the amounts of oil obtained from these wells as the basis for establishing a median estimate.
- For McDonnell Douglas's decision (figure 6–14), the firm will have information on its previous efforts to develop and sell new commercial aircraft, often in direct competition with Boeing.
- For the plea-bargain dilemma (figure 6–17), the defendant's lawyer can provide information on the length of sentences given for convictions in similar cases.
- For the book-publisher's dilemma (figure 6–18), the publisher can obtain sales data on campaign biographies of previous presidential candidates.
- Even for Ventron Corporation's plant-investment decision (figure 6–16), it may be possible to obtain some useful information on the number of new uses discovered for other chemicals, similar to $NaBH_4$.

Such background data can usually be obtained quickly and need only be in rough form, as in "In 90 percent of the wells drilled in locations with similar geological features, the amount of oil obtained (when oil was struck) was between 4 million and 40 million barrels." Having such rough information *before* making a median estimate has a most valuable impact. For now, a decision to use a median estimate below 4 million barrels or one above 40 million must be thoroughly justified (if only to oneself): Is this situation so unique that all the data on previous experiences can be safely ignored? By first obtaining some rough distributional data, a decision maker helps ensure against making a completely unrealistic median estimate.[60]

When assessing upper and lower quartiles, one should be conscious of another heuristic that Tversky and Kahneman call "availability."[61] Using this device, an individual assesses the probability that an event will occur by imagining similar events or recalling related information. The more "available" such related instances or information are, the higher the probability assigned to that event. For example, people's assessment of the probability of an airplane crash goes up significantly after one is reported on the evening news. Consequently, if someone cannot easily think of similar events occurring in the past, or ways in which such events could happen in the future, he will tend to assess the probability of that event to be too low.

This suggests a way of avoiding overconfidence in a median estimate—and thus in too-narrow interquartile ranges: Consciously create different scenarios that could result in outcomes below the lower quartile and above the upper quartile. Are there many such scenarios? Are there reasons the actual outcome could be far, far from your median?[62] If so, perhaps the interquartile range should be widened. Composing scenarios for extreme outcomes is proposed by Carl S. Spetzler and Carl-Axel S. Staël von Holstein of the decision analysis group at the Stanford Research Institute to help overcome what they call the "central bias" of too tight a distribution.[63]

The effort to create plausible scenarios that result in extreme outcomes—which, by definition, means outcomes far above or below the median estimate—must be deliberate. The median estimate may itself have been assessed by developing a "most likely" scenario, which can then dominate thinking about possible outcomes. Write Tversky and Kahneman, "The generation of a specific scenario may inhibit the emergence of other scenarios, particularly those that lead to different outcomes."[64]

One specific recommendation for creating extreme scenarios is to think about all the different possible factors that could vary to create far-out outcomes. Moreover, do not just vary one factor at a time; the most extreme scenarios will result from extreme values of several factors, not just one. This is important because, as Tversky and Kahneman observe, "people will tend to produce scenarios in which many factors do not vary at all, only the most obvious variations take place, and interacting changes are rare."[65]

When estimating the total time needed to complete a specific task, the shortest estimate will come from summing the shortest estimates for each of the subtasks. And the longest estimate for total time will come from summing the longest estimates for each of the subtasks. The median estimate will come from the different possible combinations of very short estimates for some subtasks, median estimates for others, and very long estimates for still others. When thinking analytically about median and quartile estimates of the time to complete a task, the overall assignment needs to be decomposed into smaller subtasks; then the times needed to complete each of the various subtasks need to be varied.

(The availability heuristic helps explain why the time or cost needed to complete a task is usually underestimated. There is, of course, an incentive for making a low estimate when doing the work for someone else, but even when people are making the estimate for themselves, the bias towards estimates that are too low still exists. The most "available" scenario is the "surprise-free" one—each subtask is easily completed in the minimum time—and thus the median estimate is usually derived from the no-complication scenario. Then longer times are calculated, using "extreme" scenarios, with complications developing for one or two [but not all] of the subtasks; these are assigned to the upper quartile, 90th percentile, and so forth. But do not forget Murphy's Law: If something can go wrong, it will.[66] The most available, surprise-free scenarios should be used to assess an estimate well below the median; scenarios with lots of complications, not just a few, should be used to assess high estimates.[67])

When you create scenarios, do not just rely upon memory. Check out other sources of information. When people use the availability heuristic, they assign higher probabilities to events that are easy to recall because they are reported in the news or because they have been encountered recently. Many people, write Tversky and Kahneman, "must have experienced the temporary rise in the subjective probability of an accident after seeing a car overturned by the side of the road."[68] Alternative events may be just as likely, even if they are not as immediately available for mental recall.

Calibration with Almanac Questions

It is not possible to determine for any specific subjective estimate of an uncertain quantity (that is, median plus upper and lower quartiles) whether the assessment is "accurate."[69] Just because the actual value proves to be, for example, below the lower-quartile estimate does not mean that the assessment was poor; after all, there was a 25-percent chance of that happening. It is possible, however, using a number of different assessments, to determine if the assessor is well "calibrated."[70]

For example, if an individual assesses median and upper- and lower-quartile estimates for one hundred different uncertain quantities, the actual value should fall below the lower quartile approximately twenty-five times. If the actual value was below the lower quartile forty times, this assessor has a tendency to employ a lower-quartile estimate that is too close to the median. If the actual value was below the lower-quartile estimate only three times, then the assessor had the opposite bias. A well-calibrated assessor of uncertain quantities will find that, if A is the actual value,

- 50 percent of the time, A < median;
- 50 percent of the time, lower quartile < A < upper quartile;
- 25 percent of the time, A < lower quartile;
- 25 percent of the time, median < A < upper quartile; and so on.

If, in the process of analyzing your own decisions, you need to estimate medians and quartiles, you will want to calibrate yourself—particularly so that you can become aware of the extent of your own central bias and attempt to eliminate it. There is at least some evidence that weather forecasters—experts who have much experience making probabilistic forecasts on which they ob-

FIGURE 7-4

Twenty Almanac Questions for Assessing Estimates of Uncertain Quantities	Estimates of the Uncertain Quantities					For Calibration					
	LE Lower Extreme	LQ Lower Quartile	M Median	UQ Upper Quartile	UE Upper Extreme	$x < LE$	$LE < x < LQ$	$LQ < x < M$	$M < x < UQ$	$UQ < x < UE$	$x > UE$
						a	b	c	d	e	f
1. Number of points Pete Maravich scored in his college basketball career.											
2. U.S. government income from corporation income taxes in FY 72.											
3. Number of passenger cars produced in the U.S. in 1970.											
4. Population of Moscow in 1970.											
5. Per capita income of the U.S. (1970) census).											
6. Average number of men working in U.S. coal mines in 1970 (lower 48 states).											
7. Number of listed shares of AT&T stock as of December 31, 1970.											
8. Length of the Verrazano-Narrows Bridge (in feet).											
9. Number of American battle deaths in Vietnam (1961–1972).											
10. Shipments of uranium ore from U.S. mines in 1970 (in short tons).											
Subtotals (#1–10)											

Interquartile Index (#1–10): _____

Surprise Index (#1–10): _____

	LE Lower Extreme	LQ Lower Quartile	M Median	UQ Upper Quartile	UE Upper Extreme	For Calibration					
						x > LE a	x > LQ b	LQ > x > M c	M > x > UQ d	UQ > x e	UE > x f
11. Amount of money on deposit with the Bank of America on June 30, 1973.											
12. Average Consumer Price Index in 1972. (CPI = 100.0 for 1967.)											
13. Daily circulation of the *New York Daily News* in 1970.											
14. Public debt of the U.S. in 1970.											
15. The area of Central Park in New York City (in acres).											
16. Revenue airline passengers enplaned in the U.S. in 1972 (number of passengers on domestic and international flights).											
17. Number of people executed in the U.S. in 1935.											
18. Cumulative gross income earned by the movie *Gone With The Wind* as of December 30, 1970.											
19. Civilian employment of the U.S. government as of June 30, 1973.											
20. Net profit from the pay toilets in the San Francisco International Airport in 1969.											

Subtotals (#11–20)

Totals (#1–20)

Surprise Index (#11–20): _____

Surprise Index (#1–20): _____

Interquartile Index (#11–20): _____

Interquartile Index (#1–20): _____

tain quick and unequivocal feedback—are quite well calibrated when estimating uncertain quantities, such as tomorrow's high temperature.[71] And there has been some success training people to estimate uncertain quantities.[72]

Making predictions about the future—such as estimating the Dow Jones closing industrials average next Friday or the number of electoral votes that will be won by the Democratic Party's presidential nominee in the next election—requires a delay before feedback can be obtained. Consequently, one traditional method for providing people with experience in estimating uncertain quantities is with a series of *almanac questions*, like the height of the Empire State Building or the number of babies born in France in 1975. For most people, the exact value of such quantities is unknown, though it can be easily found in an almanac. Of course, an architect might have a better idea of the height of the Empire State Building than would a lawyer, and a demographer would have a better sense of the number of births in France than would a physicist. But then their estimates (including the width of their interquartile ranges) should reflect this better knowledge. The same almanac questions can thus be given to people with widely differing backgrounds.

For several years, we have given collections of almanac questions to our students, both graduate and undergraduate. We have asked them to assess their median (M) and lower- and upper-quartile (LQ and UQ) estimates. We have also asked them to assess their 1st- and 99th-percentile estimates, often called the lower and upper extremes (LE and UE); these two estimates define a 98-percent confidence interval.

A collection of twenty almanac questions is given in figure 7–4. The summary results for 169 students who provided all five estimates for all twenty uncertain quantities are tabulated in table 7–5; thus this table summarizes the results for 3,380 assessments (169 students $\times$ 20 assessments/student). The table indicates that the actual value of the uncertain quantity, X, was below the lower extreme (or 1st-percentile) estimate 512 times out of 3,380 (15 percent of the assessments). Similarly, the actual value was below the lower-quartile estimate 1,001 times (30 percent of all assessments). And the actual value was between the median and upper-quartile estimate 336 times (11 percent).

It should be immediately obvious that these results reflect extreme overconfidence. The percentage of the time that the actual value fell within the estimated interquartile range—sometimes called the "interquartile index"[73]—was 23. If the students had been estimating their upper and lower quartiles properly, the interquartile index would have been 50. For several students the actual value of the uncertain almanac quantity *never* fell within their estimated interquartile ranges. (Note also that the percentages for the four ranges listed in the middle of the table should have been 25, 25, 25, and 25, not 30, 12, 11, and 48.)

Assessing Your Ignorance

TABLE 7-5

Summary Results of 3,380 Assessments of Uncertain Quantities: 169 Students'
Estimates of Twenty Almanac Questions

$X < $ LE	$X < $ LQ	LQ $ < X < $ M	M $ < X < $ UQ	UQ $ < X$	UE $ < X$
512	1,001	402	366	1,611	1,204
15%	30%	12%	11%	48%	37%

NOTE: X is the actual value of the uncertain almanac quantity. Note that the actual value had to be in one of the four ranges listed in the middle section of the table: (1) less than the lower quartile; (2) between the lower quartile and the median; (3) between the median and the upper quartile; or (4) above the upper quartile. Thus the four totals from these four columns sum to 3,380: 1,011 + 402 + 366 + 1,611 = 3,380. The percentages do not add to 100 because of rounding.

The bias of overconfidence is even more clearly dramatized by the *surprise index,* the percentage of actual outcomes that fall above the upper extreme or below the lower extreme. If these two estimates are assessed properly, the surprise index will be 2. For these 169 students, it was 51. Over half the time, the students' estimates were not even in the ball park. One student was surprised 18 out of 20 times.

Moreover, more than half of the time that the actual value was below the lower quartile, it also fell below the lower extreme. (512/1001 = 0.51.) And three-quarters of the time that the actual value fell above the upper quartile, it also fell above the upper extreme. (1204/1611 = 0.75.) When the students' estimates weren't in the ball park, they weren't even close to the ball park.[74]

You might try assessing your own estimates for the almanac questions in figure 7-4. Develop them for the first ten quantities and then, using the calibration instructions in the appendix to this chapter, calculate your own interquartile index and surprise index. If you, too, were overconfident (despite being forewarned), spread out your extreme, and quartile estimates when you assess the second ten quantities. As Professor Robert L. Winkler of the Graduate School of Business at Indiana University notes of the task of estimating an uncertain quantity, "What appears on the surface to be a reasonably simple procedure actually requires a tremendous amount of intellectual self-discipline."[75]

Decisions and Uncertain Quantities

Many decisions depend upon estimates of uncertain quantities. For example, the crop production forecasts released by the Statistical Reporting Service (SRS) of the U.S. Department of Agriculture (USDA) influence "decisions involving billions of dollars" each year, says the department.[76] Investors in commodities on the Chicago Board of Trade make their decisions, in part, on the basis of these forecasts. And, within three weeks after SRS released its August 1977 forecast that wheat production would be 2,041 million bushels for 1977,[77] President Carter proposed a 20-percent acreage cut in wheat for farmers who wished to be eligible for price supports and crop subsidies.[78]

Significantly, the Statistical Reporting Service does not provide point estimates only. Because it has been in the business of making crop production forecasts for the last fifty years, it has substantial experience with its prediction errors. Consequently, along with each point-estimate forecast, SRS publishes the 67- and 90-percent confidence intervals.[79]

Decisions involving crops and commodities also depend upon estimates of production in the Soviet Union and Canada. If the Soviet Union will have a poor harvest, U.S. farmers may wish to hold their crops until increasing demand for exports drives up prices. Or, if Canada is having a good year, farmers may seek to sell their production before Canadian crops flood the world's markets.

Estimates of foreign crop production are not very accurate. On April 19, 1975, USDA estimated that Soviet grain production would be 210 million tons for that year. "I'd say 210 is well on the safe side," said one USDA specialist. "It'll probably be more."[80] On July 24, USDA revised its estimate to 185 million tons of grain. On August 11, the forecast was reduced further to 180 million tons. Finally, on October 24, USDA dropped the figure to 160 million tons—25 percent less than what it had forecast only six months earlier.[81] The actual total was 140 million tons—only two-thirds of USDA's original estimate.[82] Yet none of those inherently imperfect point estimates were accompanied by any assessment of the uncertainty involved.

Business decisions often depend upon government predictions. Farmers base many of their decisions on meteorological and climatic forecasts. In March 1977, the Bureau of Reclamation predicted that in some of the irrigation districts in the Yakima River Valley (in Washington state), the water supply would be only 5 percent of what was available normally. As a result, some farmers took drastic steps, plowing their fields under and selling their water rights, drilling expensive wells, moving their crops to fields in other valleys. Then in May, the estimate was increased to 50 percent, and then later to 70 to 80 percent. An initial "overly conservative" forecast resulted in a lot of wasted money.[83]

Of course, businesses must make their own predictions, too. When deciding whether to bring out a new product, or how much production to schedule for an existing line, a firm must forecast sales (and production costs, too). When MITS Inc. of Albuquerque, New Mexico, was first considering introducing a home-computer kit, it attempted to forecast sales. "I projected 800 machines in 1975, and people said I was a wild-eyed optimist," reports the firm's president. MITS sold 5,000 that year.[84]

Similarly, decisions about the adoption of a new government program (or the expansion of an existing one) depend upon forecasts of costs—and also of benefits. As with other uncertain quantities, such factors may be quite difficult to estimate. For example, when attempting to decide whether to set up a new federal jobs-and-training program, it is necessary to predict not only the costs of training each individual and of creating each new job, but the types of additional employment that will result. Such predictions cannot be made with single, point-estimate precision. As one federal economist noted, "We think we know within a broad range what our proposals would do in the way of creating jobs, but I'd be less than frank if I didn't say that our estimates could be way off."[85]

Point Estimates Are Not Good Enough

For several reasons, point estimates are often not good enough when making decisions involving a range of risk. First, point estimates are not good enough because they are not very good. As is illustrated by OMB's predictions of federal outlays and USDA's predictions of the Soviet grain harvest, point estimates can be very wrong—misleadingly wrong.

Second, point estimates are not good enough because they fail to convey any sense of just how uncertain the estimate is. For example, a real estate reporter for the *Washington Post* notes the lack of information in the frequently publicized median price of housing:

> The median town house price in Fairfax is more than $95,000, or enough to scare budget-conscious shoppers all the way to Spotsylvania. The median price is the point at which half the new houses are more expensive and half are cheaper. But there's no indication of how much cheaper, and that's the kind of information you need if you're looking for the affordable house.[86]

Point estimates, particularly multidigit estimates, imply precision, an absence of uncertainty. They fallaciously suggest that the future can be predicted with precision.

Finally, and most significantly, point estimates are not good enough because the amount of uncertainty in a forecast can be important, perhaps critical, when making a decision. The resolution of many dilemmas will depend not only upon a best (point) estimate, but also upon the uncertainty of that estimate. A small interquartile range can imply one decision; a large one can lead to an entirely different alternative. A false faith in point estimates can result in a delusory confidence in the predicted outcome of an intrinsically risky alternative—and thus in a poor decision. (More on this in chapter 9.)

In some cases, of course, a point estimate will be helpful for a first-cut analysis *and* useful for the final resolution of the dilemma as well. For example, in analyzing the book-publisher's dilemma of chapter 2 (figure 2–12) and chapter 6 (figure 6–18), it was adequate to use a point estimate of the number of copies of a Carter biography that would be sold *if* Carter won the Democratic presidential nomination in 1976. This was because, within the range of possible outcomes of this uncertain quantity, the point estimate selected for the sales of a biography of presidential nominee Carter did not influence the decision; if Carter won the nomination, the publish-the-biography alternative would be better than publishing another book, no matter what point estimate was used for the uncertain sales. Thus, the key uncertainty was whether Carter would be the nominee.

Often, however, the uncertain quantity can be critical. Using a point estimate for an uncertain outcome can lead a decision maker to ignore a critical aspect of why his decision is a dilemma. Before stopping with a point estimate, check to see if the value of the uncertain quantity can possibly influence the decision. If it can, it may well be useful to do a second-cut analysis using upper- and lower-quartile estimates.

The Futile Quest for Accuracy

Predictably, one impact of the spending shortfall ($22 billion for FY 76, the transition quarter, and FY 77) has been an overrun of jokes. Two journalists called it "the greatest disappearing act since Houdini."[87] And Art Buchwald wondered: "How about the CIA? Couldn't they use the $22 billion to overthrow an unfriendly government?"[88]

Few learned very much from the spending shortfall. In November 1976, just after the end of fiscal year 1976 and the transition quarter, OMB's deputy director Paul O'Neill held a press conference to discuss the current services estimates for FY 77 and FY 78. One journalist was particularly unsatisfied with the four different sets of economic assumptions, or "paths," from which OMB obtained its four different sets of receipts, outlays, and deficits for FY 77 and FY 78. When O'Neill refused to pick one of the four paths for FY 78, the journalist asked: "How about in regard to Fiscal 1977, which you already have a budget for and for which you have submitted projections as of last July? Which one of these paths for Fiscal 1977 is the one that you see as most likely to prevail?"[89] Given that the federal government was already six weeks into FY 77 and that all the appropriations bills for that year had been passed, the uncertainty about revenues and outlays for FY 77 would certainly have been less than for FY 78. But the implications of the reporter's question—that OMB ought to be able to predict accurately the behavior of both the economy and federal expenditures—suggested an unwillingness to accept the inherent uncertainty of such forecasts. Indeed, the reporter seemed to imply that the four paths were the only possible ones—that in-between alternatives did not exist —and that it was possible—if you were only smart enough—to determine which one of the four would actually occur. If O'Neill had picked a "most likely" path, the "most likely" nature of that prediction would have been lost in the lead paragraph of the next day's story: "An OMB spokesman today predicted that federal expenditures for FY 77 will be. . . . "

Still, the futile search for accuracy continues. OMB director Bert Lance commented in the summer of 1977: "I think that we need to be able to move away from the short-fall situation and be able to project accurately what our expenditure levels will be and what our revenue levels will be, so that we don't have this constant change."[90]

The decision maker's Holy Grail is predictive accuracy—pinpoint accuracy. "The boss wants a single figure—not a range," reads a sign on a Pentagon desk.[91] As Rex V. Brown of Decision Science Consortium writes, "admissions of uncertainty . . . often run counter to the prevailing managerial culture."[92] Making point estimates is apparently essential for maintaining one's managerial machismo.

Because the future is inherently uncertain, it cannot be precisely predicted. It is not our own failure to think carefully enough that causes the errors in our point estimates. Better computer models may help reduce uncertainty but they cannot eliminate it. Truly "better" computer models will be those that provide not only best guesses or median estimates but also some measure of uncertainty: for example, upper- and lower-quartile estimates, 90-percent confidence intervals, upper and lower extremes.

Thinking Probabilistically

In the seventeenth century, Newton and his laws of motion so dominated scientific thinking that natural law was implicitly defined as one that made deterministic, causal predictions. By the nineteenth century, however, scientific theories that offered probabilistic and statistical predictions were quite acceptable. As Jacob Bronowski has emphasized, this progress required a revolution in scientific thinking.[93] As a result, in the nineteenth and twentieth centuries natural science made major advances with the discovery of several probabilistic laws: Mendel's laws of heredity; the kinetic theory of gases developed by Maxwell, Calusius, and Boltzmann; and the laws of radioactive decay developed by Rutherford and Soddy, and by von Schweidler.

This shift from a deterministic to a probabilistic paradigm culminated in the formulation of Heisenberg's uncertainty principle, which states the limits to the accuracy with which the physical measurements of subatomic particles can be made. No matter how sophisticated the instrumentation, there are inherent uncertainties in the measurements of position and/or momentum. Much of the research now being done in the natural sciences would not be possible without the replacement of deterministic thinking with probabilistic thinking.

A similar shift is now occurring in social science. Writes James B. Ramsey, professor of economics at New York University: "Almost all scientific disciplines have been moving in recent years from deterministic to stochastic formulations of their theories . . . . Economics is a stochastic science."[94] To Lester C. Thurow, professor of economics at Massachusetts Institute of Technology, it is "the end of Newtonian economics:" "Economics, along with much of modern science, is being drawn in a direction where events are perceived to be much more stochastic and much less deterministic than had previously been thought."[95]

In medicine, too, there is a need to think probabilistically. Harold Bursztajn of the Massachusetts General Hospital and Robert M. Hamm of Harvard University argue that physicians need to reject the "Mechanistic Paradigm," which currently guides much of clinical practice. Assuming that medical science is Newtonian—that is, can provide "straightforward and certain guidance"—physicians search for the mechanistic links that connect a disease, its causes, and its symptoms in a single, objective way. Bursztajn and Hamm stress, however, that there is "an element of irreducible statistical variability in the connections from causes to diseases," so that "the course of the disease cannot be predicted with complete confidence." Moreover, the results of diagnostic tests are inherently probabilistic. (For an example of such a test, see chapter 10.) Consequently, physicians must be prepared to combine probabilistic diagnostic evidence with their own judgment when deciding how to treat a patient.[96] Bursztajn and Hamm argue that "the wise clinician's practice is consistent with the scientific principles of the Probabilistic Paradigm."[97]

Still, probabilistic thinking has not become part of our popular culture. In the spring of 1979, when NASA's space satellite *Skylab* was about to fall from orbit, the North American Air Defense Command (NORAD) was careful to make probabilistic predictions as to when this would happen. As is illustrated in table 7–6, NORAD provided a median estimate of the reentry time, plus 5-percentile and 95-percentile estimates (which defined a 90-percent confidence interval). Yet the press coverage of *Skylab* (and even some of NASA's own press releases) often misinterpreted these predictions. For example, the prediction that NORAD made on June 6 was: a 5th percentile of July 4, a median of July 16, and a 95th percentile of July 28. But NASA's "Skylab Advisory 9" said that "as of June 6, NORAD advises that Skylab decay is

TABLE 7–6

*Predictions of Skylab's Reentry Date Made by the North
American Air Defense Command.* [98]

Date Prediction Made	Prediction of Skylab Reentry Date		
	Fifth Percentile	Median	Ninety-Fifth Percentile
March 14	May 16	May 30	June 13
April 11	June 11	June 19	July 1
April 18	June 13	June 19	July 1
April 25	June 15	June 21	July 2
May 2	June 17	June 23	July 2
May 9	June 20	June 26	July 4
May 16	June 26	July 2	July 9
May 24	June 20	July 2	July 14
May 30	June 27	July 9	July 21
June 7	July 4	July 16	July 28
June 13	July 7	July 16	July 25
June 20	July 7	July 12	July 17
June 22	July 10	July 15	July 20
June 25	July 11	July 16	July 21
June 26	July 11	July 15	July 19
June 27	July 10	July 14	July 18
June 28,29,30	July 10	July 13	July 16
July 1	July 9	July 12	July 15
July 2,3,4	July 10	July 12	July 14
July 5,6	July 9	July 11	July 13
July 7	July 10	July 11	July 12

SOURCE: International Affairs Division of the National Aeronautics and Space
Administration.

predicted July 16 (50% chance before that date and 50% chance after) with
a confidence window (95% chance) from July 4 to July 28."[99] Somehow,
NORAD's 90-percent confidence interval had become 95-percent when
relayed by NASA. And the Associated Press report on that prediction stated
that "there is a 95 percent probability the station will fall to earth between July
4 and July 28 and a 50-50 chance it will come down on July 16."[100] Like so
many other newspaper reports, AP confused NORAD's prediction that there
was a 50-percent chance that *Skylab* would fall *by* July 16 with a 50-percent
chance that it would fall *on* that day.[101] And, often, the 90-percent confidence
interval would be reported as if it were 100-percent. A story in the *Washington
Post* using NORAD's June 25 estimate reported that the agency "predicted
that Skylab will fall to Earth sometime between July 11 and July 19, with a
50 percent chance it will come down on or before July 16."[102] The probabilistic
range provided by NORAD was reported as if there existed no chance that
reentry could occur before or after this interval. (Reentry of *Skylab* occurred

on July 11, 1979, at 1637 Greenwich Mean Time—or 12:37 P.M. Eastern Daylight Time—plus or minus two minutes.[103])

Clearly, probabilistic thinking does not come easy. Before decision makers can use decision analysis and quick analysis, they will have to undergo a revolution in their approach to predictions and estimates. They will have to discard the notion of a completely causal world, in which accurate, deterministic predictions can—if only the proper information is collected—be made. They will have to accept that the future is inherently uncertain. They will have to learn to think probabilistically.

Appendix: Calibrating Assessments of Uncertain Quantities

Once the five estimates of the uncertain almanac questions in figure 7–4 have been assessed, the six columns at the right can be used along with the actual values (given in table 7–7) to calibrate an individual assessor.

First, place a check in one of the four middle columns: (b) $X < $ LQ; (c) LQ $< X < $ M; (d) M $< X < $ UQ; or (e) UQ $< X$. In other words, if the actual value, X, lies between the lower-quartile and median estimates, put a check in column c. If the actual value is greater than the upper-quartile estimate, put a check in column e. For each uncertain quantity, there must be a check in one of these four columns, because the actual value must fall within one of the four ranges defined by the lower-quartile, median, and upper-quartile estimates.

If there is a check in column b (that is, if the actual value is less than the lower-quartile estimate), determine if it is also less than the lower extreme. If so, put a check in column a.

If there is a check in column e (if the actual value is greater than the upper-quartile estimate), the actual value could also be greater than the upper extreme. If so, put a check in column f.

192

Assessing Your Ignorance

TABLE 7–7

Actual Values for Almanac Questions in Figure 7–4

Uncertain Almanac Quantity	Actual Value
1. Number of points Pete Maravich scored in his college basketball career	3,667 points
2. U.S. government income from corporation income taxes in FY 72	$32.168 billion
3. Number of passenger cars produced in the U.S. in 1970	6,550,128 cars
4. Population of Moscow in 1970	6,942,000 people
5. Per capita income of the U.S. (1970 Census)	$3,943
6. Average number of men working in U.S. coal mines in 1970 (lower 48 states)	144,000 men
7. Number of listed shares of AT&T stock as of December 31, 1970	549.3 million shares
8. Length of the Verrazano-Narrows Bridge (in feet)	4,260 feet
9. Number of American battle deaths in Vietnam (1961–1972)	45,929 deaths
10. Shipments of uranium ore from U.S. mines in 1970 (in short tons)	6,324,000 short tons
11. Amount of money on deposit with the Bank of America as of June 30, 1973	$36.862 billion
12. Average Consumer Price Index in 1972 (CPI = 100.0 for 1967)	125.3
13. Daily circulation of the *New York Daily News* in 1970	2,129,909
14. Public debt of the U.S. in 1970	$370.919 billion
15. Area of Central Park in New York City (in acres)	840 acres
16. Revenue airline passengers enplaned in the U.S. in 1972 (number of passengers; on domestic and international flights)	195,305,000 passengers
17. Number of people executed in the U.S. in 1935	199 people
18. Cumulative gross income earned by the movie *Gone With The Wind* as of December 31, 1970	$72,921,000
19. Civilian employment of the U.S. government as of June 30, 1973	2,765,662
20. Net profit from the pay toilets in San Francisco International Airport in 1969	$48,456

For example, here is a hypothetical set of estimates for the number of points scored by Pete Maravich in his college basketball career.

LE	LQ	M	UQ	UE
3,700	4,500	5,000	6,000	9,000

The actual number of points he scored was 3,667. Since the actual value is less than the lower-quartile (LQ) estimate, a check goes in column b. And the actual value is also less than the lower-extreme (LE) estimate, so a check goes in column a, too.

Now add up the number of checks in each column. Since there must be a check in one of the four middle columns (b, c, d, or e) for each uncertain quantity estimated, the summed totals for these four columns should equal the number of quantities assessed.

To calculate the interquartile index, divide the combined number of checks in columns c and d by the number of quantities estimated (and multiply by 100). For example, if after estimating the first ten quantities in figure 7–4, there was one check in column c and two checks in column d, the interquartile index would be 30. In other words, for one of the quantities estimated the actual value was between the lower-quartile and median estimates, and for two of the ten quantities the actual value was between the median and upper-quartile estimates; consequently, the actual value fell within the interquartile range 30 percent of the time.

To calculate the surprise index, divide the combined number of checks in columns a and f by the number of quantities estimated (and multiply by 100). For example, if there were two checks in column a and five in column f after estimating the first ten quantities, the surprise index would be 70. (Not too good!) That is, for two of the quantities estimated the actual value fell below the lower extreme and for five of the quantities estimated the actual value fell above the upper extreme; consequently, the actual value fell outside the two extremes 70 percent of the time.

Note that the interquartile index and the surprise index cannot add to more than 100.

Chapter 8

Money and Risk: RKO and the FCC

IN the spring of 1978, RKO General Inc. faced an important decision—whether to sell its Boston television station, WNAC-TV, for $54 million. This was the offer made by the New England Television Corporation (NETV), though the station was said to be worth approximately $80 million. But because the Federal Communications Commission had only granted RKO a temporary renewal of its license for WNAC, the firm could not sell the station's license on the open market.

In 1969, two groups of prominent black Boston businessmen, Community Broadcasting of Boston and The Dudley Station Corporation, had challenged the renewal of RKO's license to operate WNAC. In proceedings before the FCC, the two groups charged that the station's public affairs and news programming were inadequate and cited corporate misconduct of The General Tire and Rubber Company, which owned RKO. General Tire had been accused of corporate bribery overseas and illegal campaign contributions at home, and of pressuring its suppliers into purchasing advertising on RKO's sixteen radio and television stations. As a result, in 1977, the FCC issued RKO only a temporary renewal of its WNAC-TV license. This meant, according to FCC rules, that until RKO obtained a permanent license it could only sell the station to those challenging its renewal, and Community Broadcasting and Dudley Station formed New England Television for that purpose. The sale of the license to the challengers could only be completed, however, if the FCC approved the permanent license renewal. (If RKO did not have a permanent license, it could not sell it.)[1]

Thus, RKO was faced with a double-risk dilemma (figure 8–1). Whether or not RKO sold the station to New England Television, the FCC could fail to renew its license for WNAC; if so, RKO would be left with nothing.[2] Natu-

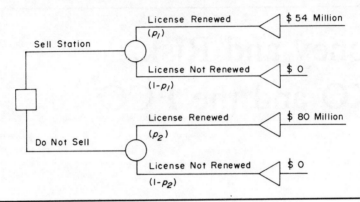

Figure 8–1. RKO's Dilemma.

rally, the best outcome would be not to sell the license to NETV but still have it renewed permanently, since then it would have a station worth $80 million. But RKO must have assumed that the probability of getting its WNAC license renewed was greater if it sold it to NETV ($p_1 > p_2$), since in this situation the FCC, if they denied the renewal request, would be in effect taking the license away from NETV, not from RKO. Indeed, if the probability of getting the license renewed was not increased by selling it to NETV, there would be no dilemma; RKO should not sell the station.

Assessing Indifference Outcomes or Certain Monetary Equivalents

With RKO's dilemma decomposed with the help of a decision tree, the next step is to work with the components—to assess probabilities and preferences. To assess the necessary preference-probability (for the $54 million outcome), $80 million and $0 are selected as the reference outcomes of the reference gamble. Then, one adjusts V, the probability of winning the reference gamble, until one is indifferent between that gamble and $54 million for sure. (See figure 8–2.)

Money and Risk

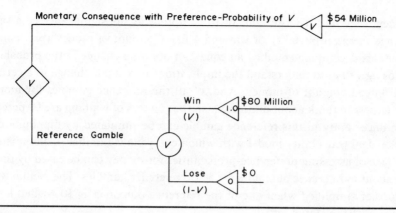

Figure 8–2. Using a Reference Gamble to Assess the Preference-Probability for the Monetary Consequence of $54 Million.

There is another way to look at the task of assessing preference-probabilities for money. Instead of picking a particular monetary outcome (such as $54 million) and assessing a preference-probability for it, one can pick a particular preference-probability (e.g., $V = 0.5$) and determine the monetary outcome that is equivalent to it. Rather than assess the *indifference probability, V,* that makes one indifferent between the two alternatives in figure 8–2, one can assess the *indifference* (interjacent) *outcome, $X,* that makes one indifferent between the two alternatives in figure 8–3.

Thinking carefully about an indifference outcome requires just as much intellectual discipline as thinking carefully about an indifference probability. Nevertheless, for most people, probabilities are a more abstruse concept than

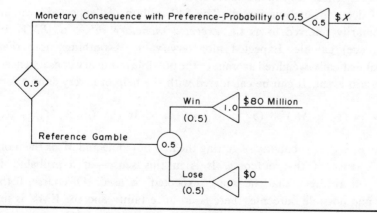

Figure 8–3. Using a Reference Gamble to Assess the Monetary Consequence with a Preference-Probability of 0.5.

money; they find it more difficult to comprehend the significance of a small change in the probability of winning a fixed amount of money (particularly since this is complemented by an equal but opposite change in the probability of losing), than to understand the implications of a small change in a certain, guaranteed amount of money. And, of all the reference gambles for money, it is easiest to think about one for which the chances of winning are 50 percent. The uncertainty in this reference gamble can be simulated by flipping a coin —the ideal probability model with which everyone is familiar. Consequently, the task of assessing preference-probabilities for money can be eased by thinking about indifference outcomes for 50-50 reference gambles. The mental work is further simplified when one of the reference outcomes is $0—when losing means just the status quo.

The indifference outcome for this reference gamble does not, of course, produce the preference-probability that is needed to resolve RKO's license-sale dilemma. Some more work must be done after this indifference outcome is obtained. But being able to think only about 50-50 reference gambles (thus avoiding other, less easily visualized probabilities) may more than compensate for this additional work (which is described shortly).

What should be the indifference outcome $X in figure 8–3? $20 million? $40 million? $60 million? Well, the "expected" outcome of the 50-50 reference gamble is $40 million. That should give some clue. Not that one could actually "expect" to get $40 million by selecting the reference gamble; the outcome will be either $80 million or $0. But if one played that gamble over and over again, say, a thousand times, one would expect to win on approximately half of the gambles (and lose on the other half). Consequently, the "expected" winnings over the long run would be $40 million (for each time the gamble is played).

Here it is necessary to introduce an unfortunate but hopelessly uneradicable bit of decision analysis jargon. The $40 million of "expected" winnings is customarily referred to as the *expected monetary value,* or *EMV,* of this (reference) gamble. Expected monetary value is nothing more than the probabilistically-weighted average of the possible monetary consequences of an uncertain event. It can be calculated with the help of a very simple formula,

$$\text{EMV} = (p_1 \times M_1) + (p_2 \times M_2) + (p_3 \times M_3) + (p_4 \times M_4) + \cdots,$$

where p_1 is the probability of getting the first outcome and M_1 is the monetary consequence of that outcome. It is in this sense—of a probabilistically-weighted average—that the word "expected" is used. (Of course, if there is only one possible outcome, there is no uncertainty and the EMV is just the certain monetary consequence of that alternative. The EMV of a certain $54 million is simply $54 million.)

What should be the indifference outcome $X in figure 8–3? The EMV of $40 million for the reference gamble provides a clue. Clearly, $40 million ought to be the upper limit on X. Who, if they actually had the right to a 50-50 chance at $80 million or nothing, would demand more than a sure $40 million to sell those rights? Even a billionaire might be somewhat reluctant to take this risk with such large stakes. So X is somewhere between $0 and $40 million.

Following the usual procedure of narrowing the range (to avoid the bias of anchoring), the next question might be Do you prefer a certain $30 million, or a 50-50 chance at $80 million or nothing? Again, for most people, the answer would be quite obvious—take the guaranteed $30 million. After all, $30 million would substantially increase most people's standard of living, and it is difficult to comprehend what additional pleasure another $50 million would buy. The first million is worth more than the second million; the first $10 million is worth more than the second $10 million; the first $30 million is worth more than the second $30 million—or even another $50 million. Few of us, if given a check for $30 million, would be willing to trade it for a 50-50 chance at $80 million or nothing (even though the gamble has the larger EMV). Even for a large corporation such as RKO, $30 million is a lot of money; it might well prefer this for sure to a 50-50 gamble on $80 million or nothing.

Now, what about a million dollars? Would you prefer a certain $1 million, or a 50-50 chance at $80 million? Undoubtedly, many people would still take the riskless alternative. Whether one's assets consist of an $800 savings account, or a $65,000 house and $10,000 in the bank, or a $250,000 house and $75,000 in stocks and long-term bonds, $1 million would substantially increase one's standard of living—so much so that the next $79 million might seem to provide only marginal benefits.

For RKO, however, this might not be true. The firm already has millions in assets in its fifteen other radio and television stations. To such a company, $1 million does not look like much more than $0. RKO might thus prefer the 50-50 gamble for $80 million or nothing to a certain $1 million.

Suppose after thinking carefully about RKO's preferences for money, the firm's executives conclude that their indifference outcome X for a 50-50 reference gamble for $80 million or nothing should be about $15 million. (It might be $14 million or $17 million—it is difficult to decide precisely—but they are convinced it is between $10 million and $20 million.) This means that for RKO, $15 million has a preference-probability of 0.5.

A decision maker's indifference outcome for a reference gamble (or, indeed, for any uncertain event) is often called a *certain monetary equivalent,* or *CME,* for that gamble. This represents the amount of certain money that the decision maker decides is equivalent in value to taking the gamble. For RKO, the CME for a 0.5 reference gamble is $15 million.

Preference Curves

This first step of assessing this preference-probability may seem like a small one. At this stage, preference-probabilities have been assessed for only three monetary consequences ($0, $15 million, and $80 million), and two of these have been arbitrarily selected. Nevertheless, determining the certain monetary outcome with a 0.5 preference-probability does provide a good picture—literally a picture—of RKO's preferences for money. In figure 8–4 are plotted these

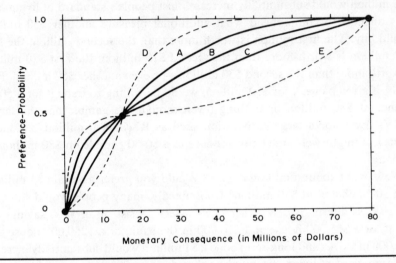

Figure 8–4. Various Possible Preference Curves Given Three Specific Points ($0/0; $15 Million/0.5; and $80 Million/1.0).

three monetary outcomes and the preference-probabilities that have been assessed for them ($0/0; $15 million/0.5; and $80 million/1.0). These three points clearly suggest the type of relationship that exists between preference-probability and monetary consequence—something like curve A, or B, or C. For unless one assumes some type of peculiar preferences (as suggested by curve D or E), there exists only a small family of smooth curves that can be drawn through these three points. Thus, a single CME for the 0.5 reference gamble defines, to a very great extent, the shape of any *preference curve* that relates preference-probability to monetary consequence.

(Note that, for all five curves in figure 8–4, preference-probabilities increase as the monetary consequence increases. It would not make sense for the preference-probability of $60 million to be less than the preference-probability of $30 million. Consequently, the shapes of even the peculiar preference curves, D and E, are constrained; even they must always be increasing. Exactly

200

why curves D and E have been labeled "peculiar" is explained in detail later. Intuitively, however, it would seem that preferences for money should change according to a smooth pattern, and not in a bumpy or irregular way.)

Incredibly, this simple analysis—assessing a CME for the 0.5 reference gamble—may be quite sufficient to make many decisions. Take, for example, RKO's dilemma about whether to sell WNAC-TV. Suppose the probability that the license will be renewed is 0.6 if RKO sells it to NETV, and 0.4 if it does not sell the station. (In figure 8–1, this means that $p_1 = 0.6$ and $p_2 = 0.4$.) Thus, the preference-probability for the do-not-sell alternative is 0.4.[3] To determine the preference-probability for the sell-WNAC-TV alternative, RKO first needs to determine the preference-probability for the $54 million outcome.

This can be found on the preference curve in figure 8–4. Well, not exactly. There are several curves. But if you eliminate the peculiar ones (D and E) and concentrate on A, B, and C, it is clear that the preference-probability for a $54 million outcome is somewhere between 0.84 and 0.97.[4] Where exactly within that range the preference-probability actually lies is inconsequential. For if the preference-probability for the $54 million outcome is between 0.84 and 0.97, then the preference-probability for the sell alternative is between 0.5 and 0.58.[5] Thus, regardless of which preference curve (A, B, or C) reflects RKO's true preferences for money, the preference-probability of 0.5 to 0.58 for "Sell" is higher than the 0.4 preference-probability for "Do Not Sell." The single step of assessing the CME for the 0.5 reference gamble is sufficient to resolve, convincingly, RKO's dilemma.

Specifying a Preference Curve with More Points

Given some different assumptions, RKO's decision concerning WNAC-TV might depend upon whether curve A or curve C reflects the firm's true preferences for money. Or, RKO might need to make other decisions involving money and risk and would thus like to have a preference curve it could use in a variety of different decision-making situations. In either case, it would be necessary to specify the firm's preference curve a little more closely. This can be done by assessing another point or two on the curve.

A quick glance at curves A and C suggests that the greatest difference between them occurs in the region above $15 million. But look again. The possible preference-probabilities for $50 million (for example) are 0.81 to 0.95 —a range of 14 percentage points. In contrast, the possible preference-probabilities for $4 million are 0.15 to 0.32—a range of 17 percentage points. In the region with lower monetary consequences, the curvature of a preference curve is the greatest; above a preference-probability of 0.5, the curve is much closer to a straight line (reflecting, as will be discussed later, the lowered risk aversion that comes with higher assets). The crucial distance is not horizontal but vertical (for this indicates the possible differences in preference-probability for any given monetary consequence), and the vertical distance between plausible curves is often greater for low monetary consequences.

Most of the effort in assessing preference-probabilities should be made in the preference-probability region below 0.5. Actually, this is also the region about which it is easiest to think, for one outcome of the gamble used to make the assessment will be $0. And, again, the probabilities for the gamble will be 50-50. For example, to specify further RKO's preference curve, the firm's executives need to assess their CME for a 50-50 gamble for $15 million or nothing. Suppose they decide that they are indifferent between this gamble and $6 million for sure. If this 50-50 gamble were a reference gamble (i.e., if $15 million had a preference-probability of 1.0, with the preference-probability of $0 still being 0), then $6 million would have a preference-probability of 0.5. But since $15 million has a preference-probability of 0.5, the preference-probability of $6 million is 0.25.

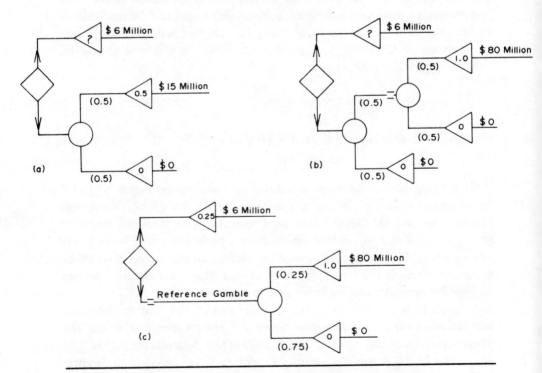

Figure 8–5. Assessing a Monetary Outcome with a 0.25 Preference-Probability.

Money and Risk

To see this, use our old friend, the substitution principle. Take the hypothetical decision indicating that RKO is indifferent between $6 million for certain and a 50-50 chance at $15 million or $0 (figure 8–5a). Substitute for the $15 million the equivalent reference gamble: a 50-50 chance at $80 million or $0 (figure 8–5b). Then, using the probability rules, reduce the resulting uncertainty (in figure 8–5b) into a single reference gamble (in figure 8–5c). The result indicates that RKO is indifferent between a certain $6 million and a 0.25 reference gamble (on $80 million or $0). This implies that RKO's preference-probability for $6 million is 0.25. (The reason for picking $15 million for one of the outcomes of the 50-50 gamble used in this assessment should now be obvious—it has a preference-probability of 0.5. If the two outcomes of a 50-50 gamble have preference-probabilities of 0.5 and 0, the CME for that 50-50 gamble will automatically have a preference-probability of 0.25.)

To double-check this assessment, RKO's executives can think about whether they are really indifferent between the two alternatives in figure 8–5c. Is their CME for a 0.25 reference gamble really $6 million? Are they really indifferent between a certain $6 million and a 25-percent chance at $80 million when it is combined with a 75-percent chance at nothing? If they decide that this is about right, then their preference-probability for $6 million is indeed 0.25.

This result can be used to specify further RKO's preference curve. In figure 8–6, the four monetary consequences for which preference-probabilities have been assessed are plotted: $0/0; $6 million/0.25; $15 million/0.5; and $80

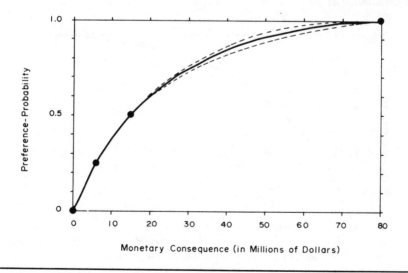

Figure 8–6. Possible Preference Curves Given Four Specific Points ($0/0; $6 Million/0.25; $15 Million/0.5; and $80 Million/1.0).

million/1.0. With these four points, the range of curves indicating the relationship between preference-probabilities and monetary consequences has been further narrowed. The shape of the curve in the region below $15 million (that is, below a preference-probability of 0.5) has been fixed, and even the possibilities above $15 million have been substantially narrowed.

The remaining ambiguity may not be significant. If it is important to decide, for example, whether the preference-probability of $54 million is 0.91 or 0.95, RKO can assess the monetary consequence with a preference-probability of 0.75. To do this, it must determine its CME for a 50-50 gamble with outcomes of $15 million and $80 million. This CME will then have a preference-probability of 0.75.[6]

Note that a 50-50 chance at $15 million or $80 million is the same as being given $15 million plus a 50-percent chance at an additional $65 million. Yet, when assessing the CME for this 50-50 chance at $65 million or nothing, the $15 million guarantee is important. With only your personal assets, your CME for a 50-50 gamble between $65 million and nothing might be $1 million or less. But if you are guaranteed assets totaling $15 million, your CME for the 50-50 gamble might well go up to $20 million. The same thing holds for RKO. Having been guaranteed $15 million, the firm's executives must decide how much more they must be guaranteed to forego the 50-percent chance at another $65 million. They decide that this should be another $15 million. That is, RKO is indifferent between $30 million (the $15 million guarantee and the $15 million CME for the 50-percent chance at the additional $65 million) and a 50-50 chance at $80 million or $15 million.

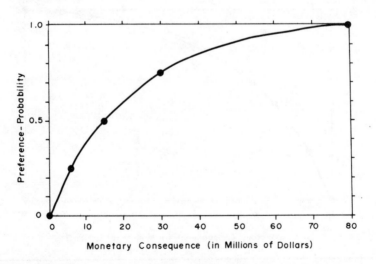

Figure 8–7. RKO's (hypothetical) Preference Curve.

Money and Risk

This 0.75 preference-probability for a $30 million monetary consequence becomes one more point on RKO's preference curve. The result of assessing only three preference-probabilities (more accurately, assessing monetary consequences for three preference-probabilities—0.25, 0.5, and 0.75) is that the preference curve is now quite well defined (figure 8-7). This curve can be used by RKO to help analyze decisions involving uncertain outcomes over the range of $0 to $80 million. For, having done the work to determine this preference curve, the firm has assessed a preference-probability for every possible monetary consequence between $0 and $80 million.

Risk Aversion

Most people dislike risk. If given a choice between $500 for sure and a 50-50 chance at $1,000 or nothing, they will take the $500. Indeed, if given a choice between $450 and the same 50-50 chance at $1,000 or nothing, many people will take the certain $450. People whose certain monetary equivalent for a gamble (either a reference gamble or any more complex uncertainty) is less than the expected monetary value of that gamble are, in the vernacular of decision analysis, *risk averse*.

As the stakes increase, so does one's risk aversion. Consider the following three choices between a certain amount and a 50-50 gamble:

A. $4, or a 50-50 chance at $10 or nothing
B. $400, or a 50-50 chance at $1,000 or nothing
C. $400,000, or a 50-50 chance at $1,000,000 or nothing

The "fairness" of these choices is the same (the certain alternative is precisely 80 percent of the EMV of the gamble). As the value of what must be sacrificed to play the gamble increases, however, the certain amount becomes more attractive. We have often asked our students to think about how they would make these three choices; one collection of ninety-eight students reported the preferences listed in table 8-1.

The degree of an individual's aversion to the risk of a particular gamble can be measured by the difference between the EMV of the gamble and the individual's CME for it. This difference, between the "objective" worth of the gamble and the value that the decision maker places upon it, can be called the "risk premium." If a decision maker is given the EMV of the gamble and then directed to turn that money in to play the gamble, his risk premium is the amount he would pay not to have to take that risk. (It is like the insurance premium he would pay to avoid that risk.) For example, the preferences

TABLE 8-1

How Ninety-Eight Students Chose between Certain Amounts and Gambles

	Percentage of Students Who—	
Choice	Preferred Guarantee	Preferred Gamble
$4, or		
50-50 chance at $10 or $0	7	93
$400, or		
50-50 chance at $1,000 or $0	54	46
$400,000, or		
50-50 chance at $1,000,000 or $0	96	4

assigned to RKO implied that the firm had a risk premium of $25 million for a 50-50 gamble on $80 million or nothing. The EMV of the gamble was $40 million and RKO's (hypothetical) CME for it was $15 million. Thus, if RKO was given $40 million and then told to play double-or-nothing (the 0.5 preference gamble), the firm would pay $25 million (keeping $15 million) to avoid that risk. The risk premium of a 0.5 reference gamble can, therefore, be taken as an indicator of the decision maker's risk aversion over the range of monetary consequences between the two reference outcomes.

A related indicator of risk aversion is the extent of the bend in the preference curve. A straight line between the two reference outcomes indicates that the decision maker's CME for the 0.5 reference gamble is identical to the EMV of that gamble and thus that the decision maker is willing to base his decisions on the expected monetary value criterion. And the more the preference curve bends away from the EMV (straight) line, the more risk averse is the decision maker. For example, examine the four preference curves in figure 8-8. The reference-outcomes are $100 million and $0. The straight line is the EMV curve; it is the preference curve used by someone—sometimes called an *EMVer* —who is not risk averse and is willing to base all decisions on expected monetary value. The horizontal distance between the EMV line and a preference curve at the 0.5 preference-probability level is the risk premium for the 0.5 reference gamble. For preference curve Z, the risk premium for the 0.5 reference gamble is (as indicated by the arrow labeled "risk premium") $20 million. For curve Y, it is $35 million. For curve X, the risk premium of the 0.5 reference gamble is $45 million. For the EMV curve, the risk premium is zero; anyone who has a CME of $50,000 for the 0.5 reference gamble between $100 million and $0 has no risk aversion. Clearly, the more a preference curve bends, the further it is from the EMV line, the larger is the risk premium, and thus the more risk averse is the decision maker.

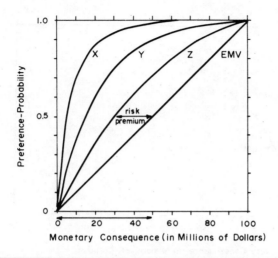

Figure 8–8. Four Preference Curves, with Different Degrees of Risk Aversion.

As the data in table 8–1 suggest, the larger the range of monetary consequences, the more risk averse a decision maker will be. Take the (hypothetical)
RKO case as an example. The preference curve in figure 8–7 indicates that the
firm's risk premium for a 0.5 reference gamble is $25 million. If a smaller range
of outcomes is considered, one would expect RKO's risk premium to become
smaller still. Consider the range of $0 to $15 million. The EMV for a 0.5
reference gamble covering this range is $7.5 million, and RKO's CME for this
gamble was assessed to be $6 million (see figure 8–5a). Consequently, RKO's
risk premium for this reference gamble is $1.5 million. Moreover, this risk
premium is only 20 percent of the EMV of the gamble: $1.5 million/$7.5
million = 0.2. Compare this with the ratio of the risk premium of the original
reference gamble to that gamble's EMV: $25 million/$40 million = 0.625.
This method of comparing the objective "worth" of a gamble (its EMV minus
the lowest possible consequence) to the risk premium provides a measure of
a decision maker's risk aversion.[7]

Actually, even the risk premium for the 50-50 gamble between $0 and $15
million can be obtained directly from RKO's preference curve, reproduced in
figure 8–9. The section of the curve above $15 million can be ignored and the
bottom half taken to be RKO's preference curve for the $0-to-$15-million
range. This requires only a change of scale on the vertical axis (since $15
million now has a preference-probability of 1.0). Then, constructing a new
EMV line, the new risk premium can be obtained by measuring the distance
between the preference curve and the EMV line at the new 0.5 preference-
probability level. As indicated above, this is $1.5 million.

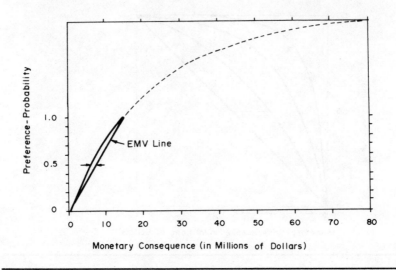

Figure 8–9. RKO's Original Preference Curve Converted into One for the $0-to-$15-Million Monetary-Outcome Range.

For any decision involving uncertainty and money, the decision maker's attitude toward risk may be a decisive factor. The risk premium is a useful idea not because it enters directly into some magic formula that dictates a decision, but because it offers a simple way of specifying one's aversion to any risk. Such fundamental concepts as the CME and the risk premium for a 0.5 reference gamble can provide a mental framework for thinking analytically—quickly yet carefully and systematically—about one's own preferences for risk over a large range of possible outcomes.

Preference Curves and Certain Monetary Equivalents

The curve specifying the relationship between preference-probability and monetary consequence is developed by assessing certain monetary equivalents for a few easy-to-think-about, 50-50 gambles. Such a preference curve can also be used in reverse: to assess, indirectly, the decision maker's CME for *any* uncertain event, no matter how complicated, for which all the possible monetary consequences are within the monetary range covered by the curve.

Suppose that RKO was presented with the opportunity to underwrite a new television series. This is not within RKO's traditional line of business, and to make such an independently produced series a success, RKO would have to either sell it to one of the three major networks or put together its own "network" of stations (the stations it owns plus others not affiliated with any of the three networks).

Such a decision might look like the following. RKO would have to put up $10 million to underwrite the series. It would then offer to sell the series to a network for $50 million; given the quality of the proposed series (combined with the networks' traditional reluctance to air shows not originated by themselves), RKO thinks that it would have a 25-percent chance to do this. If no network bought the series, RKO could attempt to set up its own network to distribute it. RKO thinks that such an effort would have a 50-percent chance of succeeding but that the series distributed by such an "independent network" would be "worth" only $20 million.[8] If RKO is unable to set up its own network to distribute the series, it is worth nothing. And, of course, if RKO decides not to invest in the series, it gets to keep its $10 million. Thus, the decision is a dilemma because of the uncertainty involved in underwriting the series; RKO does not know whether it thinks the gamble is worth more than $10 million.

This hypothetical dilemma is described by the decision tree in figure 8–10. The preference-probabilities for the various terminal outcomes have been obtained from the preference curve in figure 8–7, and the preference-probabilities for the uncertain events and the two alternatives have been determined using the usual procedure. This analysis suggests that RKO prefers to invest in the proposed series.

The preference-probability for the underwrite-series alternative is 0.45. Recall what this means: RKO is indifferent between (a) the opportunity presented by underwriting the series (that is, the combination of various uncertain out-

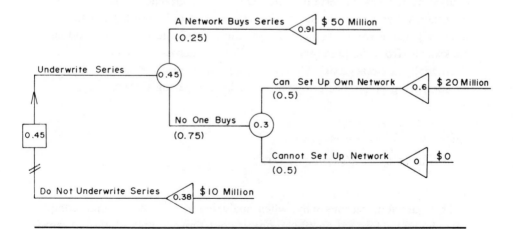

Figure 8–10. A Decision Tree for Deciding Whether to Underwrite a TV Series.

comes that could result from doing this) and (b) a 0.45 reference gamble (giving a 45-percent chance at $80 million and a 55-percent chance at nothing). This means that RKO is also indifferent between (a) the opportunity presented by underwriting the series, and (c) $12.5 million for sure.

This second equivalency is obtained by using the substitution principle. Note that the preference-probability of $12.5 million is 0.45. (This is obtained from the preference curve in figure 8–7.) That means that RKO is indifferent between (b) a 0.45 reference gamble and (c) $12.5 million. Now, if RKO is indifferent between (a) the underwrite-series alternative and (b) a 0.45 reference gamble, and also between (b) a 0.45 reference gamble and (c) $12.5 million, then it should also be indifferent between (a) and (c)—between underwriting the series and $12.5 million. This logic (based on the substitution principle) suggests that RKO thinks the series is worth $12.5 million (and thus that investing $10 million in it makes sense).

RKO's executives now have two ways to double-check their indirect assessment of the 0.45 preference-probability for underwriting the series. They can assess this preference-probability directly, asking whether they are really indifferent between this alternative and a 0.45 reference gamble. And, they can ask whether they are really indifferent between having the collection of uncertain outcomes that go with this alternative and having a certain $12.5 million. If the answer to both is yes, RKO's executives can be confident of their indirect assessment of this preference-probability. If not, they will want to rethink their analysis.

In summary, then, a preference curve can be used in two ways. It can be used to assess the preference-probability of any certain monetary outcome. And it can be used in the other direction—to determine a certain monetary equivalent for any uncertain event. Once the preference-probability of an uncertainty has been assessed (either directly or indirectly), the equivalent monetary value (or CME) can be obtained from the curve by reading it backwards (from the preference-probability axis across to the curve and then down to the monetary axis). Thus, dilemmas can be resolved analytically either by comparing preference-probabilities or by comparing CMEs.

The Shape of Preference Curves

There are four reasons why, when analyzing a decision dilemma complicated by many different possible monetary outcomes, it makes sense to assess a preference curve rather than attempt to assess, individually, a preference-probability for each monetary outcome.

Money and Risk

1. It takes less work; there are fewer assessments to make. A useful preference curve can usually be assessed by making only two or three hypothetical decisions—by determining the monetary outcomes with preference-probabilities of 0.5, 0.25, and perhaps 0.75. Then the preference-probabilities for the various possible outcomes of the dilemma can simply be read from this curve. Otherwise, it is necessary to make a separate decision about the preference-probability for every one of the possible outcomes.

2. It is simpler; it is easier to think about the decisions required to determine a preference curve. All the hypothetical indifference decisions involved in assessing a preference curve require only the determination of CMEs, or indifference outcomes, for 50-50 gambles. In contrast, directly assessing the preference-probabilities for the various monetary outcomes of the dilemma requires the determination of indifference probabilities, which for most people is a much more perplexing task.

3. It facilitates the interpretation of preference-probabilities assessed (indirectly) for uncertain events and alternatives. A preference-probability for an uncertain event (or alternative) indicates that the decision maker is indifferent between the combination of uncertain outcomes that could result from that event (or alternative) and the uncertain outcomes of the equivalent reference gamble. But, with a preference curve, it is also possible to determine the decision maker's CME for that uncertain event. Thus, the decision maker can double-check the indirectly assessed preference-probability by asking himself if he is indeed indifferent between this guaranteed amount (the CME) and the gamble involved in the uncertain event.

4. Finally, as will be illustrated in chapter 9, a preference curve facilitates simple sensitivity analysis for risk aversion. If the preference-probabilities for all the terminal outcomes have been assessed directly (and thus individually), it is quite difficult to determine how and how much each should be varied to reflect more or less risk aversion. With a preference curve, however, the CME (and thus the risk index) for the 0.5 reference gamble provides a direct measure of the decision maker's risk aversion. By systematically varying this CME, and thus the bend in the preference curve, a decision maker can analyze the sensitivity of any choice to changes in his risk aversion.

These four advantages follow from an important assumption about human values. Although each of us has different preferences, for most people, preferences for money are characterized by a regular pattern distinguished by a diminishing marginal value for money. That is, most people value the first $100,000 more than the second $100,000, which in turn they value more than the third $100,000. In terms of a preference curve, this means that the difference between the preference-probabilities for $100,000 and $0 is greater than the difference between the preference-probabilities for $200,000 and $100,000. For example, from RKO's preference curve (figure 8–7), the preference-probabilities of $0, $5 million, $10 million, and $15 million are 0, 0.21, 0.39, and 0.5, respectively. The differences between the preference-probabilities over these $5 million intervals are 0.21, 0.18, and 0.11—they are constantly diminishing. Continuing in $5 million intervals, the differences between the preference-probabilities are (approximately) 0.1, 0.08, 0.07, 0.05, 0.045, 0.035, 0.03, 0.025, 0.02, 0.015, 0.015, 0.01 and 0.005. (Note that these sixteen numbers sum to 1.0.) It is this regular pattern of a preference curve that permits its assessment with just a few points.

This helps explain why, when assessing RKO's preferences for money, the "peculiar" preference curves, D and E in figure 8–4, were eliminated from consideration. These curves are not characterized by a diminishing marginal value for money. For most people, the first $100,000 is "worth" more than the second $100,000, which is worth more than the third $100,000. That is because more additional happiness—either the hedonistic pleasure of consumption or the altruistic satisfaction of philanthropy—can be bought with the first $100,000 than with the second. But curves D and E imply (at least over certain ranges) the opposite. With curve D, for example, the difference between the preference-probability for $0 and $5 million is 0.08, while that between the preference-probability for $5 million and $10 million is 0.14.[9]

Preference curves such as D and E imply choices that most people, after careful consideration, would not make. Indeed, such preference curves imply that for some gambles the decision maker is actually risk *seeking*. Consider the decision described in figure 8–11, a choice between a certain $10 million and a 50-50 chance at $15 million or nothing. Most people—and most corporations —would undoubtedly prefer the certain $10 million. Yet preference curve D indicates, through its preference-probabilities for $0, $10, and $15 million, that the risky alternative is better.

Anyone whose preferences for monetary outcomes between $0 and $15

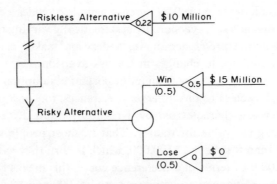

Figure 8–11. The Contradiction of a "Peculiar" Preference Curve.

million are characterized by curve D actually seeks risks rather than avoids them. Geometrically, this is indicated by the preference curve starting off with a very small slope and then becoming increasingly steep (so that the preference curve is below the straight line between $0 and $15 million rather than above it). As a result, the EMV of any gamble will be less than the CME obtained from a risk-seeking preference curve.

The EMV of the gamble in figure 8–11 is $7.5 million. The CME obtained from curve D is, approximately, $12 million. (The preference-probability of the gamble is 0.25, for which the monetary equivalent from curve D is $12 million.) This means that anyone whose preference for money can be described by curve D has a negative risk premium—he is willing to pay more than the expected monetary value of a gamble to play it. If given $7.5 million, he would be willing to pay this plus another $4.5 million (for a total of $12 million) for a 50-50 chance at $15 million or nothing.

Someone who is risk averse has certain monetary equivalents that are less than the expected monetary value of those gambles. Someone who is risk seeking has CMEs for gambles that are greater than the EMVs for those gambles. Any preference curve that is not constantly turning downwards[10]— that is, any curve with a section like that of curve D below $15 million or curve E above $15 million[11]—implies that the decision maker who assessed it is risk seeking for at least some kinds of gambles.

The world is full of examples of risk-seeking behavior. The expected monetary values of the games played in Las Vegas are clearly less than the (certain) amount you must pay to play. The people at the gambling tables are not, however, solely concerned with the monetary consequences of their (gambling) decisions. Other consequences are important too—perhaps more important. People go to Las Vegas for recreation and they are willing to pay the price of unfavorable long-run odds for the thrill of gambling. (One not-so-wealthy acquaintance devoted an evening at a Las Vegas crap table to prove—to himself and the house—that he was enough of a high roller to "earn" a free drink. That was a very expensive "free" drink, but then it was not just a drink that he was buying.)

There are other situations in which quite "rational" preferences might not involve a smooth, regular preference curve, such as being temporarily broke and owing $500 in unpaid parking tickets. Imagine someone in such a predicament who must pay the fine or spend a week in jail, starting tomorrow. Such an individual might well prefer a 10-percent chance at $500 (even when combined with a 90-percent chance at nothing) to a certain $250. The $500 can buy freedom; the $250, or even $450, cannot. Such an individual might have a preference curve similar to the one in figure 8–12.

One significant feature of the usual, regular preference curves (such as in figures 8–7 and 8–8) is that they bend very slowly. Indeed, over small ranges

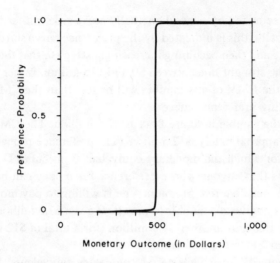

Figure 8–12. A Possible Preference Curve for an Individual Who Is Broke and Must Pay a $500 Fine or Go to Jail.

they are effectively straight lines. Thus, for decisions involving uncertain monetary outcomes that are concentrated in a relatively small range, the expected monetary value criterion may be quite appropriate. Suppose that RKO had to choose between a certain $50 million and a 50-50 chance at $45 million or $55 million. Using preference-probabilities obtained from RKO's preference curve (figure 8–7), it is clear that the firm is essentially indifferent between these two alternatives. Given the limits on the accuracy with which this curve can be read, the preference-probabilities for these two alternatives are essentially the same. (See figure 8–13.)

But that makes sense. The decision is the same as being given $45 million plus a choice between an additional (certain) $5 million and a 50-50 chance at an additional $10 million. Given $45 million in the bank, RKO may be quite willing to use the EMV criterion to make decisions involving amounts as "small" as $10 million. In fact, for any $10 million range, RKO's preference curve is very close to a straight line. If the firm finds it necessary to think more carefully about a decision involving uncertain outcomes over any such $10 million range, its executives might have to think more carefully about their preferences for money, perhaps developing another preference curve involving only monetary outcomes for that particular range. After all, the preference curve in figure 8–7 was drawn from assessments of indifference outcomes for only three 50-50 gambles, which cover a range of $80 million. It would not make sense to claim that such a curve could be very helpful in resolving dilemmas involving uncertain outcomes covering a much narrower range.

214

Money and Risk

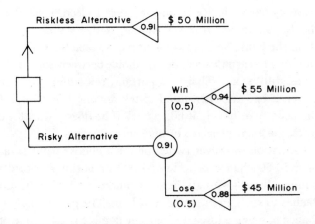

Figure 8–13. A Decision Involving Uncertain Monetary Outcomes Over a Small Enough Range that the EMV Criterion Is Appropriate.

Preferences for Losses and Losing

There does exist one set of circumstances under which humans consistently exhibit risk-seeking behavior. That is when they are asked to state their preferences for gambles that involve losses. Suppose that Joe Sturdley (our answer to John Q. Citizen) is asked to choose between $500 and a 50-50 gamble for $1,000 or nothing. He chooses the guaranteed $500. Then Sturdley is asked to choose between −$500 and a 50-50 gamble for −$1,000 or nothing. Here he chooses the gamble. Note that for both these choices, the EMV of the gamble is equal to the certain alternative. In the first situation, Sturdley's preference for the certain $500 implies that he is risk averse. In the second situation, however, Sturdley preferred the gamble to its EMV, suggesting that he is risk seeking.

These two choices illustrate how many people think about money and risk. When asked questions involving gambles and gains, they give answers that imply they are risk averse. But when asked to choose among alternatives involving losses, they appear to be risk seeking. A wide variety of psychological experiments have reproduced these results.[12] Daniel Kahneman and Amos Tversky have discussed this phenomenon,[13] as has Richard Thaler of Cornell University[14] and others.[15] But the developing explanations are still not completely satisfactory.

Perhaps part of the answer lies in our cultural attitudes towards winners and losers. In the first choice (between a certain $500 and a 50-50 chance at $1,000 or nothing), Sturdley has a chance to be a winner. Indeed, if he chooses the certain $500 he is guaranteed to be a winner, and, as well as having an additional $500 in the bank, he can take a certain satisfaction in having won. Even if he did nothing to earn this wonderful choice between $500 and double-or-nothing, he has still "won." That is important, rewarding, and satisfying. Consequently, even if he is not permitted to tell anyone about his $500 winnings (under the penalty of having it taken back if he does), Sturdley can still take some private, personal pleasure in his success.

In the second situation, however (when he must choose between a certain loss of $500 or a 50-50 chance of losing $1,000 or nothing), Sturdley is in danger of becoming a loser—with all the social and personal implications that our culture attaches to such an outcome. But look. The gamble only involves a 50-percent chance of being a loser. Indeed, the gamble is attractive precisely because it gives Sturdley an opportunity to avoid that loser image. Whether he loses $500 or $1,000 may not be as important as simply being a loser. And again, even if he could be sure that no one else would know about the loss (the family bookkeeping would be arranged to conceal the loss from even his wife), the psychological impact could not be avoided. Thus, in an effort to avoid being a loser, Sturdley behaves as if he actually seeks risks.[16]

Many people think about gambles for negative amounts as if they are mirror images of similar gambles for positive amounts. If Joe Sturdley were asked to

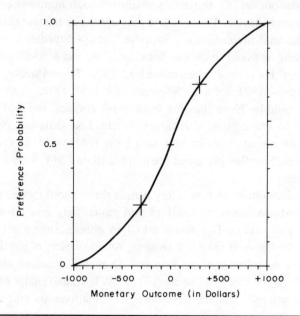

Figure 8–14. A Mirror-Image Preference Curve for Gains and Losses.

assess his CME for the 50-50 gamble for $1,000 or nothing, and concluded it was $300, then, when thinking about a 50-50 gamble for −$1000 or nothing, he might decide that his CME for this gamble was about −$300. (Kahneman and Tversky call this the "reflection effect.")[17]

This pair of CMEs suggests that, in figure 8–14, Sturdley's preference curve should be symmetrical with respect to $0 (neither loss nor gain), with the curve changing direction at this point. Above $0, the curve bends downwards, indicating that Sturdley is risk averse in this region ($0 to +$1,000). But the curve bends upwards below this point, indicating that he is risk seeking in this region (−$1,000 to $0). Note that Sturdley's two CMEs are accurately reflected by this curve. From figure 8–14, +$300 has a preference-probability of 0.75; so does a 50-50 gamble for $0 versus +$1,000. Similarly, −$300 has a preference probability of 0.25, and a 50-50 gamble for −$1,000, and $0 does too.

Now, consider the problem of assessing preferences for gains and losses of money from a different perspective. Suppose that Joe Sturdley, who has assets of $X, is given on Monday a choice between a certain $600 and a 50-50 chance at $1,000 or nothing. (Any winnings will, naturally, be added to his existing assets.) Given the preferences that Sturdley has already revealed, it is clear that he would select the certain $600 (as is indicated on the decision tree in figure 8–15).

Now suppose that instead of Monday's choice Sturdley is placed in a different situation. On Tuesday, Sturdley is given $1,000, which he deposits in his bank account. His assets are now $X + $1,000. And suppose that on Wednesday, he is forced to choose between paying $400 and a 50-50 chance at paying $1,000 or nothing. (And these payments would be subtracted from Sturdley's

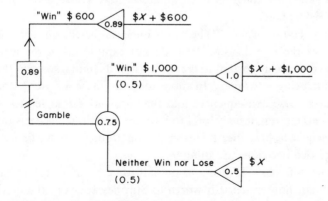

Figure 8–15. Joe Sturdley's Monday Decision.

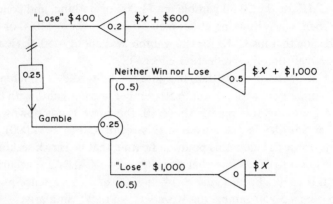

Figure 8–16. Joe Sturdley's Wednesday Decision.

assets of $X + $1,000.) Again, given the preferences he has already revealed, his choice here is also clear—he would select the gamble (as is indicated on the decision tree in figure 8–16).

But wait. Examine the monetary *consequences* of these two dilemmas. They are identical. Both decisions involve choices between guaranteed assets of $X + $600 and a 50-50 chance of assets of $X + $1,000 versus $X. In terms of the terminal outcomes, the two decisions are equivalent. The only difference is that Monday's choice is made with $X in the bank and Wednesday's with $X + $1,000 in the bank. Regardless of how much money is in the bank *before* the decision, though, the possible amounts that Sturdley will have *after* the decision are exactly the same. Can merely depositing $1,000 in his bank account so alter Sturdley's preferences for monetary outcomes—for money in the bank—that he converts from a careful, risk-averse decision maker to a carefree risk seeker?

Sturdley could argue, "The consequences listed on the consequence branches of the two decision trees do not capture all of the aspects of the outcomes that are important to me. In the first dilemma, some of the outcomes involve me being a 'winner.' In the second, I can be a 'loser.' Your decision tree ignores these consequences and they are—to me, at least—important." Consequently, it might be helpful to Sturdley to redraw his decision trees with two consequence branches for each terminal outcome. As figure 8–17 indicates, the two decisions are different.[18]

But *how* different? How important is it to be a winner rather than a loser? In particular, how much is it worth to Sturdley to avoid the image of being a loser or to take on the aura of a winner? For example, if Sturdley was to end up with $X + $600 in the bank but be a "loser," how much of his assets would he trade-in to convert his loser image into that of a winner? That is, how much

Money and Risk

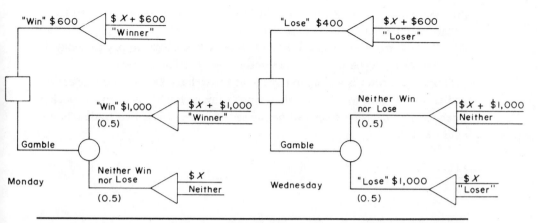

Figure 8–17. Joe Sturdley's Monday and Wednesday Decisions, with a Second Consequence Branch to Indicate Whether He is a "Winner" or "Loser."

would he pay—out of his own pocket—to be transformed from a loser into a winner? That should give Sturdley some idea of how important the winner/loser consequence really is.

Given Sturdley's previously expressed preferences, it would appear that he thinks his image—even if it is only his self-image—is quite important. It appears to be worth something in the neighborhood of several hundred dollars. But Sturdley needs to think carefully about his image. How important is it really? If he does end up a loser, how long will he have to live with this reputation? How much will it affect his social status or self-esteem? This decision does not involve any test of Sturdley's talents or intelligence. How important is image compared with the impact of his real accomplishments and real defeats? Which will have a more lasting impact?

Sturdley should not forget about the value—even today—of a hundred dollars. In most cities in the world, that amount of money can still provide two people with a most enjoyable evening. In Paris, you could have dinner at Chez Androuet. In New York, you could listen to jazz at the Knickerbocker Saloon. In Boston, you could watch the Red Sox from the box seats on the roof of Fenway Park. In Seattle, you could take in one of Wagner's *Ring* cycle of operas. In Copenhagen, you could attend the ballet at the Royal Danish Theater. Would not such an evening more than compensate Sturdley for "losing" Wednesday's gamble?

Perhaps Sturdley is a professional gambler, one whose personal pride and social access are dependent upon his continued reputation as a winner. Then his image consequence of these outcomes might be worth, to him, not hundreds but thousands of dollars. But if not—if his own sense of self-worth and his reputation with his peers is derived from other aspects of his personal and

219

professional life—then he might be willing to pay only $5 or $10 to be transformed from a winner to a loser. And do not forget that these payments are also "losses" from his assets. Whatever money he chooses to pay to avoid the loser image could be used for some other, worthwhile purpose.

Suppose Sturdley is willing to pay about $10 to have his loser's image erased, and is also willing to trade-in his winner's image for $5 more in his pocket. Then his two decision trees can be revised to reflect these two trade-offs (see figure 8–18).

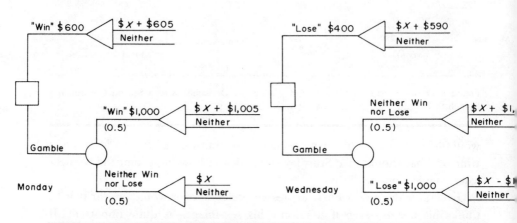

Figure 8–18. Joe Sturdley's Monday and Wednesday Decisions Revised with Trade-Offs So That Only One Consequence Branch Reflects the Differences in Outcomes.

(At Sturdley's insistence, the two dilemmas have been converted into ones with multiple consequences. Two consequences of these decisions are important to him: (1) the amount of money he ends up with in the bank, and (2) his image. And he cannot, apparently, resolve these dilemmas satisfactorily without analyzing the impact of both consequences on his preference for the terminal outcomes. The trade-offs discussed, in which Sturdley decided how much of one consequence he was willing to give up to make a gain on the other consequence, illustrate how one can think about dilemmas complicated by multiple consequences. For a more thorough examination of how to analyze such decision dilemmas, see chapter 11.)

For all outcomes on the revised decision trees, the image consequence is the same: "Neither" winner nor loser. Thus, for the revised Monday dilemma, Sturdley is faced with a choice between a certain $X + $605 and a 50-50 gamble for $X + $1,005 or $X. Wednesday's revised choice is between a certain $X + $590 and a 50-50 gamble for $X + $1,000 or $X − $10. The two dilemmas are different, but not very different. Indeed, in both cases, the certain outcome is nearly $100 greater than the EMV of the uncertain alternative. Thus, if Sturdley is indeed risk averse, he will choose the certain alternative in both gambles.[19]

There are two ways to view the role of this analysis. One is that it revealed Sturdley's true preferences about money and risk. The decision dilemma was complicated by the image consequence, but once that complexity was handled with some trade-off analysis, the true implications of the various alternatives —and thus the preferred choices—became clear.

Alternatively, the analysis may have helped Sturdley to actually develop his own values. It is not at all obvious that Sturdley had any well-established preferences for images and dollars tucked away somewhere in the back of his brain, waiting to be brought forth by sending the required electrical signal to the proper corner of his cerebrum. It may well have been that Sturdley had never thought seriously about his preferences for such consequences before. By providing a framework for thinking about the implications of his choices, the analysis helped Sturdley create a reasonable, consistent, and satisfactory set of preferences for resolving his dilemma. We cannot all be expected to have well-established preferences concerning the outcomes of every decision we will face in our lives. But thinking analytically about a decision dilemma can help develop those values needed to resolve it.

Preference Curves for Total Assets

How a decision problem is formulated can significantly affect people's thinking and their choices. We commonly use simple rules of thumb, heuristics, and other devices—focusing attention on some factors while ignoring others—so as to minimize the effort required to make decisions. And different formulations of the same problem can trigger different heuristics, thus producing different choices. The psychological literature of behavioral decision theory is replete with examples of how people can make different choices between the same alternatives depending upon how the problem is presented.[20] Baruch Fischhoff, Paul Slovic, and Sarah Lichtenstein offer one example involving gambles and losses:

> We have found that most people will prefer a gamble with a .25 chance to lose $200 (and a .75 chance to lose nothing) to a *sure loss* of $50. However, when that sure loss is called an *insurance premium,* people will reverse their preferences and forego the $50.[21]

Kahneman and Tversky observe, "Two prospects that are equivalent in probability and outcomes could have different values depending upon their formulations."[22]

In fact, it is possible to formulate decision problems so as to abet violations of what people accept as the principles of logic. One such principle is called *transitivity:* If you prefer A to B, and if you prefer B to C, then you should prefer A to C. If you do, your preferences are transitive. (If you assert, however, that you prefer A to B, B to C, and C to A, your preferences are *intransitive.)* Still, when people are given a series of decisions to make (and are hindered in their efforts to make the traditional checks for consistency), they do occasionally make intransitive choices. When the logical inconsistency of such a choice is pointed out to them, however, they immediately move to correct their "mistake."[23]

One way to elicit such intransitive choices from people is to ask them about their preferences for new cars. Among a series of questions about "why the sea is boiling hot and whether pigs have wings," people could be asked to choose between different combinations of two of the following:

A. Paying $5,000 for a Chevrolet Chevette;
B. Paying $9,000 for a Buick LaSabre; and
C. Paying $13,000 for a Cadillac Eldorado.

When asked to choose between A and B, Joe Sturdley might pick B, with reasoning something like "If I am going to buy a new car, I might as well get one that will have enough room." When choosing between B and C, Sturdley might select C, reasoning "If I am going to spend $9,000, I might as well spend $13,000 and get a really good car." Yet, when asked to choose between A and C, Sturdley might choose A, because "$13,000 is just too much to spend for a car, when I can get adequate transportation for less than half that price." When comparing cars in pairs, Sturdley may focus on those one or two features that appear to most distinguish the two alternatives. But those features need not be the same for every pair, and thus the choices that result from such disconnected reasoning may be quite inconsistent.

When these three choices are removed from the clutter of the other decisions, however, people immediately recognize that such gut reactions—it would be unfair to call them "thinking"—violate the principle of transitivity. Even if they have never heard of this concept, they will want to rearrange their choices to make them logically consistent. Formulating the car buying decision as a choice involving three alternatives thus facilitates analytical thinking. Indeed, the other presentation of the problem, a series of choices between just two cars, with the pairs mixed with other problems so as to inhibit the use of memory and any systematic comparisons, is explicitly designed to prevent any thoughtful analysis.

With decisions involving money and risk, it is also possible to create logical inconsistencies by reformulating the problem. As was illustrated earlier, if presented with choices involving gains and losses from present assets, people exhibit risk-averse behavior for gains and risk-seeking behavior for losses. But when the same choices are reformulated in terms of total assets—so that more attention is focused on how much you end up with in the bank and losses from these assets appear less important—people make choices that reflect traditional risk aversion over the entire range of total assets.

Moreover, such a reformulation of the problem—such as in figure 8–17—dramatizes to people the inconsistency of their previous choices. How can you prefer A to B, and also prefer B to A? When confronted with such logical inconsistencies, people are forced to reexamine their thinking. They feel the need to make their decisions consistent with what they themselves accept as the principles of logic (or else to argue that there is some additional factor, such as the image consequence, that has been ignored in the formulation of the problem and that, when included, eliminates the inconsistency).

As there is no single process that is always best for assessing subjective probabilities, so there is no specific formulation of even a single class of decision problems that is best for assessing preferences.[24] But there are some ways of dealing with the standard tendencies toward logical inconsistencies.

One such formulation is to think about preference for money in terms of total assets rather than changes in assets. As Kahneman and Tversky write, "The explicit formulation of decision problems in terms of final assets is perhaps the most effective procedure for eliminating risk seeking in the domain of losses."[25] Of course, changing a problem formulated in terms of gains and losses into one in which the outcomes are specified as total assets involves nothing more than a shift in perspective—a change in the origin (or zero point) of the monetary consequences axis on the preference curve. With gains and losses, this zero point on that axis is at present assets; when these consequences are expressed in terms of total assets, the origin is just shifted to the left—to where assets are zero.

Present asset position is certainly the most convenient reference point from which to measure—as gains or losses—the monetary consequences of the various outcomes of a decision, for it simplifies the calculations that must be made to specify the final consequences. But what, precisely, are present assets? Suppose Joe Sturdley has $X in the bank and is offered the choice between a certain $200 and a 50-50 chance at $1,000 or nothing. Are Sturdley's assets really $X? Or should he think about them as $X + $200, and the gamble as a choice between nothing and a 50-50 chance at +$800 or −$200? After all, once he is offered the choice, he does indeed have access to assets of $X + $200.

But reformulating the problem—redefining present assets—might change Sturdley's preferences for the two alternatives (see figure 8–19). The original formulation of the problem focused his attention on the 50-percent chance of winning $1,000, and he did not think that the certain $200 was large enough

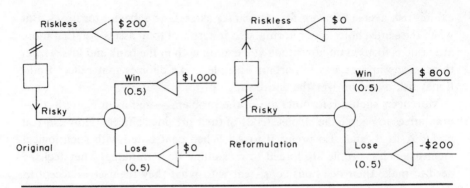

Figure 8–19. Two Ways to Formulate a Decision in Terms of Changes (Gains or Losses) from Present Assets.

for him to give up the opportunity for the larger prize. But after redefining present assets, Sturdley's thinking is so dominated by his concern for losing that $200 that he is not willing to risk it even for an equal chance of winning $800. Thus, even "present assets" are not unambiguously defined, and the perspective used in selecting the present-asset position from which changes will be calculated can affect any final choice.

In contrast, defining the consequences of a decision in terms of total assets provides a more realistic appreciation of the true implications of the various possible monetary outcomes. The amount won or lost is placed in perspective; the decision maker can evaluate the change in assets in terms of the total assets he has available. If thinking about your preferences for money in terms of gains and losses produces results that you find logically unacceptable, perhaps reformulating your thinking about preferences for money in terms of total assets is—for you—more helpful.

For example, the RKO problem at the beginning of this chapter was formulated in terms of assets. RKO has a station worth $80 million. If RKO's license is not renewed, it loses that $80 million. If it sells the station for $54 million, it loses $26 million. But the outcomes were expressed not in terms of such losses, but in terms of the assets that the firm will have in the station.

Actually, it would have been better to formulate the problem in terms of RKO's *total* assets. That is, if the firm's twenty-six stations are worth a total of $1 billion, then the firm's assets are $920 million if the license is not renewed, and $974 million if it sells the station for $54 million. Looking at the decision this way (see figure 8–20) might further modify RKO's thinking. For now the firm's executives need to think about how risk averse they are for uncertain outcomes over the range of $0 to $1 billion.

Since the range of possible outcomes has expanded by more than a factor of ten (from $80 million to $1 billion), RKO will be even more risk averse for

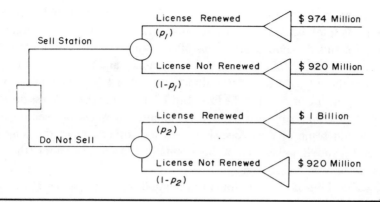

Figure 8–20. RKO's Dilemma Reformulated in Terms of the Firm's Total, Final Assets.

the entire range. For example, it might have a preference curve as shown in figure 8–21, with a risk premium of $450 million for a 50-50 gamble for $0 or $1 billion. But over the asset range of $900 million to $1 billion, this preference curve is nearly a straight line. This implies that, for decisions with outcomes in this range, RKO would almost be an EMVer. Thus, for the firm's decision concerning whether to sell WNAC-TV, RKO should have very little risk aversion.

That was not, however, the original reasoning as summarized in the preference curve in figure 8–7. The original description of the dilemma ignored the relationship of WNAC to the rest of RKO; it almost appeared as if this was

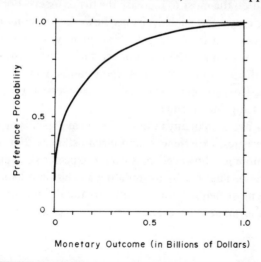

Figure 8–21. RKO's (hypothetical) Preference Curve for Total Assets.

225

the only station that the firm owned. But reformulating the problem in terms of the firm's total assets makes it clear that RKO should not have much risk aversion for this decision. RKO owns fifteen other stations and undoubtedly makes a large number of decisions involving money and risk with the possible outcomes differing by "only" $50 million or so.[26] For RKO, such decisions do not involve the life or death of the firm. Indeed, these are the business decisions (gambles) that the firm must make every month, or week, or even day. The firm will win some of these decisions and lose others. Over the long run, however, because it makes a lot of these "small" decisions, it is not in the firm's interest to be very risk averse.

The same thing holds true for an individual making a series of decisions involving monetary outcomes of "only" $100 or so. If you had a series of choices between a certain $5 and a 50-50 gamble for +$60 or −$40, you would want to choose the gamble every time. Losing $40 on any one decision —or even losing $40 several times in a row—will not bankrupt you, and you can expect to win over the long run almost exactly half the time.[27] The EMV of the gamble is $10, compared to an EMV of only $5 for the other choice. In other words, you would win some gambles and lose others, but in the long run you would win an average of $10 per gamble.

Note, however, that this is not the view of the middle managers of a business firm. They might easily have preferences that differ from those of the firm as a whole. The firm would be willing to take a variety of "small" gambles, winning some and losing others, as long as each time it was faced with such a decision it selected the alternative with the highest EMV. The result of all these decisions would do the most to increase the firm's assets. For the middle manager, who makes only a few such decisions, however, the consequences are not "small." He must demonstrate success. Consequently, such a manager will select those alternatives with modest but more certain gains, rather than those options that involve the possibility of a big success combined with a significant possibility of failure. How to encourage middle managers to take more risks is a basic problem of top management.

Obviously, the risk aversion of any individual or firm depends upon a variety of personal characteristics, experiences, and circumstances. For any specific range of possible outcomes, however, one would expect risk aversion to decrease as assets increase. That is why formulating a decision dilemma in terms of total assets is the most helpful; total assets provide the proper perspective from which a decision maker can evaluate his own risk aversion.

Money and Risk

Thinking Subjunctively: Why Preference-Probabilities Make Sense

Thinking about hypothetical future states of the world—let alone comparing them systematically—is difficult.[28] People are simply not accustomed to thinking in the subjunctive. All decisions depend upon the evaluation of potential outcomes—future outcomes that are, at present, very abstract. Some possible outcomes may appear to be remote, fantastic, incomprehensible. Many will never be realized. But to think analytically about a decision, it is necessary to decide which outcomes are better than others and by how much. Otherwise a decision will be based on only a few factors—or on pure whimsy.

Preference-probabilities can help make subjunctive thinking more analytical. They cannot provide an objective scale against which to measure any potential outcome. But they do offer a useful aid for making the subjective judgments that are required to compare the various possible outcomes of any decision.

Few people use preference-probabilities to help make decisions. In the history of human knowledge, preference-probabilities were invented very recently—indeed, only in this century.[29] As with any new and strange idea, acceptance has come slowly. When introduced to the concept, most people find it terribly awkward and circuitous to define a measure of desirability in terms of a hypothetical probability of winning a hypothetical gamble. They dismiss preference-probabilities as too illusive, too artificial, too unintuitive.

Probabilities and gambles are obscure concepts—abstractions about which it is difficult to think. And hypothetical probabilities for hypothetical gambles can be perfectly confusing. Little wonder that the human mind employs a variety of heuristics to eliminate most factors as "extraneous," so that a decision can easily be made by directly comparing only one or two factors. This avoids the difficulty of dealing with perplexing probabilities and unnerving uncertainty. As Henry S. Rowen of Stanford Business School points out, however, analysis itself can serve as a "heuristic aid."[30] It provides a framework for thinking about a problem without unknowingly ignoring some important factors. If one must make a decision involving uncertainty, preference-probabilities provide a useful heuristic to help evaluate outcomes and alternatives. If one needs to resolve a puzzling dilemma—and is willing to do the hard work of thinking systematically about the various alternatives—then it makes sense to use the best tools available. And, for three important reasons, preference-probabilities are a most valuable heuristic.

First, preference-probabilities are defined precisely and can thus be unambiguously explained. Once the two reference outcomes, the *Best* and the *Worst*, have been designated, the meaning of any preference-probability is clear. By assessing (either directly or indirectly) a preference-probability of, for example, 0.7 for an outcome, a decision maker is stating that he is indifferent between that outcome and a gamble that gives a 70-percent chance at the *Best* reference outcome and a 30-percent chance at the *Worst*. For the decision maker, both the outcome and the reference gamble are hypothetical; until the decision is made, neither exists and all their possible consequences and subtle ramifications are difficult to comprehend. But the decision maker has been able to decide that, for him, the worth of the outcome and the worth of the reference gamble are identical.

This leads to the second advantage of preference-probabilities: Decisions that are dilemmas because of uncertainty about the outcome of one or more alternatives can be readily resolved by assessing preference-probabilities for each outcome. Once the decision maker has decided upon his equivalent reference gamble for each possible outcome of his decision, each outcome can be replaced with its equivalent reference gamble, and the probability rules used to determine the chance of getting a *Best* outcome from each alternative. Then, because of the substitution principle—because replacing an outcome with an equivalent reference gamble does not affect a decision maker's preferences for any of the alternatives—the decision maker prefers the alternative with the largest chance of getting a *Best* outcome, meaning the one with the largest preference-probability.

The third advantage of preference-probabilities is that they are universally applicable. Preference-probabilities can be used whether the consequences of a decision are wealth, health, or happiness. They can be used when a decision concerns election to public office or the outcome of a football game, bypass surgery on an individual or health policy for a nation, the verdict of a jury or the choice of a consumer. They can be used to help resolve decisions in government, business, law, medicine, education, labor, or journalism. In any situation, a decision maker can use preference-probabilities to assess his relative preferences for each of the outcomes—and thus for each of the alternatives.

To think about the desirability of an outcome in terms of preference-probabilities, it is necessary to think about uncertainty and probabilities. To think subjunctively, one must first be able to think probabilistically. That is the big hurdle. Until a decision maker is willing to make probabilistic predictions and is confident of his own ability to assess judgmental probabilities for uncertain events, he will be unable to use the idea of preference-probabilities to make judgments about the relative desirability of different outcomes. Future outcomes are hypothetical, in part, because they are uncertain. Thinking about them analytically requires an intuitive feel for probabilities that takes some practice to develop.

Money and Risk

Appendix: Sunk Costs Don't Count

A generic decision dilemma that occurs in personal, business, and governmental situations is whether to follow through on a project after an initial investment has been made. Some of the costs of the project have already been spent, reducing the total cost to complete it. And, given that the benefits will not be received until the project is completed, it may be even more desirable to follow through than it was to start the project originally.

But what if the other circumstances affecting the decision have also changed? Indeed, unless such an additional change has occurred, there would be little reason to reconsider the original choice. For example, suppose that even though the project is partially complete, it has become apparent that finishing it will be much more expensive than originally predicted. Then, in analyzing whether or not to follow through on the project, exactly what costs are relevant to the decision is important.[31] Here the basic rule is a simple one: *Sunk costs don't count.* Unfortunately, applying this rule is not as simple.

Consider the hypothetical decision discussed in this chapter concerning whether RKO should invest in the development of a new TV series. That decision involves monetary consequences covering a range of "only" $40 million, so the decision tree (in figure 8–10) can be redesigned with expected monetary value as the criterion (see figure 8–22a). The preferred alternative is the same—to invest in the series—but, since the choices have been reevaluated in terms of EMV (rather than on the basis of risk-averse preferences), this preference is even stronger.

Note that this decision could have been formulated in terms of gains and losses from present assets (figure 8–22b). Not to underwrite the series now has a monetary consequence of $0—neither a loss nor a gain. And from the sales of the series is subtracted the $10 million cost of developing it. Still, since RKO is using the EMV criterion, the decision is unchanged. All that has happened is that RKO is now measuring its monetary consequences from a different point. The difference in EMV between the two alternatives is still $10 million.

Now, suppose that, after investing a total of $10 million in developing the series, RKO concludes that it will have to spend a total of $35 million to complete the project (the $10 million already spent, plus an additional $25 million). What should it do now? Decision trees for this reevaluation decision are shown in figure 8–23. With the dilemma formulated in terms of project assets (figure 8–23a), the EMV of completing the project is $20 million; but the EMV of stopping is $25 million. Thus, it makes sense to stop the project.

Note that the $10 million already spent on the project has been ignored in this analysis. Whatever RKO decides to do now, it cannot recover that $10

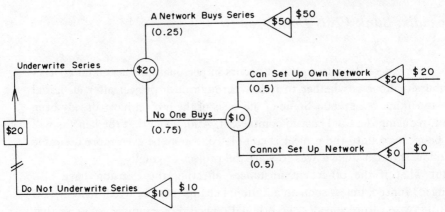

(a) Formulated in Terms of Project Assests.

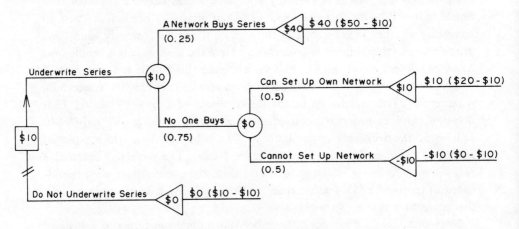

(b) Formulated in Terms of Gains and Losses from Present Assets.

Figure 8–22. RKO's Decision about Whether to Underwrite a TV Series, with EMV as the Criterion (All Dollar Figures in Millions).

million. It has already been spent. The $10 million is a sunk cost, and whether it is $10 thousand or $10 billion makes no difference. What do make a difference are the potential gains and losses of the alternatives that the firm *now* has available. Taking these gains and losses into account, the expected monetary consequence of stopping the project is better than that of continuing.

This decision, too, could have been formulated in terms of gains and losses from present assets (figure 8–23b). This would involve merely subtracting the $25 million cost of completing the project from all the outcomes, thereby affecting both alternatives equally. Thus, it would not affect the relative ranking of the two alternatives. The EMV of stopping is still $5 million higher than the EMV of continuing.

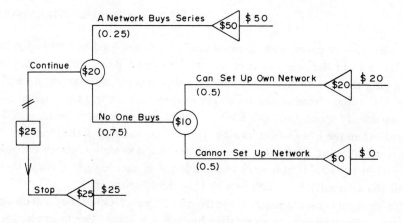

(a) Formulated in Terms of Project Assets.

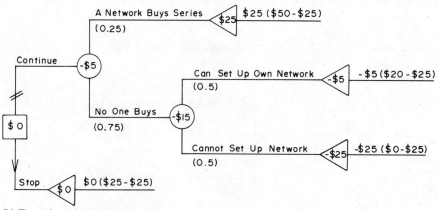

(b) Formulated in Terms of Gains and Losses from Present Assets.

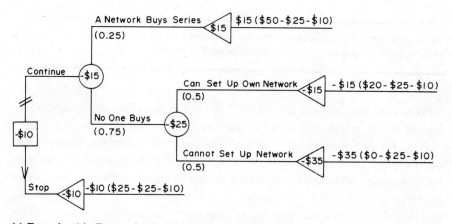

(c) Formulated in Terms of Gains and Losses from Original Assets.

Figure 8–23. RKO's Decision about Whether to Continue Investing in a TV Series, with EMV as the Criterion (All Dollar Figures in Millions).

Finally, this stop/continue decision could be formulated in terms of gains and losses from the original asset position (before RKO spent anything on developing the series) (figure 8–23c). This would mean subtracting an additional $10 million from all the monetary outcomes, to reflect the original $10 million already spent. Still, the EMV of the stop alternative is better—by $5 million—than the EMV of continuing. The relative ranking of the two alternatives is not affected. This is because the $10 million in sunk costs affects both alternatives equally. If you want to include them, you have to include them for all the alternatives—which is why they don't count.

This logic causes some people some trouble, however. Often they will charge the sunk costs against one alternative but not the other. For example, they might charge it against the stop alternative, but not against the one for continuing the project (see figure 8–24). The reasoning might go something like "If

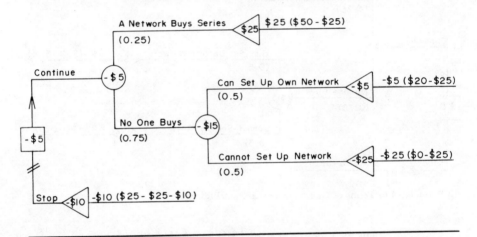

Figure 8–24. RKO's Decision about Whether to Continue Investing in a TV Series, with Sunk Costs Applied to Only One Alternative (All Dollar Figures in Millions).

we stop now, we will have wasted the $10 million, but if we continue developing the series, it will only cost $25 million to complete it."

It is this desire to avoid "wasting" the sunk costs that leads people and governments (and occasionally, though less often, businesses) to continue half-completed projects even though it should be clear—if the analysis is done correctly and the sunk costs ignored—that the potential payoff is less than the additional cost.[32] In a desire to justify sunk costs, people often pursue projects that should be terminated.[33]

The easiest way to avoid this mistake is always to formulate a decision problem in terms of final assets. This puts all costs on an equal basis—they

Money and Risk

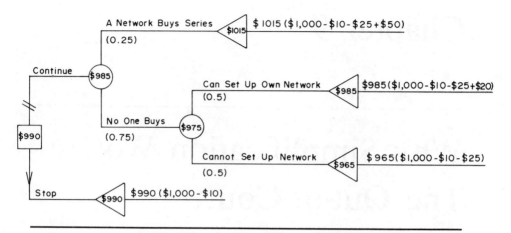

Figure 8–25. RKO's Decision about Whether to Continue Investing in a TV Series, Formulated in Terms of Final Assets (All Dollar Figures in Millions).

all must be subtracted from the original asset position to produce final assets. And, again, this formulation puts the decision in the proper perspective; costs and benefits are viewed not as losses or winnings but merely as debits or credits to be subtracted from or added to other assets. The decision tree in figure 8–25 thus provides the least-delusive view of RKO's stop/continue decision.

Chapter 9

Why Simplification Works: The Out-of-Court Settlement Decision Revisited

FLASHBACK to J. C. "Cookie" Phillips. The last time we saw him, he was sitting in a courtroom doing a bit of quick analysis to help decide whether to accept a $400,000 out-of-court settlement. Phillips had been injured in an automobile accident and had filed suit for $1.5 million; the defendant's insurance company had offered to settle for $400,000.

For his first-cut analysis, Phillips used a decision sapling and a median estimate of $1.1 million for the uncertain amount of any jury award. This analysis suggested that the settlement was slightly—just slightly—better (see figure 6–7). Then, Phillips took a second cut at his decision, approximating the range of possible jury awards with a two-branch outcome fork, with $1.3 million for his upper-quartile estimate and $750,000 for his lower quartile. The results of this analysis were also close, again slightly favoring a decision to accept the settlement (see figure 6–10, reproduced below as figure 9–1).

Now what should Phillips do? So far, his analysis has hardly been convincing enough to help much in making the decision. Should Phillips undertake some additional work with a more sophisticated (less drastic) simplification for the range of risk? Or is now the right time to do some sensitivity analysis?

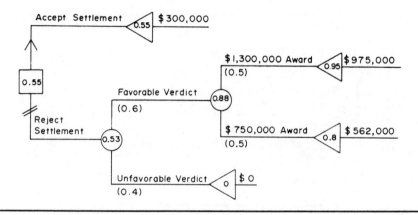

Figure 9–1. The Second-Cut Analysis of J. C. Phillips's Out-of-Court Settlement Dilemma.

Phillips's Preference Curve

Before these questions are answered, a confession is in order. The preference-probabilities used in chapter 6 to help analyze Cookie Phillips's dilemma were not each assessed individually. Rather, a preference curve was first assessed (figure 9–2), and *then* the necessary preference-probabilities were simply read off this graph.

For this dilemma, the range of possible monetary outcomes (after the lawyer's fee) is $0 to $1.2 million. With these two amounts as the reference outcomes, Phillips decides that he is indifferent between a 50-50 chance at $1.2 million or nothing and a certain monetary equivalent of $250,000. In other words, for Phillips, the preference-probability for $250,000 is 0.5, and this point is marked with a ○ in figure 9–2. (See chapter 8 for a discussion of how to develop preference curves. Using that process, he determines the monetary outcomes for which his preference-probabilities are 0.25 and 0.75—$90,000 and $500,000, respectively. These points are also marked with a ○ on figure 9–2, and a preference curve is fared through the five monetary-outcome/preference-probability points: $0/0; $90,000/0.25; $250,000/0.5; $500,000/0.75; $1,200,000/1.0.)

Phillips is obviously very risk averse. (His risk premium for a 50-50 gamble on $1.2 million or $0 is $350,000. His risk index for this range is 0.58.) But this is quite reasonable, since a $1 million award—or even $400,000—would overwhelm his present assets.

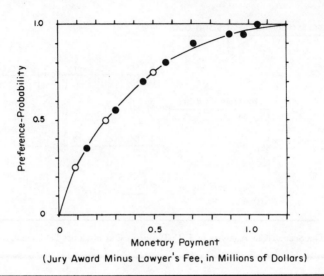

Figure 9–2. J. C. Phillips's Preference Curve.

The black dots on the preference curve are not the points used to assess it but those needed to analyze Phillips's dilemma. For example, in the second-cut analysis (figure 9–1), it was necessary to assess preference-probabilities for outcomes of $0, $300,000, $562,500, and $975,000. The preference-probabilities for these outcomes were read from the preference curve as 0, 0.55, 0.8, and 0.95.

Note that the preference-probability for $975,000 is 0.95, not 0.963. Preference-probabilities are not read from the curve to three significant figures; that would just be another example of phoney precision, since the preference curve itself was developed from the certain monetary equivalents for just a few 50-50 gambles. And these CMEs were not precise numbers. Phillips did decide that $250,000 was his CME for the 0.5 reference gamble between $0 and $1.2 million, but that just reflected his conviction that the CME should be somewhere between $200,000 and $300,000—or maybe somewhere between $150,000 and $350,000. Consequently, the $250,000/0.5 point on the preference curve is not a precise one, and it would be absurd to claim that a curve fared through this and a few other points is accurate to three significant figures. Accordingly, all the preference-probabilities read from Phillips's preference curve have either only one significant figure (e.g., 0.3 or 0.9) or two digits, of which the second is a five (as in 0.65 or 0.85).

Why Simplification Works

A Third-Cut Analysis

With a preference curve now providing the basis for assessing a preference-probability for any possible outcome, Phillips can undertake further analysis. For Phillips is not too confident about the results of his second cut; the preference-probabilities for the two alternatives (0.55 and 0.53) are still very close. And this result is based on the assumption that the entire range of possible jury awards (from $0 to $1.6 million) could be approximated by just two outcomes ($750,000 and $1.3 million). To Phillips, this seems like too much of a simplification. This analysis does not take into account the benefits that might be gained in the admittedly unlikely event that the jury made an award greater than $1.3 million. Nor does it reflect the possibility that the award might be quite small—as small as the $400,000 settlement offer, or even smaller.

Consequently, Phillips decides to undertake a more sophisticated, third-cut analysis by using four possible outcomes to represent the uncertainty of the jury award. This additional analysis is designed to give him a better assessment of his preference for the uncertain outcome of a favorable verdict, and thus for the reject-settlement alternative.

Phillips subdivides the two ranges he used in his second-cut analysis (high award and low award) into two ranges each. The high award range, $1.1 million to $1.6 million, which was previously approximated by a $1.3 million award, is now approximated by two, equally probable awards: $1.2 million and $1.4 million. Similarly, the low award range, $0 to $1.1 million, which was previously approximated by a $750,000 award, is now represented by two, equally probable outcomes: $400,000 and $950,000 (figure 9–3).

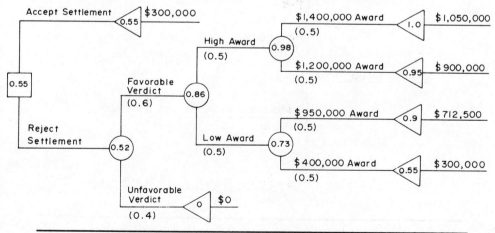

Figure 9–3. A Third-Cut Analysis of Phillips's Out-of-Court Settlement Dilemma.

Now there are six monetary outcomes, but their preference-probabilities can be easily assessed using the preference curve (of figure 9–2). Then, applying the substitution principle, the preference-probabilities for a high award, a low award, a favorable verdict, and the reject-settlement alternative can be assessed indirectly (using the procedure described in the appendix to chapter 6). The results are shown in figure 9–3.

Compared with the second cut, this third-cut analysis changes several preference-probabilities (as can be seen by comparing figures 9–1 and 9–3). The preference-probability of a high award has increased slightly (from 0.95 to 0.98), while that for a low award has decreased more (from 0.8 to 0.73). The result is a slight decrease in the preference-probability of a favorable verdict (0.88 to 0.86) and an even smaller decrease in the preference-probability of the reject-settlement alternative (from 0.53 to 0.52). Again, it looks like Phillips prefers the certain alternative of accepting the settlement, but the preference-probabilities for the two choices (0.55 and 0.52) are still not very far apart.

Note that subdividing each of the two, equally probable outcomes (the high award and the low award) into two equally probable outcomes is the same as approximating the entire range of possible jury awards by four outcomes of equal probability. On the third-cut decision tree (figure 9–3), the probability that a favorable verdict will result in a $1.4 million award is $0.5 \times 0.5 = 0.25$. This calculation also applies to the other three possible awards. Consequently, another way to diagram the four possible final outcomes of a favorable verdict is with a four-point, equiprobable outcome fork (figure 9–4). The two collec-

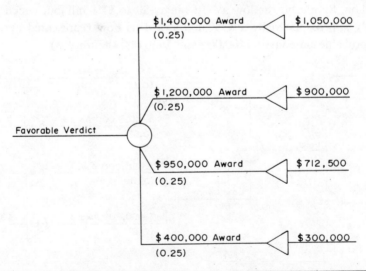

Figure 9–4. Approximating the Uncertain Jury Award with a Four-Branch, Equiprobable Outcome Fork.

tions of nodes and branches attached to the favorable-verdict outcome branch in figures 9–3 and 9–4 indicate identical chances of getting the four representative jury awards. The first diagram (figure 9–3) was used for the third-cut analysis, however, so that Phillips could compare the preference-probabilities he assessed in the second and third cuts for a high award and a low award.

Specifying Uncertainty: Octiles

The four estimates used to approximate the entire range of possible jury awards in the third-cut analysis are often called the *octiles;* $400,000 was the lower octile, $950,000 was the third octile, $1.2 million the fifth octile, and $1.4 million the upper octile. These four estimates are called octiles because, along with the two quartiles and the median, they divide the range of possible outcomes into eight equiprobable subranges. As figure 9–5 indicates,

- The lower octile is also the 12.5th percentile.
- The lower quartile (or second octile) is the 25th percentile.
- The third octile is the 37.5th percentile.
- The median (or fourth octile) is the 50th percentile.
- The fifth octile is the 62.5th percentile.
- The upper quartile (or sixth octile) is the 75th percentile.
- The upper octile is also the 87.5th percentile.

Accordingly, there is a 12.5-percent or one-eighth chance that the actual outcome will fall within any one of these eight subranges defined by the seven octile estimates. (Note also that there is a 75-percent chance that the actual outcome will be between the lower and upper octile estimates—the lower and upper octiles define a 75-percent confidence interval.)

As figure 9–5 also shows, the lower-quartile, median, and upper-quartile estimates divide the range of possible jury awards into four subranges of equal likelihood. And at the probabilistic midpoint of each of these four ranges is one of the octile estimates. For example, there is a 25-percent chance that the award will be between $750,000 (the lower quartile) and $1,100,000 (the median), and dividing that range into two subranges is the third octile, at $950,000. This means that *if* the award falls between the lower-quartile and median estimates, it is as likely that it will be below the third octile (though above the lower quartile) as it is that it will be above the third octile (though below the median).

This explains why, in the third-cut analysis, all the possible jury awards could be approximated by these four estimates—the lower, third, fifth, and

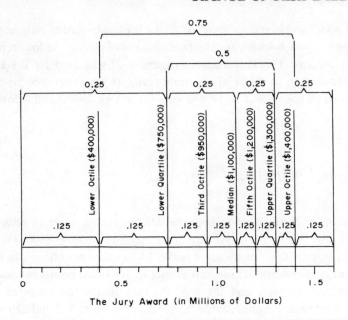

Figure 9–5. Eight Equiprobable Ranges for the Jury Award, Created by Phillips's Octile, Quartile, and Median Estimates.

upper octiles. The entire range of awards is first divided into four subranges. Then, each of these four subranges is approximated by a single number—by the award that is at the probabilistic midpoint of that subrange. (In the first cut, all of the possible outcomes were approximated by a single number, the median estimate, which is at the probabilistic midpoint of the whole range of possible outcomes. In the second cut, the approximation was based on two estimates, the upper and lower quartiles, which are at the probabilistic midpoints of the two equiprobable subranges.) On the third-cut decision tree, each of these four awards has a 25-percent chance of being the outcome of a favorable verdict, for they are each approximating a range of possible outcomes into which there is a 25-percent chance that the jury award will actually fall.

Specifying Uncertainty: Uncertainty Curves

There is one more concept that helps one think about estimates of uncertain quantities: the *uncertainty curve*. This simple graph specifies the probability that the actual outcome will be below any particular number. For example, given J. C. Phillips's previous assessments, he thinks that there is a 12.5-percent chance that a jury award would be less than $400,000. He also thinks

Why Simplification Works

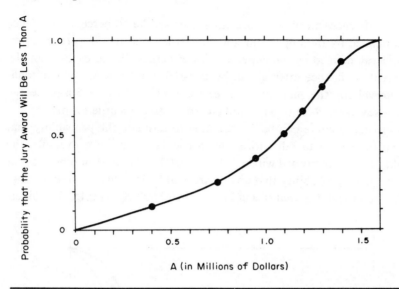

Figure 9–6. Uncertainty Curve for a Jury Award.

there is a 25-percent chance that any award will be less than $750,000, a 37.5-percent chance that it will be below $950,000, etc. Phillips's seven estimates can be plotted on a graph, and a curve fared through these points (see figure 9–6).

To determine from an uncertainty curve the probability that the actual outcome will be below any specific number, read up from that number on the bottom axis to the curve and then across to the left axis. The probability that the jury award will be less than $900,000, for example, is 0.34.

Conversely, to determine a specific percentile estimate for the uncertain outcome (i.e. that estimate for which there is a given probability that the actual outcome will fall below it), read across from the given probability (or percentile) on the left-hand axis to the curve and then down to the estimate on the bottom axis. For example, the tenth-percentile estimate of the jury award is $330,000. This means there is a ten-percent chance that the jury award will be less than $330,000.

An uncertainty curve is also called a *cumulative probability distribution,* since it indicates the probability that the actual outcome will fall in the range below any given number; it "cumulates" the probabilities of all the possible outcomes below that number. The uncertainty curve is thus always ascending; the probability that any jury award will be less than $800,000 clearly must be as large or larger than the probability that any award will be less than $700,000. (These two cumulative probabilities could be the same only if there were no chance that the award could be between $700,000 and $800,000.)

Note that once an uncertainty curve has been assessed, it can be used to estimate confidence intervals. There already exists the 50-percent confidence interval, defined by the upper and lower quartiles, and the 75-percent confidence interval, defined by the upper and lower octiles. But also, for example, a 90-percent confidence interval can be assessed. Phillips's 90-percent confidence interval for the jury award goes from $170,000 (the 5th-percentile estimate—see figure 9–6) to $1.5 million (the 95th-percentile estimate).

An uncertainty curve can be further used to estimate the probability that the actual outcome will fall within any particular range. For example, the probability that a jury award will be between $500,000 and $1 million is about 25 percent. (The probability that any award will be less than $1 million is 41 percent. The probability that it will be less than $500,000 is 0.15. The differ-

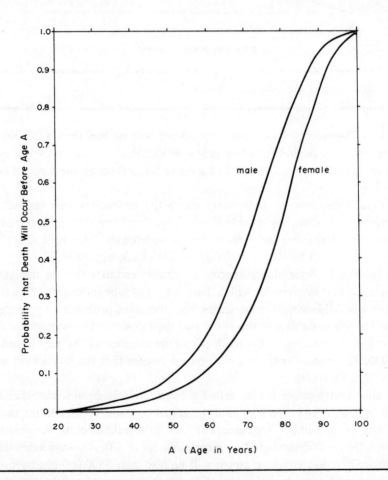

Figure 9–7. Lifespan Estimates: Uncertainty Curves of Age at Death for Two Healthy Twenty-Year-Old College Students, One Male and One Female.

ence, 0.41 − 0.15, is 0.26. For additional characteristics of uncertainty curves, see the appendix to this chapter.)

Clearly, an estimate in the form of an uncertainty curve provides much more information than a point estimate. It includes not only a median, or "best-guess" estimate but a very specific indication of the assessor's uncertainty about that best guess over the entire range of possible outcomes. Take, for example, the lifespan estimates in figure 9–7. These uncertainty curves are for two healthy twenty-year-old college students, one male and one female. They do not reflect the group statistics for all twenty-year-olds, but rather subjective judgments about the lifespans of two individual students with particular health characteristics.

These curves provide much more information than a single point estimate of life expectancy. For the male, there is a 50-percent chance that he will live to age 72[1], but a 10-percent chance that he will die before 51. There is also a 10-percent chance that he will live to be 87. For the female, there is only a 28-percent chance that she will die before age 72. She has a 50-percent chance of living to 80 and a 10-percent chance to live to be over 92. And she has a 10-percent chance of dying before age 58.

A Final Cut

The analytical process of subdividing equally probable intervals into smaller intervals can be continued to obtain a more detailed approximation of the possible outcomes for an uncertain quantity. For example, Cookie Phillips could subdivide the four ranges for the jury award into eight subranges. Indeed, the octile estimates developed in the second cut already do that (see figure 9–5); all that must be done now is to determine the probabilistic mid-points of each of the eight ranges so that these eight estimates can be used on an eight-branch, equiprobable outcome fork. The lowest subrange (below the lower octile), for example, would be approximated by the 6.25th-percentile estimate; this estimate would be assigned to the lowest outcome branch on the eight-branch outcome fork and given the probability 0.125 (which is the probability that the actual jury award will fall below the lower-octile estimate). This general procedure for subdividing intervals is just an extension of the particular ones used to develop the two-branch and four-branch outcome forks. Equally probable intervals are defined and then the possible outcome that is at the probabilistic midpoint of each interval is selected as a representative outcome to stand for the entire interval.

In some situations, however, it may not be necessary to subdivide further all of the intervals; it may be helpful to subdivide only some. Decision analysis is not a mechanical process; to help resolve a dilemma, its concepts need to be adapted to the specifics of the decision. For Cookie Phillips, who needs to decide whether to accept the out-of-court settlement, the most difficult issue is determining his preference-probability for the reject-settlement alternative, which is in turn very dependent upon the preference-probability for the outcome of a favorable verdict, the jury award. So far, Phillips has concentrated most of his analytical energies on determining his preference-probability for the uncertain jury award. And he could get a better handle on that preference-probability by approximating the entire range of possible awards by eight rather than four outcomes. But it is not clear that the results of all this analytical work would be justified. The preference-probability of a high award (that is, for awards above the median estimate of $1.1 million) is up around 0.95 or 0.98. This assessment is not apt to change much even with a more sophisticated analysis. This is because Phillips, with assets significantly less than $1 million, has a difficult time distinguishing the differential impact of getting $1.05 million as opposed to "only" $900,000.

The same is not true, however, for the lowest jury awards. There is a 25-percent chance (according to Phillips's assessments) that the award will be between $0 and $750,000, and where the award falls in that range could be significant. To Phillips, whether he receives $200,000 or $400,000 is important. (This is indicated by the shape of the preference curve in figure 9–2. At the upper end of the curve, the monetary outcomes can change by several hundred thousand dollars without affecting the preference-probability significantly. At the lower end, however, a change in the monetary outcome of $100,000 has a significant impact upon Phillips's preference-probability.)

For this reason, Phillips decides to focus his additional energies on only the range of possible outcomes below the lowest quartile ($750,000). In the third-cut analysis, he approximated this range by his lower-octile estimate of $400,000; the monetary outcome for Phillips was 75 percent of this, or $300,000, with a preference-probability of 0.55. Now he decomposes that range into two subranges: $0 to $400,000 (below the lower octile), and $400,000 to $750,000 (between the lower octile and the lower quartile). There is a 12.5-percent chance that the actual award will fall in either of these two ranges.

The remaining task is to determine the two estimates that will be used to approximate these two ranges. Since the lowest range of $0 to $400,000 goes from 0 to the 12.5th percentile, the probabilistic midpoint of this range is the 6.25th-percentile estimate. From Phillips's uncertainty curve (figure 9–6), this is just about $200,000. The other range, $400,000 to $750,000, goes from the 12.5th to 25th percentiles, so the probabilistic midpoint of this range is the 18.75th percentile, or about $600,000 (from figure 9–6). Consequently, the very low award of $400,000 in the third-cut analysis can be replaced with two

Why Simplification Works

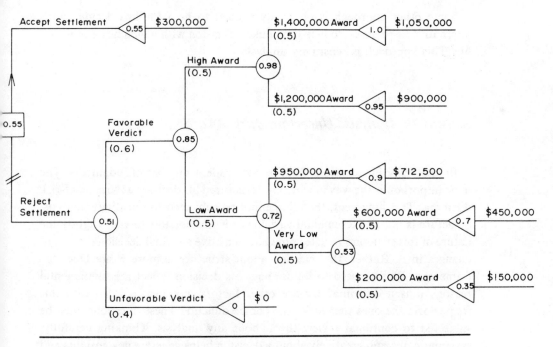

Figure 9–8. A Final-Cut Analysis of Phillips's Out-of-Court Settlement Dilemma.

outcomes: $200,000 and $600,000 (see figure 9–8). If there is a favorable verdict, the probability that the jury award will be $600,000 is 0.125. (0.5 × 0.5 × 0.5 = 0.125.) Similarly, the probability that a favorable verdict will result in a $200,000 award is also 0.125.

If the award were $600,000, Phillips would receive $450,000, and his preference-probability for this outcome is 0.7 (from his preference curve, figure 9–2). From a $200,000 award, Phillips would receive $150,000, for which his preference-probability is 0.35.

As always, Phillips uses the substitution principle to resolve his dilemma. The results are shown in figure 9–8. The preference-probability for a very low award has dropped from 0.55 (for the third cut) to 0.53; the preference-probability for a low award has declined from 0.73 to 0.72; that for a favorable verdict is also down, from 0.86 to 0.85. And thus the preference-probability for the reject-settlement alternative drops as well—from 0.52 to 0.51.[2]

The results of these two more sophisticated analyses, the third and final cuts, have caused Phillips to reassess his preference-probability for the reject-settlement alternative downward, but only slightly. This preference-probability has dropped from 0.53 in the second cut to 0.51 in the final cut. This has not helped him much in his effort to compare this option with the accept-settlement alternative. And that, after all, is the purpose of the analysis.

Some other approach is obviously needed to help Phillips decide which alternative he prefers—to help him make a decision with which he is comfortable. This approach is sensitivity analysis.

Sensitivity Analysis: Uncertain Jury Award

In analyzing his decision, Phillips has made a number of judgments. The most important is the way in which he structured his decision as a range-of-risk dilemma. This judgment, though, cannot be subjected to sensitivity analysis. Structure is not an incremental variable; it is not possible to vary slightly the nature of this structure to determine how sensitive any final decision is to small changes in it. Rather, the question about structure is more basic: Does the framework Phillips used to think about his decision reflect the fundamental reasons it is a dilemma? Or are other factors, not incorporated into this framework, the ones that make the choice difficult? These questions must be subjected to continual review throughout any analysis. Thinking carefully, systematically, and creatively about a decision helps generate new insights and can suggest whether it is necessary to try an entirely different approach. If Phillips is having a difficult time making this decision precisely because he is faced with a choice between a riskless alternative and a risky one that is complicated by a range of risk, then this structure is indeed appropriate. The only question that remains is how detailed to make that structure—how simplified can the analysis be and still resolve the decision to his satisfaction?

Phillips has made three assessments that are subject to sensitivity analysis: the uncertainty concerning the verdict, the range of risk involved in the uncertain jury award, and his preferences for the monetary outcomes. For no particular reason, he begins his sensitivity analysis by looking at the uncertainty involved in the jury award.

Two general factors are involved in assessing the range of risk for any uncertain quantity: the probabilistic "center" of the range of possible outcomes, which is indicated by the median estimate;[3] and the dispersion of possible outcomes around that center, which is described by the interquartile range (or the 75-percent confidence interval, or the 90-percent confidence interval, or whatever). An uncertainty curve captures both of these characteristics. Varying the center of the uncertainty simply means moving that curve to the left or right. Varying the dispersion means spreading out the interquartile range or squeezing it together. (See the appendix to this chapter.)

For Phillips's assessment of his uncertainty about the jury award (figure 9–6), it is not really possible to increase the dispersion very much, since the range of possible outcomes has fixed bounds of $0 and $1.6 million. The curve could be made steeper near the median, to indicate greater certainty about the size of the jury award, but this would reflect unwarranted overconfidence, since the base-rate data from similar law suits would indicate that the range of possible jury awards is quite large. (See the discussion under "Assessing Medians and Quartiles" in chapter 7.)

It also does not make much sense to check the sensitivity of the decision to a lowering of the median estimate for the jury award. This would mean that any jury award would be, on the average, less, and thus the reject-settlement alternative would be even less attractive. Such a reevaluation would only reinforce the current conclusion to accept the settlement.

But what happens if the median estimate of the jury award is increased? This would increase Phillips's preference-probability for the outcome of a favorable verdict and thus for the reject-settlement alternative. It might make rejecting the settlement more desirable than accepting it.

Suppose he reassesses his median estimate for the jury award to be $1.2 million rather than $1.1 million. Since the award cannot be greater than $1.6 million, his median estimate cannot be too close to that. Indeed, even though the award will be made by a jury that has already rendered a favorable verdict, $1.2 million is quite a high median estimate. Still, thinks Phillips, it might be possible for a number as high as $1.2 million to divide the range of possible jury awards into two, equiprobable subranges.

An uncertainty curve for the award with $1.2 million as the median estimate

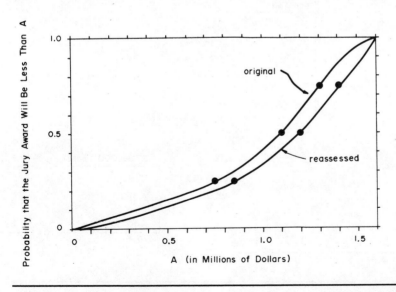

Figure 9–9. Sensitivity Analysis: Reassessing the Uncertainty Curve for the Jury Award.

and $850,000 and $1.4 million as the lower and upper quartiles, respectively, is shown in figure 9–9. (The original uncertainty curve is also shown here.) This new curve can be used to test whether Phillips's decision to accept the settlement (based on his final-cut analysis) is sensitive to an upward shift of about $100,000 in his uncertainty curve.

From this new uncertainty curve, Phillips obtains the estimates needed to approximate the range of possible jury awards on the final-cut decision tree (figure 9–10). Then, he obtains the necessary preference-probabilities from his preference curve (figure 9–2) and, using the substitution principle, assesses indirectly his preference-probability for the reject-settlement alternative. It is 0.52—up only slightly from the 0.51 obtained using the original uncertainty curve.

Why is this decision so insensitive to a hundred-thousand-dollar shift in the uncertainty curve? Part of the reason is that the preference-probabilities do not change very much for the larger jury awards. In fact, the preference-probability for a high jury award, which is used to approximate all the outcomes greater than the median, is still 0.98. It cannot go much higher, but the reason for this is not some mathematical quirk. Rather, it is the result of the difficult time Phillips has had distinguishing among monetary payments such

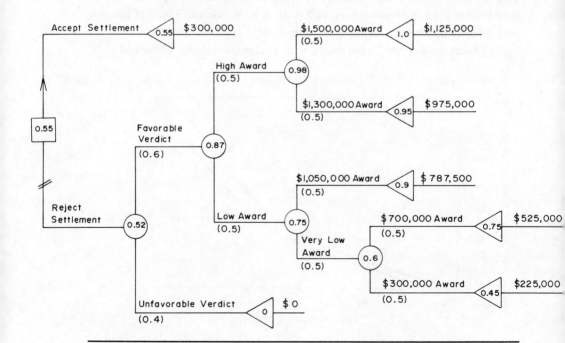

Figure 9–10. A Sensitivity Analysis for a $100,000 Shift in the Uncertainty Curve.

Why Simplification Works

as $900,000, $1 million, and $1.1 million. To Phillips, it makes little difference whether he approximates the upper half of the range of jury awards with two payments of $1,125,000 and $975,000 or of $1,050,000 and $900,000. If he had to choose, he would, of course, choose the pair with the larger payments. But given his financial position, either combination is so fantastic that it is hard to determine the differential happiness that the larger pair would bring.

The preference-probability for the range of outcomes below the median (those outcomes approximated by a low award) did increase, from 0.72 to 0.75. That was not significant enough, however, to have much impact upon the preference-probability for the reject-settlement alternative.

Rather, the major reason why Phillips's decision is quite insensitive to a reassessment of the possible jury awards is that he cannot get any jury award until after there is a favorable verdict. And he thinks there is only a 60-percent chance of getting a favorable verdict.

Here a little switch-point analysis is revealing. If V_r is the preference-probability for the reject-settlement alternative and V_f is the preference-probability for a favorable verdict, then the relationship between the two is given by $V_r = 0.6 \times V_f$. Given this, how large must V_f be to make V_r greater than 0.55 (which is the preference-probability for the accept-settlement alternative)? The answer is obtained by solving the above equation for V_f: $V_f = V_r/0.6$. Then, for V_r to be 0.55, V_f must be 0.55/0.6 = 0.92. Thus, for the preference-probability of rejecting the settlement to be greater than for accepting it, the preference-probability for the outcome of a favorable verdict must be greater than 0.92.

This, in turn, has implications for how high the preference-probability for the lower half of the jury awards must be. Let V_{la} be the preference-probability of a low award, and let V_{ha} stand for the preference-probability of a high award (the upper half of the awards). Then, even if V_{ha} goes all the way up to 1.0, the preference-probability for the lower half must go up to at least 0.84 for V_f to be 0.92. This can be seen by substituting $V_f = 0.92$ and $V_{ha} = 1.0$ in the equation that expresses the preference-probabilities for a favorable verdict in terms of the preference-probabilities of the high and low awards:

$$V_f = [(0.5 \times V_{ha}) + (0.5 \times V_{la})].$$
$$0.92 = [(0.5 \times 1.0) + (0.5 \times V_{la})].$$

Solving for V_{la} gives

$$V_{la} = \frac{(0.92) - (0.5 \times 1.0)}{(0.5)} = \frac{0.42}{0.5} = 0.84.$$

Thus, for Phillips to switch from accepting to rejecting the settlement, the preference-probability for a low award would have to increase from the 0.72

of the final cut of the original analysis to 0.84, from this sensitivity analysis. That is a very large change—too large to result from some small reassessment of his uncertainty about the amount of any jury award. Phillips's uncertainty curve would have to shift drastically to the right for V_{la} to get as high as 0.84. This sensitivity analysis helps confirm his decision to accept the settlement.

Sensitivity Analysis: Preferences

Phillips also needs to check if his decision is sensitive to his preferences—to the preference-probabilities he assessed for the various monetary outcomes. These preference-probabilities were all assessed indirectly, however, using a preference curve. Consequently, this sensitivity analysis involves checking to see how sensitive his decision is to change in his preference curve, for which the basic parameter is risk aversion. So what he really needs to do is to determine how sensitive his decision is to changes in his risk aversion as expressed by his CME (or risk premium) for a 50-50 gamble for $1.2 million and $0.

Originally, he had decided that he was indifferent between this 50-50 reference gamble and $250,000 for sure. But maybe he is more risk averse than that. Would he really give up a certain $250,000 for only a 50-percent chance at $1.2 million, when there was also a 50-percent chance he would end up with nothing? Perhaps. But such a reassessment would only reenforce his original decision. From his final-cut analysis, Phillips concluded that he still preferred the riskless alternative to the risky one. If he now decides that he is more risk averse than he originally thought (if he decides to use a preference curve reflecting greater risk aversion to help assess his preference-probabilities for the different monetary outcomes), then any reanalysis would only make the risky alterative look even worse in comparison with the riskless choice. Greater risk aversion can only make a riskier alternative less desirable. Consequently, Phillips would gain nothing by analyzing the implications of using a preference curve with greater risk aversion, for he already knows the implications of that change.

But suppose Phillips, upon rethinking his CME for the 50-50 gamble for $1.2 million or $0, decides he is really *less* risk averse than he originally thought? Maybe, he thinks, his CME should be $300,000, or even $400,000. If he is really less risk averse, it might shift his choice in favor of the risky alternative. How can he check this out?

The first thing to do might be a simple EMV analysis based on the assumption that Phillips is not at all risk averse—that he is risk neutral. This can be done either by using a straight-line preference curve or by simply determining

Why Simplification Works

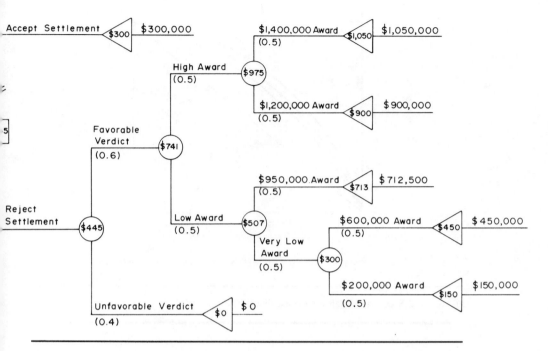

Figure 9–11. An EMV Analysis of Phillips's Out-of-Court Settlement Dilemma (All Dollar Figures Inside Nodes Are in Thousands).

the expected monetary outcome for each uncertainty (as was done in the appendix to chapter 8). This EMV analysis is shown in figure 9–11. Clearly, the expected monetary value of the risky, reject-settlement alternative is much higher than the certain $300,000 obtained by accepting the settlement. If Phillips were not at all risk averse, he would certainly reject the settlement.

This EMV analysis may appear to have been unproductive. But what if it had revealed that Phillips preferred the accept-settlement alternative even if he was risk neutral? Then, there would have been no need to do any more sensitivity analysis for Phillips's preferences—such results of an EMV analysis would have indicated that he preferred to accept the settlement under all possible degrees of risk aversion. This was not the case, but the EMV calculations are so easy to do that it is worth making this small effort.

Moreover, the EMV analysis does reveal that there exists a preference curve, somewhere between the original one assessed by Phillips and the straight EMV line, that will make him exactly indifferent between the two alternatives. This *switch curve* will divide all possible preference curves into two categories. For preference curves with greater bends in them than the switch curve (reflecting greater risk aversion), Phillips will prefer the riskless alternative. (These curves will all lie to the left of the switch curve.) For preference curves with less bend

251

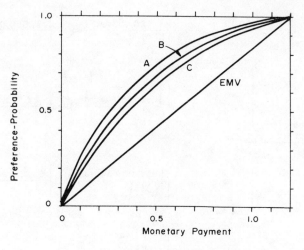

(Jury Award Minus Lawyer's Fee in Millions of Dollars)

Figure 9–12. Sensitivity Analysis: Reassessing the Preference Curve.

(indicating less risk aversion), he will prefer the risky alternative. (These curves will all lie to the right of the switch curve.)

To find the switch curve, Phillips draws two more preference curves (figure 9–12). The A curve is the original one, with a CME of $250,000 for the 50-50, $1.2 million/$0 reference gamble. The B curve is one for which this CME is $300,000. For the C curve, this CME is $350,000. The B curve reflects less risk aversion than A, and curve C indicates still less risk aversion. As a reference, the EMV line is also shown.

From these three preference curves, the preference-probabilities for the various monetary outcomes of the final cut are assessed and shown on figure 9–13. Inside each node are three preference-probabilities. The upper one is for the original, A, curve and is the same as on the final-cut decision tree of figure 9–8. The middle one is for preference curve B, and the lower is for C.

As risk aversion decreases, the related preference curve moves toward the EMV line, downward and to the right. Thus, as risk aversion decreases, the preference-probability for any particular monetary outcome (except for the two reference outcomes) also decreases. For example, the preference-probability for a $300,000 outcome is 0.55 for curve A, 0.5 for the B curve, and 0.45 for C. Accordingly, for all the terminal nodes on the decision tree of figure 9–13 (except the one for the reference outcome of $0), the preference-probabilities decrease from top to bottom as risk aversion decreases from A to B to C.

Why Simplification Works

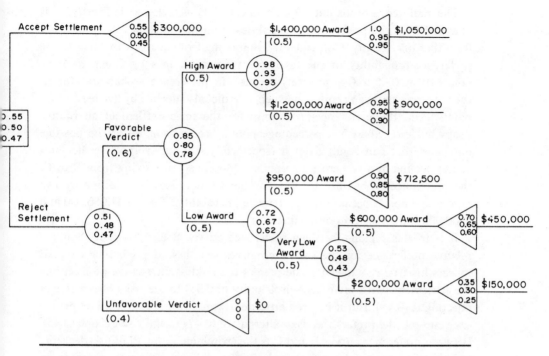

Figure 9–13. A Sensitivity Analysis for Preferences, Using Three Different Preference Curves, Reflecting Different Degrees of Risk Aversion.

This means that the preference-probabilities inside all the uncertainty nodes will also decrease from top to bottom as risk aversion decreases. Significantly, however, the preference-probability for the riskless (accept-settlement) alternative drops more rapidly (from 0.55 to 0.5 to 0.45) than does the one for the risky (reject-settlement) alternative. This phenomenon—as risk aversion decreases, the preference-probability drops more quickly for the least risky alternative—is a characteristic of risk aversion itself.

The preference-probability does not drop as fast for the riskier alternative because it involves a chance at both higher and lower outcomes than the outcome(s) of the less risky alternative. That, after all, is why the riskier alternative is riskier. But because the preference curve is bowed above the EMV line more at the middle than at the ends, the preference-probabilities for extreme outcomes (near $0 and $1.2 million) do not change as rapidly as do those for outcomes nearer the middle of the range. In fact, the preference-probability for the outcome of an unfavorable verdict ($0) remains unchanged at 0 regardless of the degree of risk aversion. And the preference-probabilities for the high-award outcomes of $900,000 and $1,050,000 change negligibly as risk aversion declines from B to C.

The preference-probability for an uncertainty is assessed indirectly; it is obtained from the preference-probabilities of all the outcomes that can result from that uncertainty. Consequently, in moving from curve A to curve B, the preference-probability of the favorable verdict declines by five percentage points (from 0.85 to 0.8) precisely because the preference-probabilities for *all* the outcomes that can result from such a verdict also decline by five percentage points.[4] But the preference-probability for the reject-settlement alternative drops by fewer than five percentage points because not all of the possible outcomes that can result from it (specifically, the unfavorable-verdict outcome) decline by five percentage points. Moreover, in moving from B to C, the preference-probability for a favorable verdict does not decline by five percentage points because the preference-probabilities for the $1,050,000 and $900,000 outcomes do not decline at all.

It is in this region—between preference curves B and C—that Phillips's relative preference for the two alternatives switches. If preference curve B reflects his true risk aversion, he prefers the riskless alternative of accepting the settlement (with preference-probability of 0.55) to the risky alternative of rejecting it (0.48). But if his true attitude towards risk is expressed by preference curve C, he prefers the risky alternative (0.47) to the riskless one (0.45). Between preference curves B and C is the switch curve for Phillips's decision.

This sensitivity analysis thus leads Phillips to concentrate his thinking on curves B and C—or, more specifically, on the CMEs that define these two curves. Somewhere between CMEs of $300,000 and $350,000—approximately $325,000—is the CME switch point (which defines the switch curve). Does Phillips think that his CME for the 50-50 gamble for $1.2 million or $0 is less than $325,000? If so, he is too risk averse (for this out-of-court settlement decision, anyway) and should take the riskless alternative of accepting the settlement. Or does he think that his CME for this gamble is more than $325,000? If so, he is not very risk averse (at least in terms of this decision) and should take the risky option of rejecting the settlement.

Preference curves provide an easy way to test the sensitivity of a decision to the decision maker's risk aversion. For it is relatively simple to develop a new set of internally consistent preference-probabilities for *all* the possible outcomes of a decision by just reassessing a CME or two. For Cookie Phillips's decision, the fundamental question concerning his preferences for the various possible outcomes is whether his CME for this 50-50 gamble for $1.2 million or $0 is $300,000 or less, or $350,000 or more. It is the answer to this single question that determines how Phillips's attitude towards risk affects his decision.

Why Simplification Works

Sensitivity Analysis: Uncertain Verdict

To examine the sensitivity of Phillips's decision to the probability that the jury verdict will be favorable, switch-point analysis is helpful. Let V_a, V_f, and V_u be the preference-probabilities for the accept-settlement alternative, the favorable verdict, and the unfavorable verdict, and let p be the probability of a favorable verdict. Then, if he is indifferent between the two alternatives, $V_a = ([p \cdot V_f] + [(1-p) \cdot V_u])$. Noting that V_u is always 0 and solving for p gives $p_{switch} = V_a/V_f$. Thus, for the preference-probabilities assessed in the final cut ($V_a = 0.55$, $V_f = 0.85$), p_{switch} is 0.55/0.85, or 0.65. This means that if Phillips thinks p is greater than 0.65 he should reject the settlement; if he thinks p is less than 0.65 he should accept the settlement.

Phillips's original analysis plus these three sensitivity analyses lead him to the following conclusions:

A. If he believes that he has a 60-percent chance of getting a favorable verdict from the jury, and if his median estimate for any jury award is $1.1 million, with lower- and upper-quartile estimates of $750,000 and $1.3 million, and if he is indifferent between $250,000 for sure and a 50-50 gamble for $1.2 million or $0, then he should accept the out-of-court settlement.

B. But, if he believes that there is a 65-percent or greater chance of getting a favorable verdict, then (all other factors remaining as in A) he should reject the settlement.

C. Or, if he decides that he prefers $350,000 for sure to a 50-50 gamble for $1.2 million and $0, then (all other factors remaining as in A) he should reject the settlement.

D. There is no reasonable shift in his assessment of the uncertain jury award that would by itself convince him to reject the settlement.

Phillips's sensitivity analysis helps him decide what to do for a range of possible assessments of the factors crucial to his decision.

Note that the switch point for each factor depends upon the assessments used for the other two factors. For example, the switch point for p depends upon the uncertainty curve and preference curve used to assess, indirectly, preference-probabilities V_a and V_f. If Phillips decided that his attitude towards risk aversion was reflected better by preference curve C, then p_{switch} would be 0.45/0.78, or 0.58.

The three sensitivity analyses for each of the three factors were done while holding the other two factors constant at their original assessments. But this is not necessary. If, in rethinking his attitude towards risk, Phillips decides that he is less risk averse than he originally thought—if he concludes that his CME for the reference gamble is greater than $250,000, then he will want not only to develop a new preference curve but also to recalculate the switch point for

p using this new curve. For example, doing the sensitivity analysis for p using preference curve C produces the following conclusions:

E. If his median estimate for any jury award is $1.1 million (with lower and upper quartiles of $750,000 and $1.2 million), and if he is indifferent between $350,000 for sure and a 50-50 chance at $1.2 million or $0, then he should reject the settlement if he thinks the probability of getting a favorable verdict is greater than 0.58, but accept it if he thinks this probability is less than 0.58.

F. If he thinks his chance of getting a favorable verdict is 0.58, and if his median estimate for any jury award is $1.1 million (with lower and upper quartiles of $750,000 and $1.2 million), then he should reject the settlement if he thinks he prefers a 50-50 chance at $1.2 million or $0 to a certain payment of $350,000, but he should accept the settlement if he is willing to accept something less than $350,000 rather than take this 50-50 gamble.

Finally, note that this type of thinking can also provide some insight into what is an acceptable out-of-court settlement. For the final-cut analysis, the preference-probability for the reject-settlement alternative was 0.51. The monetary outcome with this preference-probability is (from the preference curve in figure 9–2) $260,000. The insurance company settlement that would give Phillips this payment is $260,000/0.75 = $347,000. This analysis produces the following conclusion:

G. If Phillips thinks he has a 60-percent chance of getting a favorable verdict, and if his median estimate for any jury award is $1.1 million (with lower and upper quartiles of $750,000 and $1.3 million), and if he is indifferent between $250,000 for sure and a 50-50 gamble for $1.2 million or $0, then he should accept any out-of-court settlement greater than $347,000.

It is conditional conclusions such as this that help the decision maker relate his fundamental preferences and beliefs to the immediate decision he must make.

The Importance of Sensitivity Analysis

Sensitivity analysis provides a decision maker with much more insight than does an analysis based on a single assessment of the various factors. The latter provides information of this form: If factor A is 0.5, and factor B is 9 and factor C is 0.7, then you should choose alternative X rather than alternative Y. A sensitivity analysis, however, provides much more useful information: If A is 0.5 or greater, and B is 9 or less, and C is 0.7 or more, then choose alternative X, but if A drops to 0.4, or if B increases to 11, or if C declines to 0.6, then choose Y. A sensitivity analysis provides information about which alternative to choose for a range of assessments of the important factors. Rethinking one's analysis to see how sensitive the conclusions are to the original assessments is an essential part of analytical thinking.

The benefit of sensitivity analysis is that in the process of thinking carefully and specifically about the impact of changes in the factors that create the dilemma, a decision maker can develop new insights into his own beliefs about uncertainty and his own preferences for outcomes. And when he has such insights—when thinking about a factor causes him to reassess it—he then needs to consider the implications of that reassessment by doing a sensitivity analysis based upon it. Doing this will help the decision maker develop a set of conditional decisions (such as B through G), which relate appropriate combinations of the factors to which the decision is most sensitive to the various courses of action.

Why Point Estimates Are Not Good Enough—Continued

In chapter 7, several dangers of using point estimates to make decisions were discussed: (1) Point estimates are often very far off. (2) Point estimates fail to convey any sense of just how uncertain an estimate is. (3) Point estimates prevent a decision maker from taking into account how the range of risk involved in an uncertain outcome might affect the decision. Why the extent of the uncertainty about an outcome can influence a decision can now be examined in more detail. The reason is risk aversion.

Suppose that before Cookie Phillips decided whether to accept or reject the $400,000 out-of-court settlement, the jury reached a favorable verdict.[5] Now the insurance company offers a $1 million out-of-court settlement. Given these new conditions, should Phillips accept this new settlement?

The new situation changes several aspects of Phillips's decision, as is illustrated by the new decision tree, in figure 9–14. But it does not change his attitude towards risk, and it does not necessarily change his assessment of the amount of the uncertain jury award. Remember, the original uncertainty curve was assessed on the assumption that the jury's verdict would be favorable. The only way that the jury can make an award is if it reaches a favorable verdict first, so the median, quartile, and octile estimates used to assess the uncertainty curve of figure 9–6 all assumed that the award would be made by a jury that thought Phillips had been at least somewhat wronged.

It could have been that in announcing its verdict the jury gave some hint

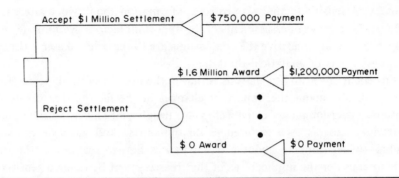

Figure 9–14. J. C. Phillips's New Out-of-Court Settlement Dilemma.

as to whether it was sympathetic towards Phillips's plight, or whether it was philosophically opposed to million-dollar law-suit payments, or whatever. Even the amount of time the jury took deliberating might be interpreted by Phillips's lawyer as providing more information as to the size of the award. But because there exists no such additional information, Phillips decides that he still thinks his original uncertainty curve reflects his best estimate of the uncertain amount of the award.

Were he to use a point estimate to approximate the entire range of possible jury awards, his decision tree would look like that in figure 9–15a. Phillips would make his decision by directly comparing the $1 million settlement with his median (point) estimate of a $1.1 million jury award (though the two monetary payments of $750,000 and $825,000 and their preference-probabilities[6] are also shown on this decision tree). Clearly, an analysis based upon a point estimate suggests that Phillips should reject any settlement less than $1.1 million but accept any offer greater than this.

Is this analysis adequate? Is a point estimate good enough? Does it make any difference if the range of possible jury awards is approximated by a two-branch outcome fork? Figure 9–15b provides the answer. If the range of risk is approximated by a 50-50 chance at the lower- and upper-quartile estimates ($750,000 and $1.3 million), the preference-probability of the risky alternative drops below that of the riskless one. The preference-probability for rejecting the settlement is 0.88, which is the preference-probability for a payment of $720,000. Thus, this analysis, based on a two-branch estimate for the range of risk, implies that Phillips should reject any settlement that is less than $720,000/0.75 = $960,000, but accept any offer over this figure.

What happens if a more sophisticated approximation is used? In the decision tree of figure 9–15c, the range of risk is approximated by a four-branch outcome fork. Using the lower, third, fifth, and upper octile estimates, the

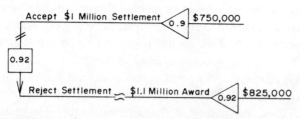

Accept $1 Million Settlement ◁0.9 $750,000

0.92

Reject Settlement ～ $1.1 Million Award ◁0.92 $825,000

(a) Point Estimate

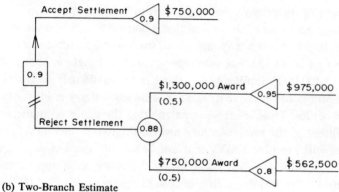

Accept Settlement ◁0.9 $750,000

0.9

$1,300,000 Award ◁0.95 $975,000
(0.5)

Reject Settlement ○0.88

$750,000 Award ◁0.8 $562,500
(0.5)

(b) Two-Branch Estimate

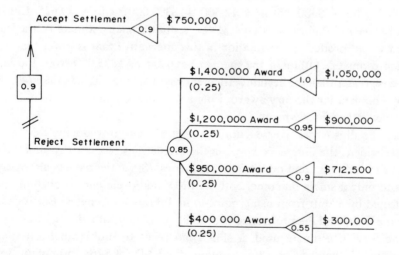

Accept Settlement ◁0.9 $750,000

0.9

$1,400,000 Award ◁1.0 $1,050,000
(0.25)

$1,200,000 Award ◁0.95 $900,000
(0.25)

Reject Settlement ○0.85

$950,000 Award ◁0.9 $712,500
(0.25)

$400 000 Award ◁0.55 $300,000
(0.25)

(c) Four-Branch Estimate

Figure 9–15. Why a Point Estimate Is Not Good Enough: Three Different Analyses of J. C. Phillips's New Out-of-Court Settlement Dilemma.

preference-probability for the risky, reject-settlement alternative drops further, to 0.85,[7] which is equivalent to a certain payment of $670,000. According to this four-branch estimate, Phillips should reject any settlement less than $670,000/0.75 = $893,000, and accept anything greater.

This simple example illustrates why point estimates are not good enough—they can result in poor decisions. Making decisions is, after all, the purpose of any analysis, and thus the quality of the decision is the sole basis for evaluating any analysis or any analytical tool. A point estimate is not good enough when it leads to a decision that does not adequately reflect the decision maker's assessment of uncertainty and/or his attitude towards risk.

In J. C. Phillips's case, part of the reason that a point estimate is inadequate is that his uncertainty curve is not symmetrical; the lower-quartile estimate is below the median by $350,000, but the upper-quartile estimate is above the median by only $200,000. Similarly, the third octile is further below the median than the fifth octile is above it, and the same asymmetry holds for the lower and upper octiles. Thus, even when calculating the expected monetary value of the payment of the uncertain jury award, the two-branch and four-branch estimates will produce EMVs that are below the median payment, which is $0.75 \cdot \$1.1$ million = $825,000. Using the two-branch approximation, the estimate of the EMV for this uncertain payment is ($975,000 + $562,500)/2 = $768,750. Using the four-branch approximation, this estimate is ($1,050,000 + $900,000 + $712,500 + $300,000)/4 = $740,625. Consequently, even if Phillips was an EMVer, a multibranch estimate of the jury award would produce an evaluation of this alternative that is lower than the median estimate. Although the median payment of $825,000 from the jury award is greater than the certain settlement payment of $750,000, the $740,625 EMV, obtained for the jury award using a four-branch approximation, is less than the settlement payment.

Also, Phillips is risk averse—not risk neutral—and introducing this factor further widens the difference between the evaluations of the risky alternative obtained from point and multibranch estimates. (Since the riskless alternative leads to only a single outcome, both its EMV and preference-probability are unaffected by a shift from using point to multibranch estimates. But because both the EMV and the preference-probability of a range of risk can be affected by the type of estimate used, a shift from point to multibranch estimates can also shift the decision.) For example, the EMV of $768,750 obtained by using the two-branch estimate for the risky alternative is still larger than the $750,000 payment from the riskless settlement. But the preference-probability of 0.88 assessed indirectly for the risky alternative using this two-branch approximation is less than the 0.9 preference-probability for the riskless settlement.

Consequently, the conclusion Phillips draws from his analysis depends upon whether he uses a point or multibranch estimate to approximate his range of

TABLE 9–1

How Phillips's Analysis is Affected by the Type of Estimate Used for the Range of Risk and His Attitude Toward Risk

		Attitude Toward Risk	
		Risk Neutral	Risk Averse
Type of Estimate	Point Estimate	Riskless EMV: $750,000 *Risky EMV: $825,000	Riskless Pref-Prob: 0.9 *Risky Pref-Prob: 0.92
Used for Range	Two-Branch Estimate	Riskless EMV: $750,000 *Risky EMV: $768,000	*Riskless Pref-Prob: 0.9 Risky Pref-Prob: 0.88
of Risk	Four-Branch Estimate	*Riskless EMV: $750,000 Risky EMV: $740,625	*Riskless Pref-Prob: 0.9 Risky Pref-Prob: 0.85

The asterisk indicates which alternative the analysis suggests is best.

risk, and upon whether he is risk neutral or risk averse (see table 9–1). Using a point estimate, he concludes that he prefers the risky alternative of rejecting the settlement. (This is true regardless of whether he is risk averse or risk neutral, since with no uncertainty, risk aversion cannot affect the analysis.) Using a two-branch estimate, he concludes, if he is an EMVer, that he still prefers the risky alternative. If, however, he uses a two-branch estimate *and* is risk averse, he does conclude from his analysis that he should choose the riskless alternative.

The importance of the attitude towards risk is due to the bowed shape of a risk-averse preference curve. As you move downwards along such a preference curve, the preference-probability drops off faster than it increases as you move upward along the same curve. For example, the preference-probability of Phillips's median estimate of $825,000 is 0.92. The preference-probability of an outcome of $600,000 ($225,000 below this median) is 0.83, while the preference-probability of an outcome of $1,050,000 ($225,000 above the median) is 0.98. Decreasing the outcome $225,000 below the median estimate lowers the preference-probability by nine percentage points, but increasing the outcome by $225,000 only raises it six percentage points. The more risk averse the decision maker, and thus the more bowed the preference curve, the more dramatic is this differential.

The bowed shape of a risk-averse preference curve means that replacing a single, point estimate with a two-branch estimate is apt to lower the preference-probability assessed for any range of risk.[8] For Phillips's uncertain jury award, for example, the preference-probability of the upper quartile is 0.95 (only three percentage points above the median's), while the preference-probability of the lower quartile is 0.8 (or twelve points below the median's). These combine (using the substitution principle) to produce a preference-probability that is $(12 - 3)/2 = 4.5$ percentage points below the one obtained using only the median estimate.[9]

Whenever a decision maker is strongly risk averse, a point estimate for a range of risk simply will not do. It is necessary to take into account—explicitly and carefully, if also quickly—how this risk aversion may affect the decision. To do this, it helps to decompose the uncertainty involved by using at least a two-branch outcome fork and using a preference curve to indirectly assess one's preference for the range of risk. This type of analysis is necessary to prevent a point estimate from leading to an inappropriate decision.

Why Simplification Works

As Cookie Phillips's dilemma illustrates, a very simplified analysis can be quite valuable. In fact, little insight is gained by using a more detailed decomposition, such as a ten-branch approximation for the range of risk. In such an analysis, each of the ten branches, following the logic of the two-branch and four-branch approximation, represents a range into which there is a one-tenth chance that the actual award might fall. These ten ranges run between the 0th- and 10th-percentile estimates, 10th- and 20th-percentile estimates, and so forth. Then, to represent each range, the probabilistic midpoint is used, including the 5th-percentile estimate, the 15th, the 25th, and so forth. The resulting ten-branch outcome fork (perhaps it should be called an outcome fan) is shown in figure 9–16. Phillips then assesses his preference-probabilities for these ten terminal outcomes using his preference curve (figure 9–2) and, applying the substitution principle, indirectly assesses his preference-probability for an uncertain jury award.

(The rationale for this ten-branch approximation is to obtain a more "accurate" assessment of Phillips's preference-probability for the uncertain jury award. Accordingly, to obtain the numbers in figure 9–16, both the uncertainty curve and the preference curve have been read as "accurately" as possible, and the preference-probabilities for the terminal outcomes are given to two significant figures.)

This ten-branch approximation yields a preference-probability of 0.83—just two percentage points below the 0.85 assessed (in figure 9–15c) using a four-branch approximation and only five percentage points below the 0.88 assessed (in figure 9–15b) using a two-branch approximation. And, significantly, that downward movement was predictable. Phillips's uncertainty curve is skewed towards the lower outcomes (for example, the 5th-percentile estimate is farther below the median than the 9th-percentile estimate is above it) and his preference curve is significantly risk averse. These characteristics of the two curves guarantee that as he uses a more detailed approximation for the uncertain jury

Why Simplification Works

award he will lower (slightly) his indirectly assessed preference-probability for the range of risk.

Using a more detailed approximation for the range of risk means adding more branches, both above and below the median.[10] But, because Phillips's preference curve is skewed, the outcomes for the lower branches are further below the median than the outcomes for the upper branches are above it; thus, the more detailed the approximation, the lower will be the EMV assessed for the entire range of risk. Moreover, with a bowed, risk averse preference curve (rather than a straight, EMV line), the preference-probabilities for the lower

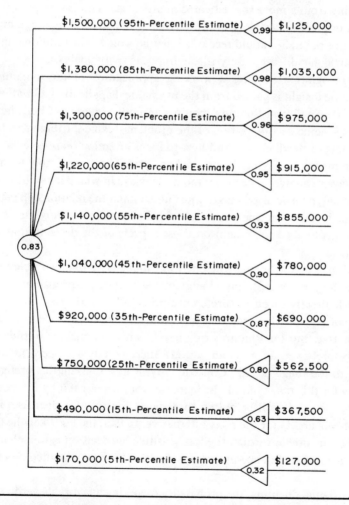

Figure 9–16. Using a Ten-Branch Outcome Fan to Help Assess Phillips's Preference-Probability for the Uncertain Jury Award.

outcomes drop off further from the preference-probability of the median than the preference-probabilities increase above the median's for the higher outcomes. Using a more detailed approximation can only result in a lowering of Phillips's assessment of his preference-probability for his range of risk.[11]

The four-branch approximation was more than adequate. Indeed, once Phillips had discovered, using only a two-branch approximation, that his preference-probability for the risky alternative was less than that for the riskless choice, he should have realized (given the nature of his problem) that a more detailed approximation of his range of risk could *only* lower his indirectly assessed probability for the risky alternative. Given this discovery, Phillips gains nothing from a more sophisticated analysis based on his original assessments (his original uncertainty and preference curves) for this range of risk. Rather, at this point, he should recognize that he would gain additional insight into *his* particular dilemma only through a sensitivity analysis.

Such a recognition requires a working appreciation of the dynamics of analysis. Little insight is gained from the mechanical application of mathematical formulas. Analytical thinking requires an understanding of both how an analysis—a specific decomposition of the problem—can contribute to a better understanding of the dilemma, and how to focus attention on selected aspects of the dilemma by modifying the original analysis. There are simply too many different ways to analyze a decision, too many ways in which it can be decomposed. An analytical decision maker must understand the relationship between the dilemma he faces and the analytical tools he commands. Only then can he use these tools to shed some light on those aspects of the decision that make it a dilemma.

For Phillips's new dilemma (the one to be made after the favorable verdict but before the jury award), any change in the preference-probability for the range of risk directly affects the preference-probability for the risky alternative. The range of risk for the uncertain jury award is the immediate outcome of that alternative. But for Phillips's original dilemma, in chapter 6 (the one to be made before a verdict was announced), there is only a 60-percent chance of getting to the range of risk. Consequently, if in rethinking his preference-probability for this range of risk, he increases (or decreases) it by five percentage points, the result will be only a three-point increase (or decrease) in the preference-probability for the risky alternative. In fact, the less likely he thinks he is to get a favorable verdict, the less sensitive his decision is to a change in his assessment of preference-probability for the (uncertain) outcome of that verdict.

For his original dilemma, the probability of getting a favorable verdict is (as depicted in the decision sapling of figure 6–5) a critical factor. Unless he gets a favorable verdict, he cannot even get to the uncertain jury award; this decision warranted a second-cut analysis only because, in the first cut, his 0.6 assessment for the probability of a favorable verdict made the decision too close to call. Had he thought this probability was 0.4 or 0.8, a simple, first-cut analysis would have been quite adequate.

After a second cut (which gave him a better handle on the range of risk), Phillips should have realized that attempting to wring more accuracy from his rough preference and uncertainty curves would do little to increase his understanding of his dilemma. Rather, he should have concentrated on determining how sensitive his decision was to those rough curves themselves. Because the switch point for p had only increased from 0.61 for the first-cut analysis to 0.63 for the second cut, it should have been clear to Phillips that using a more detailed approximation would not increase p_{switch} by very much. It went up to 0.64 for the third cut and 0.65 for the final cut. These additional cuts did not change Phillips's understanding of how sensitive his decision is to his assessment of this fundamental probability—an understanding which can be easily summarized:

- If Phillips thinks p is less than 60 percent, he should (given his preference and uncertainty curves) accept the settlement.
- If he thinks p is greater than two-thirds, he ought to reject it.
- In between, his preferences for the two alternatives are just about the same.

When does simplification work? When is a point estimate not good enough? How simplified should an analysis be? The answer depends upon the nature of the decision. The decision maker needs to be sufficiently familiar with the character of his dilemma that he can predict the implications, in direction if not degree, of introducing more complications. Analysis needs to be concentrated on those factors that most influence the decision, but it is impossible to identify those factors without understanding the nature of the dilemma.

As a good rule of thumb, however, it is dangerous (if one is risk averse) to approximate an important range of risk with only a point estimate. It is best to check how a two-branch approximation affects the preference-probability for the alternative. If the change is small, the effect of more-detailed approximations will (unless the nature of the problem suggests otherwise) be smaller still.

That is why simplification works. If the initial, drastically simplified analysis really captures the essence of the dilemma, adding additional complications will only slightly modify your conclusions concerning relative preferences for the alternatives. And each succeeding complication will result in even smaller modification. The key to making simplification work is to properly define the basic reason why the decision is a dilemma.

A Complicated Decision Tree is Not a Virtue

A decision problem is not characterized by only one, "correct" decision tree. Rather, there exist a variety of different decision diagrams that can describe the various factors influencing the decision. Some of these decision trees can be quite simple; some will be complex. Different decision trees will emphasize different factors. The key to resolving a decision dilemma lies not in discovering *the* decision tree—for it does not exist—but in developing the one that best helps to analyze the problem. And designing the most appropriate decision tree depends upon which factors the decision maker believes are most important and upon the detail that he needs to convince himself that the resolution of his dilemma is satisfactory.

When designing a decision tree, one of the most important decisions concerns where to cut it off. Indeed, the triangular outcome nodes that terminate each sequence of alternatives and outcomes might best be called "cut-off" nodes. These nodes represent not the actual, final outcome, but rather the point at which the decision maker decided to cut off the analysis. Any cut-off node can always be replaced by a more complex collection of uncertainty nodes, outcome branches, and consequence branches, as well as additional decision nodes and alternative branches. When constructing a decision tree, the question is not what are the ultimate outcomes and thus the true outcome nodes, but where is it most appropriate to cut off the analysis. Ward Edwards of the Social Science Research Institute at the University of Southern California writes:

> Since it is always necessary to cut the decision tree somewhere—to stop considering outcomes as opportunitites for further decisions and instead simply to treat them as outcomes with intrinsic values—the choice of what to call an outcome becomes largely one of convenience.[12]

For the out-of-court settlement dilemma, Cookie Phillips used terminal nodes that looked natural enough. Once he receives his payment, the decision has played itself out. But not really. Unless Phillips, like Scrooge McDuck, takes particular pleasure in the physical size of his fortune—enjoys just looking at the piles of coins or stock certificates in his basement vault—the money itself is not the ultimate consequence of his decision. The real consequences are the types of pleasure, satisfaction, objects, freedom, or whatever that the money will provide. When assessing his preference curve, Phillips had to decide upon a CME for a 50-50 gamble between $1.2 million and $0. But such a decision can only be based on what he would do with the $1.2 million or the CME. What will $1.2 million and $250,000 (Phillips's CME) buy him? This is the comparison that must be made whenever thinking about outcomes that involve money. Yet those consequences are rarely introduced explicitly; rather, the cut-off node usually has money itself as the consequence.

Still, the sophistical siren of scientism is seductive. To be scientific, it would seem decision making should be comprehensive, complete, exhaustive. John D. Steinbruner of the Brookings Institution writes that "the quintessential analytical decision maker is one who strains towards as complete an understanding as possible of the causal forces which determine outcomes."[13] Charles E. Lindblom, director of the Institution for Social and Policy Studies at Yale University, in his classic article, "The Science of 'Muddling Through,' " distinguishes between his "method of successive limited comparisons" and the more "scientific" approach, "the rational comprehensive method." Writes Lindblom, "Ideally, rational-comprehensive analysis leaves out nothing important."[14]

These caricatures of analytical thinking are, however, misleading. The pursuit of completeness is attractive, but quite unscientific. In *The Encyclopaedia of Ignorance,* Sir Hermann Bondi, professor of mathematics at King's College of the University of London, writes about the "lure of completeness" in science.

> Science is only possible because one can say something without knowing everything. To aim for completeness of knowledge can thus be essentially unsound. It is far more productive to make the best of what one knows, adding to it as means become available.[15]

The same can be said of decision making. It is only possible to make a decision because one can analyze the problem without knowing everything. To aim for a complete analysis is essentially unsound. It is far more productive to make the best decision possible given what one knows, and to revise it if more information becomes available.

Elsewhere in this "encyclopaedia," another scientist notes that "even today, three centuries after Newton, there still remain puzzling features of the lunar motion."[16] Nonetheless, even though scientists do not possess complete knowledge about the motion of the moon, engineers know enough about its trajectory to decide how best to send three men over 200,000 miles through space and land them safely on the lunar surface. The engineers do not miss. They may not be able to explain the moon's movements perfectly, but this ignorance is unimportant. For the purposes of landing spacecraft on the moon, our knowledge of lunar motion is quite adequate.

Still, in both business and government, "improving" decision making usually means making it more comprehensive—collecting more data and manipulating those data with computer programs that are ever more sophisticated. In "A Heretical View of Management 'Science,' " Theodore Levitt of the Harvard Business School criticizes such efforts to make business management more "scientific."

> Management "scientists" in business schools, consulting organizations, and the larger corporations themselves are pressing ever harder for the use of ever more elaborate forms of mathematicized analyses of an expanding variety of corporate activities . . . . They build intricate decision trees whose pretension to utility is exceeded only by the awe in which high-level managers hold the technocrats who construct them.[17]

A complicated decision tree is not a virtue. In most cases, it is best to begin any decision analysis with a very simple decision tree—perhaps the decision sapling—which can capture the essence of why the decision is a dilemma. Then, even if a first-cut analysis does not resolve the problem, it can illuminate what factors require further, more detailed work. And, if the decision can be satisfactorily made without a complicated decision tree, it is silly—indeed stupid—to draw one. The time and effort devoted to making a decision must be based on the significance of the consequences involved.

A complete understanding of any decision problem is not only wasteful but unattainable; there are always too many factors. In fact, a comprehensive analysis is incomprehensible. A complex analysis of all factors and their interconnections inevitably evolves into an impenetrable maze that obliterates the decision maker's intuitive feel for the nature of the dilemma, the relative significance of the individual factors, and the interactive relationships among them.

It is impossible to think analytically without simplifying. Thinking requires abstraction, selecting from the myriad of facts and factors those few on which to focus attention. The first step when thinking about a decision is to convert a complicated reality into a simplified abstraction. If both the process of creating that simplification and working with it are analytical—that is, thoughtful, careful, systematic, and explicit—then the thinking can be quite valuable.

Such an approach permits the decision maker to maintain an intuitive grasp of the problem. The role of decision analysis is not to replace intuition but to aid it. Decision analysis merely makes the intuitive judgments explicit. Designing a decision tree forces the decision maker to specify why his intuition tells him the decision is a dilemma. Assessing probabilities forces him to specify his intuitive judgments about the uncertainties that create the dilemma. Assessing preference-probabilities forces him to think carefully about his own values and to specify his relative preferences for the few outcomes involved in his analysis. Using the substitution principle forces the decision maker to rethink whether his indirectly assessed preferences for the various alternatives reflect his better understanding of the dilemma.

Why Simplification Works

By using a simplified framework, a decision maker can ensure that his intuition will be engaged throughout the analysis. If the simplification of a decision tree captures the essence of the decision, it will concentrate the decision maker's intuition on the basic nature of the dilemma. The result will be a better understanding of both the character of the dilemma and the decision to be made.

Appendix: The Shape of an Uncertainty Curve

An uncertainty curve is usually steepest near the median, where it is most likely the uncertain outcome will fall, and gently approaches a cumulative probability of 1.0 for high outcomes and a cumulative probability of 0 for low outcomes. Unless the uncertain quantity is bounded (as Phillips's jury award was), it may make sense to estimate that there is some small probability that the outcome will be above any high figure or below any low figure.[18] Such uncertainty curves—for example, those for life span in figure 9–7—are shaped like a flattened S, and called an *ogive*.

The steeper an uncertainty curve, the more confidence its assessor has that the actual outcome will be close to the median. Consider the three different uncertainty curves for federal outlays in FY 86 shown in figure 9–17. The median estimate for all three is $912 billion, which is the FY 86 "target outlay ceiling" presented in President Reagan's *Fiscal Year 1982 Budget Revisions.*[19] Uncertainty curve A is the steepest, reflecting the greatest confidence in President Reagan's ability to come close to his target; the interquartile range for

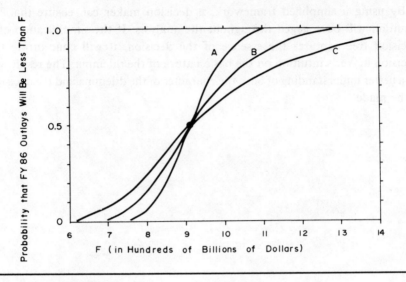

Figure 9–17. Three Uncertainty Curves for Federal Outlays in FY 86.

this assessment is $860 billion to $970 billion. Uncertainty curve B reflects less confidence in the median estimate; the interquartile range runs from $830 billion to $1,020 billion. Uncertainty curve C reflects the greatest uncertainty about FY 86 outlays, though the target ceiling is still used as the median; the interquartile range runs from $800 billion up to $1,080 billion. Curve A suggests that there is an 80-percent chance that FY 86 outlays will be between $800 billion and $1,000 billion. B indicates that there is a 55-percent chance that outlays will be in this range, and C says the chance is only 40 percent.

Uncertainty curves are smooth. There are no kinks in them. An uncertainty curve is rarely horizontal; a horizontal uncertainty curve between $800 billion and $900 billion would indicate there was no chance for outlays to fall in this region (for the probability that outlays would be less than $900 billion would be identical to the probability that they would be less than $800 billion). Also, uncertainty curves do not jump up quickly; a curve that increased from a cumulative probability of 0.4 for $899 billion to a cumulative probability of 0.5 for $900 billion would indicate that there was a 10-percent chance that FY 86 outlays would be in this narrow one-billion-dollar range. If an uncertainty curve had a sharp bend at $900 billion, so that the slope just before the kink was much steeper than the slope just after it, it would mean that there was a significantly greater probability of outlays being in the range $890–$900 billion than in the range $900–$910 billion. Unless a particular characteristic of the uncertain quantity gives the uncertainty curve one of these features, the curve should be a smooth one.

PART III

Complications and Dynamics

Chapter 10

Compound Decision Dilemmas: Rufus Edmisten, Ruth Mason, and Light Beer

IN the fall of 1977, Rufus L. Edmisten, attorney general of North Carolina and former aide to U.S. Senator Sam J. Ervin, Jr., had to decide whether to seek the Democratic senatorial nomination and challenge incumbent Senator Jesse A. Helms. Edmisten's dilemma was complicated by the need to decide, if he did win the Democratic nomination, whether or not to resign his state office. If he did resign as attorney general, he would have a better chance of unseating Helms, for there was some sentiment in the state against a politician who uses one office to seek a higher one; the state's other senator, Robert Morgan, had resigned as attorney general after he won the Democratic nomination in 1974. If Edmisten did resign, however, and then lost to Helms, he would be out of a job—and out of public office.

The decision tree for Edmisten's dilemma (figure 10–1) looks like a basic decision sapling followed by a double-risk decision tree. Indeed, if he were to win the Democratic senatorial nomination, Edmisten would face a double-risk dilemma structurally identical to the one faced by senatorial candidate Daniel P. Moynihan in chapter 5. For one alternative (resign, either as attorney general or Harvard professor) the probability of winning is greater; for the other alternative (do not resign) the consequences of losing are better. And

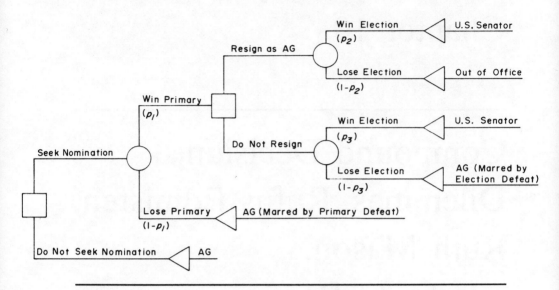

Figure 10–1. Rufus Edmisten's Compound Decision Dilemma.

Edmisten's initial decision looks like the basic dilemma faced by any politician who must give up a safe office if he wishes to take the chance of winning a higher post.

Edmisten need not commit himself initially as to whether he would, if he won the nomination, resign as attorney general. After he won the primary, he would want to think carefully about this decision and choose the alternative he thought was best. Nevertheless, to make the immediate decision about whether or not to seek the nomination, he has to make a preliminary judgment about whether or not it would be better, if nominated, to resign. (In fact, when Edmisten himself actually considered whether or not he should run for the Senate, he devoted most of his thinking to the question of whether, if nominated, he should resign.[1])

Consequently, when Edmisten analyzes the seek-nomination alternative, he needs to specify his preference for the win-primary outcome, and he can do this only if he determines what will be the consequence of winning the primary: (1) a p_2 chance at being senator combined with a $1-p_2$ chance of being out of office; or (2) a p_3 chance at being senator combined with a $1-p_3$ chance of being attorney general marred by an election defeat. If he does not make a preliminary decision as to what he will do if nominated, he might undervalue the win-primary outcome and thus also undervalue the seek-nomination alternative.

Several pieces of information provide a basis for assessing the probabilities and preference-probabilities needed to resolve the dilemma.[2]

Compound Decision Dilemmas

- The "view in the Edmisten camp" was that "he could win the nomination in a crowded primary field, but would face an uphill fight against Helms."
- As a "top aide" put it, "Many people felt that after the primary, he would have to resign because of the pressure brought to bear by his opponent and the media."
- In a meeting with "financial backers," only "about a third of the 175 persons present recommended he resign if he wins the primary."
- "Rufus has no money. . . . He hasn't gotten rich over here."
- "Rufus loves being attorney general."

This information suggests that the following probabilities and preference-probabilities represent one set of possible assessments.

- The probability of winning the nomination is 0.75.
- The probability of winning the election, if he resigns, is 0.4.
- The probability of winning the election if he does not resign is 0.3 (substantially less).
- The *Best* outcome is being a U.S. senator, so this gets a preference-probability of 1.0.
- The *Worst* outcome is being defeated and out of public office, so this gets a preference-probability of 0.
- Since Edmisten "loves" being attorney general, he is indifferent between this outcome (unmarred by any defeat) and a 50-50 chance at being senator or out of office.
- Being attorney general but marred slightly by a primary defeat is a little worse and thus is equivalent to a 0.45 reference gamble.
- Being attorney general but marred slightly more by a general-election defeat is somewhat worse and thus equivalent to a 0.4 reference gamble.

To resolve Edmisten's dilemma, the first step is to decide what he should do if he wins the nomination. As is indicated in figure 10–2, *based on the probabilities and preference-probabilities assessed now* (i.e. in the fall of 1977), he should not resign as attorney general if he wins the nomination. If he does

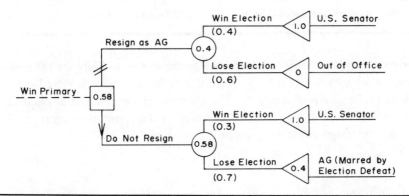

Figure 10–2. Resolving Edmisten's Future Decision First.

actually win the primary, he might then, using new information and new insights, change his assessment of some of the probabilities and preference-probabilities and thus change his decision. But with the information he has now (fall of 1977), he would not resign.

The implication of this (tentative) decision not to resign if nominated is that the win-primary outcome should have a preference-probability of 0.58. This was assessed indirectly for the do-not-resign alternative by using the substitution principle. (The preference-probability of 0.4 for the alternative of resigning is clearly not as good, and it would make little sense to use it when a higher one can be obtained from the other alternative.) This 0.58 preference-probability has thus been inserted in the decision node at the end of the win-primary outcome branch on the decision tree for the entire problem (figure 10–3).

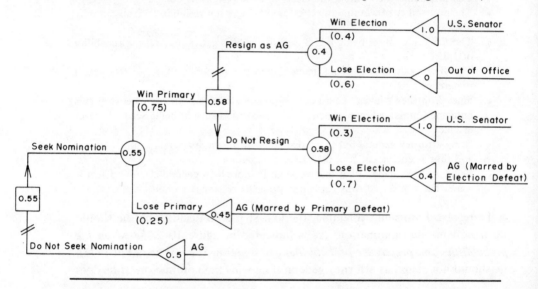

Figure 10–3. Resolution of Rufus Edmisten's Compound Decision Dilemma.

The next step is to assess indirectly the preference-probability for the seek-nomination alternative. It is 0.55. Since this is higher than the 0.5 (directly assessed) preference-probability for the do-not-seek-nomination alternative, the immediate decision is to seek the nomination. The (tentative) future decision is not to resign as attorney general if nominated.

Compound Decision Dilemmas

A Second Approach

Another way to approach Rufus Edmisten's dilemma is to analyze, independently, two different decisions. First, Edmisten could decide whether or not to seek the nomination, assuming that, if nominated, he *would* resign as attorney general. Second, he could decide whether or not to seek the nomination, assuming that, if nominated, he *would not* resign. Then, if the analyses based on these two assumptions resulted in conflicting conclusions, he would need to decide which strategy, resign or do not resign, produced the most favorable initial decision.

If he adopts the strategy of resigning as attorney general if nominated, winning the primary would lead to a gamble giving a 40-percent chance at being a senator and a 60-percent chance of being out of office. Using the preference-probabilities previously assessed for these and the other outcomes, this first decision can be resolved. The preference-probability for the seek-nomination alternative is 0.41, and that for the do-not-seek-nomination alternative is 0.5. Thus, if Edmisten plans to resign if nominated, he should not seek the nomination (see figure 10–4a).

If, however, he adopts the do-not-resign strategy, the win-primary outcome leads to a gamble giving a 30-percent chance at being a senator and a 70-percent chance of continuing as attorney general, though marred by a general-election defeat. Again, using the preference-probabilities previously assessed, this decision can be resolved. The preference-probability for seeking the nomination is now 0.58; for not seeking the nomination it is, as before, 0.5. If Edmisten plans not to resign if nominated, he should seek the nomination (see figure 10–4b).

Clearly, what he should do *now* depends upon what he plans to do in the *future* if nominated. Indeed, it makes sense to seek the nomination *only if* he plans not to resign if nominated. Of course, he could change his mind after actually winning the primary; at that time he would have more information to use in assessing the probabilities of winning with and without resigning, and perhaps a different perspective on the relative desirability of the three outcomes: U.S. Senator, Out-of-Office, and Attorney General (Marred by Election Defeat). Still, if he was now to decide that he would, in fact, resign if nominated, it is clear that he should not seek the senatorial nomination.

This second analytical approach is described by the decision tree in figure 10–5. Edmisten first must choose between two strategies, resign or do not resign. Then, for each strategy, he decides whether or not to seek the nomination. Since the do-not-resign strategy has the higher preference probability, and since this comes from the seek-nomination decision, the conclusion is the same as before—the immediate decision is to seek the senatorial nomination; the (tentative) future decision is not to resign as attorney general.

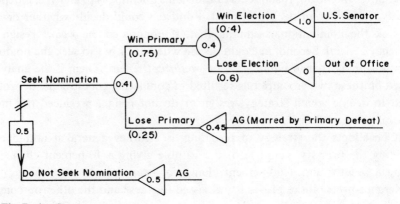

(a) The Resign Strategy

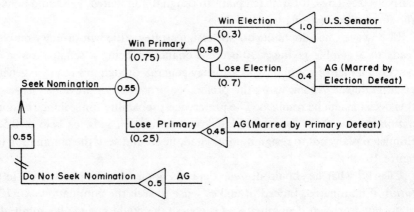

(b) The Do Not Resign Strategy

Figure 10–4. Using Two Different Strategies for Edmisten's Future Decision to Help Analyze His Immediate Decision.

Compound Decision Dilemmas

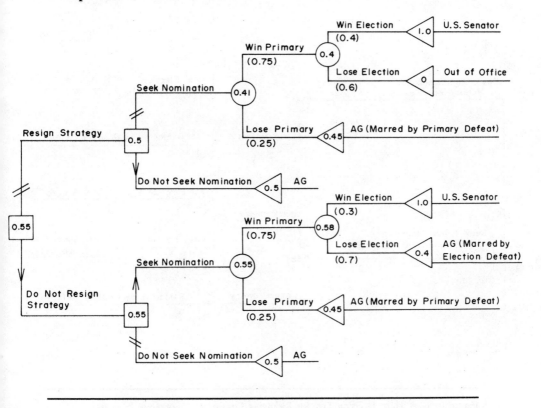

Figure 10–5. Another Decision Tree for Resolving Edmisten's Compound Dilemma.

A Third Approach

There is one more way to think about Rufus Edmisten's dilemma.[3] The immediate decision can be viewed as presenting three alternatives: (1) seek nomination and, if nominated, resign; (2) seek nomination and, if nominated, do not resign; (3) do not seek nomination. The third alternative leads directly to a terminal node. The first two alternatives lead to a 75-percent chance at winning the primary and a 25-percent chance at losing it. If the primary is won, the probability of winning the general election and the consequence of losing it depend upon which of the first two alternatives has been chosen (see figure 10–6).

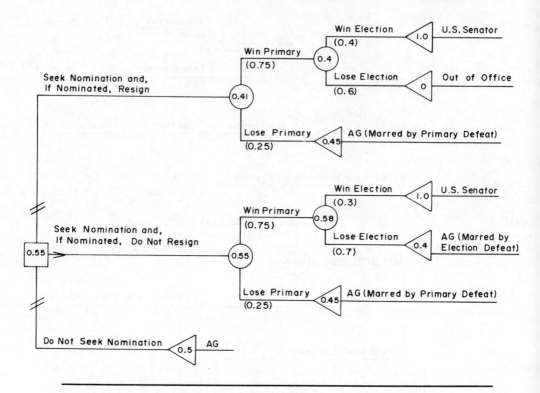

Figure 10–6. A Third Decision Tree for Resolving Edmisten's Compound Dilemma.

Using this third approach, the conclusion is the same as before—seek the nomination and, if nominated, do not resign. But again, the future, do-not-resign component of the decision is not binding. It can be changed after the primary if new information and a new perspective significantly affect Edmisten's indirect assessment of his preference-probabilities for the then-immediate alternatives, resign and do not resign.

Compound Decision Dilemmas and the Future-First Principle

Compound decision dilemmas involve not only immediate but future decisions although, as the third approach for resolving Edmisten's dilemma illustrates, all future decisions can be converted into the present by increasing the number of immediate alternatives. The immediate decision presented by a compound dilemma can be made only by also making a tentative decision about the future choices that must eventually be made. Such decisions about the future can of course be changed when it actually comes time to make them, as Edmisten's dilemma also illustrates.

Compound decision dilemmas are difficult to resolve intuitively because it is not easy to see how an immediate decision may be influenced by the possible outcomes of some decision that must be made in the future. In this way, the complication presented by a future decision is similar to that posed by uncertainty—when it is difficult to see how an immediate decision may be influenced by the potential outcome of some future uncertain event. There is also a similarity in the analytical approaches used to resolve such dilemmas.

When a decision is complicated by a future, uncertain event, the decision maker tries to make a probabilistic prediction of the outcome by assessing a probability for each possible outcome. When the decision is complicated by a future decision, however, the nature of the difficulty is different—the future outcome will be chosen by the decision maker himself, not by someone or something else. To think analytically about the outcome of that future decision, the decision maker tries to predict which alternative he will choose. To do this, he applies to the future decision the same analytical concepts that he uses to resolve an immediate decision.

This, then, is the rationale for the *future-first* approach to resolving compound decision dilemmas. As with the analysis of any type of decision problem, the first step is to decompose the problem into smaller components, in this case into a series of simple (noncompound) decisions. Each simple decision is analyzed separately and the pieces recombined to give the overall decision. But, since the outcomes of the immediate decisions cannot be evaluated until the future decisions are made, the future decisions must be analyzed first. Then, once the least preferable future alternatives are eliminated, the immediate decision can be analyzed. In the jargon of decision analysis, this is called "folding back" or "working backwards," or the "backward induction of dynamic programming."[4]

Ruth Mason's Dilemma

Another excellent example of a compound decision dilemma (and of the applicability of the future-first principle) is the following case in bioethics posed by Robert M. Veatch, senior associate at the Hastings Center.

Ruth Mason's sister has just had a child—a boy. Within hours it is clear that the child has classic hemophilia. Among the children of Ruth's sisters he is the second son to be born with hemophilia. Because hemophilia of this kind (type A) is caused by a gene on the X-chromosome, which is passed from mother to daughter, Ruth has a one in two chance of being a carrier herself. If she is, approximately half of her male offspring would receive the X-chromosome with the hemophilia gene and half of her daughters would be carriers like herself; the other half would be normal. She had been planning to have a child and now wants desperately to know what she can do in these circumstances.

Her obstetrician tells her about a new test which she could take before becoming pregnant to determine if she were a carrier of hemophilia. He emphasizes that if the test were positive, it definitely means she has the gene, but that it would only pick up 80–95 percent of the women who are carriers. Should she become pregnant, the obstetrician informs her that a prenatal test called amniocentesis could be done around the 16th week of her pregnancy which would tell her within days whether or not she was carrying a male fetus. In the current state of our technology, however, he points out that there would be virtually no way to ascertain whether the fetus was normal or destined to be a hemophiliac. The doctor tells Ruth that she could then choose an abortion during the second trimester of her pregnancy. Ruth realizes that if she were positively identified as a carrier, she would then be faced with the prospect of an abortion where there would be a 50:50 chance of aborting a hemophiliac male —or a normal son. And if she were negative, she still couldn't be sure of not having a hemophiliac because the carrier detection test misses almost one in every five who have the hemophilia gene.

Ruth Mason decides to find out more about the disease and calls the National Hemophilia Foundation which tells her of new developments in the care and treatment of hemophiliac boys. There is a new means of preparing the anti-clotting factor (cryoprecipitate) and home therapy programs which greatly reduce the cost of home treatment to approximately $6,000 per year. She also learns that a prophylactic schedule of treatments greatly reduces the insidious bleeding which in the past caused much of the disability (by causing joint problems) experienced by hemophiliacs. She returns to the obstetrician, troubled and confused. Should she go ahead and take the test to determine if she is a carrier? How should she go about deciding whether or not to become pregnant and possibly have to abort?[5]

The compound decision that Ruth Mason faces has no easy or obvious answer about which all rational and moral individuals would immediately agree. Two distinguished ethicists, Sissela Bok, of Harvard Medical School, and Mark Lappé, chief of the Office of Planning and Evaluation of the California State Department of Health Services, considered the dilemma and reached radically different conclusions. Bok suggested three options: (1) "forego pregnancy," (2) "become pregnant with the intention of undergoing amniocentesis and aborting the fetus if it should be male," and (3) "decide in favor of becoming pregnant and giving birth." Bok found "the first alternative preferable" and "the third alternative . . . the least defensible." Lappé, on the other hand, concluded, "I think the Masons could go ahead and have a child. I know I would."[6]

Ruth Mason's dilemma is perplexingly complex. It is puzzling, in part, because the consequences of selecting the different alternatives are uncertain.

Compound Decision Dilemmas

If Mason becomes pregnant, she might have a boy—or a girl. If she has a boy, he might be a hemophiliac—or not. If she takes the carrier test, it might be positive—or negative. And if the test is negative, she still might have the gene. The consequences of her various alternatives are shrouded in a fog of uncertainty.

Beyond this, Mason's problem is complicated by a clash of conflicting consequences. She wants a child, but she feels that giving birth to a hemophiliac son would have great costs for herself, her family, the child, and society. She would prefer not to take the painful, somewhat dangerous, and costly amniocentesis test, but she knows that taking the test is the only way to learn if the fetus is male or female. She would prefer not to have an abortion, and she knows that, if she aborts a male fetus, the chances (in most situations) are greater than 50 percent that the fetus would have been a normal child; however, the fetus might be a hemophiliac and Mason would prefer not to give birth to a hemophiliac. The deepest ethical dilemmas in Ruth Mason's problem stem from these conflicting values concerning parenthood, abortion, the pain and other costs of hemophilia, and from the weight given to the interests and preferences of Ruth Mason, her husband, the child, and society. (How to consider explicitly conflicting consequences when analyzing a decision is the topic of the next chapter.)

Finally, the dilemma is perplexing because Mason must make four sequential decisions rather than one. She has to decide whether to take the carrier test. She has to decide whether to become pregnant. If she does, she has to decide whether to take the amniocentesis test and, then, whether to have an abortion or give birth. Her later decisions will be influenced by the results of her earlier decisions. For example, her decision about whether to have an abortion will be affected by whether she took the carrier test and, if so, by whether the result was positive or negative. Conversely, her earlier decisions depend on what she thinks her later decisions will be. Her decision about whether to take the amniocentesis test, for example, depends on whether she would be willing to abort a male fetus. Mason's dilemma is compounded by four separate but interdependent decisions.

How should Mason go about deciding what to do? Clearly, she should think long and hard about the problem and talk it over at length with her husband (as joint decision maker), her friends, and trusted counselors. But how should all the pieces of her decision puzzle be put together? She could make the decisions "holistically," balancing and weighing the decision alternatives, uncertain outcomes, and competing values "in her head." That is what most people would do if confronted with a dilemma as complex and emotionally charged as Ruth Mason's. But doing so makes as much sense as trying to multiply multidigit numbers mentally; indeed, it makes much less sense, since Mason's dilemma is many times more complicated and important than a multiplication problem. The intricate interplay of compound decisions, the uncertainty about outcomes, and the clash of conflicting consequences make it particularly worthwhile for Ruth Mason to think about her decision systematically.

Structuring Ruth Mason's Dilemma

When a decision dilemma is as complicated as Ruth Mason's, structuring the problem with a decision tree can be very informative. Such a diagram displays, clearly, the important sequential relationships among the various decision alternatives, uncertain outcomes, and resulting consequences.

For Mason's dilemma, the decision tree (figure 10–7) indicates that her first decision is whether to take the carrier test. If she does, the result will be either positive or negative. In either case, or in the case where she decides not to take the carrier test, her next decision is whether to become pregnant. If she decides not to become pregnant, she must decide whether to try to adopt a child.

If she decides to become pregnant, Mason's next decision is whether to take the amniocentesis test. If she does not, then she will give birth either to a boy or a girl. If she has a boy, he will be either a hemophiliac or normal; if she has a girl, she will be either a carrier or normal. If Mason takes the amniocentesis test, the test will indicate either a male or a female fetus. If the fetus is male, Mason can either abort the fetus or give birth. If she gives birth, her son will be either a hemophiliac or normal.

But what if the amniocentesis test indicates a female fetus? Mason could decide to have an abortion. If she felt that way, however, it seems clear that she would also decide to abort a male fetus; after all, having a female carrier is a better outcome than having a male hemophiliac (and in all situations, the probabilities for those two outcomes are the same). Thus, if she decided to abort a female fetus, there would be no reason to take the amniocentesis test, since she would have an abortion regardless of the result. Indeed, there would be no reason to become pregnant, since she would abort any pregnancy.

Consequently, in constructing the decision tree, it was assumed that Mason would give birth to any female fetus. If this were not the case, there would be no dilemma about whether to become pregnant or take the amniocentesis test. Since the carrier test cannot prove that Mason *is not* a carrier (though it can prove that she *is* one), if she would abort any fetus with the slightest chance of being either a carrier or a hemophiliac, she would simply not become pregnant. This illustrates, again, how future decisions can affect—indeed, sometimes determine—present decisions.

284

Compound Decision Dilemmas

It is assumed that, if Mason has an abortion, the fetus would be studied to determine whether the child would have been a hemophiliac. It is further assumed that Ruth Mason would be told the result. This knowledge would be important if she subsequently considered whether she should become pregnant again. If the fetus proved to have been a hemophiliac, Mason would know she was a carrier; if the fetus were normal, the probability that Mason was a carrier would be reduced.

Complex as the decision tree in figure 10–7 is, it is not complete. To make it possible to analyze the dilemma, the decision tree has been simplified by truncating it with a series of terminal nodes. Each terminal node (on this or any other decision tree) represents not an ending but a cut-off point. For example, if Mason becomes pregnant, there is some chance the child will be deformed or seriously ill. Although these and other possibilities certainly exist, they are not central to Mason's dilemma. It thus makes sense to ignore them, at least initially.

The diagram is also truncated so that various possible future decisions are not included. For example, suppose Mason becomes pregnant and gives birth to a normal boy. She now faces the decision of whether to have a second child. If she does, she will face the decision of whether to have a third child, and so on. Since including such decisions would make an elaborate diagram many times more elaborate, it is reasonable, at least as a first cut, to not include such future decisions in the diagram. When evaluating the desirability of the various possible outcomes, however, Mason should consider the consequences that may follow from these outcomes.

Not only have decisions concerning subsequent children been left off the decision tree, but the different possible consequences of trying to adopt a child have also been ignored. Will the Masons be able to adopt a child? How long will it take to do so? What type of child will it be? Ignoring such complications will make no difference if the Masons prefer remaining childless to trying to adopt a child, and it is quite possible that they would; an increasing number of couples have decided not to have children. If, however, the Masons preferred—or thought they might prefer—trying to adopt a child, the decision diagram would have to be enlarged to include the various possible consequences of such a choice.[7] For simplicity's sake (and since no information on adoption possibilities was provided in Veatch's case), from here on it is assumed that the Masons would rather remain childless than try to adopt a child.

The probabilities for the various uncertain outcomes are shown on the decision tree. The probability that any fetus will be male is actually 51 percent, though for simplicity it is taken to be 50 percent. The other probabilities were calculated (in the appendix to this chapter) from the information in the case, the laws of genetics, and some probability rules.

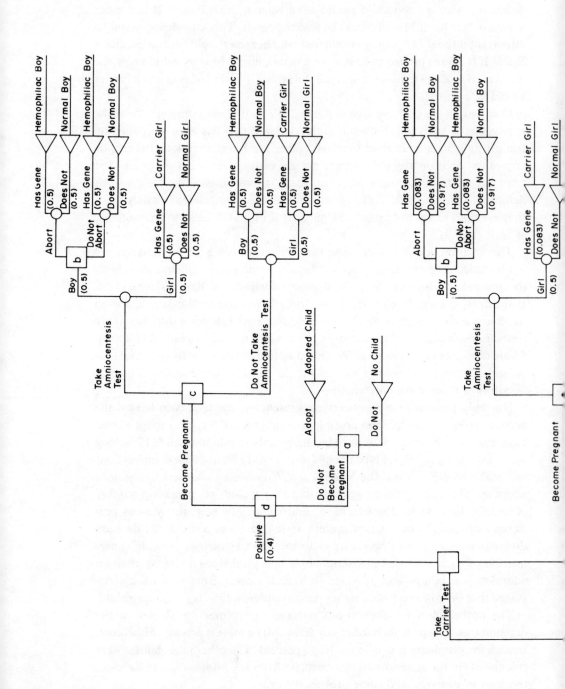

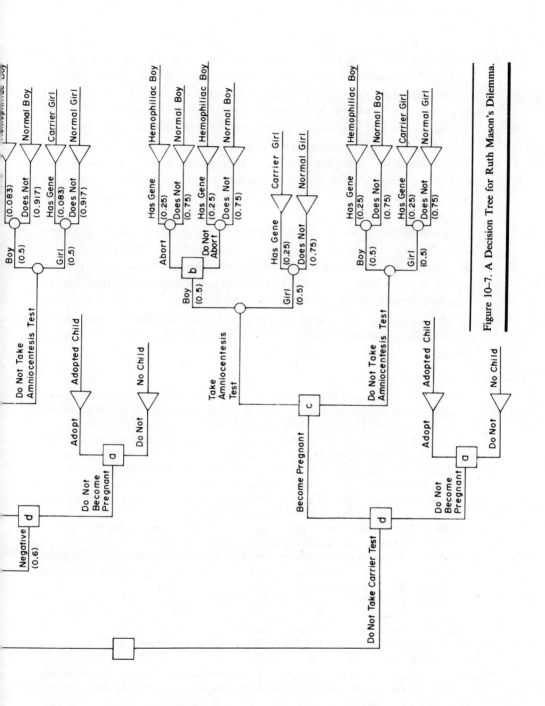

Figure 10–7. A Decision Tree for Ruth Mason's Dilemma.

Resolving Ruth Mason's Dilemma

The following conversation between Ruth Mason and a "decision analyst" suggests how Mason might go about resolving her dilemma. For clarity of exposition, the dialogue is purposefully made terse and unemotional. The value judgments Mason must make, however, are not at all simple or uncontroversial. In reality, she might have great difficulty and suffer considerable emotional strain answering the analyst's questions. She might well want to make the decisions jointly with her husband and discuss her answers with some close friends or counselors. The following dialogue is not designed to be true to life but to illustrate how to organize one's thinking about a compound decision dilemma.

On the decision tree for Mason's dilemma, it should be noted, the same structures of uncertain events and future decisions follow from (1) not taking the carrier test, (2) having a negative result from the carrier test, and (3) having a positive result from the carrier test. The probabilities are different, but the structures are identical. Consequently, the following dialogue exploits the similarities among these three sections of the decision tree by considering together the four trios of similar decisions (which are identified with the lower case letters "a," "b," "c," and "d").

ANALYST: In your decision tree, a number of simpler decision problems are embedded. Let's resolve these one by one, starting with the ones farthest in the future. There are three decisions (labeled "a") involving the choice between trying to adopt a child and remaining childless. You said before that you preferred remaining childless; so let's consider these decision problems resolved, at least for the time being. There are also three decisions (labeled "b") involving a double-risk dilemma—aborting versus giving birth to a male fetus. In the top one of these decisions, there is a 50-percent chance of this male fetus being a hemophiliac. Would you have an abortion in that case?

MASON: That would be an extremely difficult choice for me to make, but I think I would choose, with much trepidation, to have an abortion.

ANALYST: How about the other two abortion decisions? In one, the chance that a male fetus is a hemophiliac is a little more than 8 percent; in the other, the probability is 25 percent.

MASON: I definitely wouldn't have an abortion in either of these two cases.

ANALYST: Now, let's consider your three decisions about whether or not to take the amniocentesis test (decision nodes labeled "c"). In the two situations where you would not abort a male fetus (after a negative carrier test, and without any carrier test), it would hardly make sense to take the amniocentesis test; after all, if the information you collect from the test (whether the fetus is male or female) would not influence your decision, there is no point in collecting the information. But what about the first case, where you said you would have an abortion if the test indicated a male fetus?

Compound Decision Dilemmas

MASON: Well, that is a very hypothetical situation. For it, I've gotten a positive result on my carrier test—which means I know I have the hemophilia gene—and I become pregnant; thus, there is a 50-50 chance that the fetus I'm carrying has the gene. I have already decided that if I know the fetus is a male, I will abort it. In that situation, it seems to me that I ought to take the test to find out whether or not the fetus is male.

ANALYST: Don't forget—there is some risk, discomfort, and cost to taking the test. That might tip your decision, especially since you apparently feel that having an abortion is only slightly better, here, than giving birth.

MASON: I see that. But I really do think I'd prefer taking the test to having a 25-percent chance that I would give birth to a hemophiliac male.

(In this dialogue, the analyst consciously asks Mason to resolve her future decisions first. This is because her decisions about whether to have an abortion influence the chronologically prior decisions about whether to take the amniocentesis test. She decided not to have an abortion in two situations; that decision dictated the "prior" one, since there was no need to take the amniocentesis test if an abortion was not contemplated. In the other situation, Mason decided she would abort a male fetus; that decision strongly influenced her decision to take the amniocentesis test.)

ANALYST: Okay. Continuing to work backwards on your diagram, the next decision is whether or not to become pregnant. That decision also appears three times (decision nodes labeled "d") and, given the choices you've already made, these three decisions can now be diagrammed more simply. (See figure 10–8.)

MASON: What I should do in the first of these three cases (figure 10–8a) seems clear to me; I just wouldn't want to become pregnant if I knew that it was as likely as not that I'd then have an abortion. But what I should do in the other two cases is not obvious to me at all. I think I need to assess some preference-probabilities to analyze these two choices.

ANALYST: I suppose you feel that having a hemophiliac son is the worst outcome. But what is the best?

MASON: Having a normal child, boy or girl.

ANALYST: In that case, we can simplify these two decision trees by combining the normal-boy and normal-girl outcomes into a single, normal-child outcome and then making a few probability calculations [as described in the appendix to chapter 4]. (See figure 10–9.)

MASON: There are two interjacent outcomes—having a carrier daughter and remaining childless. The second will be easier for me to think about, so let's look at that one first.

ANALYST: You have to compare remaining childless with a "reference-gamble" with having a normal child as the *Best* and having a hemophiliac son as the *Worst*. Suppose the probabilities were 50-50? What would you prefer?

MASON: I'd definitely remain childless. I've thought about this long and carefully, and I'd remain childless unless there was only one chance in ten—or less—of having a hemophiliac son. That means my preference-probability for remaining childless is 0.9.

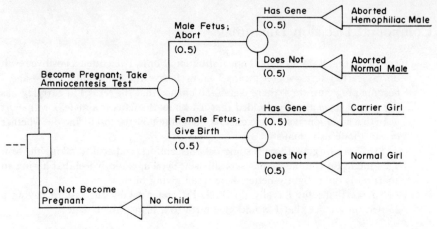

(a) Positive Carrier Test

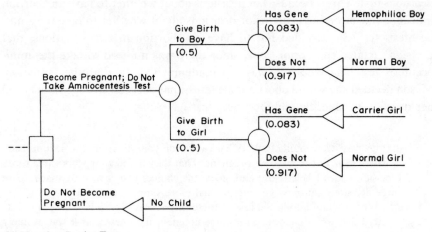

(b) Negative Carrier Test

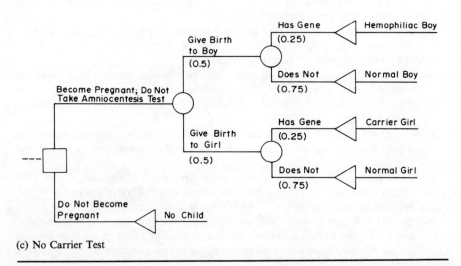

(c) No Carrier Test

Figure 10–8. Ruth Mason's Three Pregnancy Decisions (For a Positive Carrier Test, a Negative Carrier Test, and No Carrier Test).

Compound Decision Dilemmas

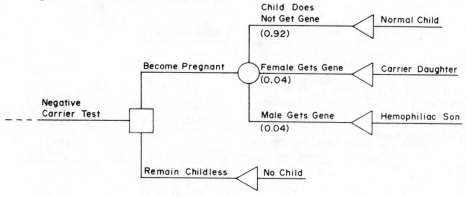

(a) Pregnancy Decision After Negative Carrier Test

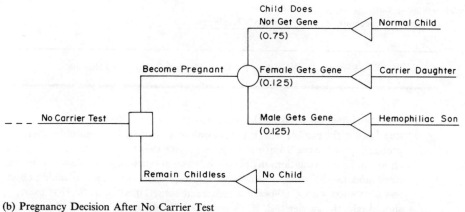

(b) Pregnancy Decision After No Carrier Test

Figure 10–9. Ruth Mason's Two Remaining Pregnancy Decisions.

ANALYST: If you feel that way, you don't have to assess a preference-probability for having a carrier girl. In the case where you have a 92-percent chance of having a normal child (figure 10–9a), even if having a carrier girl was as undesirable as having a hemophiliac boy, you'd still become pregnant. And, in the other case (figure 10–9b), there's a 12.5-percent chance of having a hemophiliac boy; thus, even if you decided that having a carrier girl was as good as having a normal child, you would still not become pregnant, since you said you would remain childless if the probability of having a hemophiliac son was more than 10 percent.

MASON: That's right. So now we've resolved all the subdecisions except the first one —whether to take the carrier test.

ANALYST: Given your other decisions, that one can now be diagrammed quite simply. You can see from this reduced decision tree (figure 10–10) that if you take the carrier test you'll have a 40-percent chance of remaining childless and a 60-percent chance at a gamble with three outcomes.

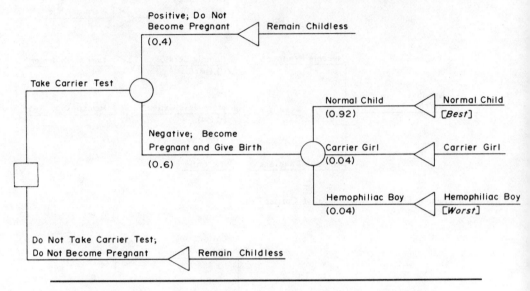

Figure 10–10. A Reduced Decision Tree for Ruth Mason's Compound Dilemma.

MASON: Looking at the decision that way makes the choice clear. I have already said that I prefer the gamble with the three outcomes—indeed, any gamble where the probability of having a normal child is greater than 90 percent—to remaining childless. In this situation, my choice is between remaining childless, on the one hand, and, on the other, a gamble with a 40-percent chance at remaining childless combined with a 60-percent chance at something better. So that means I should take the carrier test. If it's positive, I'll remain childless. If it's negative, I'll become pregnant and give birth.

Ruth Mason's Decision-Making Process

Ruth Mason would surely agonize much more over her decisions than is suggested by this intentionally rapid and straightforward dialogue. The decisions reached, however, are quite reasonable. Mason chose to take the carrier test but not the amniocentesis test. She decided to remain childless, rather than trying to adopt a child, if the carrier test were positive. But if the test were negative, she would become pregnant and give birth; she would not have an abortion.

Mason's choices clearly are based on her value judgments concerning parenthood, hemophilia, abortion, the interests of the child, and the interests of society. Other women, in different circumstances, with different beliefs, preferences, and values, might choose other courses of action. A number of people with whom we have discussed this dilemma concluded that they would either remain childless or try to adopt a child, regardless of the outcome of the carrier test—indeed, that they would not take the carrier test. Other people, who valued parenthood highly and who were not strongly opposed to abortion, said that they would become pregnant, take the amniocentesis test, and abort all male fetuses. Others, who also valued parenthood highly and felt that a hemophiliac could lead a worthwhile life but were deeply opposed to abortion, decided that they would simply go ahead and have a child. And still other people suggested alternative courses of action, which depended on the results of the carrier test and amniocentesis test. We have discussed Ruth Mason's problem with several hundred friends, colleagues, and students; there is no consensus, not even a majority view.

Not only might other individuals choose a course of action different from what Ruth Mason decided in the dialogue above; Mason herself might choose differently if she thought about her dilemma some more. As discussed earlier, her decision tree is incomplete; it is a clear and conscious simplification of reality. It does not, for example, include the decision about whether or not to have a second child. Mason might want to expand her diagram to include some additional factors. And if she did so, she might change her mind about what to do. Chapter 12, on the dynamics of analysis, includes a discussion of how a decision maker can decide whether to do a more elaborate analysis.

Mason's dilemma dramatizes the advantage of systematically decomposing a puzzling problem into more manageable subproblems, which can be analyzed one by one. In the dialogue, Mason resolved her dilemma by resolving a series of less complicated decisions, such as whether she would remain childless or try to adopt a child, or whether she would have an abortion if she knew the fetus she was carrying was a male with a 50-percent chance of being a hemophiliac. *These* decisions are by no means simple to make, but they are easier to think about than Mason's total dilemma. Indeed, most of these subdecisions —once they were defined—were so clear to her that she could resolve them without explicitly assessing any preference-probabilities. In the entire analysis, she assessed only one preference-probability, that for the remain-childless outcome. Thus, as described here, Ruth Mason's decision was a dilemma because it was very complex—because it was a decision problem involving an intertwined series of successive decisions. For such compound decisions, the process of decomposition and the future-first principle can be the key to a useful analysis and a successful resolution of the dilemma.

Deciding Whether to Obtain More Information

Two of the decisions that compounded Mason's dilemma concerned whether to obtain additional information before making the main decisions of the dilemma. Before she decided whether to become pregnant, she could obtain information by taking the carrier test. And before deciding whether to have an abortion, she could obtain information by taking the amniocentesis test. Indeed, any decision dilemma can be compounded by the opportunity to collect more information before making the main decision.

Such information can be valuable if it alters the decision maker's uncertainty about future events by changing the probabilities for various possible outcomes. The information would be "perfect" if it eliminated all uncertainty and permitted a faultless prediction of the future. The amniocentesis test provides perfect information on whether a fetus is male or female. The information collected would be "imperfect" if it changed the uncertainty but did not eliminate it; in terms of whether or not a fetus is a male hemophiliac, the amniocentesis test provides only imperfect information,[8] since it changes the probabilities of having a male hemophiliac but does not eliminate the uncertainty about whether the fetus is a male hemophiliac.

Since the decision about collecting the information must be made before the main decision, it appears before the main decision on the decision tree (figure 10–11). Then, the decision branch for not collecting the information and the

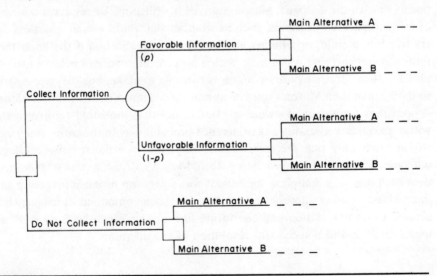

Figure 10–11. The Prototypal Tree for a Decision Dilemma, Compounded by the Opportunity to Collect Information.

Compound Decision Dilemmas

various outcome branches for all the different possible types of information that might be obtained lead to the same primary choice (in figure 10–11, between "Main Alternative A" and "Main Alternative B"). This was indeed the fundamental structure of Ruth Mason's dilemma (figure 10–7) and of a vast variety of dilemmas where such preliminary informational decisions naturally arise.

For many decisions about whether to collect information, the various uncertain informational outcomes will not be limited to a few possibilities (such as positive and negative, or favorable, ambiguous, and unfavorable). The information may be an uncertain quantity, so that there is a spectrum of possible outcomes. This, for example, is usually the case when a business's main decision about whether to introduce a new product (see figure 6–14) is compounded by the informational decision concerning whether to test market the new product.

The Test-Market Compound Dilemma

Test marketing can provide information on consumer acceptance of a new product (and, perhaps, on the effectiveness of various marketing techniques). Of course, a firm carrying out such testing would be uncertain about what that information would be—if it were certain, there would be no need to gather the information—and the types of possible information could cover an entire spectrum of outcomes. If the market test produced a favorable consumer response, the decision would be to introduce the product; if the test were unfavorable, the product would not be introduced. Regardless of whether the firm decides to test market the product, and regardless of the information obtained, the firm must still make the main decision about whether to introduce the product. In fact, the decision-tree segments that follow any (informational) outcome branch and that follow the decision branch for no test market have the same structure; the results of test-market information change only the probabilities of getting high, medium, and low sales. The basic structure of this test-market compound dilemma, as illustrated in figure 10–12, is thus similar to the prototype in figure 10–11.

A compound decision of this kind faced the marketing executives of the major U.S. breweries in 1977 as they raced to introduce a new product—low calorie, "light" beer. As each company sought to establish its market share, it shortened the time usually devoted to test marketing. The *Wall Street Journal* reported:

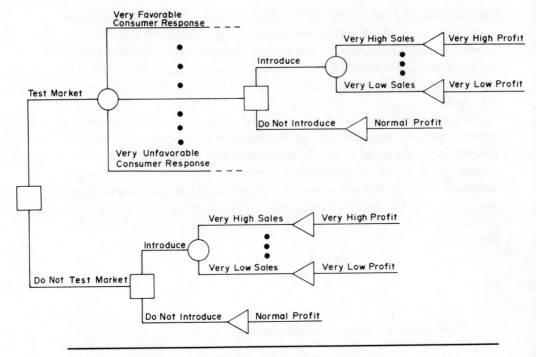

Figure 10–12. A Decision Tree for a Test-Market Compound Dilemma.

Anheuser-Busch . . . introduced its Natural Light in 15 test markets in January 1977—and went national in June. The company "felt safe in rolling ahead faster than expected," says Jack MacDonough, product marketing manager.[9]

Later, Anheuser-Busch introduced its premium brand, Michelob Light. This time the company decided to shun what Robert E. McDowell, Michelob marketing manager, called the "conventional three, six or twelve-month test market."[10]

For a first-cut analysis of the test-market dilemma for light beer, the decision tree can be reduced. Because of the "unprecedented" and "intensified" competition in the light-beer market,[11] the choice may have been strictly between a short, three-month test and immediate introduction. Further, for a first cut it may be helpful to divide the entire spectrum of possible consumer responses into just two categories, favorable and unfavorable. A favorable consumer response would lead directly to a decision to introduce the product; an unfavorable response would lead to the opposite decision. This substantially reduces the decision tree for this dilemma; indeed, it reduces it to a single (noncompound) decision (see figure 10–13).

Compound Decision Dilemmas

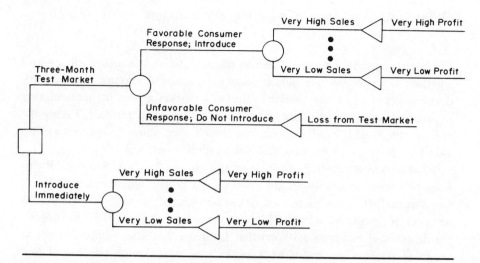

Figure 10–13. Reduced Decision Tree for a First-Cut Analysis of the Test-Market Dilemma.

Resolving a test-market dilemma requires the use of the future-first principle. A firm cannot decide whether to test market a product until it decides what it might do with the various possible results of such a test. For the reduced, first-cut analysis it is necessary to decide on a switch point on the scale of possible consumer responses. At what point, as the consumer response improves from very unfavorable to very favorable, does the firm switch from not introducing the product to introducing it?

Deciding upon such a switch point, and assessing the probabilities that the consumer response will be above and below it, may require considerable thought. Indeed, to develop an uncertainty curve for the results of a test market and to determine how different types of consumer responses can be used to make probabilistic predictions of future sales, a marketing executive may wish to obtain the services of an experienced statistician. Resolving a test-market dilemma may require some researched analysis,[12] but an initial quick analysis of the problem, based on something like the reduced decision tree in figure 10–13, may help a marketing executive organize his thinking about the decision and determine what information he really needs to make the final judgment.

Other Decisions About Collecting Information

A politician attempting to decide whether to seek another office—and whether to commission a public opinion poll before making that primary decision—is in a position similar to that of a marketing executive attempting to decide whether to introduce and/or test market a new product. Taking the poll produces additional information, which then must be translated into assessments of the probability that the candidate will win.

When he was attempting to decide whether to run for the U.S. Senate, Rufus Edmisten spent fifteen thousand dollars on a poll of seven hundred North Carolinians.[13] If he had been in doubt about whether to take this survey, his decision tree might have looked like the one in figure 10–14. Here, to simplify the diagram, it has been assumed that Edmisten has already decided not to resign as attorney general if he wins the primary—though the information obtained from the poll could influence that decision too.

Again, after receiving "favorable" polling results, Edmisten would run, and with "unfavorable" results he would not. Analyzing this compound decision requires determining how the poll results will affect p_1 and p_2, the probabilities of winning the primary and the election, and then determining the switch point for the poll results.

This decision tree (figure 10–14) can also be reduced by using the future-first principle; for each of the different types of polling information that he can obtain, Edmisten could make a conditional decision about whether to run. To do this, Edmisten would decide what poll responses would cause him to run and what responses would result in the opposite decision. And he would also decide what he would do if he did not take a poll. Then, the decision tree could be reduced to one with a single, immediate decision: whether or not to take the poll.

In addition to the dilemma confronting women who, like Ruth Mason, are potential carriers of the hemophilia gene, a variety of other medical problems involve deciding whether to collect more information by performing diagnostic tests. For example, the angina decision dilemma of chapter 2 can be compounded by the requirement that an angiogram (or aniography) be taken prior to having coronary-artery bypass surgery. (In chapter 2, this dilemma was analyzed *after* the angiogram had been taken.) This diagnostic test is painful, costly, and dangerous. Thomas A. Preston, professor of medicine at the University of Washington in Seattle, concludes that "the risk of death . . . averages approximately 0.2 to 0.5% for all cases, and about 3% with major lesions of the left coronary artery."[14]

Thus, the decision tree for the compound angina dilemma is complicated by the need to include not only the various possible results of the angiogram, but

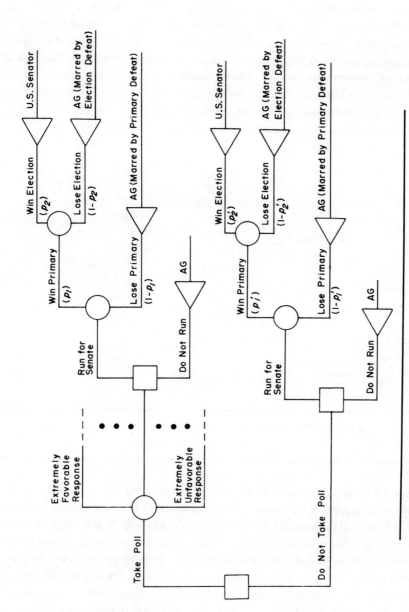

Figure 10–14. Edmisten's Dilemma, Compounded by the Polling Decision.

also by the question of whether the patient survives the test. Still, the tree can be reduced to a form that is simpler than the prototypal one for any dilemma compounded by the opportunity to collect more information (figure 10–11). First, a preliminary decision not to have the test precludes surgery (and thus ensures continued medical treatment). Further, by dividing the possible results of the angiogram into two categories—those that imply surgical treatment and those that imply continuing with the medical treatment—the decision tree can be further simplified. It can, in fact, be reduced to a single decision about whether to have the angiogram—for the main decision can be made automatically once the results of the test are known (see figure 10–15).

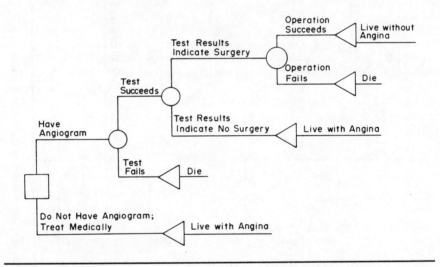

Figure 10–15. A Reduced Decision Tree for the Angina Dilemma, Compounded by the Angiogram Decision.

This is a direct result of the future-first principle. One cannot decide whether to take the angiogram until one determines whether the information might be worthwhile, that is, whether it can affect one's decision. It is no more difficult to decide, before one takes the angiogram, whether a particular result would cause one to have surgery or to continue medical treatment, than it is to make that same decision after actually receiving that result. Of course, an analysis of the entire compound dilemma requires making a decision for all the possible diagnostic results, but all one must really determine is one's switch point.[15]

Much of the initial research in decision analysis concerned the question of whether more information should be collected before making main decisions. As a result, a large literature now exists on the subject, including some excellent textbooks.[16] Most of it is devoted to questions of researched analysis—how to use statistical data to improve one's probabilistic predictions for uncertain outcomes.[17] Nevertheless, even in those situations where a researched analysis is necessary to process the data, an initial quick analysis can help structure the dilemma and reveal what type of information may be most useful.

Information and the Future-First Principle

The future-first principle applies to all simple decisions compounded by the opportunity to collect additional information. In some situations, the information can be obtained at no, or very little, cost. This was the case with the carrier test for Ruth Mason. In such circumstances, it usually makes sense to obtain the information before making the main decision.

In other situations, the same alternative (of the main decision) would be chosen regardless of what type of information is obtained. For example, Ruth Mason (after she had received a negative carrier test) would not have an abortion regardless of whether the amniocentesis test revealed the fetus to be male or female. In such circumstances, there is no reason to bother obtaining the (useless) information.

In other circumstances, additional information may make the main decision obvious. After obtaining one informational result, the decision maker will clearly choose a particular (main) alternative; with different information, however, he will easily choose a different (main) alternative. In this situation, structuring the problem—organizing one's thinking—may be sufficient to reveal which alternative is preferred. This was the case for Ruth Mason; she needed to assess only one preference probability to resolve her dilemma.

In many situations, however, the dilemma will be sufficiently puzzling that a more thorough analysis is required. It will be necessary to decompose the problem into the various informational results that might be obtained, and to decide how the future, main decision will be made for each possible result. Then, it will be necessary to consider all of these future, main decisions to make the immediate one about whether to collect additional information.

All this reveals the importance of the future-first principle. In nature, the present influences, and often limits, the future. In decision making, however, the future can influence—and also limit—the present. Analytical decision makers need to exploit foresight about their future decisions in order to make better immediate ones and thus create a more desirable future.

Appendix: More on Working with Probabilities

To assess the probabilities necessary to resolve Ruth Mason's dilemma, one more concept concerning probabilities (beyond the four rules explained in the appendix to chapter 4) must be introduced. This idea is known as *Bayes's Theorem,* but the same result can be obtained by "flipping" a probability tree. This is done when you know Prob $(B|A)$ but need Prob $(A|B)$ to resolve your decision dilemma. That is, you know the probabilities in the tree in figure 10–16a, but need the ones in the tree in figure 10–16b. Essentially, this second probability tree is just the reverse of the first; the first uncertain event concerns B or $\bar{B}$, and the second concerns A or $\bar{A}$. Thus, to obtain Prob $(A|B)$ you need to flip the original probability tree on the top in figure 10–16 to obtain the one on the bottom.

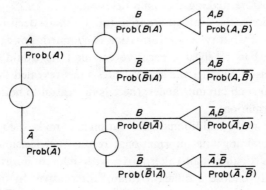

(a) The Original Tree

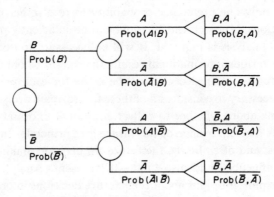

(b) The Flipped Tree

Figure 10–16. "Flipping" a Probability Tree.

Compound Decision Dilemmas

The probabilities on the second tree in figure 10–16 can be obtained from those on the first tree with a few simple steps that make use of the probability rules described in the appendix to chapter 4.

Step 1. Obtain the terminal probabilities on the original tree. Use the six outcome branch probabilities—Prob(A), Prob($\bar{A}$), Prob($B|A$), Prob($\bar{B}|A$), Prob($B|\bar{A}$), and Prob($\bar{B}|\bar{A}$)—to obtain the four terminal outcome probabilities —Prob(A,B), Prob($A,\bar{B}$), Prob($\bar{A},B$), and Prob($\bar{A},\bar{B}$)—by multiplying the branch probabilities along the paths from the original uncertainty node to the various terminal nodes. (This is probability rule 2 in the appendix to chapter 4.) For example,

Prob(A,B) = Prob(A) $\times$ Prob($B|A$).

Step 2. Obtain the *terminal probabilities* for the flipped tree. Observe that Prob(A,B) must equal Prob(B,A), since the probability that A and B will occur is exactly the same as the probability that B and A will occur. Thus, the probabilities for the terminal outcomes on the flipped tree (figure 10–16b) can be obtained directly from the corresponding terminal outcomes on the original tree (figure 10–16a).

Step 3. Obtain the *unconditional probabilities* for the initial uncertain event of the flipped tree. Do this by adding up the probabilities for all the terminal outcomes that correspond to each outcome (B and $\bar{B}$) of that uncertain event:

Prob(B) = Prob(B,A) + Prob($B,\bar{A}$).
Prob($\bar{B}$) = Prob($\bar{B},A$) + Prob($\bar{B},\bar{A}$).

(This is probability rule 4.)

Step 4. Obtain the *conditional probabilities* for the flipped tree. To do this, use the rule about multiplying the outcome branch probabilities along the path from the original uncertainty node to obtain the probability for a terminal outcome (rule 2). For example, since

Prob(B,A) = Prob(B) $\times$ Prob($A|B$),

both sides of this equation can be divided by Prob(B), so that

$$\text{Prob}(A|B) = \frac{\text{Prob}(B,A)}{\text{Prob}(B)}.$$

This gives the conditional probability, Prob($A|B$), that created the need to flip the tree; the conditional probability Prob($B|A$) was known, but the conditional probability Prob($A|B$) was needed.

The other three conditional probabilities for the flipped probability tree can be obtained from similar equations:

$$\text{Prob}(A|\bar{B}) = \frac{\text{Prob}(\bar{B},A)}{\text{Prob}(\bar{B})};$$

$$\text{Prob}(\bar{A}|B) = \frac{\text{Prob}(B,\bar{A})}{\text{Prob}(B)};$$

$$\text{Prob}(\bar{A}|\bar{B}) = \frac{\text{Prob}(\bar{B},\bar{A})}{\text{Prob}(\bar{B})}.$$

This process of flipping the probability tree—of reversing the order of the uncertain events—is mathematically identical to using the formula known as *Bayes's theorem*.

Indeed, Bayes's theorem can be derived from this tree-flipping process. Take the final formula in step 4 for the conditional probability Prob($A|B$) and insert the formula from step 1 for the joint probability Prob(B,A):

$$\text{Prob}(A|B) = \frac{\text{Prob}(B,A)}{\text{Prob}(B)} = \frac{\text{Prob}(A,B)}{\text{Prob}(B)} = \frac{\text{Prob}(A) \times \text{Prob}(B|A)}{\text{Prob}(B)}.$$

This is one expression for Bayes's theorem. Another can be derived by replacing the denominator, Prob(B), with the formula for it from step 3:

$$\text{Prob}(A|B) = \frac{\text{Prob}(A) \times \text{Prob}(B|A)}{\text{Prob}(B,A) + \text{Prob}(B,\bar{A})}.$$

And, finally, the two joint probabilities in the denominator can be replaced with the formula from step 1:

$$\text{Prob}(A|B) = \frac{\text{Prob}(A) \times \text{Prob}(B|A)}{[\text{Prob}(A) \times \text{Prob}(B|A)] + [\text{Prob}(\bar{A}) \times \text{Prob}(B|\bar{A})]}.$$

This formula is usually given as the full expression of Bayes's theorem.

When the probabilities in question become more complex—when there are more than two uncertainties or more than two outcomes—using the formula can become difficult and confusing. The process of flipping the probability tree remains essentially the same, however, regardless of how complicated the uncertainties are.

The value of knowing how to flip a probability tree is demonstrated by the probabilities that need to be assessed to resolve Ruth Mason's dilemma. These are the probabilities that a fetus will have the hemophilia gene "given" three different circumstances: Mason takes the carrier test and it is positive; she takes the carrier test and it is negative; and she does not take the carrier test.

Compound Decision Dilemmas

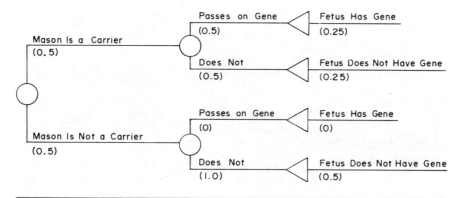

Figure 10–17. The Probability Tree for Assessing the Probability that Mason's Child Has the Hemophilia Gene, Given No Carrier Test.

Take the third situation first—no carrier test. The case states that there is one chance in two that Mason is a carrier. If she is, there is one chance in two (given the laws of genetics) that she will pass on the hemophilia gene to her child. This information can be organized on a probability tree (see figure 10–17). Multiplying along each path from the initial uncertainty node to the terminal node and then adding up the probabilities for all the terminal outcomes for which the fetus has the gene gives the probability as 0.25: Prob(Fetus Has Gene|No Carrier Test) = 0.25.

If Mason takes the carrier test and the result is positive, there is a 100-percent chance, according to the case, that she has the gene. Thus, in this situation, the probability that any child of Mason's will have the gene is 0.5: Prob(Fetus Has Gene|Positive) = 0.5.

If, however, she takes the carrier test and the result is negative, the task of assessing the probability that any child of hers will have the gene becomes more complicated. This is because the information given in the case is that the test will only pick up 80 to 95 percent of the women who are carriers, that is, Prob(Positive|Carrier) = 0.80 to 0.95, or Prob(Negative|Carrier) = 0.05 to 0.20. The case does *not* give one of the conditional probabilities that is necessary to resolve the dilemma, Prob(Carrier|Negative). To obtain this probability, it is necessary to flip a probability tree.

The information that is given is displayed on the probability tree in figure 10–18. Here it is assumed that, for Mason, the probability of getting a positive test if she is a carrier is 0.8. This is the "worst case" situation; the probability at the "least reliable" end of the 80–95 percent range has been selected so that there is a high, 20-percent chance that a carrier will get a negative test result. This will give the highest possible probability for Mason having the gene given a negative test. If some other value (say, 85 or 95 percent) for the probability of getting a positive test from a carrier seems more appropriate, it could be used

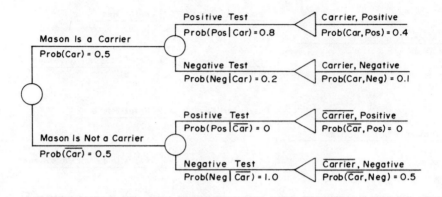

Figure 10–18. The Probability Tree for Ruth Mason's Dilemma (for Which the Probabilities Are Given).

instead. Note that on the probability tree, the probability that the test will be positive if Mason is not a carrier, Prob(Pos|$\overline{\text{Car}}$), is given as 0. If (as the case states) a positive result gives a 100-percent guarantee that the woman has the gene, such a result cannot come from a woman who is not a carrier. Thus, Prob(Pos|$\overline{\text{Car}}$) = 0.

To obtain the probabilities needed to resolve the dilemma, Prob(Car|Neg) and Prob($\overline{\text{Car}}$|Neg), it is necessary to develop a probability tree on which these probabilities appear explicitly. Then, the probabilities from the original tree (figure 10–18) can be used to obtain the probabilities for this flipped tree (figure 10–19).

The first step is to calculate the terminal probabilities for the original tree, which has already been done. Then, these probabilities are used to obtain the corresponding (identical) terminal probabilities for the flipped tree, such as Prob(Pos,Car) = Prob(Car,Pos) = 0.4.

The third step is to calculate the probabilities of getting a positive test and a negative test:

Prob(Pos) = Prob(Pos,Car) + Prob(Pos,$\overline{\text{Car}}$) = 0.4 + 0 = 0.4.
Prob(Neg) = Prob(Neg,Car) + Prob(Neg,$\overline{\text{Car}}$) = 0.1 + 0.5 = 0.6.

These numbers are then placed under the outcome branches attached to the first uncertainty node in figure 10–19.

The final step is to calculate the conditional probabilities that motivated the entire analysis:

$$\text{Prob(Car|Neg)} = \frac{\text{Prob(Neg,Car)}}{\text{Prob(Neg)}} = \frac{0.1}{0.6} = 0.167.$$

Compound Decision Dilemmas

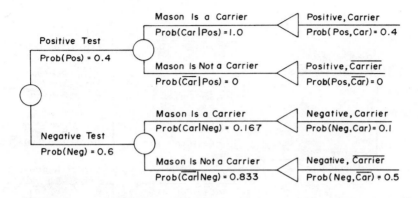

Figure 10–19. The Flipped Probability Tree for Ruth Mason's Dilemma (for Which the Probabilities Have Been Calculated).

$$\mathrm{Prob}(\overline{\mathrm{Car}}|\mathrm{Neg}) = \frac{\mathrm{Prob}(\mathrm{Neg},\overline{\mathrm{Car}})}{\mathrm{Prob}(\mathrm{Neg})} = \frac{0.5}{0.6} = 0.833.$$

Note also that this type of calculation can be used to double-check the conditional probabilities given a positive test, which were previously determined.

$$\mathrm{Prob}(\mathrm{Car}|\mathrm{Pos}) = \frac{\mathrm{Prob}(\mathrm{Pos},\mathrm{Car})}{\mathrm{Prob}(\mathrm{Pos})} = \frac{0.4}{0.4} = 1.0.$$

$$\mathrm{Prob}(\overline{\mathrm{Car}}|\mathrm{Pos}) = \frac{\mathrm{Prob}(\mathrm{Pos},\overline{\mathrm{Car}})}{\mathrm{Prob}(\mathrm{Pos})} = \frac{0}{0.4} = 0.$$

Of course, these are not exactly the probabilities needed for Mason's decision tree (figure 10–7). The probability that is really important is the probability that a fetus has the gene given a negative test. If Mason is a carrier, there is a 50-percent chance that any child of hers will receive the hemophilia gene. Thus, there is a 0.5 × 0.167, or 0.083, chance of this happening if the carrier test is negative:

Prob(Fetus Has Gene|Negative) = 0.5 × 0.167 = 0.083.

This was the probability used on the decision tree (figure 10–7).

This probability can also be obtained directly by "flipping" the slightly more complicated probability tree in figure 10–20. This tree is the same as the one in figure 10–18, *but* with the addition of the uncertainty about whether the hemophilia gene will be passed on to a fetus. Consequently, there is a third series of uncertainty nodes, and the terminal outcomes involve three consequences: (1) whether or not Mason is a carrier; (2) whether the test is positive

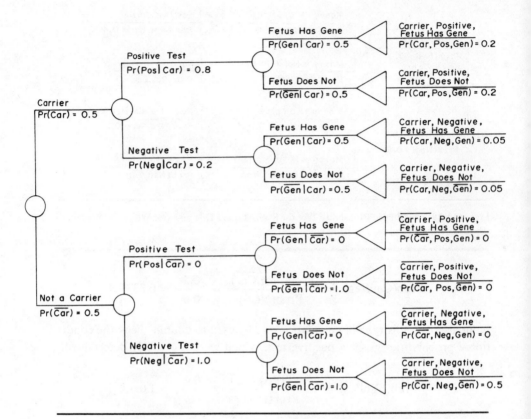

Figure 10–20. Another "Original" Probability Tree for Ruth Mason's Dilemma.

or negative; and (3) whether or not the fetus has the gene. All the branch probabilities on this tree were given in the case, and the terminal probabilities were calculated from them by multiplying along a path from the original uncertainty node to each terminal node.

To obtain the two probabilities needed to resolve Mason's dilemma, Prob (Gen|Neg) and Prob($\overline{Gen}$|Neg) (where "Gen" indicates a fetus has the gene), it is necessary to construct a probability tree on which this conditional uncertainty appears explicitly. This means that there will have to be an outcome branch to indicate a negative result of the carrier test, followed by an uncertainty node with two possible outcomes—"Fetus Has Gene" and "Fetus Does Not." This is all that is necessary, for the required probabilities will appear directly on this new probability tree.

Such a flipped probability tree is shown in figure 10–21. Note, however, that this tree does not really reverse the order of the uncertain events from that of the "original" tree. Rather, since the probability of Mason being a carrier is not needed on the decision tree used to analyze her dilemma (figure 10–7), this

Compound Decision Dilemmas

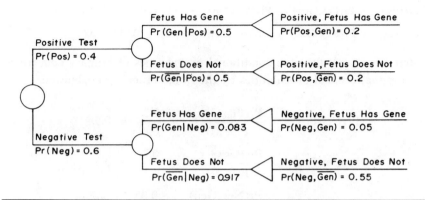

Figure 10–21. A Flipped Probability Tree for Ruth Mason's Dilemma, Giving Directly the Probability that a Fetus Has the Gene.

uncertain event has been eliminated. The result is that the two conditional probabilities of primary concern, Prob(Gen|Neg) and Prob($\overline{\text{Gen}}$|Neg), appear explicitly on the flipped probability tree. On the original probability tree (figure 10–20), whether the fetus had the gene was conditional *only* on whether Mason was a carrier; on the flipped tree (figure 10–21), it is conditional *only* on whether the results of her carrier test are positive or negative.

To calculate the probabilities of primary concern on the flipped tree, just follow the four-step process described at the beginning of this appendix. The terminal probabilities on the original tree (figure 10–20) have already been calculated. So step 2 is to determine the terminal probabilities for the flipped tree by comparing them with the terminal probabilities on the original. There is no one-to-one comparison, since there are more terminal outcomes on the original than on the flipped tree. But the probability for each terminal outcome on the flipped tree can be obtained (using probability rule 4 from the appendix to chapter 4) by adding up the probabilities for the corresponding terminal outcomes on the original tree:

$$\text{Pr(Pos,Gen)} = \text{Pr(Car,Pos,Gen)} + \text{Pr}(\overline{\text{Car}}\text{,Pos,Gen}) = 0.2 + 0 = 0.2.$$

$$\text{Pr(Pos,}\overline{\text{Gen}}\text{)} = \text{Pr(Car,Pos,}\overline{\text{Gen}}\text{)} + \text{Pr}(\overline{\text{Car}}\text{,Pos,}\overline{\text{Gen}}\text{)} = 0.2 + 0 = 0.2.$$

$$\text{Pr(Neg,Gen)} = \text{Pr(Car,Neg,Gen)} + \text{Pr}(\overline{\text{Car}}\text{,Neg,Gen}) = 0.05 + 0 = 0.05.$$

$$\text{Pr(Neg,}\overline{\text{Gen}}\text{)} = \text{Pr(Car,Neg,}\overline{\text{Gen}}\text{)} + \text{Pr}(\overline{\text{Car}}\text{,Neg,}\overline{\text{Gen}}\text{)} = 0.05 + 0.5 = 0.55.$$

Note that these four terminal probabilities sum to 1.0, as should be the case by probability rule 3.

Step 3 is to calculate the unconditional probabilities for the original uncertainty node, Pr(Pos) and Pr(Neg). These can be obtained by adding up the corresponding terminal probabilities (from either the original or flipped tree):

$$\text{Pr(Pos)} = \text{Pr(Pos,Gen)} + \text{Pr(Pos,}\overline{\text{Gen}}) = 0.2 + 0.2 = 0.4.$$

$$\text{Pr(Neg)} = \text{Pr(Neg,Gen)} + \text{Pr(Neg,}\overline{\text{Gen}}) = 0.05 + 0.55 = 0.6.$$

Step 4 is to calculate the conditional probabilities of primary concern by dividing the terminal probabilities by the initial branch probabilities:

$$\text{Pr(Gen|Pos)} = \frac{\text{Pr(Pos,Gen)}}{\text{Pr(Pos)}} = \frac{0.2}{0.4} = 0.5.$$

$$\text{Pr(}\overline{\text{Gen}}\text{|Pos)} = \frac{\text{Pr(Pos,}\overline{\text{Gen}})}{\text{Pr(Pos)}} = \frac{0.2}{0.4} = 0.5.$$

$$\text{Pr(Gen|Neg)} = \frac{\text{Pr(Neg,Gen)}}{\text{Pr(Neg)}} = \frac{0.05}{0.6} = 0.083.$$

$$\text{Pr(}\overline{\text{Gen}}\text{|Neg)} = \frac{\text{Pr(Neg,}\overline{\text{Gen}})}{\text{Pr(Neg)}} = \frac{0.55}{0.6} = 0.917.$$

These four probabilities were used on the decision tree for Mason's dilemma (figure 10–7). The conditional probability of 0.5 for a fetus having the gene given a positive test was easy enough to determine; a positive test guaranteed that Mason was a carrier, and there is a 50-percent chance that a carrier will pass the gene on to any fetus. Without analysis, however, it is more complicated to think about the conditional probability for a fetus having the gene given a negative test. But, by constructing a flipped probability tree that involves this probability directly it is not difficult to obtain this conditional probability of primary concern.

Chapter 11

Conflicting Consequences and Trade-Off Analysis: The Raleigh-Durham Airport Decision

IN April 1976, the Raleigh-Durham Airport Authority faced a major decision. The main runway at RDU Airport had begun to break up and was very much in need of repair. Since this was the only runway that could handle commercial air traffic, the airport authority had two alternatives:

1. Close down the airport for approximately one month and reconstruct the entire runway. This rebuild-runway alternative would cost $1.5 million and the rebuilt runway would last for 10 to 12 years.
2. Repair the existing runway at night while the airport was not in use. This mend-runway alternative would cost $2 million (because the work would have to be done at night, piecemeal), and the mended runway would last 5 to 7 years.

(Of course, as one member of the airport authority pointed out, there was a third alternative—do nothing. But this, observed the airport engineer, would mean that RDU would "face a closure this winter."[1])

For each alternative, there are three important consequences: runway life, operational status of the airport during the repair period, and cost. A decision tree describing this dilemma thus will have three *consequence branches* attached to each of the outcome nodes (figure 11–1). As is necessarily the case,

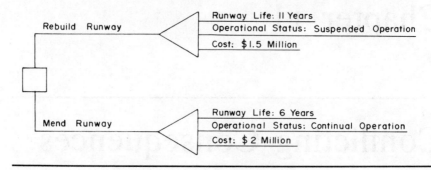

Figure 11–1. A Decision Tree for the Airport-Repair Dilemma.

this decision tree is a simplification. There was some uncertainty about how long the mended and rebuilt runways would last. Further, how long the airport would have to suspend operation to rebuild the runway was also uncertain; it might take three, four, or five weeks. But these uncertainties were not the central reasons why this decision was a dilemma, and thus they can be ignored (at least for an initial analysis).

The airport-repair decision is a dilemma because of the conflicting consequences. For each alternative there exists more than one important consequence—more than one consequence that must be taken into account when evaluating and comparing the alternatives—and neither of these alternatives produces the best result for all of the different consequences. The rebuild alternative is best for runway life and cost; the mend alternative is best for the other consequence, operational status. To make this type of decision, to resolve this conflict between consequences, it is necessary to make trade-offs—to decide how much of one consequence to give up to gain more of another. For example, how many years of runway life is the airport authority willing to sacrifice to have continual rather than suspended operations?

This trade-off between runway life and operational status is the essence of the airport-repair dilemma. For a first-cut analysis, it can be assumed that the $500,000 difference in cost between the two alternatives is much less important than the 5-years difference in runway life and the difference between continual operation of the airport and a month of suspended operation. This does not mean that money is unimportant to the airport authority; for some of its decisions, money is very important. But the *difference* between these two alternatives in terms of the cost consequence is much less significant than the *difference* between the two alternatives in terms of the runway-life consequence and the operational-status consequence. If the cost *difference* between the two alternatives were $10 million, the monetary consequence would be very important—perhaps so important that it would overwhelm all other

Conflicting Consequences and Trade-Off Analysis

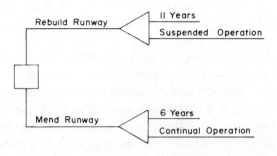

Figure 11–2. A Decision Tree for a First-Cut Analysis of the Airport-Repair Dilemma.

consequences and dictate the decision. But for this decision, the two conse-quences that the airport authority considers to be the most important are runway life and operational status. The cost consequence can be ignored for the first-cut analysis, and the decision tree simplified so that each outcome is characterized by only two consequences (figure 11–2).

Which of many consequences to include on a decision tree (and thus to consider in a decision analysis) cannot be determined in the abstract. It is impossible to develop an all-purpose ranking of the importance of possible consequences. Which consequences are most important depends upon the specific dilemma. For it is the *range* of any possible consequence—the differ-ence between the highest and the lowest possible value of that consequence—that determines how important it is. The greater the difference between the various outcomes in terms of a particular consequence, the more important is that consequence. For the RDU Airport Authority, the $500,000 cost range between the two alternatives is sufficiently small, when compared to the range of the other two consequences, that cost can be ignored in a first-cut analysis. The airport-repair decision is a dilemma because if the airport is kept open, only a short-term repair can be made, but to make a long-lasting repair, the airport must be closed. This is the fundamental trade-off.

A First-Cut Analysis

An initial analysis of this decision must compare two outcomes in terms of two consequences. To analyze the trade-off between runway life and opera-tional status, the airport authority must specify how much of one consequence it is willing to sacrifice to gain the other. For example, given that the airport authority can have a 6-year runway without closing the airport, how many years of runway life must it gain if it is to give up continual operation of the airport?

Clearly, the addition of just one more year to the runway's life would not be sufficient to compensate the airport authority for suspending operation. That is, the airport authority prefers the outcome of the mend-runway alternative (a 6-year runway, and continual operation) to the hypothetical outcome of a 7-year runway obtained at the price of one month of suspended operation (figure 11–3). On the other hand, the authority would be more than willing to suspend operations for a month if that would add 25 years to the runaway's life (figure 11–4). Thus, the basic question is, Exactly how many more years must be added to the life of the runway to compensate the airport authority for suspending operations? Or, from figure 11–5, what should Y be (in years) so that the airport authority is indifferent between the outcome of the mend-runway alternative and the hypothetical outcome?

Given the preferences expressed in figures 11–3 and 11–4, Y is somewhere between 7 and 31 years. Now, the best process for assessing the hypothetical consequence Y that makes the airport authority indifferent between the two outcomes is to narrow the range of possibilities. (This avoids our old nemesis,

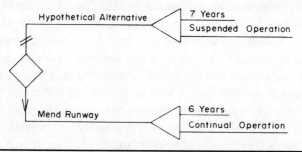

Figure 11–3. Comparing the Mend-Runaway Alternative with a Hypothetical Alternative.

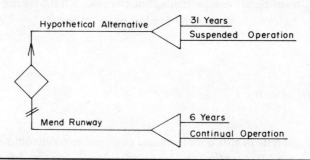

Figure 11–4. Comparing the Mend-Runway Alternative with Another Hypothetical Alternative.

Conflicting Consequences and Trade-Off Analysis

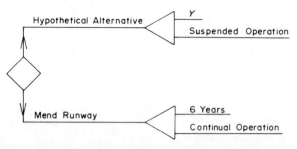

Figure 11–5. The Basic Indifference Question for the Airport-Repair Dilemma.

the anchoring and adjustment heuristic.) Suppose that the airport authority determines that if $Y = 9$ years, it prefers the outcome of the mend-runway alternative, but if $Y = 20$ years, it prefers the hypothetical outcome. Finally, suppose the airport authority decides that the runway life that makes it indifferent between the two outcomes is just about 15 years.

The reason for developing the hypothetical indifference decision in figure 11–6 may be obscure, but by using the substitution principle the motivation will become clear. Since the airport authority is indifferent between the two outcomes in figure 11–6, it can substitute one for the other. In particular, on the first-cut decision tree (figure 11–2), it can replace the outcome of the mend-runway alternative with the hypothetical outcome in figure 11–6, without affecting its relative preferences for the two original alternatives.

Expressed this way (figure 11–7), the best choice is obvious. Since the second consequence (operational status) is the same for both outcomes, it can be ignored and the decision based on the first consequence. This is called the *independence principle:* If one consequence is the same for all outcomes, the decision is independent of the value of that consequence and thus can be made by comparing all the outcomes in terms of the remaining consequence(s).[2] Since a 15-year runway is preferred to an 11-year runway, the mend-runway

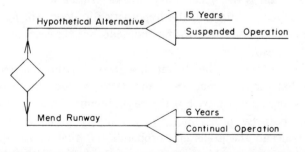

Figure 11–6. An Indifference Relation for the Outcome of the Mend-Runway Alternative.

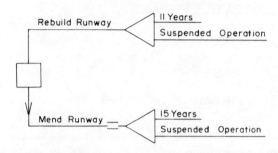

Figure 11–7. Using the Substitution and Independence Principles to Resolve the Airport-Repair Dilemma.

alternative is preferred as well. Developing the indifference relation in figure 11–6 was motivated by the desire to replace (on the decision tree) the outcome of the mend-runway alternative with an indifference outcome, one consequence of which was identical to the corresponding consequence of the rebuild-runway alternative.

Of course, it is not really necessary to make formal, explicit use of the substitution principle to resolve this dilemma. The preferred alternative is obvious from figure 11–6. This indifference relationship indicates that the airport authority is indifferent between the hypothetical outcome and the mend outcome. Thus, if the runway-life consequence of the hypothetical outcome is reduced from 15 to 11 years—so that this outcome is worsened and becomes the rebuild outcome—then the authority would prefer the mend outcome. But recognizing this implication of the hypothetical indifference decision in figure 11–6 is nothing more than an implicit, application of the substitution principle.

Furthermore, it is not really necessary to specify precisely the runway-life Y that makes the airport authority indifferent between the two outcomes in figure 11–5. All that is really necessary is to determine whether Y is greater or less than 11 years. After all, the hypothetical outcome in figure 11–5 is merely the rebuild outcome with the first consequence (11 years of runway life) replaced by the unspecified Y.

The logic used to resolve this dilemma, with two conflicting consequences, is similar to that used (in chapters 2 and 3) to examine the basic decision dilemma involving uncertainty. For the basic dilemma, it is not really necessary to specify both the probability p of getting the *Best* outcome from the risky alternative and the preference-probability V that makes the decision maker indifferent between the consequence of the riskless alternative and the reference gamble. To resolve the basic dilemma it is only necessary to determine which is greater, p or V. Nevertheless, the roles of p and V are explained

Conflicting Consequences and Trade-Off Analysis

when the basic dilemma is first introduced because they are essential tools for analyzing decisions with more complex uncertainties. Similarly, the reason for analyzing the dilemma with two conflicting consequences by specifying Y, the *indifference consequence,* is to lay the groundwork for the analysis of decisions complicated by three or more conflicting consequences.

Reanalyzing the First Cut

The first-cut analysis of the airport-repair dilemma was based on the question implicit in figure 11–5: How many years *more* than 6 does the runway have to last to compensate the airport authority for suspending operation? The answer was 9 years more than it would last if the runway were not closed (15 years total). This 9 years could be called the *compensating change, X*—the amount that one consequence must be adjusted to just compensate for a change in another consequence.

There is another way to look at the first-cut dilemma: How many years *less* than 11 can the runway last to compensate for not having to close the airport to make the repairs? This question is equivalent to determining the hypothetical runway life, Y' (a new indifference consequence), such that the airport authority is indifferent between the two alternatives in figure 11–8. Or, another way to look at the question: What is the new compensating change, X' ($= 11 - Y'$), in years of runway life, that will just balance the change in operational status from suspended to continual?

Significantly, X' and X are not necessarily the same—9 years. Just because the airport authority needed to add 9 more years to the life of a 6-year runway to compensate it for closing the airport does not mean that it would necessarily be willing to subtract exactly 9 years from the life of an 11-year runway just

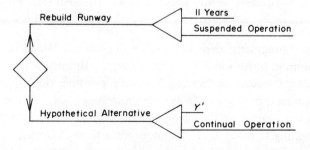

Figure 11–8. Another Basic Indifference Question for the Airport-Repair Dilemma.

to keep the airport open during the repair period. After all, suppose that the airport authority had assessed the original indifference consequence Y (of figure 11–5) to be 20 years; then X would be 14 years, meaning that the airport authority would need 14 more years of runway life to compensate it for suspending operation. But would this mean that X' was also 14 years? If so, then Y' would be 11 years minus 14 years = negative 3 years. A negative runway life does not make sense.

The reason that X' is not necessarily equal to X is that the original position —the outcome from which the trade-offs are made—is important. How many additional years of runway life are needed to compensate for the loss of continual operation depends not only upon the amount of disruption that suspending operation would cause but also upon how long the runway built with continual operation would last. If the runway was to last 5 years when rebuilt with continual operation, the airport authority might demand only 5 additional years of runway life to compensate it for suspending operation. But if the runway was to last 20 years when rebuilt with continual operation, the airport authority might require an additional 30 years in runway life before it was willing to suspend operation to make the repair. There is thus nothing inconsistent about the airport authority being indifferent about both the hypothetical decisions in figure 11–9.[3]

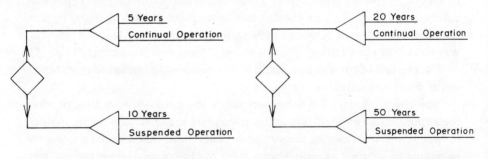

Figure 11–9. Two Compatible (Not Necessarily Inconsistent) Hypothetical Indifference Relations.

All trade-off judgments depend upon one's position. For example, in general, a kingdom is worth much more than a horse. But this is not always true; such a statement assumes a "normal" starting position, that is, a reasonably normal existence. But if your life were in danger and only a horse could save you—if you were caught in the battle on Bosworth Field—you, too, would be more than willing to trade your "kingdom for a horse." Similarly, there is no way to specify for all possible situations how many years of runway life it is worth to keep the airport open during the repair period. The number of years of runway life that the airport authority is willing to sacrifice to keep the

Conflicting Consequences and Trade-Off Analysis

airport open depends upon how long the runway will last when repaired by suspending operations.

Considering the indifference question in figure 11–8, the airport authority decides that if Y' is 10 years it prefers the hypothetical outcome, but if Y' is 1 year it prefers the rebuild outcome. Narrowing the range, the authority finally concludes that $Y' = 4$ years makes it indifferent between the two outcomes. Again, the substitution and independence principles makes this indifference decision helpful. Since the airport authority is indifferent between the hypothetical outcome in figure 11–10 and the rebuild outcome, the former

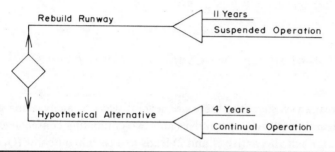

Figure 11–10. An Indifference Relation for the Outcome of the Rebuild-Runaway Alternative.

can be substituted for the latter on the first-cut decision tree (figure 11–2) without affecting the authority's relative preference for the two original alternatives (see figure 11–11).

As before, because the second consequence of both outcomes is the same (although this time it is continual operation rather than suspended operation), the independence principle applies. The decision can be based on the first consequence alone, and clearly a 6-year runway is preferred.

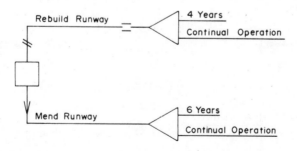

Figure 11–11. Using the Substitution and Independence Principles to Resolve the Airport-Repair Dilemma.

This reanalysis confirms the original decision: The airport authority prefers to mend the runway (maintaining continual operation and getting a runway that will last approximately 6 years) rather than rebuild the runway (suspending operation to get a runway that would last 11 years). If, however, the airport authority had decided that Y' was 7 years—that it was only willing to give up 6 years of runway life to ensure continual operation—this reanalysis would have contradicted the original decision; then the airport authority would have had to reexamine completely both indifference consequences, Y and Y', and thus both compensating changes, X and X'.

Trade-Off Analysis for Two Conflicting Consequences

As this reanalysis suggests, there are several ways to analyze the general decision dilemma with two alternatives and two conflicting consequences (see figure 11–12). Each alternative (1 and 2) leads to a certain outcome (Q_1 or Q_2), and each outcome has two important consequences (A and B). The consequences of outcome Q_1 are A_1 and B_1; the consequences of outcome Q_2 are A_2 and B_2. The decision is a dilemma because consequence A is better for one outcome while consequence B is better for the other (that is, A_1 is better than A_2 while B_2 is better than B_1, or vice versa).

One approach to resolving this general dilemma is to develop a hypothetical indifference outcome, Q_2^*, with two characteristics:

1. The decision maker is indifferent between Q_2^* and Q_2.
2. One of the consequences of Q_2^* is the same as the corresponding consequence of Q_1; for example, $B_2^* = B_1$.

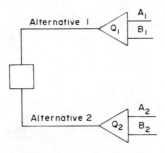

Figure 11–12. The Conflicting-Consequences Dilemma with Two Alternatives and Two Consequences.

Conflicting Consequences and Trade-Off Analysis

Then a decision can be made by simply comparing the two outcomes Q_1 and Q_2^* in terms of the only consequence that is different, A. If A_1 is better than A_2^*, then outcome Q_1 is preferred; if A_2^* is better than A_1, outcome Q_2 is preferred.

Figure 11–13c is the hypothetical indifference relationship that the decision maker develops. Since the decision maker is indifferent between the hypothetical indifference outcome, Q_2^*, and outcome Q_2 (by characteristic 1), the substitution principle applies. Q_2^* from figure 11–13c can be substituted for Q_2 on figure 11–13a to produce a new decision tree, figure 11–13b. (The double-shafted arrow means that figure 11–13c "implies" the change in figure 11–13a that results in figure 11–13b.) Now, since the second consequence of Q_2^* is the same as the second consequence of Q_1 (by characteristic 2), the independence principle can be applied to figure 11–13b—the two alternatives can be compared in terms of the only consequence that is different, consequence A. Thus A is called the *comparison consequence*. Note that the difference between A_2 and A_2^* is the compensating change $(X = A_2 - A_2^*)$; this is the shift in the comparison consequence that just compensates for the change in the other consequence, from B_2 to $B_2^* (= B_1)$.

A decision with two conflicting consequences (figure 11–12) is a dilemma because, with the first alternative preferred in terms of one consequence and

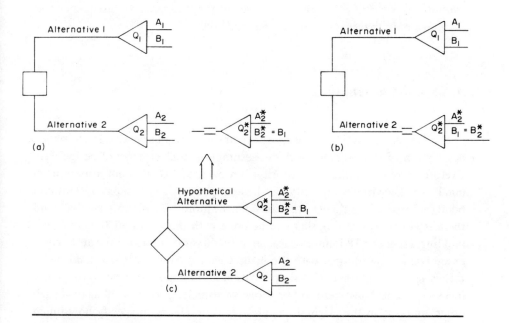

(a)

(b)

(c)

Figure 11–13. Using Trade-Off Analysis to Resolve a Decision Dilemma with Two Alternatives and Two Conflicting Consequences.

the second alternative preferred in terms of the other, it is difficult to compare the two consequences simultaneously. It is therefore necessary to undertake a trade-off analysis—to determine exactly how much of one consequence you are willing to give up to get more of the other. To do this, the decision maker selects a comparison consequence (either A or B) and develops a hypothetical indifference outcome (either Q_1^* or Q_2^*). Thus, for a conflicting-consequences dilemma with two alternatives and two consequences, there are (potentially) four ways to undertake the trade-off analysis.

Trade-Off Approach	Comparison Consequence	Indifference Outcome	Comparison Used to Make Decision
1	A	Q_1^*	A_2 with A_1^*
2	A	Q_2^*	A_1 with A_2^*
3	B	Q_1^*	B_2 with B_1^*
4	B	Q_2^*	B_1 with B_2^*

Note, however, that the comparison consequence must be an incremental quantity, something that can be adjusted by small amounts to just compensate for a change in another consequence. Thus, if one of the two consequences takes on only discrete values (for example, operational status can be only continual or suspended), it cannot be used as the comparison consequence and there are only two ways to make the trade-offs.

A Second-Cut Analysis

The first-cut analysis of the airport-repair dilemma was based on a simplified description of the problem—on the assumption that cost could be ignored. Even for a regional airport authority, however, $500,000 is not a mere marginal cost. The airport authority has the financial capacity to repay a $2 million bond (otherwise it could not even consider the more expensive alternative), and there is always something that can be done with that extra $500,000 (if only building a bigger VIP lounge or leasing more luxurious cars for the authority's executives). Accordingly, with the insight gained from a first-cut analysis, it makes sense to eliminate this simplification and include the cost consequence in a second cut. Now there will be three consequences to trade off against each other, and—as in the original analysis—it is necessary to specify how much of one consequence the airport authority is willing to give up to obtain more of another. (See figure 11–14, where Q_R stands for the outcome of the rebuild-runway alternative, and Q_M for the mend-runway outcome.)

Conflicting Consequences and Trade-Off Analysis

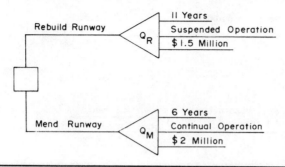

Figure 11–14. A Decision Tree for a Second-Cut Analysis of the Airport-Repair Dilemma.

For example, given that the airport authority can have a 6-year runway at a cost of $2.0 million (with continual operation), how much of the runway's 6-year life would the authority give up to reduce the cost to $1.5 million (still with continual airport operation)? Suppose that the authority decides it is willing to give up 1.5 years of runway life to reduce the cost by $500,000 (see figure 11–15). That makes sense. It would mean that the authority is indifferent between buying a 6-year runway for $2 million and a 4.5-year runway for $1.5 million. Either way, each year of the runway's life costs $333,333.[4]

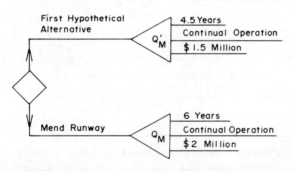

Figure 11–15. An Indifference Relation for the Outcome of the Mend-Runway Alternative.

Having made the trade-off between runway life and cost (while keeping operational status fixed), the next step is to make a second trade-off, this time between runway life and operational status (keeping cost fixed). To do this involves answering the question posed in figure 11–16: How many years more than 4.5 must the runway last to compensate the airport authority for suspending operation (given that the authority is spending $1.5 million on the runway)?

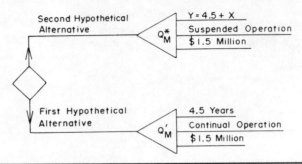

Figure 11–16. An Indifference Question.

The authority decides that Y (in figure 11–16) should be 9 years. This means that it is indifferent between a 9-year runway obtained at a cost of $1.5 million and suspended operation, and a 4.5-year runway obtained at a cost of $1.5 million but with continual operation. Or, to put it another way, if the authority can obtain a 4.5-year runway for $1.5 million with continual operation, it would need 4.5 more years of runway life to compensate it for suspending operation (see figure 11–17).

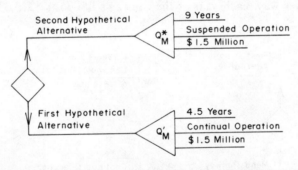

Figure 11–17. An Indifference Relation Between Two Hypothetical Outcomes.

The motivation for developing the hypothetical indifference decisions in figures 11–15 and 11–17 may not be obvious. Neither of the two hypothetical outcomes in figure 11–17, Q_M^* and Q_M', appears to be related to either of the two outcomes of the original dilemma. Nonetheless, there is a clear relationship, as indicated in figure 11–18. Since (from figure 11–15) the authority is indifferent between the outcome of mending the runway, Q_M, and the first hypothetical outcome, Q_M', it can substitute Q_M' for Q_M on the original decision tree; this is the first step in figure 11–18. Further, since the authority is also indifferent between Q_M' and Q_M^* (from figure 11–17), it can substitute

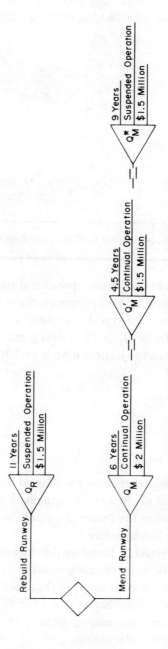

Figure 11–18. Using the Substitution Principle.

Q_M^* for Q_M'; this is the second step in figure 11–18. Finally, because the authority is indifferent between Q_M and Q_M', and also between Q_M' and Q_M^*, it must also be indifferent between Q_M and Q_M^*. Thus, Q_M^* can be substituted for Q_M on the original decision tree, creating a choice between Q_R and Q_M^*. (See figure 11–19.)

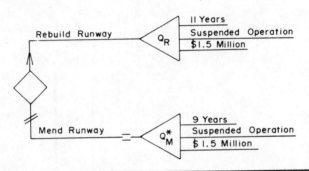

Rebuild Runway — Q_R
- 11 Years
- Suspended Operation
- $1.5 Million

Mend Runway — Q_M^*
- 9 Years
- Suspended Operation
- $1.5 Million

Figure 11–19. Using the Independence Principle to Resolve the Airport Dilemma.

Now the choice is quite obvious. Since operational status (suspended) and cost ($1.5 million) are the same for both outcomes, the independence principle applies, and a decision can be based on the comparison consequence, runway life. And since the runway life for Q_R of 11 years is greater than for Q_M^*, which is only 9 years, the rebuild-runway alternative is preferred.

A Third-Cut Analysis

Unfortunately, the decision reached on the basis of the second-cut analysis contradicts the conclusion of the first cut. Originally, it looked as if repairing the runway was best; but after the financial consequences were introduced, reconstructing the runway looked better.

This reversal is certainly possible. Mending the runway (the more expensive alternative) looked best until its extra cost was taken into account. Then the $500,000 saved by suspending operation tipped the scales in favor of rebuilding the runway. (If the first-cut analysis had resolved the dilemma in favor of the less-expensive rebuild-runway alternative, introducing cost considerations could only have reinforced that decision.)

The difference in the conclusions drawn from the two analyses suggests that one more look at the problem might be helpful. This will be done by using the

Conflicting Consequences and Trade-Off Analysis

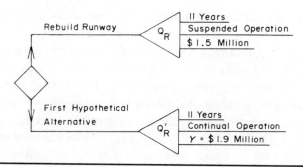

Figure 11–20. An Indifference Relation for the Rebuild-Runway Outcome.

same definition of the decision as employed in the second cut (figure 11–14), but with the trade-offs made in dollars instead of years; cost, not runway life, will be the comparison consequence.

Beginning this time with the rebuild-runway alternative, one consequence of which is suspended operation, the first step is to ask: If the airport authority is going to buy an 11-year runway, how much more than $1.5 million is it willing to spend to have continual rather than suspended operation? After thinking about this trade-off, the authority decides that this compensating change, X, should be $400,000. That is, the authority decides that Y (in figure 11–20) should be $1.9 million. (Y = $1.5 million + X = $1.9 million.)

With the trade-off between the operational-status consequence and the cost (comparison) consequence made, the next step is to trade off runway life for cost. The question now is, What should Y' (in figure 11–21) be, so that the airport authority is indifferent between paying $1.9 million for an 11-year runway and Y' for a 6-year runway (both obtained without closing the airport)?

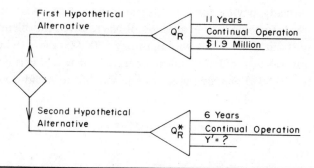

Figure 11–21. An Indifference Question.

But wait. Suppose we take the results of the first trade-off (figure 11–20) and apply the substitution principle at this stage in the analysis. Substituting Q'_R (from figure 11–20) for Q_R on the original decision tree (figure 11–14) is quite revealing (figure 11–22). Not that all but one of the consequences are the same for both alternatives; both runway life and cost differ. (The middle consequence, concerning operational status, is the same for both alternatives and thus, by the independence principle, can be ignored in making a decision.) But look carefully. The hypothetical outcome Q'_R, which has been substituted for the rebuild-runway outcome, is better than the mend-runway outcome, Q_M, in terms of *both* runway life *and* cost. Clearly, then, the rebuild alternative is preferred.

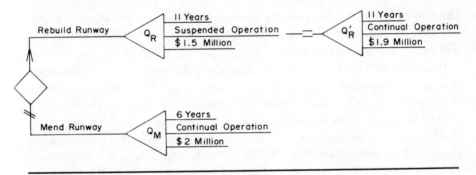

Figure 11–22. Resolving the Airport-Repair Dilemma.

In fact, as long as the indifference consequence Y in figure 11–20 is less than $2 million, the airport authority prefers to rebuild the runway. The authority should now concentrate its analytical attention on its compensating change (X, in dollars) for shifting from suspended to continual operation. If it is convinced that it would not pay more than $500,000 (in addition to the $1.5 million it is already paying for the 11-year runway) to avoid suspending operation, it needs to do no further analysis. It has resolved the dilemma. After all, if the airport authority is not willing to pay $500,000 more (when getting an 11-year runway) to avoid suspending operation, it would certainly not be willing to pay $500,000 *and* five years of runway life to avoid doing so.

Conflicting Consequences and Trade-Off Analysis

Some Reflections on These Trade-Off Analyses

Often, people faced with a public investment decision similar to the airport-repair dilemma immediately commission a cost-benefit analysis. Such an undertaking is inherently complex; it requires a specification of many more factors than were included in the sequential steps of the preceding trade-off analysis, particularly the specification of how costs and benefits will be distributed over time. And then, to compare the alternatives, it is still necessary to make the trade-off judgments for all these conflicting factors. As Richard A. Musgrave of Harvard University notes, "Cost-Benefit analysis provides no substitute for the basic problem of evaluation in the case of final social goods. All it can do is to expedite efficient decision-making after the basic problem of evaluation is solved."[5] Whether or not you use cost-benefit analysis, you must still make the basic judgments concerning how much of one consequence you are willing to sacrifice to gain a certain amount of another.

Consequently, a sophisticated cost-benefit study may not be appropriate, especially at the beginning of an analysis. Indeed, it may obscure, behind a plethora of factors, the basic reason that the decision is a dilemma. As a result, the decision maker may be forced to either (1) accept, unquestioningly, the recommendations of the professional analyst who performed the cost-benefit calculations, or (2) resort to pure intuition. Neither course is very satisfactory.

Any decision maker (even the sophisticated analyst) has much to gain—and little to lose—by undertaking the kind of quick trade-off analysis described above. No mathematical sophistication is required to make the series of trade-offs—only careful, disciplined thought. Moreover, as the trade-offs specified here suggest, it may be possible to resolve the dilemma satisfactorily without a more sophisticated approach.

It is, of course, possible that a trade-off analysis will not satisfactorily resolve the dilemma. For example, after careful thought, the airport authority might conclude that the value it assesses for the runway-life consequence of the second hypothetical alternative in figure 11–16, Q_M^*, is very close to 11 years. In this case, it would be impossible to decide, based on this analysis at least, which alternative is preferred. Then, however, there are several possible courses to take. One is to rethink the original analysis, focusing particular attention upon those judgments to which the decision is most sensitive. Sensitivity analysis should have the first priority, for any change in one of the original assessments could change the conclusion. A second course is to introduce some additional consequences, minor ones perhaps, but consequences that might just, as a group, tip the nearly balanced scales in one direction or the other. A third possible course is to commission a more detailed and sophisticated analysis of the problem; such an undertaking might uncover additional information or produce insights that make the choice clear.

On the other hand, further work might not prove any more satisfactory; it might suggest that the airport authority is indeed indifferent between the two alternatives. Thus, a fourth course to follow after an initial trade-off analysis fails to uncover a preferred alternative is to accept that, although the two alternatives are quite different, one's preferences for the two are indistinguishable. Despite the emphasis in this book on selecting the preferred alternative, it is always possible that two or more alternatives are equally desirable. Indeed, analysis is useful even when it reveals that one alternative is as good as a second.

Inherent in any cost-benefit analysis is the trade-off between costs expended and benefits received. All the trade-offs are implicitly made with money as the comparison consequence. The airport-repair dilemma is interesting because money does *not* enter into the fundamental trade-off between runway life and operational status. As the second-cut analysis reveals, cost, too, is often one of the conflicting consequences that creates a dilemma. And many people do find it easiest to think about trade-offs using money as the comparison consequence. That is, they are willing to specify the "worth" in dollars of some change in another, nonmonetary consequence—to determine exactly how much of a change in the monetary consequence is required to just compensate them for a change in the nonmonetary consequence. But there is no reason, even when cost is one of the consequences of the decision, that some other quantity, such as runway life, might not be the most appropriate comparison consequence.

The Ubiquity of Trade-Offs

Life is full of trade-offs. We must constantly make decisions that are complicated by multiple consequences—and by our inability to find an alternative that is best in terms of every one of these consequences. A baseball player who wants to hit more home runs next season must accept that his batting average will fall as a result; attempting to hit home runs means, among other things, striking out more often. Alternatively, if he wants to raise his batting average, he must accept that he will hit fewer home runs. "That it is impossible simultaneously and continually to realize all social and political goods," writes philosopher Robert Nozick, "is a regrettable fact about the human condition."[6]

In our personal lives, whenever we make a choice about a job, we must make trade-offs involving a wide variety of consequences: salary, living environment, job responsibilities, educational opportunities for the children, career oppor-

Conflicting Consequences and Trade-Off Analysis

tunities for a spouse, and recreational opportunities for all. More families are being confronted these days with the need to make trade-offs between the career interests of husband and wife. Further, there always exists the trade-off between one's professional career and one's avocational interests, be they a relaxed family life, playing with an amateur jazz quartet, or racing a sailboat competitively.[7] Moreover, some jobs, such as being a construction worker on a skyscraper or suspension bridge, present conflicts between salary and safety. And many people choose, as Achilles did, a short, glorious life rather than a long, uneventful one.

In government, too, there are always trade-offs to be made, if only because there are limited financial resources with which to fund the various programs that people wish government to undertake. "We cannot have more flood control *and* more education and more of everything else," writes A. Myrick Freeman, III, of Bowdoin College. "It is 'either/or.' Choices must be made."[8] For example, efforts to reform the American system of public welfare have been complicated by the necessity of making trade-offs between three important consequences of any welfare reform plan: (1) the strength of the plan's work incentive, (2) the benefit floor provided to the neediest individuals and families, and (3) cost. As any alternative is modified to improve consequences 1 and 2, the third consequence necessarily becomes worse. Or, if you keep cost fixed, there is a direct trade-off between the benefit floor and the incentive.[9] Moreover, in addition to the funding conflicts between different programs— between guns and butter—there are the conflicts over how society's limited resources should be allocated: to public spending, to capital formation, or to private consumption. As Senator Mark Hatfield, chairman of the Senate Appropriations Committee, observed before the beginning of the 1981 session, "I think we're going to have some tradeoffs; I don't think we can have a 10 percent tax cut, increase the military and balance the budget."[10]

Also, whenever government makes a decision about health, safety, or environmental regulations, there occurs a trade-off between the consequences for people's health and the consequences for their (or others') economic well-being. Industrial plants such as the copper smelter of Asarco in Ruston, Washington and the iron ore processor of the Reserve Mining Company in Silver Bay, Minnesota provide jobs for thousands of people and useful products for many others. But arsenic or asbestoslike fibers are by-products of these production processes and can create health hazards. So the government, which cannot shut down every firm that creates a health hazard without destroying the economy, must make some trade-offs between conflicting consequences. Similarly, when making decisions about air emission standards for automobiles, the government must make trade-offs involving air quality, fuel economy, and automobile prices. Or when the Food and Drug Administration makes decisions about the levels of hazardous substances it will permit in the

331

food we eat, it too must make trade-offs, for requiring that no impurities be permitted in our food would effectively ban everything we eat. Similarly, society has made trade-offs between rapid transportation and safe transportation (by automobile, train, bus, ship, or plane); we have not, in order to maximize safety, decided to reduce transportation speed to zero. As William D. Nordhaus, a former member of the President's Council of Economic Advisors, notes, "we know that many fewer people will be killed at a 45-mile-per-hour speed limit than at 55, but that doesn't mean we automatically lower it."[11]

Further, there is what the late Arthur M. Okun of the Brookings Institution called "our biggest socioeconomic tradeoff": economic efficiency versus social equality. To the extent that we create an efficient economy, we increase our economic output and society's wealth; at the same time, however, we exacerbate the disparities of income among members of that society. The "pursuit of efficiency necessarily creates inequalities," writes Okun. "And hence society faces a tradeoff between equality and efficiency. . . . We can't have our cake of market efficiency and share it equally."[12]

Finally, the proposals made to reform the structure and processes of government involve trade-offs. For not only are there the intended consequences of the reform—greater citizen participation, better government responsiveness, more open government, greater public accountability—but there are the unintended consequences that plague any public program or decision. Rep. Morris K. Udall has discovered "Udall's Fourth Law: Every reform always carries consequences you don't like."[13]

Trade-Offs in Business

Multiple and conflicting consequences obviously complicate many decisions faced by public policy makers and by all of us in our personal lives. Business, however, is concerned with a single objective—profit—and business decisions are often thought to be dilemmas primarily because of the uncertainty about the profit to be earned from any investment.[14] Yet there exists no single, simple index of a firm's financial well-being. Indeed, to provide useful information to the managers, owners, and creditors of a business (as well as to other interested parties, such as labor, government, and society as a whole), there are multiple measures of business performance: the gross margin, profit margin (return on sales), expense ratio, contribution to fixed cost and profit, turnover ratio, inventory ratios, return on owner's equity, earnings per share, price/earnings ratio, cash flow per share, dividends per share, current ratio, debt-to-equity

Conflicting Consequences and Trade-Off Analysis

ratio, and many others.[15] Business decisions are indeed complicated by conflicting consequences, and business executives—just as their public sector cousins—are constantly forced to make trade-offs.

The most fundamental business trade-off is between short-term and long-term income.[16] Given limited financial resources, a firm's manager must decide whether to generate profits immediately or to invest the firm's cash to ensure profits in the future. Writing in the *Harvard Business Review,* Robert L. Banks and Steven C. Wheelwright note:

> The tug-of-war between short-term and long-term goals is a dilemma that corporations face recurrently. The conflict is basic. The attainment of long-range goals often involves resource commitments that may adversely affect profits in the current period, even though these investments may provide significant return in later years.[17]

Banks and Wheelwright offer a number of examples of business managers making decisions involving such a short-term/long-term trade-off. For example, they report on one firm that had to decide whether or not to replace its existing steam boilers with ones that were more efficient. Replacing the boilers now (before inflation drove the price of the new boilers even higher) would adversely affect short-run profits; though operating costs for the new boilers would be lower, the firm would immediately incur significant capital costs. Keeping the existing boilers would delay these capital costs but significantly increase long-run costs, thus decreasing long-run profits (see figure 11–23).[18]

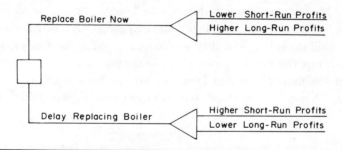

Figure 11–23. A Business Decision with Conflicting Consequences.

This firm, deciding that the long-run consequences were more important in this case, replaced the boilers immediately. Similarly, American Bakeries decided in the mid-1970s to embark upon what one executive called "the biggest capital spending program—$84 million—in our history, over the five years that ended in 1980." Thus, despite increasing sales, profitability as a percent of sales dropped from 1.38% in 1975 to 0.39% in 1980; between 1977 and 1980, earnings per share declined from $2.73 to $0.85, and annual dividends per share were cut from $1.10 to $0.65. The result was a proxy fight initiated by a group upset with the firm's "dismal performance" and resisted by the existing management, which claimed that its program was "absolutely crucial to this company's competitiveness and growth prospects."[19] At the 1981 annual meeting, the dissidents won the four seats that were up for election on the firm's twelve-member board of directors.[20]

Some business observers argue that, when confronted with the conflict between short-run and long-run profits, American firms have placed undue emphasis upon short-run profits rather than the development, over the long run, of new products and innovative production processes. Examining the "marked deterioration of competitive vigor" experienced by U.S. business (particularly compared with Europe and Japan), Robert H. Hayes and William J. Abernathy of the Harvard Business School conclude that it is the result, in part, of American management's preference for "short-term cost reduction rather than long-term development of technological competitiveness."[21] Reginald H. Jones, the former chairman of General Electric, says, "What we have today is a bunch of money managers who are under tremendous pressure from Wall Street to have every quarter a little bit better than the last." Jones argues that American firms have to "make investments that will enhance the long-range opportunities of the corporation."[22]

Still, not all the consequences affecting a business trade-off concern only money and profit. For example, when Capital Cities Communications proposed to buy the *Hartford Courant* in 1978, one editor and stockholder commented: "Money isn't the only factor. We couldn't find a better employer anywhere." Many of the newspaper's 800 employees also owned stock in the privately held company, and they considered working for a newspaper that was, as one reporter put it, "paternalistic in the best sense" to be more important than the money obtained from the sale of their stock. Observed this journalist, "A good place to work is worth more than a quick profit." Further,

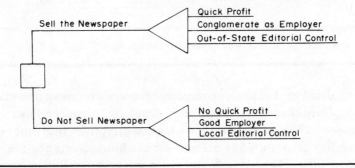

Figure 11–24. Selling the *Hartford Courant:* The Trade-Offs.

if the paper was sold to Capital Cities, a communications conglomerate, it would lose its independent status and, perhaps, its local editorial control. "Local ownership leads to local accountability," argued the reporter. Thus, for many stockholders, this business decision involved a trade-off with three conflicting consequences: money, employment, and independence (figure 11–24). In the end, the holders of a majority of the newspaper's stock voted not to sell, and so did the directors of the paper.[23]

The Odiousness of Explicit Trade-Offs

Making explicit trade-offs is unpleasant. We all feel there is something distasteful about making specific trade-off statements, such as "I am willing to give up repairing the 500 potholes in the city so that we can hire 10 more teachers for the schools; but if we can get only 5 more teachers, I would rather have smooth roads." We cringe from the unsavory idea of stating how much of a child's education we are willing to sacrifice to avoid some broken axles. We particularly do not like making trade-offs between monetary and non-monetary consequences. Who is willing to state unambiguously, even if only to himself, "If I take this high-pressure job, I will be able to spend very little time with my kids, but we will be more than compensated for that loss by the extra $12,000 I will earn each year"?

Trade-offs become completely unpalatable when we begin comparing mere money with human health—what Professors Howard Raiffa (Harvard), William B. Schwartz (Tufts), and Milton C. Weinstein (Harvard) call "a highly emotional and treacherous domain of discourse."[24] No one wants to say that we, as a society, should be willing to spend $1 million to prevent an automobile accident fatality, but not $2 million. No public official is willing to assert that a human life is anything but priceless.

Yet, despite our unwillingness to admit it, our actions belie the notion that human life is priceless. We do not reduce highway speed limits to forty-five miles per hour, let alone to zero, even if doing so would save some lives. If a human life—any human life—were in fact priceless, the next time a human life was endangered (and that is right now) we would immediately devote all of society's resources to saving it. We do not do this, of course. We *do* make the trade-off between money and human lives. What we do not do is admit it—such an admission is too distasteful. For the public official, the admission may also be politically costly. For the individual, the admission may create greater emotional costs than the benefits obtained from making a more explicit and carefully thought-out decision. But whether it is explicit or implicit—whether one admits it or not—the judgments about trade-offs will be made. As Raiffa, Schwartz, and Weinstein write, "Analysis must be done either implicitly or explicitly; by not doing it explicitly, decision makers may try to escape making vexing value judgments and tradeoffs, but these judgments are, nevertheless, implicit in their decisions."[25]

Unfortunately, we are all taught at an early age that "you can't add apples and oranges." This justifies our unwillingness to state, for example, how many billion dollars of GNP we are willing to sacrifice to reduce air pollution from sulfates from six to three micrograms per cubic meter. "You can't add apples and oranges" is the easy retort. But this is just an excuse for not thinking carefully about whether or not we should make greater efforts to reduce air pollution.

Certainly there is no objective way to add apples and oranges, but you can do it subjectively. If you have to choose between a crate of oranges and a bushel of apples, you can decide that one orange is worth, say, two apples—that you are willing to give up exactly one orange to gain two apples. You may make that judgment because you find the pleasure of eating a single orange equivalent to that obtained from eating two apples, or because you believe the nutritional value of one orange is the same as that of two apples, or because you think the beauty that one orange contributes to the fruit basket on your kitchen table is equal to the beauty of two more apples.[26] As Garrett Hardin writes in his classic essay, "The Tragedy of the Commons":

> Comparing one good with another is, we usually say, impossible because goods are incommensurable. Incommensurables cannot be compared. Theoretically this may be true; but in real life incommensurables *are* commensurable. Only a criterion of judgment and a system of weighting are needed.[27]

Of course, finding the criterion of judgment and the system of weighting for making choices between apples and oranges is relatively straightforward. Such a task becomes distasteful only when the consequences of the decision are more incommensurable than are different fruits. Raiffa, Schwartz, and Weinstein put it this way: "In the literature one talks about the problem of comparing 'apples and oranges'; it would be more appropriate if we talked about comparing apples with sexual joy or with political prestige, or with pleasant landscapes."[28] This is when we find making explicit trade-offs most odious.

Conflicting Consequences and Trade-Off Analysis

Expedients for Avoiding Trade-Offs

When we wish to avoid the political costs, emotional discomfort, and mental effort required to make thoughtful trade-offs between conflicting consequences, we employ a number of simplifying strategies, as we do in coping with uncertainty, in an attempt to avoid the "cognitive strain"[29] of a careful analysis. After surveying a number of psychological studies, Paul Slovic of Decision Research concluded that

> the amalgamation of different types of information and different types of values into an overall judgment or decision is a difficult cognitive process and, in our attempts to ease the strain of processing information, we often resort to judgmental strategies that may do an injustice to our underlying values.[30]

There is, for example, the simplifying strategy defined by Amos Tversky, "elimination by aspects." To avoid thinking directly about the conflict between consequences, we concentrate on one consequence at a time, eliminating alternatives that do not measure up to some minimum level for that factor. An example offered by Tversky concerns the choice of a new car. Clearly, this decision involves many conflicting consequences: One car may have better mileage but cost more, another may have more room and comfort but handle less well, while another may have better safety features but poorer styling. Tversky argues that, to cope with such a multitude of consequences (aspects), people start off by eliminating those cars that do not measure up to a certain standard in the dimension chosen. First they may eliminate all cars that get less than twenty-five miles per gallon; then they eliminate all cars without front-wheel drive; then they eliminate all cars without room for four adults. They continue this process—eliminating by aspects—until only one car remains.[31]

Of course, it may be that no trade-off exists, that there is a *dominant* alternative that is best in terms of all important consequences. For example, for the trade-off between equality and efficiency, Arthur Okun argues that eliminating discrimination in employment is best for *both* consequences, because it will result in the fairest distribution of jobs and in the most-productive people getting those jobs. This, writes Okun, "illustrates the general possibility that what is good for equality may be good for efficiency" too.[32]

Dominant solutions are rare, however. It is not often that we can have both guns and butter—at least not without more inflation in the bargain. Still, the attraction is there; asserting that a dominant alternative exists—or simply that two apparently conflicting objectives can actually be pursued independently—is another way to avoid confronting trade-offs. Taking note of the "psychological pain" imposed by thinking about trade-offs, John D. Steinbrunner of the

Brookings Institution surveys some of the work on cognitive psychology and concludes:

> Decision makers . . . can be expected primarily to deny the trade-off relationship in their minds and to assume that they are pursuing the separate values simultaneously and independently. Some decision makers will actually reverse the relationship and see the two objectives as mutually supportive.[33]

For example, President Carter stated in his first environmental message, on May 1977:

> I believe environmental protection is consistent with a sound economy. Previous pollution control laws have generated many more jobs than they have cost. And other environmental measures whose time has come—measures like energy conservation, reclamation of stripmined lands, and rehabilitation of our cities—will produce still more new jobs, often where they are needed most. In any event, if we ignore the care of our environment, the day will eventually come when our economy suffers from that neglect.[34]

Yet, two years later, in his second environmental message, he said:

> I do not pretend that all new replacement sources of energy will be environmentally innocuous. Some of the new technologies we will need to develop pose environmental risks, not all of which are yet fully understood. I will work to ensure that environmental protections are built into the process of developing these technologies, and that when tradeoffs must be made, they will be made fairly, equitably, and in the light of informed public scrutiny.[35]

Apparently, to the president, there was no trade-off between the environment and the economy, but there was one between environmental protection and energy development. A few months before the president sent his second message to Congress, however, his Council on Environmental Quality had published a report, *The Good News About Energy*, stating:

> if we take energy productivity seriously, we can have a healthy, expanding economy in the coming decades with energy growth far below that predicted only a few years ago . . . . The feasibility of low energy growth is indeed good news, for it means that the tremendous difficulties posed by high energy growth to the environment and to the economy can be largely avoided.[36]

It is not just political leaders who have trouble facing up to the existence of trade-offs. When the *New York Times* asked 420 New Yorkers in July 1975 what the city should do about its budgetary crisis, it found that "a majority of people polled favored cutting services rather than increasing taxes, but they did not want services cut either." Of the respondents who answered the question, 60 percent said they wanted to "keep taxes as low as possible, even though this might require reductions in services," while 65 percent said they dissapproved of trying "to make ends meet by laying off employees and by reducing city services."[37] That means at least one quarter of the respondents offered inconsistent opinions.

Another political mechanism for coping with conflicting consequences is to obscure the objectives of any undertaking. Such ambiguity facilitates the formation of a coalition to support the project, for the members of the group need not confront the disruptive task of resolving the conflicts among their respective interests and the outcomes they hope to achieve. An alternative political strategy is to confess that such conflicts exist; then, to resolve them all, prescribe a platitudinous principle that is so vague as to offer no real guidance as to how any actual trade-offs will be made. For example, Gifford Pinchot, the founder of the National Forest Service, once declared, "Where conflicting interests must be reconciled the question will always be decided from the standpoint of the greatest good of the greatest number in the long run."[38] This is no more helpful than the statement of the mayor of Sidney, Nebraska that "our intent is to buy the best snowplow for the least money,"[39] or the 1969 comment of Secretary of Defense Melvin Laird that U.S. military strategy in Vietnam was to keep "maximum military pressure on the enemy consistent with the lowest possible casualties."[40] Such ridiculisms give no hint as to how the required trade-offs will actually be made.

Despite this wide variety of expedients for avoiding trade-offs, we must frequently make decisions complicated by conflicting consequences. And when we do, we must either undertake some explicit trade-off analysis or hope that the circumvention we employ to escape thinking about the real conflicts between consequences can produce a decision with which we are satisfied.

Once Again—The Importance of Simplification

So how can one cope with the complexity created by conflicting consequences? How is it possible to think carefully about such decisions? The answer —again—lies in the imperative of simplification. As with decisions complicated by uncertainty, the human mind will simplify the task anyway. The only question is whether the process of simplification will focus attention on the essence of the decision—on the most important conflicting consequences that create the dilemma.

Roger N. Shepard of Bell Telephone Laboratories writes of "man's demonstrable inability to take proper account, simultaneously, of the various component attributes of the alternatives." From a review of a variety of psychological experiments, Shepard found "a systematic bias" in human judgment—"a consistent tendency" for the subjects of these experiments to restrict the number of factors considered and to rely "too heavily on one or two of these factors while, in effect, ignoring the significant contribution of the remaining factors." Concluded Shepard, "In making an evaluative judgment a subject can take account of only a very limited number of factors at any one time."[41]

Paul Slovic ran a series of such experiments, giving the subjects a choice between two alternatives each of which was defined by two important consequences. In one experiment, individuals were asked to choose the more valuable of two baseball players: Player A, with a batting average of .287 and 20 home runs; and Player B, with a .273 average and 26 homers. The subjects had been asked at a previous session to adjust one of the four consequences so that the two players were "of equal ability and value to their teams." Yet, when asked to choose between the players that they themselves had made equally valuable, more than two-thirds of the subjects concentrated their attention on one consequence as the basis of their choice.[42]

Slovic suggests that the subjects resolved their dilemma of conflicting consequences not by making trade-offs but by selecting a most important dimension and basing their choice solely on it. Such a process not only produces a relatively quick, consistent, predictable, and painless decision, but is also easy to justify and explain. Shepard writes that "at the moment when a decision is required the fact that each alternative has both advantages and disadvantages poses an impediment to the attainment of the most immediate subgoal: namely, escape from the unpleasant state of conflict induced by the decision problem itself." Consequently, he argues, there is an advantage to a process that "clearly favors one alternative over its competitors and permits the decision to be consummated."[43]

We resist the idea that we would (or should) simplify any decision. Someone living in Louisiana who was considering a move to Fort Thomas, Kentucky sent the city clerk there a post card requesting information.

Moving soon. Considering your area. Please send info schools, busing for integration? Dope, alcohol problems? Teacher and pupil ratio. Band, academic achievement. College? Hospital of specialists? Churches. Temp. extremes, tornados, floods, snow slides, quakes? Elevation, 24 hour drug stores, gas stations? TV, Cable, PBS? Suburb plazas, K-Mart, Sambos? Rabies, mosquito control? Water source, hard chlorine?

Police protection, fire department rating. Crime, vandalism, gun control? Minorities and percent of population? Nuclear plant, sanitarium, penitentiary, Housing project near? Gas available for heating new homes? Solar energy? Basements? Please have savings and loan send certificate savings information. Please send address of closest military base, large Sunday paper, local realtor and new suburb developments.[44]

Conflicting Consequences and Trade-Off Analysis

Would the existence of twenty-four-hour drug stores, a sanitarium, gun control, or a nearby military base really affect this decision to move? Why is this decision a dilemma anyway? Why is it worth spending some time thinking about this decision? Might not this Louisiana resident be better off to determine first why *this* decision about moving creates a dilemma and then concentrate on those consequences that directly affect it, rather than seek a plethora of information about every possible factor that might somehow influence the generic decision about whether to move anywhere?[45] Notes Shepard, "Possibly our feeling that we can take account of a host of different factors comes about because, although we remember that at some time or other we have attended to each of the different factors, we fail to notice that it is seldom more than one or two that we consider at any one time."[46]

It would be nice if there existed a subtle, wholistic, complex style of decision making that employed a large number of factors.[47] But all the available evidence suggests that simplification is inherent in human decisions. Writes Robin M. Hogarth of the Center for Decision Research at the University of Chicago's Graduate School of Business:

> A key aspect in choice is human incapacity to process information. We simply cannot handle all the information inherent in complex choice situations and, in particular, to make the many kinds of trade-offs implied by choices involving several conflicting dimensions. Intuitive judgment is deficient and requires "decision aids."[48]

Indeed, using the decision aid of trade-off analysis, it may be possible to consider carefully three or four consequences rather than the one or two that are employed when a decision is made solely through unaided intuition.

Analysis and Values

Conflicting consequences make a decision perplexing. How do the various consequences influence the overall desirability of the outcomes? How much of a gain in one consequence is necessary to just balance a specific loss in another? How does a small change in one consequence affect the relative desirability of a particular outcome? When a decision involves multiple conflicting consequences, it may even be quite difficult just to keep all of them straight in one's head.

In such situations, a simple trade-off analysis can be very helpful. Decomposing the various outcomes into their component consequences and keeping track of these components with a pencil and paper—a wonderful decision aid

—permits a decision maker to think carefully about the conflicts arising from the various consequences that create the dilemma. But careful thinking is not necessarily easy thinking. Trade-offs imply that some consequences must be sacrificed to gain others, and acceptance of such losses can be painful.

Thinking carefully about trade-offs requires us to specify our values—to appraise the relative worth of different incommensurables about which we have never had to think in this way before. Frequent Gallup and Harris polls create the impression that all humans (with the exception of those 4 percent undecideds) have well-formed views about all sorts of questions and issues. Do we really all hold the well-formed, well-established, well-thought-out values necessary to guide all of the decisions we will ever have to make? Henry S. Rowen argues:

> The analytic process will contribute to beliefs about facts and relationships and will help in the construction of value preferences. The phrase "construction of value preferences" is deliberately chosen. This reflects the view that preferences are generally built through experience and through learning about facts, about relationships, and about consequences. It is not that values are latent and only need to be "discovered" or "revealed." There is a potentially infinite number of values; they are not equally useful or valid, and part of the task of analysis is to develop ones that seem especially "right" and useful and that might become widely shared.[49]

Analysis (that is, thoughtful, structured thinking) can provide a process for developing our own values—helping us think through just how much of a consequence we are willing to sacrifice to gain some of another.

Of course, no single analysis provides the key to the construction of needed values. "Expressed values seem to be highly labile," write Baruch Fischhoff, Paul Slovic, and Sarah Lichtenstein; how these values are elicited "can have marked effects on what people express as their preferences." They argue that the best way to help people "make value judgments in their own best interest is to provide them with new analytical tools. Such tools would change respondents by deepening their perspective." The "theme" of their article is: "Consider more than one perspective."[50]

Even when using the simple analytical tool of trade-off analysis, it helps to think about the dilemma from several different perspectives. Doing a second analysis with a different consequence as the comparison consequence (as was done for the runway-repair dilemma) can help do just that. Not only does such a second cut reveal the sensitivity of the decision to different values of the consequences, but it also exposes how sensitive the decision is to a different trade-off perspective.

Making sequential trade-offs involving various consequences does not automatically produce a miraculous, optimal decision. The process is necessarily subjective. The judgments require work, meaning careful, disciplined thought. The decision is a dilemma because of the messy conflicts among the consequences—among the values reflected in each outcome. All trade-off analysis does is to provide a framework for thinking carefully about trade-offs, a structure within which it is possible to organize one's intuition to specify how much of a gain in one consequence will just balance the loss in another. Specifying that balance may be psychologically painful but not as costly as a decision based solely upon wholistic—and inherently simplistic—hunches can be.

Appendix: Generalized Trade-Off Analysis

The second-cut analysis of the airport-repair dilemma suggests the general approach for analyzing decision dilemmas with multiple, conflicting consequences. This is to make a series of trade-offs between just two of the consequences, keeping the others fixed, until a hypothetical outcome is developed that has two characteristics:

1. The decision maker is indifferent between this hypothetical outcome and one of the actual outcomes of the original dilemma.
2. All the consequences of this hypothetical outcome except one are the same as the corresponding consequences of another one of the actual outcomes of the original dilemma.

Then the two outcomes can be compared in terms of the single comparison consequence that is different.

To see this, consider the general dilemma of conflicting consequences with three alternatives and five consequences, as shown in figure 11–25. To resolve this dilemma, the first step is to select a comparison consequence. Usually, it is most convenient to order the consequences so that *A* is the comparison consequence. The only requirement for a comparison consequence is that it be some kind of incremental quantity, such as dollars or years of runway life. The decision maker must be able, when making the trade-offs with other consequences, to make small adjustments in the value of the comparison consequence so as to develop indifference relationships. Thus, a consequence that can take on only discrete values, such as the operational status of an airport, cannot be used as the comparison consequence.

It is strictly a matter of convenience which consequence is selected to be the comparison consequence. Disposable income might be a useful comparison consequence for analyzing the choice among several job offers when not only salary, but also location, employer, job responsibilities, and opportunities for

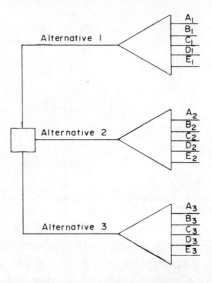

Figure 11–25. A General Conflicting-Consequence Dilemma.

advancement are important consequences. For a business firm, after-tax earnings, sales, or market share might be useful comparison consequences. For some kinds of medical decisions, life expectancy or days in bed might be appropriate. The unemployment rate (or inflation rate) could be a helpful comparison consequence when making choices about a nation's economy.

For some dilemmas, none of the important consequences is a continuous quantity. In such situations, it is necessary to introduce an extra consequence (a "dummy variable," as the computer buffs would call it) that would be the same for all the other alternatives; this consequence would then be used as the comparison consequence to make the necessary trade-offs. For example, two

Conflicting Consequences and Trade-Off Analysis

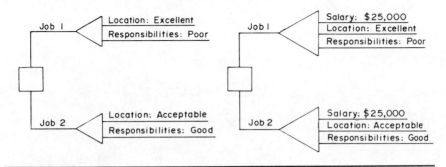

Figure 11–26. Introducing an Extra, Comparison Consequence.

jobs might have the same salaries, but one might have more responsibility while the other might be in a better location. In that case, salary could be introduced as the comparison consequence (as in the right-hand diagram in figure 11–26) even though it was the same for both alternatives.

Having selected a comparison consequence, the next step is to select a base outcome—the one with which all the other outcomes will be compared. Again, which outcome is selected is strictly a matter of convenience. For the general dilemma in figure 11–25, outcome Q_1 has been selected as the base outcome.

Finally, the decision maker needs to make a series of sequential trade-offs to develop an indifference outcome, Q^*, for each of the remaining, non–base outcomes. That is, for the general dilemma in figure 11–25, the decision maker must develop Q_2^* and Q_3^*. Such indifference outcomes have two important characteristics:

1. The decision maker is indifferent between the non–base outcome and its indifference outcome (here, between Q_2 and Q_2^*, and between Q_3 and Q_3^*).
2. All the consequences of the indifference outcome *except one* (which is the comparison consequence) are identical with the corresponding consequences of the base outcome (that is, $B_2^* = B_1$, $C_2^* = C_1$, and so forth).

Then the various indifference outcomes can be compared directly with the base outcome by looking solely at the comparison consequence (for it is the only one that differs) and a decision can be made using such comparisons.

Figure 11–27 illustrates how to make the series of trade-offs necessary to develop the required indifference outcomes. First, the decision maker trades off consequences A and B, to develop a new (hypothetical) outcome, Q_2', such that (1) the B consequence of this outcome is identical with the B consequence of outcome Q_1 (that is, $B_2' = B_1 = B_2^*$), and (2) he is indifferent between this outcome, Q_2', and the original outcome for this alternative, Q_2. The decision maker does this by adjusting the (incremental) comparison consequence, mov-

345

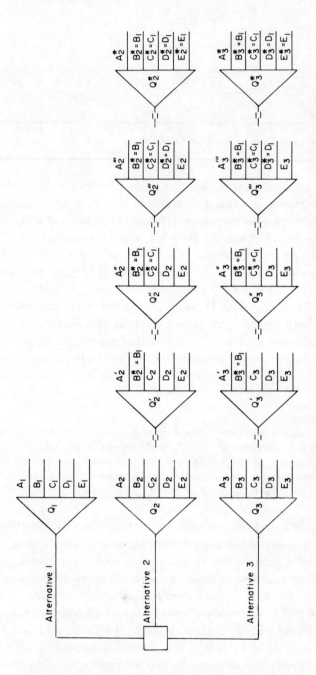

Figure 11-27. The Series of Trade-Offs Necessary to Resolve a Conflicting-Consequences Dilemma with Three Alternatives and Five Consequences.

Conflicting Consequences and Trade-Off Analysis

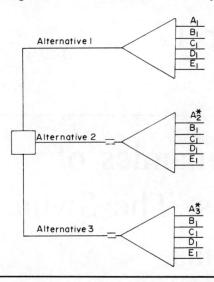

Figure 11–28. Resolving a General Conflicting-Consequences Dilemma Using the Substitution and Independence Principles.

ing A_2 to A_2', so as to just compensate for the shift from B_2 to B_1. Next, he trades off consequences A and C, using a similar process. A new (again, hypothetical) outcome, Q_2'', is developed such that (1) the C consequence of this outcome is identical with the C consequence of outcome Q_1 ($C_2'' = C_1 = C_2^*$), and (2) he is indifferent between this outcome, Q_2'', and the first hypothetical outcome for this alternative, Q_2', and thus between Q_2'' and the original outcome, Q_2. This process of sequential trade-offs continues until Q_2^*, with the two characteristics previously described, is developed. Similarly, a series of trade-offs are made to develop Q_3^* for the third alternative. Then, using the independence principle, a decision can be based solely on which of the comparison consequences, A_1, A_2^*, or A_3^*, is the best, as is made clear in figure 11–28.

Chapter 12

The Dynamics of Analysis: The Swine Flu Dilemmas

OCTOBER 7, 1976. The students in the engineering school were scheduled to be vaccinated against the swine flu the following day. There was talk of a potential epidemic—even a pandemic—and David Garric, a twenty-six-year-old graduate student in biochemical engineering, was having a quiet lunch and thinking about whether to get the shot.

Dave did not know much about influenza other than the few bits and pieces of information he had picked up from reading the newspapers and talking with friends. He recalled President Ford announcing in March that an epidemic was "a very real possibility."[1] He suspected that if an epidemic swept the country, his chance of catching the swine flu would be substantial but by no means certain; he had had flu two or three times before, but most winters had managed to stay well.

Dave had never been inoculated against flu before—in fact, he had taken very few shots in his life, partially because he felt they were unpleasant and partially because he was reluctant to take any form of medication unless it was absolutely necessary. He had read that the swine flu inoculation was safe and effective, but neither perfectly safe (the pharmaceutical companies supplying the vaccine insisted that the federal government assume liability[2]) nor 100 percent effective. Given that the consequences of his choice could be significant—he might come down with the flu this coming winter, or he might waste all

348

of tomorrow afternoon standing in line to get shot up with something he did not need—David Garric decided that it was worth some of his time to do a quick analysis of his decision about whether to get the swine flu shot.

A First-Cut Analysis

Dave decided to keep his analysis as simple as possible by concentrating on what he thought was the major risk—catching the swine flu if he did not get the inoculation. As Garric saw it, his dilemma was whether to (1) get the shot and play it safe by avoiding the possibility of coming down with the flu, or (2) not get the shot and gamble on not catching the flu. On a paper napkin, Garric sketched a decision sapling that described the essence of his dilemma (figure 12–1).

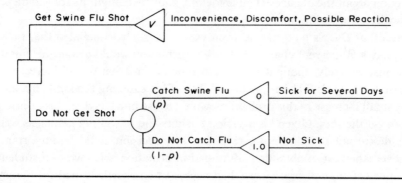

Figure 12–1. David Garric's Swine Flu Dilemma: First-Cut Decision Sapling.

To resolve his dilemma, Dave needed to specify the probability that he would catch the flu, and his (relative) preference for the three outcomes. Tentatively, he decided that V should be something like 0.9. That is, only if he had more than a 10-percent chance of getting the swine flu would he accept the inconvenience, discomfort, and possible side effects of getting the inoculation. Since this judgment was based on very limited information, Dave recognized that he might well revise his assessment if he learned more about the severity of contracting the flu or the possible side effects of getting the shot. For the moment, however, he decided that a preference-probability of 0.9 was appropriate.

Specifying the probability of catching the swine flu if he skipped the shot seemed more difficult. What on earth did President Ford mean by "a very real possibility" of an epidemic? And if the epidemic struck, how likely would it be that he would get sick? A 50-percent chance of an epidemic and a 50-percent chance of then catching the flu would imply a 25-percent chance of his getting sick; in that case, it seemed clear that he should be inoculated. Maybe, however, "a very real possibility" only meant something like one chance in four, and perhaps there was also only one chance in four of catching the flu if there were an epidemic; in that case, he would only have one chance in sixteen of getting sick and the inoculation would not be worthwhile.

Dave decided that if he had to make the decision right now, he would assess the chance of an epidemic as one-in-three and the chance of his then catching the flu as one-in-three as well. So he would use a p of one-in-nine, or around 0.11, in his analysis and would decide—but just barely—to get the shot. Still, Garric felt uncomfortable about these guesstimates, and he did not have to resolve his dilemma immediately. He had some free time and his curiosity was aroused; perhaps a quick trip to the medical school library would help. Some of the medical specialists on influenza might have published a more helpful prediction about the chances of an epidemic, and there might be some data on the incidence of swine flu.

Given that Dave's tentative decision was so close, he concluded that there was nearly a 50-percent chance that new information would change his mind. It was just as likely, thought Dave, that new information would increase as decrease his judgment about the probability of his catching the swine flu, and even a small increase in this probability would cause him to switch his decision and not get the shot. Given his aversion to shots and to waiting in line, as well as his desire not to get the flu, reversing this decision could be important. Moreover, the cost of obtaining additional information was low; as a student in biomedical engineering, Garric had access to an excellent medical library and he knew how to use it. Furthermore, he did not think he was so much "spending" his time, as "using" it to satisfy his curiosity and "investing" it to learn more about medical decision making. Consequently, Dave decided to obtain more information.

In a recent issue of the *New England Journal of Medicine,* Garric found an article, "The Swine-Influenza Decision," which contained just the probability estimates he needed.[3] From a survey of experts in the fields of influenza epidemiology and virology, the authors of the article estimated that there was only a 10-percent chance of an epidemic. That was an interesting surprise— was that what President Ford meant by "a very real possibility"? Also, for people his age, the experts predicted a 30-percent "attack rate." Dave thought he was healthier than average, but living in a university community, his exposure to the flu would also be higher than average. Consequently, he decided that his personal chances of catching the flu if there were an epidemic were 30 percent. Thus, given that the chance of an epidemic was 10 percent,

The Dynamics of Analysis

Garric's chances of getting the flu if he did not get the shot were only 3 percent. Clearly, he decided, he should skip the shot.

Sensitivity Analysis

Still, Dave knew, he had better check to see how sensitive this decision was to his various assessments. Given the preference-probability of 0.9 that Dave had assessed for the interjacent outcome, the probability of his getting the flu would have to be greater than 10 percent before he would decide to get the shot. Thus, Dave reexamined the two probabilities (the chance of an epidemic and the chance that he would catch the flu given an epidemic) that he used to assess, indirectly, his own probability, p, of getting the flu.

The 10-percent chance of an epidemic given in the article was the median of the estimates of five experts, with the individual assessments ranging from 2 to 25 percent. Dave realized that the 10-percent figure reflected the best available information. Nevertheless, he found it reassuring to calculate that even if the chance of an epidemic was 25 percent his personal chance of catching the flu was still less than 10 percent ($0.25 \times 0.3 = 0.075$).

For the other probability, the attack rate, Dave quickly realized that his decision would remain the same even if it were much greater than the 30-percent figure provided in the article. Indeed, given a 10-percent chance of an epidemic and his 0.9 preference-probability for getting the shot, Dave would decide against the inoculation even if the attack rate was 99 percent.

Now, how sensitive was his decision to his 0.9 preference-probability? With a 10-percent chance of an epidemic and a 30-percent chance of catching the flu given an epidemic, Dave knew that his preference-probability for the interjacent outcome would have to exceed 0.97 before he would switch his decision and get the shot. If he thought harder about his preferences, he might assess a value higher than his original (and tentative) judgment of 0.9, though he did not see how he could end up with a preference-probability greater than 0.97. Nonetheless, this component of his analysis seemed to be the shakiest, and thus Dave decided to focus his attention on it.

A Second-Cut Analysis

To indirectly assess a preference-probability for the interjacent outcome of the basic sapling, Dave decided to decompose this cut-off outcome into some of *its* outcomes. The article in the *New England Journal of Medicine* gave the probability of getting a reaction to the swine flu shot (0.02), as well as the probability that the vaccine would not protect an individual from the flu (0.3). In his first-cut analysis, Dave had ignored this possibility by assuming that getting the shot was riskless; that is, this alternative led directly to a terminal node rather than an uncertainty. On his second-cut decision tree, however, he included the possibility of catching the flu even if he got the shot. Also, he further decomposed his chance of getting the flu by including the probability of an epidemic and his "own" attack rate on the decision tree (see figure 12–2).

Dave's second cut involved not only more uncertainties, but also more outcomes, complicating the task of assessing preferences. Clearly, the best outcome was to skip the shot and stay well; the worst outcome was to get the shot and catch the flu anyway. Skipping the shot and then catching the flu was a shade better than this, but Dave decided that the difference was so small that his preference-probability for this outcome should be zero, too. This left two other outcomes: getting the shot but not getting sick, and getting the shot plus a reaction to it.

According to the article, there was a 2-percent chance of having a "serious systemic reaction" to the swine flu vaccine. What did this mean? How did this compare with coming down with the flu? The article estimated that, on average, there would be "one day lost from work" by each employee who had a "serious systemic reaction," while there would be "an average loss of 2.8 days per [swine flu] episode."[4] Days of "work" lost presumably did not include weekends and holidays, so Dave interpreted these numbers to mean that a "serious systemic reaction" would result (on average) in being sick for a day and a half, and that the swine flu would result (again, on average) in being sick for four days. And, for his purposes, these point estimates seemed to be adequate; the range of risk involved in being sick was not a factor that would change his decision.

To help him think about his relative preferences for being sick for four, one and a half, and no days, Dave constructed a hypothetical gamble (see figure 12–3). Which did he prefer: being sick for a day and a half (starting the day after tomorrow), or a gamble with an X chance of not being sick and a $(1 - X)$ chance of being sick for four days (sometime during the winter)? Or, putting the question in a way that helped him resolve his dilemma: What is X so that he is indifferent between these two alternatives? To determine X, Dave found it easier to think in terms of the number of days he would be well rather than in terms of sick days, for the desirability of the outcome increased with the number of "well days." Further, Dave reasoned, since two and a half well days was slightly more than two-thirds of four well days, and since he was just slightly averse to risks involving his health (at least for gambles involving between zero and four days of sickness), an X of about two-thirds would make

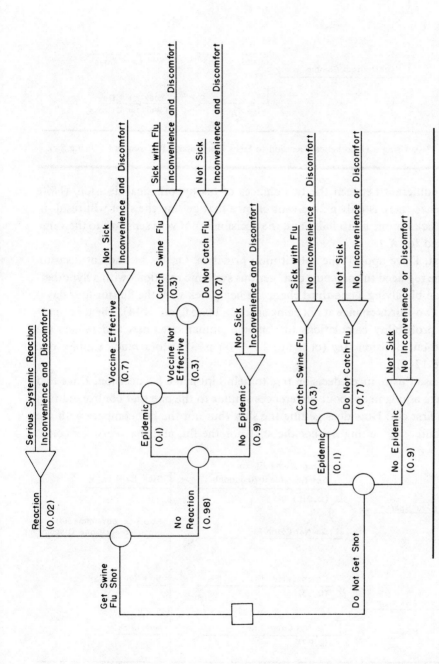

Figure 12-2. A Second-Cut Decision Tree for David Garric's Swine Flu Dilemma.

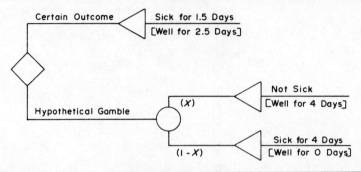

Figure 12–3. Using a Hypothetical Decision to Help Think about Preferences for Being Sick.

him indifferent between the two choices of his hypothetical decision. (Note that since there is only a 2-percent chance that getting the shot will result in being sick for one and a half days, the decision is not very sensitive to the value assessed for X.)

Next, Dave applied the substitution principle. On his second-cut decision tree, he replaced the outcome of a "serious systemic reaction" with a hypothetical gamble giving a one-third chance at being sick with the flu (for four days) and a two-thirds chance at not being sick at all (see figure 12–4). Then, he made some probability calculations to combine similar outcomes and reduce the second-cut decision tree (of figure 12–4, on p. 355) to a much simpler one (figure 12–5).

To use this reduced decision tree to help him make his decision, Dave had to make a judgment about preferences similar to the one that confronted him in his first cut: How does getting the shot (but not the flu) compare with the *Best* outcome, getting neither the shot nor the flu, and the *Worst* outcome,

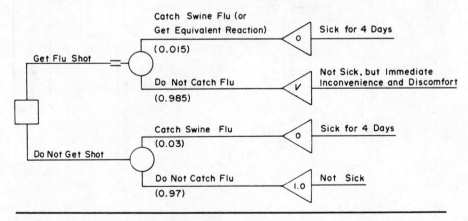

Figure 12–5. The Reduced Second-Cut Decision Tree.

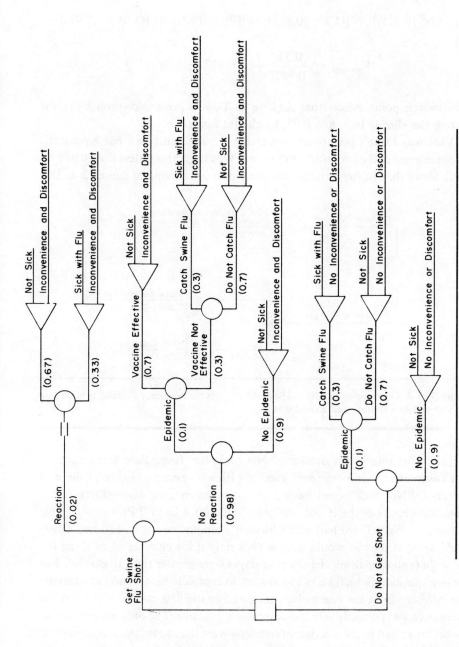

Figure 12–4. Second-Cut Tree with Equivalent, Hypothetical Gamble Substituted for "Reaction" Outcome.

getting the flu (with or without the shot)? Before assessing this preference-probability, V, however, Dave decided to calculate the switch point for it:

$$[(0) \times (0.015)] + [(V) \times (0.985)] = [(0) \times (0.3)] + [(1.0) \times (0.97)]$$

$$V_{\text{switch}} = \frac{0.97}{0.985} = 0.98477 \approx 0.98.$$

This switch point means that as long as Dave's preference-probability for getting the shot is less than 0.98, he should not get it.

What was Dave's preference-probability for not being sick but having the inconvenience and discomfort of the shot? Was it greater or less than 0.98? To think about this, he drew the hypothetical decision sapling of figure 12–6. Did

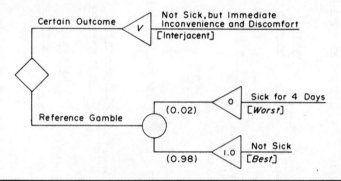

Figure 12–6. A Key Question for Garric's Second Cut: Does the Preference-Probability of Getting the Shot and Not Getting Sick Exceed 0.98?

he prefer the interjacent outcome "Not Sick, but Immediate Inconvenience and Discomfort," or a reference gamble with a 98-percent chance of the *Best* outcome, "Not Sick" (and having no inconvenience or discomfort), and a 2-percent chance of the *Worst* outcome, "Sick for 4 Days"? Previously, in his first-cut analysis, Dave had asked himself a similar question, and had tentatively decided that he would get the shot only if his chances of catching the swine flu (and thus being sick for four days) were greater than 10 percent. But the new question (which he had to answer to complete his second-cut analysis) was different from the one he had answered in the first cut. Now the riskless alternative was perfectly safe and completely effective. The only adverse consequences involved in the interjacent outcome were the immediate inconvenience of standing in line and the discomfort of the shot itself. The other possible adverse consequences of getting the shot—a reaction to it, or catching the flu anyway—had already been incorporated into the analysis explicitly. (These factors affect the value of V_{switch}, though it is not very sensitive to them.)

Still, Dave decided, he would not get even this shot. If given a choice between the inconvenience and discomfort of the shot, and a gamble with a 2-percent chance of being sick for four days (and a 98-percent chance of not being sick at all), Dave preferred to take the gamble. He realized that many of his friends would disagree with him about this, but he so disliked the hassle of standing in line and so hated shots that this hypothetical decision (of figure 12–6) seemed clear to him. And thus so did his choice about his real decision (figure 12–2): He would not get the shot.

A Third-Cut Analysis

Thinking about why some of his friends would disagree with him, Dave remembered the conjecture that the swine flu might be a "killer flu" like the influenza of 1918. That pandemic struck down young, healthy people at uncommonly high rates. He decided to consider hospitalization and death explicitly, and drew a third-cut decision tree (figure 12–7, p. 358), with outcome branches for these possibilities.

As before, the article in the *New England Journal of Medicine* provided some helpful information[5]: For people in the 25–44 age bracket, there would (given an epidemic) be 15,884,000 cases of the swine flu, 1 percent of which would result in hospitalization. Also, of these 15,884,000 cases, 9,000 would result in death, meaning that if an individual of age 25–44 caught the flu, the probability of death was $(9,000/15,884,000 =) 0.0005666$. Thus, Dave calculated, someone of age 25–44 who did not get the shot would have a probability of dying from the flu of $(0.1) \times (0.3) \times (0.0005666) = 0.000017$. Further, the article divided each age bracket into a high-risk and a low-risk group, and since he thought he belonged in the low-risk category, he calculated the probabilities for it. For the low-risk 25–44 group, the chance of dying from a case of the flu was only 0.00024; thus, he concluded, his own chance of dying from the flu if he did not get the shot was 0.0000072, or approximately seven chances in a million.

Of course, even if Dave did get the shot, he might still die from the flu. The chances of this would simply be 0.3 times the chance of dying if he did *not* get the shot (since the probability that the shot would not be effective was 0.3). Thus, for those in the 25–44 age bracket, the probability of dying from the flu if you did get the shot was 0.000005. For the low-risk 25–44 group, the probability was 0.0000022, or approximately two chances in a million.

Unfortunately, the *New England Journal of Medicine* offered no estimate of

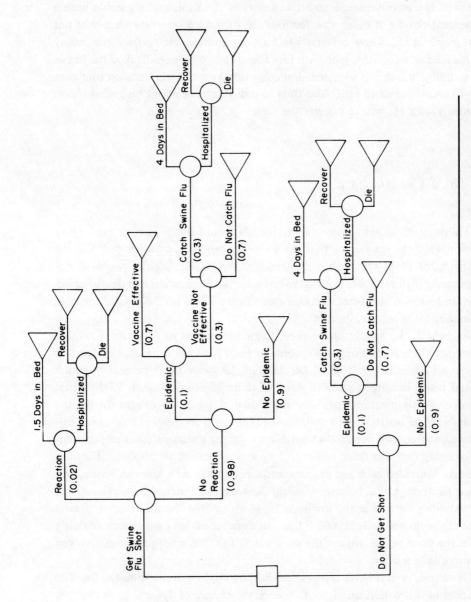

Figure 12-7. A Rough Third-Cut Decision Tree for David Garric's Swine Flu Dilemma.

the probability that a "serious systemic reaction" would lead to hospitalization or death, although Dave suspected that this was a possibility. He checked the references at the end of the article and discovered one (but only one) that seemed relevant, a report of the field trials that had been conducted the previous spring on the swine flu vaccine.[6] This report, published by the Center for Disease Control, found that "the bulk of the side effects" were "fever, malaise, myalgia, and other systemic symptoms of toxicity occurring 6–12 hours after vaccination and persisting 1–2 days." Further, these side effects "should occur in less than 2–3% of vaccinees 18 years of age or older." In addition, the report noted that allergic response and "various respiratory expressions of hypersensitivity" were "exceedingly uncommon but can occur after influenza vaccination," and that neurologic disorders have been observed in "at least temporal association with influenza vaccination." The report concluded that "influenza vaccine has only rarely, if ever, been associated with severe adverse reactions or permanent disability."

The report provided no specific probabilities, though it noted that of the more than 5,200 people involved in the field trials, only "three fatalities have been reported in temporal association with influenza vaccination." In two of these cases other causes were "strongly suggested" and "the third was equally compatible with another viral disease." Dave reasoned that "half a death" (that is, a 50-percent chance of one death, the last mentioned) out of 5,200 people vaccinated implied that the risk of dying from the shot was about one in 10,000. This was, however, clearly a very shaky estimate. Moreover, for a healthy individual like Dave, the risk might be only a tenth or a hundredth of that. Consequently, he tentatively decided to assess his chances of dying from a reaction to the shot as one in one hundred thousand (or 0.00001) and the risk of hospitalization to be ten times that (or 0.0001).

Having considered the probabilities, Dave now turned his attention to his preferences. He quickly realized that assessing preference-probabilities would not be easy. The *Worst* outcomes were those involving death, and the *Best* were those where he skipped the shot and stayed well. But what should be his preference-probabilities for the interjacent outcomes? Should the preference-probability for getting sick and spending four days in bed be 0.999 or 0.9999 or 0.999999? Dying would be so bad that all the outcomes in which he ends up living—even if he must first suffer through several days of misery—should have preference-probabilities very close to 1.0.[7] But how close? Would he prefer a reference gamble for which the probability of dying was one in a thousand (with 999 chances in a thousand of being well) to a certain four days in bed with the flu? Or would the chance of dying have to be lowered to one in ten thousand, or one in a million before he would be willing to gamble on his life?

Although it is difficult to think about probabilities, it is even more difficult to think about extremely small, minuscule probabilities.[8] Realizing this, Dave decided to make 1.0 the preference-probability for all the outcomes in which he lived (and 0 the preference-probability for all those in which he died). He knew that in doing this, he was reducing his complicated, third-cut analysis to a simple double-risk dilemma (see figure 12–8), with his decision being based

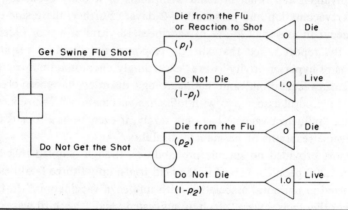

Figure 12–8. A Reduced Third-Cut Decision Tree.

on a single criterion—which alternative gave him the best chance of living. This simplification eliminated a variety of consequences, from the inconvenience of standing in line to the misery of contracting the flu, and focused attention on just one consequence—whether he lived or died. Nevertheless, this approach could be helpful, for it would give him an entirely different perspective on his decision, one not provided by his first or second cut.

Quick analysis (as we have continually emphasized in this book) is not the unthinking application of a set of mathematical formulas but the creative yet systematic process of discovery. The fundamental ideas of decision analysis provide the basis for thinking about a decision dilemma from a number of different perspectives, with each analysis reflecting a different view of why the decision is a dilemma. Consequently, what type of information and insight a decision maker seeks from a third-cut analysis depends upon what he has already learned from his first two approaches. If the possibility that the swine flu might become a "killer flu" was one reason why David Garric thought the decision about whether to get the shot was a dilemma, then he ought to analyze explicitly his chances of dying.

Dave had already assessed the probability that he would die from the swine flu if he did not get the shot: 0.0000072, or seven chances in a million. And the probability that he would die from the flu even if he *did* get the shot was

0.0000022, or two chances in a million. That meant that getting the shot reduced his chances of dying from the swine flu by five out of a million. To Dave, this was not a particularly large gain; specifically, he thought that this small benefit was outweighed by the cost of the shot—its inconvenience and discomfort.

Moreover, there was the chance that he would die from a reaction to the shot itself. And this risk would have to be less than five in a million (0.000005) if he was to have a better chance at living by getting the shot than by not. He had already tentatively assessed his chances of dying from the shot to be one in a hundred thousand (0.00001)—a probability *greater* than his chance of dying from the swine flu if he did *not* get the shot. This was, Dave had noted, a "shaky estimate," based on the little data available from the swine flu trials. Nevertheless, it was the best information he had, and this was the probability he *decided* to use in his analysis: Dave decided that he would have the same chance of living if he gambled on an urn in which were 99,999 balls labeled "live" and one ball labeled "die" as he would if he gambled on getting the shot.

Thus, Dave concluded, his chance of dying if he got the shot was 0.00001 + 0.0000022 = 0.000012, or twelve chances in a million. That was nearly double his seven-in-a-million chance of dying if he did not get the shot. For Dave Garric, that clinched it.

Deciding How to Decide

David Garric did not just decide to skip the swine flu shot. He also *decided* to do a simple, first-cut analysis of his dilemma. He *decided* to gather more information at the library. He *decided* to do a second-cut analysis. He *decided* to do a third cut. And, finally, he *decided* to stop analyzing his dilemma. He made not a single decision but a series of decisions about how he would make that decision.

All decision makers face similar decision-making decisions. As was emphasized in chapter 1, it is impossible to do a complete, comprehensive analysis of any decision. There are simply too many factors that might have some bearing on the choice, and the limits of time, information, and human cognitive abilities prevent the decision maker from analyzing the impact of all of them. Consequently, when making a decision, a decision maker must decide how to decide.

There are a large number of decision-making decisions. A decision maker must decide what factors to consider and which ones to ignore. He must decide how much time and other resources to devote to making the decision. Then, he must decide how to allocate this time between the task of gathering information and the task of thinking. Further, thinking involves a number of subtasks —designing alternatives, selecting what factors to consider, predicting the likelihood of future outcomes, appraising the desirability of these outcomes— and the decision maker must decide how to allocate his thinking time among them. And, after an initial analysis is complete and an initial decision made, he must decide whether to do some further analysis, and if so on what factors to concentrate this additional work.

Most decision-making decisions are made quickly and informally, with little or no explicit analysis. David Garric did not draw a decision tree when he decided to go to the library, or when he decided to do a second- or then a third-cut analysis, or when he decided to stop. He thought about each choice, but not in a thorough and systematic manner. In some situations, such as deciding whether to undertake an expensive sample survey before making a final decision, explicit analysis is warranted. (How to analyze compound decision dilemmas was discussed in chapter 10.) In most situations, however, informal judgments will be the basis for making decision-making decisions, particularly third- and higher-order decisions, (that is, decisions about how to make decisions about how to make decisions about . . .). Indeed, one reason why a decision maker can never do a complete analysis is that at some point he must start thinking about a decision without first thinking about how to think about the decision.

Nevertheless, the general problem of deciding how to decide is an important one—worthy of some analysis in its own right. Moreover, one type of decision-making decision—deciding whether to do additional analysis—occurs in every decision-making situation. An analysis of this generic decision-making decision can be quite revealing. All decision makers need to be able to think analytically about whether to do more analysis.

The pD > C Rule

"Life is not long, and too much of it must not pass in idle deliberation how it shall be spent," Samuel Johnson advised the young James Boswell two centuries ago.[9] Because life is not long, the benefits of analysis must be balanced against the costs of analysis to determine whether an analysis should be done and how complete it should be. As we noted in chapter 1, the basic rule has been stated succinctly by philosopher John Rawls: "We should deliberate up to the point where the likely benefits from improving our plan are just worth the time and effort of reflection."[10]

The Dynamics of Analysis

Thus, to decide whether or not to do more analysis, three factors are important: (1) the probability, p, that additional analysis will yield a different decision; (2) the difference, D, between the decision maker's preference for this different alternative and his preference for the alternative he otherwise would have chosen; and (3) the cost, C, of doing the additional analysis. The expected benefits of the additional analysis are simply $p \times D$—the probability of making a different decision times the difference between that decision and the original one. Thus, a decision maker should continue to think about his dilemma as long as $p \times D$ is greater than C. This is the $pD > C$ rule.

Since deciding whether to do additional analysis (or, indeed, whether to do any analysis at all) is a decision problem, it can be analyzed with the help of decision analysis. In fact, the $pD > C$ rule can be derived by analyzing this decision-making decision as a basic decision dilemma (see figure 12–9).

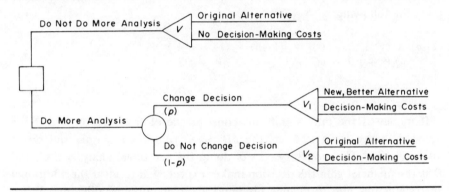

Figure 12–9. A Basic Decision Sapling for the Further-Analysis Dilemma.

For the further-analysis dilemma, there are two alternatives. The riskless alternative is to do no more analysis, for then the outcome is certain—stick with the decision already made (either through analysis or unaided intuition) for the original dilemma. The preference-probability for this riskless alternative is V, the preference-probability for the alternative already chosen for the original dilemma. The risky alternative for the further-analysis dilemma is to do more analysis, because the outcome is uncertain—the decision maker (as the result of this additional analysis) may change his mind about the original dilemma, or he may not. The worst outcome of additional analysis is to not change the decision, for then the decision maker must incur the costs (C) of the additional analysis without gaining any benefits for his original dilemma. The preference-probability for this outcome is $V_2 = V - C$. The best outcome is for the additional analysis to change the decision maker's mind about his original decision, since he would not make such a change unless the additional

363

analysis revealed a better alternative. It is better by the difference D, but since this outcome also involves the cost of the additional analysis, its preference-probability is $V_1 = V + D - C$. (Obviously, if the cost, C, of doing the additional analysis is greater than the potential benefit, D, of a changed decision, then V_1 will be less than V, and there is no dilemma. In that case, both V_2 and V_1 will be less than V, so it makes no sense to do any more analysis.)

The $pD > C$ rule can be derived from this analysis by noting that the decision maker should do more analysis as long as his preference-probability for this alternative, $(p \times V_1) + [(1-p) \times V_2]$, is greater than the preference-probability, V, for doing no more analysis. That is, do more analysis if

$$(p \times V_1) + [(1-p) \times V_2] > V.$$

Then, substituting $(V + D - C)$ for V_1 and $(V - C)$ for V_2 in this inequality gives the following:

$$[(p) \times (V + D - C)] + [(1-p) \times (V - C)] > V;$$
$$pV + pD - pC + V - C - pV + pC > V;$$
$$pD - C > 0;$$
$$pD > C.$$

If money is the only significant consequence of the decision and if the decision maker is an EMVer, the $pD > C$ rule has a simple and direct interpretation. The monetary cost of doing the additional analysis is C, and D is the financial gain the decision maker expects will result if the additional analysis causes him to change his mind about his original dilemma. When preferences for the outcomes are expressed in terms of preference-probabilities, however, C and D are differences between preference-probabilities and their interpretation is not so straightforward. Nevertheless, the $pD > C$ rule can be quite helpful in an informal way.

For a decision maker familiar with this rule, using it may become second nature, so that it is employed frequently to a host of decision-making decisions. When the decision about whether to make an incomplete analysis a bit more complete is particularly puzzling and important, the explicit use of the $pD > C$ rule may be appropriate. In most cases, however, the rule will be applied in a rough, implicit manner to decide whether to examine additional alternatives, whether to gather some more information, or whether to decompose some outcome further, into additional uncertainties or consequences.

Recall, for example, Dave Garric's decision about whether to go to the library. Because after his preliminary analysis his preferences for the two alternatives were so close and because he knew so little about the swine flu, Dave thought that additional information could significantly change his probability assessments, that collecting more information would have close to a

50-percent chance of changing his decision. That is, p was nearly 0.5. Further, he thought that changing his preliminary decision could be significant. Because the consequences affected by changing his decision involved the inconvenience and discomfort of standing in line as well as the possibility of catching the flu, he thought that the difference, D, which changing his decision might make, could be large. At the same time, he thought the cost, C, of spending an hour or so in the library to obtain the information would not be very great; indeed, that might be an interesting (and educational) way to spend an afternoon. In effect, Garric implicitly concluded that for his decision about whether to collect more information, p times D was certainly greater than C.

Another Swine Flu Dilemma

On the ides of March, 1976, another decision maker, President Gerald R. Ford, was confronted by the swine flu. On that day, the president was first informed by his staff that the Department of Health, Education, and Welfare was requesting a $135 million supplemental appropriation for a nationwide swine flu vaccination program. Within nine days, Ford made his decision. On March 24, the president announced the program "to inoculate every man, woman, and child in the United States."[11] As Dr. Theodore Cooper, then the assistant secretary of HEW for health, observed, the proposed program "dwarfs in scope even the massive polio campaign which was undertaken in the 1950's after the licensure of Salk vaccine."[12]

The swine flu vaccination program resulted from a rather traditional decision-making process. Dr. David J. Sencer, then the director of the Center for Disease Control, drafted an "ACTION" memorandum that was sent from Cooper to HEW Secretary David Mathews. The memo presented four options, though, as Richard E. Neustadt and Harvey V. Fineberg of Harvard University note in their study, *The Swine Flu Affair*, "three [were] framed to be rejected by the reader."[13] Indeed, much of the effort of those involved in the decision-making process seems to have been devoted to ensuring that the president made the "correct" choice rather than to informing his decision. Most of those in and out of government who were consulted apparently thought, as did one former assistant secretary of health, that immunizing 213 million people in three months was "the only possible course."[14]

Sencer's memo was given to the president and provided the basis for the adopted program, though Ford did not finally commit himself until he had met personally with a group of distinguished scientists, including the two most famous gurus of the immunization business, the rivals Jonas E. Salk and Albert

B. Sabin. No dissent or qualifications were presented to the president and, when he asked the scientists for their objections, none were forthcoming. So, given the unanimity of his scientific advisors, President Ford announced his swine flu decision to the press with Salk and Sabin standing by his side.

President Ford had to make his decision quickly, for if the nation was to be immunized against the swine flu, production of the vaccine would have to begin immediately. Yet there was very little information available to him. There were fears that the swine flu could recreate the pandemic of 1918. But no one knew for sure. Not the doctors at the Center for Disease Control; not the president. How then, could he have thought about his decision?

Decision analysis could have provided some help. Undertaking such an analysis might not have ensured an escape from the political box in which the president was trapped by the Sencer memorandum and the actions of officials and scientists, but thinking analytically about the decision might have generated some insight into the nature of the dilemma. Moreover, a decision analysis might have revealed that there were indeed reasonable alternatives to a massive, comprehensive immunization program. In fact, discovering such alternatives was the only way out of the president's political trap.

The president did not have much time, and he did not have much data. Still, he could have asked a staff assistant to do a quick analysis of his swine flu decision.

A First Cut at President Ford's Swine Flu Dilemma

The alternatives for any swine flu vaccination program had a number of dimensions. Who should pay the cost, the consumers or the government? How should responsibility be divided between business and government, and among federal, state, and local agencies? How should the program be publicized and implemented? The major factor that distinguished the alternatives, however, was the scale of the program: Should the government attempt to vaccinate "every man, woman, and child," half the public, just those for whom the swine flu posed the greatest risk, or no one? Shortly after President Ford made his announcement, public health officials began to realize that it was impossible to manufacture 213 million doses of the swine flu vaccine on such short notice; at the same time, bureaucratic pressures seemed to rule out ignoring the swine flu and continuing with the traditional efforts against the Victoria strain. Consequently, as a first cut, it would have made sense (in the spring of 1976) to focus on two alternatives: (1) a general program that would attempt to vaccinate approximately two-thirds of the public (140 million people) and (2)

The Dynamics of Analysis

a targeted program that would focus on those 48 million people for whom the flu presented a high risk of complications and death (of whom 28 million people might be vaccinated).[15] (There was, of course, the stockpiling alternative—manufacture the vaccine, then wait to see how many more people contract the swine flu before deciding how many people to vaccinate—though this alternative was given little attention by eager public health officials.)

The decision tree for this first cut at President Ford's swine flu decision (figure 12–10) is similar to the double-risk trees presented in chapter 5 for the dilemmas posed to public officials by various natural disasters—volcano, earthquake, hurricane. For Ford, the riskier alternative was the targeted program, as the uncertain outcomes for this alternative could be better than anything that would result from the general program (if there was no epidemic) or worse (if there was an epidemic). The less risky alternative was the general program, since it narrowed the range of possible outcomes. An epidemic is just another natural disaster, and thus thinking about the dilemma it creates as a double-risk decision can be quite helpful.

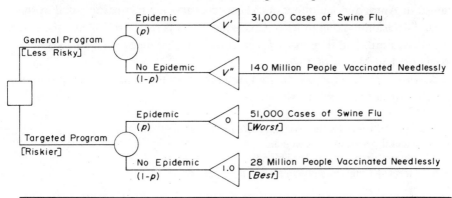

Figure 12–10. President Ford's Swine Flu Decision as a Double-Risk Dilemma.

Once the decision has been structured as a double-risk dilemma, the next question is obvious: What is the probability of a swine flu epidemic? Incredibly, however, President Ford was never given a specific assessment of this uncertainty. The memo written by Sencer simply stated:

> Present evidence and past experience indicate a strong possibility that this country will experience widespread A/swine influenza in 1976–77. Swine flu represents a major antigenic shift from recent viruses and the population under 50 is almost universally susceptible. These are the ingredients for a pandemic.[16]

Estimates of the probability by the public health officials involved in the decision were between 2 and 20 percent.[17] When HEW Secretary Mathews asked, "What's the probability?", the deputy assistant secretary for health, James F. Dickson, III, responded, "Unknown."[18] Cooper appears to have thought the chance was 1 percent, but Neustadt and Fineberg report that "Sencer and Cooper were proud of their refusal to put numbers on the possibility of a pandemic."[19]

Nonetheless, any decision obviously depended upon a judgment about this probability. If there was a 20-percent chance of an epidemic, the less risky alternative might be better. If the chance was only 2 percent, however, the riskier approach might make more sense. President Ford later recalled, "I think you ought to gamble on the side of caution."[20] With his swine flu decision, both alternatives were gambles, and which alternative was the more cautious—the more prudent—depended upon the probabilities.

The median estimate of 10 percent that was published in the *New England Journal of Medicine* appears to be a reasonable one to use.[21] The article by Stephen C. Schoenbaum, Barbara J. McNeil, and Joel Kavet, of Harvard University, did not appear until September 1976, but the estimates were obtained in April, and a number of the experts surveyed had participated in the federal decision-making process. Consequently, it is reasonable to assume that President Ford, had he pressed for it, could have obtained such a probability assessment in March of 1976.

Assessing preferences for the four outcomes can begin with the easy step of ranking them from best to worst:

1. targeted program, no epidemic (*Best*);
2. general program, no epidemic;
3. general program, epidemic; and
4. targeted program, epidemic (*Worst*).

Note that since whether or not an epidemic occurs is the major factor in determining the desirability of an outcome, the second outcome (general program, no epidemic) is significantly better than the third outcome (general program, epidemic).

To evaluate the third outcome, it is helpful to compare it with the fourth. Here three considerations are important.[22]

1. Deaths. If there were an epidemic, there would be 50,000 deaths with no program, about 33,000 deaths with a targeted program, and about 28,000 deaths with a general program. That means that the larger, general program would reduce the number of swine flu deaths by only about 15 percent below what would occur with the targeted program. This is because without any program three-quarters of the deaths would occur in the high-risk population; a swine flu epidemic (the experts thought) would not kill large numbers of healthy, young people, as did the 1918 flu. Consequently, most of the lives saved by any vaccination program would be those of people in the high-risk population.

The Dynamics of Analysis

2. Cases of Swine Flu. If there were an epidemic, there would be 56,561,000 cases of the flu with no program, 53 million cases with a targeted program, and 31 million cases with a general program. (This is because only 16 percent of the cases would occur in the high-risk group.) Consequently, the general program would reduce the number of cases to 60 percent of what would occur with a targeted program.

3. Other Costs. Five times as many people (140 million versus 28 million) would be inoculated under the general program. This means five times as many people suffering the inconvenience and discomfort of getting the shot, perhaps five times the number of serious reactions to the shot (depending upon whether the high-risk group is more vulnerable than the general public to such reactions), and perhaps five times the monetary costs (depending upon whether there existed economies of scale.)

These three considerations suggest that, in the event of an epidemic, the general program would not be all that much better than the targeted program. Thus, a reasonable preference-probability (V') for the general-program, epidemic outcome might be about 0.1 or 0.2. Even if the incidence of the swine flu were the dominant consideration (with deaths and other costs ignored), the preference-probability for this outcome could hardly be larger than 0.4, since the general program would reduce the incidence of the flu by only 40 percent.

The remaining preference-probability to be assessed (V'') is for the general-program, no-epidemic outcome. Here, calculating the switch point can be instructive. The general switch-point equation is

$$[p \times V'] + [(1-p) \times V''] = [p \times 0] + [(1-p) \times 1.0].$$

Using the judgments previously made ($p = 0.1$ and $V' = 0.2$), this becomes

$$[0.1 \times 0.2] + [0.9 \times V''] = [0.1 \times 0] + [0.9 \times 1.0];$$

$$0.9 \times (V'') = 0.9 - 0.02;$$

$$V'' = \frac{0.88}{0.9};$$

$$V''_{switch} = 0.98.$$

This means that the preference-probability for the general-program, no-epidemic outcome would have to be at least 0.98 before the general program would be preferred to the targeted program. But given the additional costs of the general program (inconvenience and discomfort, reactions, budgetary expenditures), an appropriate preference-probability would certainly be less than 0.98. Furthermore, even if V' (the preference-probability for the general-program, epidemic outcome) were as high as 0.4, V''_{switch} would only decline from 0.98 to 0.96.

This quick analysis—it certainly would not have taken a White House staffer very long to do—clearly suggests that, if a decision had to be made in March of 1976, a vaccination program targeted at the high-risk population would have been superior to an effort to vaccinate the general public.

A Second-Cut Analysis of the President's Swine Flu Dilemma

A second cut might be valuable, though, particularly if it means a closer examination of the consequences of the four possible outcomes. Five different consequences might be important: the number of deaths,[23] the number of people sick, the number of days they were sick, the financial costs of the program, and the number of people vaccinated. These are all given on the second-cut decision tree in figure 12–11.

Most of these consequences can be derived from the data provided by Schoenbaum, McNeil, and Kavet. The number of days sick from the flu was obtained by multiplying the number of flu cases by 2.8 days lost from work, and then by seven-fifths. The consequences of the vaccine (but not the flu) were calculated assuming that 2 percent of the people vaccinated would have reactions to the shot, and that each reaction would result (on average) in one day lost from work, or seven-fifths of a day sick. Schoenbaum et al. provided no data on the probability of dying from the vaccination, and the results of the Center for Disease Control's field trials were not available when President Ford made his decision. Moreover, the probability of death that David Garric obtained from the field trials—one chance in ten thousand—would have seemed much too high in March of 1976.[24] Thus, the consequences presented on the decision tree are based on a probability of dying from the vaccine of one in fifty thousand for the high-risk group and one in one hundred thousand for the general population. Note that the sickness and deaths that result from the vaccine occur whether or not there is an epidemic.

Next, the expected value of each of these consequences is calculated and noted inside the large, circular uncertainty node. Compared with the general program, the targeted program has a lower expected number of deaths (3,900 versus 4,500), approximately the same number of people sick (5.9 million), but more sick days (22 million versus 16 million). Also, the targeted program would cost less ($24 million versus $100 million) and would inoculate fewer people (28 million versus 140 million). If one wishes to focus on a single consequence, the number of deaths is clearly the most important. (The cost of either program is really quite small, both in absolute terms and in terms of the cost per life saved.)[25] The sickness caused by the flu is important too, though, and if necessary the differences in the consequences can be taken into account

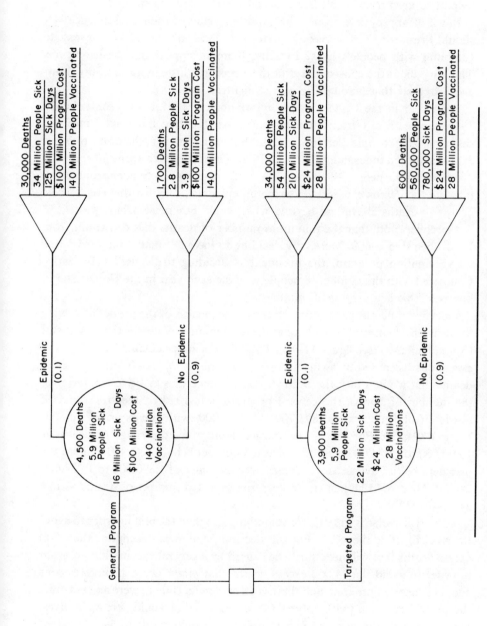

Figure 12–11. A Second-Cut Decision Tree for President Ford's Swine Flu Decision.

by doing some trade-off analysis. For the moment, however, it may be more helpful to keep track of all five consequences and their expected values.

But is it appropriate to use the expected value of each consequence? Or should President Ford be risk averse for this decision? Should he be averse to gambling with people's lives? Initially, it might appear that he should be. Thinking about the consequences of this decision a little more carefully, however, suggests that he ought to be risk neutral.

Each year in the United States, approximately 1.9 million people die. In 1975, the death rate from influenza was 2 per hundred thousand,[26] meaning that over 4,000 people died from the flu that year. (In 1976, the death rate was 3.7 per hundred thousand;[27] that is, in 1976—even without a swine flu epidemic —nearly 8,000 people died from the flu.) Thus, when Schoenbaum et al. tabulate the deaths caused by a swine flu epidemic, they list them as "excess deaths"—deaths above and beyond what would otherwise occur.

Moreover, note that the minimum number of deaths that can result from Ford's decision is 600. Merely by deciding to have a "small," targeted swine flu vaccination program, the president is deciding to "cause" 600 deaths. Compared with the number of people who die each year in the United States, however, this is a very small number.

Indeed, a different perspective on the consequences of the president's swine flu decision is obtained by looking at the total number of deaths that will result (from all causes) (see figure 12–12). Total deaths are calculated by adding the excess deaths caused by swine flu or the vaccine to 1,890,000, the number of deaths that would otherwise occur in the United States in 1976.[28] In terms of the number of deaths, the general program is less risky, since the range of possible (total) deaths is 1,891,700 to 1,920,000, with the expected number being 1,894,530. For the riskier, targeted program, the range of deaths is 1,890,600 to 1,924,000, with the expected number being 1,893,940. Should the president be risk averse for outcomes over the range of 1,890,600 to 1,924,000 deaths? Or should he just try to keep the expected number of deaths as low as possible?[29]

To be risk averse is to settle for something less than the best in order to avoid the risk of getting the worst. For this decision, that means accepting the 1,700 excess deaths that will necessarily be caused by a general vaccination program in order to avoid the 34,000 excess deaths that *might* occur if the president adopts a targeted program and there is an epidemic. If there were an epidemic, the general program (with only 30,000 excess deaths) would save 4,000 lives, compared with the targeted program (which would result in 34,000 excess deaths). If there were no epidemic, however, the targeted program (with 600 excess deaths) would save 1,100 lives, compared with the general program (which would result in 1,700 excess deaths). Are the 4,000 deaths that would be avoided by the general program *if* there were an epidemic so important that

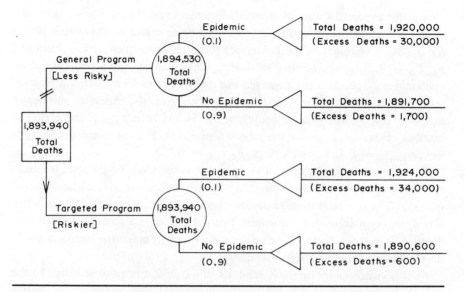

Figure 12–12. Making President Ford's Swine Flu Decision by Minimizing the Expected Number of Deaths.

they override the significance of the 1,100 deaths that will be avoided by the targeted program in the nine-times more likely event of no epidemic? When the president is making a decision about the lives of several thousand people, should he not focus his attention on saving the largest expected number of lives?

The consequence that may cause the president—or at least the president's staff—to be averse to taking the risk of the targeted program is the political consequence. If the president chooses the targeted program and there is an epidemic, he can be accused by his political opponents of causing 4,000 needless deaths. Actually, they might accuse him of causing all 34,000 deaths, since the president's political critics could charge that their (somehow miraculous) program would have prevented all those deaths. But, as President Ford's advisors told him, this was a "no-win" political situation.[30] No matter what he did, people were going to die, and he could be accused of causing those deaths. There is nothing illegitimate about adding the political consequence to all of the outcomes on the second-cut decision tree. In this case, however, the political consequences—all of which will be bad—will be roughly proportional to the number of people who die.[31]

Since the exact number of deaths, people sick, and sick days that will result from either decision and either uncertain outcome is uncertain, the next step in this analysis might be to construct a range of risk for each of these possible consequences. That would be quite a laborious task, however, and might not change the expected values of these consequences very much. Rather, an easier —and perhaps more revealing—step would be to calculate the switch points for p (the probability of an epidemic) for each consequence. For example, $p_{switch} = 0.22$ for the number of deaths. That is, when the probability of an epidemic is 22 percent, the expected number of deaths from both alternatives is the same: 7,900 deaths. If p is greater than 0.22, the expected number of deaths is less for the general program; if p is less than p_{switch}, the expected number of deaths is less for the targeted program. For the number of people sick, $p_{switch} = 0.1$. For sick days, $p_{switch} = 0.035$.

If you think the probability of an epidemic is less than 3.5 percent, it makes sense—in terms of all three of these consequences—to select the targeted program. If p is greater than 22 percent, however, the general program is better for all three of these consequences. For p between 3.5 and 22 percent, the decision is more difficult (unless you are willing to make the decision solely on the basis of the number of deaths).

As this switch-point analysis suggests, the decision is quite sensitive to the probability of an epidemic—which the deputy assistant secretary for health said was "unknown." As time goes on through the spring and summer of 1976, policy makers could obtain more information (such as the types of flu viruses circulating in the southern hemisphere during their winter, our summer) about the chances of an epidemic. Certainly it would be easier to make an intelligent judgment in September of 1976 than in March about the probability of a swine flu epidemic occurring in the winter of 1976–77.

Thus, a quick analysis that reveals how important the probability of an epidemic is to the president's swine flu decision also suggests the value of the stockpiling alternative: Manufacture the vaccine, but wait until the probability of an epidemic can be assessed with more confidence before deciding what type of vaccination program to have.

The Dynamics of Analytical Thinking

Decisions sometimes seem obvious, even important ones that boldly launch untried programs affecting millions of people and costing millions of dollars. President Ford's swine flu decision was certainly depicted, at the time, as being the obvious choice. HEW Secretary Mathews asserted, for example, "We have not found anyone who would recommend any course of action other than the President is taking."[32]

When an unimportant decision, like which movie to see tonight, seems obvious, then no analysis is needed. When, however, a decision "of vast impor-

The Dynamics of Analysis

tance to all Americans"[33]—the phrase President Ford used to characterize his swine flu recommendation—seems obvious, some analysis of whether the decision is really obvious may be very worthwhile. In terms of the $pD > C$ rule, even if p is very low, if D is great enough, then the product of p times D may well exceed the cost of a few hours of concentrated, disciplined thinking.

As the $pD > C$ rule implies, analytical thinking is a dynamic process—an iterative search for insights about the dilemma and the best decision. In general, however, the first step in analyzing a decision is to identify the essence of the dilemma, the few crucial factors upon which the choice depends. It may take some searching—and some thinking—to discover this essence (it might even be helpful to create an elaborate decision tree and then prune it back ruthlessly until only the essential features remain). Once this essence is discovered, it forms the basis for a drastically simplified first-cut analysis.

Then the question is, What does the first cut reveal? A simplified analysis may indicate unambiguously which alternative is the best. Or the first cut may reveal that the decision is dependent upon the value of a particularly illusive factor and suggest the need to obtain more information or perhaps (if time permits) to do some researched analysis to pin down that crucial factor. Or an initial analysis may indicate that introducing some additional factors could have a significant impact upon the decision. Or a first cut may suggest that another, unanalyzed alternative should be given serious consideration in the next cut. It is the nature of the insights obtained from the first-cut analysis that suggest what (if anything) is to be done next.

Will additional thinking be worthwhile? The $pD > C$ rule provides the basis for making that judgment. If the first cut suggests that further analysis might (p) result in a different and significantly better (D) decision, and if the costs (C) of doing that additional work seem low enough (compared with p times D), then the decision warrants a second cut. And so on for a third, fourth, and perhaps seventeenth cut. At each stage, however, the type of additional thinking that would be most helpful can be derived only from the perceptions and wisdom obtained through the previous analyses.

Making decisions in such a dynamic, adaptive fashion not only avoids the waste of needlessly complex analysis, but encourages the decision maker to chew over his problem in manageable bits. An elaborate decision tree may make sense, but only if it is derived from more-simplified analyses that indicate which additional complications might affect the decision. Decision trees should be grown in stages, beginning with a simple decision sapling. Otherwise, the complexity of the analytical structure can overwhelm the cognitive capabilities of the decision maker. An analysis that becomes too big too soon turns out to be a bully, terrorizing the decision maker with its impenetrable complexity. A decision maker needs to keep the analysis simple and under control so that he can push it around to serve his needs.

375

The analyses of the two swine flu dilemmas presented in this chapter illustrate the dynamics of analytical thinking. The process does not involve constructing *the* model for the problem, solving the mathematics of this model, and then assuming that the solution of the model simultaneously and automatically solves the real problem, too. Analytical thinking involves the sequential considerations of different descriptions of the problem. Complications are added only when the decision maker finds that his analytical framework is too simple to permit him to determine what he really thinks about his relative preferences for the alternatives, and when his analysis suggests which additional factors might improve his thinking about those preferences.

Decision making is not a mechanical, cookbook process. It is a subtle, dynamic, iterative search for a satisfactory resolution of an important and puzzling problem. In some situations, merely drawing a decision tree may, through its structure, make the best decision immediately obvious. Or a simple decision tree may suggest upon which factor additional work and thinking should be concentrated. In other situations, a thorough analysis, complete with the specification of probabilities and preference-probabilities for a large number of uncertain outcomes, may be required. And the simple calculation of a few switch points provides some insight into the best decision for an entire range of probabilities and preference-probabilities. The type and extent of the analysis always depend upon the nature of the decision and the needs of the decision maker.

The purpose of quick analysis is to help make a decision. The analysis itself has no value; it is useful only if it provides some insight into which alternative is best. Neither the decision tree nor the preference-probabilities are the ends of the analysis; they are merely the means. The only suitable end is a resolution of the dilemma—a decision maker who is satisfied that he has identified the best alternative given the limited information available, and the limited time for thinking about the decision.

NOTES

Preface

1. For a more detailed discussion of why this is so, see Robert D. Behn and James W. Vaupel, "Why Decision Analysis Is Rarely Used and How It Can Be," Duke University, Institute of Policy Sciences, Working Paper #12762, December 1976.

2. Aaron Wildavsky, *The Politics of the Budgetary Process,* 2d ed. (Boston: Little, Brown, 1974), p. 152.

3. Paul Slovic, "Toward Understanding and Improving Decisions," in W. C. Howell and E. A. Fleishman, eds., *Human Performance and Productivity:* vol. 2, *Information Processing and Decision Making* (Hillsdale, N.J.: Erlbaum, 1981).

4. Personal communication from Richard Zeckhauser, August 4, 1978.

5. George Bernard Shaw, *Complete Plays with Prefaces,* Volume 1 (New York: Dodd, Mead, 1963), p. 58.

Chapter 1

1. Scott is quoted by Philip Shabecoff in the *New York Times,* "Budget Maker Switched From Millions to Billions," February 5, 1974.

2. McCall is quoted by E. J. Kahn, Jr., in *The New Yorker,* "Letter from Oregon," February 25, 1974, p. 97.

3. Richard F. Fenno, Jr., "The Internal Distribution of Influence: The House," in Raymond E. Wolfinger, ed., *Readings on Congress* (Englewood Cliffs, N.J.: Prentice-Hall, 1971), p. 200.

4. William James, "Habit," *The Writings of William James,* ed. John J. McDermott (New York: Modern Library, 1968), p. 13.

5. In his book *The Cybernetic Theory of Decision* (Princeton, N.J.: Princeton University Press, 1974), John Steinbrunner suggested (p. 16) that a complex decision problem had the following characteristics:

  1. (a) Two or more values are affected by the decision.
     (b) There is a trade-off relationship between the values such that a greater return to one can be obtained only at a loss to the other.
  2. There is uncertainty. . . .
  3. The power to make the decision is dispersed over a number of individual actors and/or organizational units.

Since we assume in this book that the decision maker has the responsibility and authority to make the decision, we do not include the last factor in our definition of a complex decision.

6. Garry Brewer's maxim is from a talk he gave at Duke University on December 3, 1973.

7. For a discussion of the relationship between formal models and real policy problems, see Ralph E. Strauch, " 'Squishy' Problems and Quantitative Methods," *Policy Sciences* 6, no. 2 (June 1975): 175–184.

8. Muller is quoted by Edward B. Fiske, "Trying to Define the Liberal Arts Program," *New York Times,* November 14, 1976.

9. Richard Zeckhauser's observation is from a talk he gave at Duke University on November 25, 1974.

10. One interesting example of inconsistencies in decision making is reported by Sarah Lichtenstein and Paul Slovic in "Reversals of Preference Between Bids and Choices in Gambling Decisions," *Journal of Experimental Psychology* 89, no. 1 (1971): 46–55. Lichtenstein and Slovic presented people with two different gambles. For one gamble, the probability of winning

was higher; for the second, the amount won was larger. Many of the subjects, when given a choice between the two gambles, chose the first, but, when asked how much they would pay to play each gamble, were willing to pay more for the second.

11. George A. Miller, "The Magical Number Seven, Plus or Minus Two: Some Limits on Our Capacity for Processing Information," *The Psychological Review* 63, no. 2 (March 1956): 81–97.
12. Herbert A. Simon, *Models of Man* (New York: John Wiley, 1957), p. 198.
13. For a survey of these limitations, see Paul Slovic, Baruch Fischhoff, and Sarah Lichtenstein, "Behavioral Decision Theory," *Annual Review of Psychology* 28 (1977): 1–39.
14. In the part of their survey that covers "decision aids," Slovic et al. write: "Most of these decision aids rely on the principle of divide and conquer. This 'decomposition' approach is a constructive response to the problem of cognitive overload." Ibid., p. 17.
15. Simon, *Models of Man*, p. 204. Simon's two most fundamental articles on the subject are "A Behavioral Model of Rational Choice," *Quarterly Journal of Economics* 69, no. 1 (February 1955): 99–118, and "Rational Choice and the Structure of the Environment," *Psychological Review* 63, no. 2 (March 1956): 129–138.
16. William Strunk, Jr., and E. B. White, *The Elements of Style,* 3d ed. (New York: MacMillan, 1979), p. 21.
17. Ibid., p. 79. The last section of this book, "An Approach to Style," was written solely by White.
18. George Orwell, "Politics and the English Language," in *The Orwell Reader* (New York: Harcourt Brace 1956), p. 355.
19. As Strauch, " 'Squishy' Problems," p. 183, notes, "Subjectivity thus means both the use of judgment, and it means a prejudiced approach to a problem, trying to come to a particular answer." We, of course, are using the first definition.
20. John Rawls, *A Theory of Justice* (Cambridge, Mass.: Harvard University Press, 1971), p. 418.
21. Slovic et al., *Decision Theory*, p. 22.

Chapter 2

1. For a detailed survey of the effectiveness of coronary bypass surgery in relieving angina, see Eldred D. Mundth and W. Gerald Austen, "Surgical Measures for Coronary Heart Disease," *New England Journal of Medicine* 293, nos. 1, 2, and 3 (July 3, 10, and 17, 1975): 13–39, 75–80, and 124–130.
2. This problem was developed with the assistance of Dwight L. Robertson, M.D.
3. Bernard C. Chaitman et al., "Operative Risk Factors in Patients with Left Main Coronary-Artery Disease," *New England Journal of Medicine* 303, no. 17 (October 23, 1980): 953–957.
4. See Howard Raiffa, *Decision Analysis* (Reading, Mass.: Addison-Wesley, 1968), p. 62.
5. For an example of researched decision analysis applied to the angina/bypass surgery dilemma, see Stephen G. Pauker, "Coronary Artery Surgery: The Use of Decision Analysis," *Annals of Internal Medicine* 85, no. 1 (July 1976): 8–18; and Milton C. Weinstein, Joseph S. Pliskin, and William B. Stason, "Coronary Artery Bypass Surgery: Decision and Policy Analysis," in John P. Bunker, Benjamin A. Barnes and Frederick Mosteller, eds., *Costs, Risks, and Benefits of Surgery* (New York: Oxford University Press, 1977), pp. 342–371.
6. Robert Schlaifer, *Analysis of Decisions Under Uncertainty* (New York: McGraw-Hill, 1969), p. 3.
7. Allen is quoted by Robert Lindsey in "High Roller at Boeing," *New York Times,* August 17, 1975.
8. Jeffrey L. Pressman and Aaron B. Wildavsky, *Implementation* (Berkeley: University of California Press, 1973), p. 125.
9. Joseph Alsop, "The Decay of the West," *Washington Post,* October 30, 1974.
10. Ruth is quoted by Bob Kutter in "Pardon Challenge was Considered, Ruth Says," *Washington Post,* October 27, 1975.
11. Dashiell Hammett, *The Maltese Falcon* (New York: Vintage, 1972), p. 162. In the movie, Sam Spade was played by Humphrey Bogart and Casper Gutman by Sidney Greenstreet.
12. Throughout this book, the various inadequacies of unaided human cognitive abilities are pointed out. When these statements are made, references to the literature of cognitive psychology are given to document the particular inadequacy. A general reference, however, is Robin M. Hogarth, *Judgement and Choice* (Chichester, England: John Wiley, 1980).

378

13. A reference gamble is what Raiffa, *Decision Analysis*, p. 57, calls a "Basic Reference Lottery."
14. A preference-probability is what Raiffa, *Decision Analysis*, p. 57, calls a "Basic Reference Lottery Ticket" or "BRLT," and what others call "utility" or "utils." The others include: R. G. Moore and H. Thomas, *The Anatomy of Decisions* (Harmondsworth, England: Penguin, 1976), chapter 9; and Edith Stokey and Richard Zeckhauser, *A Primer for Policy Analysis* (New York: Norton, 1978), chapter 12.
15. For a description of this takeover attempt, see "Piper Proves Elusive Prize," *Business Week*, August 16, 1969: 62–64; and Walter Guzzardi, Jr., "The Casualties Were Staggering in the Battle for Piper Aircraft," *Fortune* 43, no. 4 (April 1976): 90–95 passim. Obviously, using the basic dilemma to analyze this dilemma is a simplification; it does not include, for example, the possibility that Chris-Craft would get into trouble with the Securities and Exchange Commission for violating federal securities laws, or that the firm might benefit from someone else's violation. In fact, the Second U.S. Court of Appeals awarded Chris-Craft $36 million in damages from Bangor Punta and its investment banking firm, First Boston Corporation. In 1977, however, the Supreme Court overturned the ruling. The takeover fight took nine months; the legal battle took nine years.
16. The executive is quoted by Atsuko Chiba, "Mitsui-Led Group Must Pay More Money Or Pull Out of Iran Petrochemical Project," *Wall Street Journal*, November 25, 1980. Also see Henry Scott Stokes, "Iran's Japanese Hostage: A $3.5 Billion Petrochemical Plant," *New York Times*, November 30, 1980.
17. For a brief description of this decision dilemma, see Christopher Lydon, "Book Publishers Caught Unprepared For Carter's Fast Rise as Candidate," *New York Times*, June 14, 1976.
18. The geophysicist was quoted by Andrew H. Malcolm in "A Volcano in West Showing Signs of Life," *New York Times*, July 3, 1975.
19. The spokesman for the U.S. Geological Survey was quoted by Robert Cooke in "Mt. Baker's Belching Concerns Scientists," *Boston Globe*, July 6, 1975.
20. BART's problems with the gophers were described by Charles G. Burck in "What We Can Learn from BART's Misadventures," *Fortune* 42, no. 1 (July 1975): 105.
21. Thomas O'Toole, "Shuttle Lacks Abort System: Space Agency Defends Decision, Notes Safeguards," *Washington Post*, May 7, 1976.

Chapter 3

1. For a discussion of why assessments of probabilities and appraisals of preferences are not merely estimates of unknown quantities but decisions themselves, see Robert Schlaifer, *Analysis of Decisions Under Uncertainty* (New York: McGraw-Hill, 1969), pp. 126–127.
2. Carl S. Spetzler and Carl-Axel S. Staël von Holstein of the decision analysis group at the Stanford Research Institute "stress the interaction between interviewer and subject" when analyzing decisions, particularly when assessing probabilities.

   We find that having the subject assign a probability distribution without the help of an analyst often leads to poor assignments. This is true even for subjects who are well trained in probability or statistics. The main reason for our emphasis on interaction is that it is difficult to avoid serious biases without having an analyst present.

   "Probability Encoding in Decision Analysis," *Management Science* 22, no. 3 (November 1975): 356.

   This advice from professional analysts sounds a little self-serving. Indeed, it brings to mind Daniel S. Greenberg's Second Law of Expert Advice: "Never Ask a Barber Whether You Need a Haircut." Nevertheless, we have found that discussing the various aspects of a decision with someone familiar with decision analysis does help work through an analysis and leads to a more satisfying decision.
3. For a report on that Rose Bowl game, see William N. Wallace, "Two-Point Play is Decisive in the Rose Bowl," *New York Times*, January 2, 1975.

Chapter 4

1. Greenspan is quoted by James L. Rowe, Jr., "U.S. Statistics—All but the Ball Scores," *Washington Post*, July 11, 1976.

2. Ford is quoted by James M. Naughton, "Ford Bids Public Accept Increased Cost of Fuel," *New York Times,* August 16, 1975.

3. Dingell is quoted in an Associated Press report, "Rep. Dingell Sees Costlier Gasoline," *New York Times,* August 21, 1975.

4. Zausner is quoted in a United Press International report, "3¢-A-Gallon Rise in Gasoline is Due," *New York Times,* August 19, 1975.

5. Rosenberg is quoted by Steve Mott, "Refiner Facing Squeeze," *Washington Post,* August 24, 1975.

6. Ilacqua is quoted by James C. Tanner, "Decontrol Will Cause Petroleum Price Rise, But Less than Feared," *Wall Street Journal,* August 8, 1975.

7. Chapin is quoted by Robert Irvin, "American Motors Has an Egg but Boxes Are in Style," *New York Times,* August 22, 1976.

8. McLaughlin is quoted by William K. Stevens, "Chrysler Emphasis Placed on Compacts as '77 Line Is Shown," *New York Times,* September 10, 1976.

9. Matthiesen is quoted in "Why the Fertilizer Forecast Was Wrong," *Business Week,* April 19, 1976, p. 134.

10. Caplan is quoted in "Raw-Materials Prices Ease, Promising Help in Checking Inflation," *Wall Street Journal,* September 10, 1976.

11. Rosen is quoted by Isadore Barmash, "Upsurge in Digital Watches," *New York Times,* July 20, 1975.

12. Ward is quoted by Ted Morgan, "The Good Life (Along the San Andreas Fault)," *New York Times Magazine,* July 4, 1976, p. 18.

13. Church is quoted by Tom Braden, "The Next Secretary of State," *Washington Post,* August 21, 1976.

14. Arthur M. Schlesinger, Jr., *The Imperial Presidency* (Boston: Houghton Mifflin, 1973), p. 366.

15. Meyer is quoted by Roy J. Harris, Jr., "Early Revival Unlikely As Jumbo-Plane Sales Continue to Languish," *Wall Street Journal,* August 10, 1976.

16. *Deterrence and Survival in the Nuclear Age* (The "Gaither Report" of 1957), Joint Committee Print (Washington, D.C.: U.S. Government Printing Office, 1976), pp. 26–27. The "Gaither Report" was prepared by the Security Resources Panel of the Science Advisory Committee, November 7, 1957, declassified in 1973, and released by the Joint Committee on Defense Production in 1976.

17. Blauvelt is quoted by James C. Tanner, "No Crippling Shortage Of Energy Expected, But Cost Will Be High," *Wall Street Journal,* March 29, 1976.

18. White is quoted by Daniel Q. Haney (Associated Press), " 'Blue Flu' Hits Boston on Eve of Busing," *Washington Post,* September 8, 1975.

19. Jackson is quoted by William Chapman, "Atlantic Bids Gamble on Natural Gas," *Washington Post,* August 22, 1976.

20. The text of this news conference appeared in the *Washington Post,* February 26, 1974.

21. Jordon is quoted by Seth S. King, "Low Reserves of Wheat By Spring Are Foreseen," *New York Times,* January 24, 1974.

22. This quotation is from luncheon remarks to the Overseas Writers Association at the International Club in Washington, D.C. A transcript was provided by the Department of Defense.

23. This statement was made on the NBC "Today" show. A transcript was provided by NBC News.

24. *Draft Environmental Statement on Operation Giant Patriot* (Washington, D.C.: Department of the Air Force, 1974), pp. iii, 3–50.

25. William N. Wallace, "N.F.L. Players' Strike Appears Likely," *New York Times,* February 17, 1974.

26. Press Conference of Hon. Elliot L. Richardson, former attorney general of the United States, with members of the press, October 23, 1973, Washington, D.C. Transcript provided by the Department of Justice.

27. Donald H. Woods, "Improving Estimates That Involve Uncertainty," *Harvard Business Review* 44, no. 4 (July–August 1966): 91–98.

28. Others have found similar disagreements about the interpretation of ambiguous probability words. See, for example, Sarah Lichtenstein and J. Robert Newman, "Empirical Scaling of Common Verbal Phrases Associated with Numerical Probabilities," *Psychonomic Science* 9, no. 10 (December 5, 1967): 563–564; and Geoffrey D. Bryant and Geoffrey R. Norman, "Expressions of Probability Words and Numbers," *New England Journal of Medicine* 302, no. 7 (February 14, 1980): 411.

380

29. C. W. Kelly III and C. R. Peterson, *Probability Estimates and Probabilistic Procedures in Current-Intelligence Analysis,* (Gaithersburg, Md.: International Business Machines Corporation, 1971), pp. 4–1, 4–2.
30. Quoted by Peter Wyden, *Bay of Pigs* (New York: Simon and Schuster, 1979), pp. 89–90.
31. Rita James Simon and Linda Mahan, "Quantifying Burdens of Proof: A View from the Bench, the Jury and the Classroom," *Law and Society Review* 5, no. 3 (February 1971): 319–331.
32. Kenneth S. Broun and Douglas G. Kelly, "Playing the Percentages and the Law of Evidence," *University of Illinois Law Forum* 1970, no. 1: 34–35.
33. Alan G. Greene, "Defining the Indefinable," *New England Journal of Medicine* 295, no. 13 (September 23, 1976): 737.
34. For a "historical perspective" on the interpretations of probability, see Howard Raiffa, *Decision Analysis* (Reading, Mass.: Addison-Wesley, 1968), pp. 273–278.
35. Joseph D. McNamara, "FBI Statistics," *Washington Post,* August 6, 1976.
36. For a more detailed discussion of judgmental probability, see Bruno de Finetti, "Foresight: Its Logical Laws, Its Subjective Sources," in Henry E. Kyburg, Jr., and Howard E. Smokler, eds., *Studies in Subjective Probability* (New York: John Wiley, 1964).
37. Okay! Okay! So it's only 1 percent.
38. James Boswell, *The Life of Samuel Johnson,* abridged by Bergen Evans (New York: Modern Library, 1967), p. 352.
39. Amos Tversky and Daniel Kahneman, "Judgment Under Uncertainty: Heuristics and Biases," *Science* 185, no. 4157 (September 27, 1974): 1124–1131.
40. Robert Schlaifer, in *Analysis of Decisions Under Uncertainty* (New York: McGraw-Hill, 1969), emphasizes this same point (p. 126): "Neither probabilities nor preferences should be thought of as possible erroneous 'estimates' of 'true values' that exist even though they may be unknown. Probabilities and preferences are *decisions.*"
41. Pierre Simon, Marquis de Laplace, *A Philosophical Essay on Probabilities* [Essai philosophique sur les probabilités, 1819] translated from 6th French edition by Frederick Wilson Truscott and Frederick Lincoln Emory (New York: Dover, 1952), pp. 1–2.
42. Ibid., p. 6.
43. In fact, if you roll a die 100 times, the probability that a "four" will turn up only 8 times or fewer is approximately 0.75 percent. This can be calculated using basic probability theory and the binomial probability model.
44. *Statistical Abstracts of the United States, 1980* (Washington, D.C.: U.S. Government Printing Office, 1980), p. 227, Table 388. During the fifteen years ending in 1978, the average number of days with precipitation of 0.01 inches or more in Jackson, Mississippi was 111 per year, 12 per January, and 5 per October.
45. See, for example, Baruch Fischhoff, Paul Slovic, and Sarah Lichtenstein, "Knowing with Certainty: The Appropriateness of Extreme Confidence," *Journal of Experimental Psychology: Human Perceptions and Performance* 3, no. 4 (November 1977): 552–564.
46. Joan E. Sieber, "Effects of Decision Importance on Ability to Generate Warranted Subjective Uncertainty," *Journal of Personality and Social Psychology* 30, no. 5 (November 1974): 688–694.
47. Baruch Fischhoff, "Hindsight ≠ Foresight: The Effect of Outcome Knowledge on Judgment Under Uncertainty," *Journal of Experimental Psychology: Human Perception and Performance* 1, no. 3 (August 1975): 288.
48. Baruch Fischhoff and Ruth Beyth, " 'I Knew It Would Happen': Remembered Probabilities of Once-Future Things," *Organizational Behavior and Human Performance* 13 (1975): 1–16.
49. Baruch Fischhoff, "Hindsight: Thinking Backward?" manuscript, 1975.
50. See, for example, Baruch Fischhoff, "Debiasing," in Daniel Kahneman, Paul Slovic, and Amos Tversky, eds., *Judgment Under Uncertainty: Heuristics and Biases* (New York: Cambridge University Press, 1981).
51. Allan H. Murphy and Robert L. Winkler, "Can Weather Forecasters Formulate Reliable Probability Forecasts of Precipitation and Temperatures?" *National Weather Digest* 2 (1977): 2–9; Murphy and Winkler, "Reliability of Subjective Probability Forecasts of Precipitation and Temperature," *Journal of the Royal Statistical Society,* series C 26, no. 1 (1977): 41–47.
52. Sarah Lichtenstein and Baruch Fischhoff, "Training for Calibration," *Organizational Behavior and Human Performance* 26, no. 2 (October 1980) 149–171.
53. "Receiving outcome feedback after every assessment is the best condition for successful training," conclude Sarah Lichtenstein, Baruch Fischhoff, and Lawrence D. Phillips in "Calibration of Probabilities: The State of the Art in 1980," in Kahneman et al., (eds.), *Judgment Under Uncertainty.*

54. Leonard Silk, "Year of Twin Crises: Wall Street Is Up Against Persistence in Uncertainties on Presidency and Oil," *New York Times,* November 8, 1973.
55. Ralph E. Winter, "Fuel Shortage Fails To Change '74 Budgets At Many Corporations," *Wall Street Journal,* December 27, 1973.
56. Graham T. Allison, *Essence of Decision* (Boston: Little, Brown 1971), pp. 171–172, 178.
57. Paul Slovic, "From Shakespeare to Simon: Speculations—And Some Evidence—About Man's Ability To Process Information," *Oregon Research Institute Research Monograph* 12, no. 12 (April 1972): 20.
58. H. L. Mencken, *Prejudices, First Series* (New York: Knopf, 1919), p. 46.
59. Ernest R. May, *"Lessons" of the Past* (New York: Oxford University Press, 1973).
60. Donald H. Woods, "Improving", p. 95.
61. Arthur M. Schlesinger, Jr., *The Bitter Heritage: Vietnam and American Democracy* (Boston: Houghton Mifflin, 1966), p. 91.
62. William Shakespeare, *Timon of Athens,* act 5, scene 1, line 207.

Chapter 5

1. See "Moynihan Continues To Teach at Harvard," *New York Times,* September 29, 1976. The analysis in this chapter is not Moynihan's.
2. William B. Schwartz, "Decision Analysis: A Look at the Chief Complaints," *New England Journal of Medicine* 300, no. 10 (March 8, 1979): 557.
3. M. J. Moroney, *Facts From Figures* (Baltimore: Penguin, 1951), p. 3.
4. "The Outlook: Senate, House and Governors," *Congressional Quarterly Weekly Report* 34, no. 41 (October 9, 1976): 2830.
5. Alain C. Enthoven, "Ten Practical Principles for Policy and Program Analysis," in Richard Zeckhauser et al., eds., *Benefit-Cost and Policy Analysis 1974* (Chicago: Aldine, 1975), pp. 456–457.
6. For these data see Stephen G. Pauker and Jerome P. Kassirer, "Therapeutic Decision Making: A Cost-Benefit Analysis," *New England Journal of Medicine* 293, no. 5 (July 31, 1975): 229–234.
7. Note that the appendectomy dilemma as described in figure 5–12 is not a double-risk decision but a basic decision dilemma, for both outcome branches of the operate decision have the same consequence, a 0.001 chance of death. Yet the overall decision dilemma, as dramatized by figure 5–16, is clearly double-risk, for both alternatives involve uncertainty about life and death. Thus, the dilemma can be resolved by determining which decision alternative gives the patient the better chance of living.
8. For some researched analysis of the appendectomy dilemma, see Pauker and Kassirer, "Therapeutic Decision Making"; Nava Pliskin and Amy K. Taylor, "General Principles: Cost-Benefit and Decision Analysis," in John P. Bunker, Benjamin A. Barnes, and Frederick Mosteller, eds., *Costs, Risks, and Benefits of Surgery* (New York: Oxford University Press, 1977), pp. 5–27; and Raymond Neutra, "Indications for the Surgical Treatment of Suspected Acute Appendicitis: A Cost-Effectiveness Approach," also in Bunker, Barnes, and Mosteller, pp. 227–307.
9. For more detailed discussions of the application of decision analysis to medical dilemmas, see Pauker and Kassirer, "Therapeutic Decision Making"; William B. Schwartz et al., "Decision Analysis and Clinical Judgment," *American Journal of Medicine* 55 (October 1973): 459–472; Barbara J. McNeil, Emmett Keeler, and S. James Adlestein, "Primer on Certain Elements of Medical Decision Making," *New England Journal of Medicine* 293 (July 31, 1975): 211–215; and a number of the chapters in Bunker, Barnes, and Mosteller, *Costs of Surgery.*
10. See "Guadeloupe Volcano Expected to Erupt; 72,000 Evacuated," *New York Times,* August 16, 1976; and "Guadeloupe's Volcano Explodes," *New York Times,* August 31, 1976.
11. "Predicting Earthquakes," *Washington Post,* December 11, 1977.
12. Michael Knight, "Quakes in New England: Common but Mysterious," *New York Times,* April 19, 1979.
13. "Geologist Warns California of 'Imminent' Earthquake," *Washington Post,* May 2, 1979.
14. Dr. E. L. Quantarelli of the Disaster Research Center at Ohio State University in Columbus argues that there is a "panic myth" about how people respond to disaster warnings. Still, public officials may be sufficiently concerned about the chance of a panic that they would want

to consider this factor when making a decision. If so, it might be best to incorporate the uncertainty about a panic into any analysis by adding another uncertainty node to the decision tree, with outcomes for "public panics" and "public does not panic." Quantarelli is quoted by Joanne Omang, "Expert Says People Take Disaster Warning Well," *Washington Post,* January 28, 1978.

15. For a more detailed discussion of how to use quick analysis to make the evacuation decision and other crisis decisions, see Robert D. Behn and James W. Vaupel, "Fighting the *Next* War: Or Preparing to Analyze the *Next* Crisis," paper presented at Research Conference on Public Policy and Management, Chicago, October 19, 1979, mimeo.

16. This "sleeper" status is reported by Robert H. Williams, "PostScript," *Washington Post,* October 24, 1977.

17. With apologies to Joseph Heller.

Chapter 6

1. For reports on Gail Kalmowitz's decision, see Lawrence Van Gelder, "Nearly Blind Student Accepts $165,000, Forfeiting $900,000 Award From Jury," *New York Times,* March 27, 1975; Richard Haitch, "Big 'If,'" *New York Times,* June 22, 1975; "Blind Student Settles Suit, Loses $735,000," *Washington Post,* March 27, 1975; and Karen F. Oliver, "Blind Student Settles Suit A Moment Too Soon," *Boston Globe,* March 28, 1975.

2. For reports on the decision of Mr. and Mrs. Farrell, see Felicity Barringer, "Jury Verdict: $500,000 Too Late," *Washington Post,* July 30, 1976; and "Hospital, 2 Doctors Pay $500,000 to Blind Boy," *New York Times,* July 30, 1976.

3. For a report on Thomas Zarcone's decision, see Tom Goldstein, "Vendor Abased by L.I. Judge Given $141,000," *New York Times,* July 21, 1977.

4. For a discussion of how to undertake a researched analysis of the new-product decision problem, see Edgar A. Pessemier, *New-Product Decisions: An Analytical Approach* (New York: McGraw-Hill, 1966).

5. For a discussion of this dilemma, see David P. Garino, "McDonnell Douglas, Fokker to Decide Soon Whether to Build 150-Passenger Plane," *Wall Street Journal,* May 15, 1981.

6. For a detailed examination of the uses of decision analysis in oil prospecting when there exists a lot of time and data, see C. Jackson Grayson, Jr., *Decisions Under Uncertainty: Drilling Decisions by Oil and Gas Operators* (Boston: Harvard Business School, 1960); and Arthur W. McCray, *Petroleum Evaluations and Economic Decisions* (Englewood Cliffs, N.J.: Prentice-Hall, 1975), especially chapter 6, "Decision Trees and Economic Models," pp. 157–189.

7. For a discussion of Ventron's decision, see Liz Roman Gallese, "Ventron Gambles on White Powder to Produce a Bigger Black-Ink Flow," *Wall Street Journal,* June 8, 1976.

8. The juror is quoted by Lawrence Van Gelder, "Nearly Blind."

9. Kalmowitz is quoted by Karen F. Oliver, "Blind Student."

10. Kalmowitz is quoted by Van Gelder, "Nearly Blind."

11. Kalmowitz is quoted by Richard Haitch, "Big 'If.'"

12. William B. Schwartz, "Decision Analysis: A Look at the Chief Complaints," *New England Journal of Medicine* 300, no. 10 (March 8, 1979): 558.

Chapter 7

1. *Budget of the United States Government: Fiscal Year 1977* (Washington, D.C.: U.S. Government Printing Office, 1976).

2. Office of Management and Budget, "Mid-Session Review of the 1977 Budget," July 16, 1976, p. 5.

3. Office of Management and Budget, "Joint Statement of William E. Simon, Secretary of the Treasury, and Paul H. O'Neill, Acting Director, Office of Management and Budget, on Budget Results for Fiscal Year 1976," July 26, 1976, p.1.

4. Office of Management and Budget, "Joint Statement of William E. Simon, Secretary of the Treasury, and James T. Lynn, Director, Office of Management and Budget, on Budget Results for the Transition Quarter," October 27, 1976, p.1.

5. U.S., Congress, House, Committee on the Budget, *Federal Outlay Shortfall for Fiscal Year 1976 and the Transition Quarter,* Hearings before the 94th Cong., 2d sess., Nov. 22 and 23, 1976 (Washington, D.C.: U.S. Government Printing Office, 1976), p. 32.
6. Ibid.
7. Ibid., p. 24.
8. See O'Neill's testimony, ibid., pp. 32–51. Also see Eileen Shanahan, "House Hearing Studies 'Shortfall' in Federal Spending," *New York Times,* November 23, 1976.
9. *Federal Outlay Shortfall,* p. 50.
10. Ibid., p. 68.
11. Ibid., pp. 82 and 83.
12. Ibid., p. 24. (Of course, the law of large numbers would suggest that the percentage errors would be larger for a three-month period than for a twelve-month period.)
13. Ibid., p. 33.
14. Ibid., p. 28.
15. Ibid., p. 34.
16. Ibid., p. 33.
17. CBO lists as sources of "potentially correctable misestimates": (1) "faulty models or inaccurate programmatic assumptions," which result from, for example, the failure to employ in the forecasting model the correct relationship between the unemployment rate and unemployment-compensation expenditures, and (2) "inaccurate spending rates and other estimating problems," which result from, for example, the failure to distinguish between policy objectives (and the spending rates needed to achieve those objectives) and realistic estimates of what will be spent and achieved. For "intrinsic uncertainties," CBO lists four sources: (1) inaccurate assumptions concerning future congressional actions to establish new programs or to expand or cut back existing ones, (2) unexpected administrative actions by the executive branch, (3) inaccurate economic assumptions, and (4) abnormal weather conditions and disasters. *Analysis of the Shortfall in Federal Budget Outlays for Fiscal Year 1978,* Staff Working Paper, Congressional Budget Office, March 1979, chapter 2, "The Reasons for the 1978 Shortfall," pp. 11–31.
18. For FY 78, outlays were $8.4 billion below the level specified by the second congressional budget resolution (which is based on CBO spending estimates). CBO concluded that it overestimated spending rates by $10.6 billion. The shortfall was only $8.4 billion, however, because faulty models accounted for a $0.9 billion underestimate in expenditures, and intrinsic uncertainties contributed another $1.3 billion overrun. ($10.6 − 0.9 − 1.3 = $8.4.) If CBO's estimates of spending rates had been right on target and there had been no errors in forecasting models, there would still have been a $1.3 billion error. See ibid., p. xii.
19. For a more detailed discussion of the factors that contribute to the uncertainties in federal spending estimates, see Office of Management and Budget, *Overview of the Current 'State-of-the-Art' of Federal Outlay Estimating,* Technical Paper Series BRD/BPB 77-1, December 15, 1977, pp. 3–6.
20. *Federal Outlay Shortfall,* p. 45.
21. Ibid., p. 72.
22. Ibid., p. 76.
23. The Congressional Budget Office reports:
    While fluctuations in some of these highly variable individual programs will always be difficult to predict, it is expected that the procedures CBO had already developed and has underway will result in significantly improved estimates of total outlays, bringing the accuracy to within 1 percent.
    "Estimates of Federal Budget Outlays," Staff Working Paper, February 1978, p. 28.
24. *Federal Outlay Shortfall,* pp. 46–47.
25. Ibid., p. 46.
26. "Half a Percentage Point's Difference," *Washington Post,* May 31, 1980.
27. Rudolph G. Penner, "Charades: The Budget Debate in Congress," *New York Times,* June 1, 1980.
28. Office of Management and Budget, *Current Services Estimates for Fiscal Year 1978,* November 1976 (Washington, D.C.: U.S. Government Printing Office, 1976), p. 8.
29. Ibid., p. 9.
30. Congressional Budget Office, *Five-Year Budget Projections: Fiscal Years 1978–1982,* December 1976 (Washington, D.C.: Congressional Budget Office, 1976), p. 4.
31. Ibid., pp. 4 and 53.

32. *Current Services Estimates,* p. 9.
33. Paul H. O'Neill et al., Office of Management and Budget, "News Conference," held on November 12, 1976, in the Old Executive Office Building, p. 4. Transcript provided by the Office of Management and Budget.
34. *Current Services Estimates,* p. 3.
35. *Special Analyses, Budget of the United States Government, Fiscal Year 1979,* (Washington, D.C.: U.S. Government Printing Office, 1978), p. 10.
36. *Federal Outlay Shortfall,* p. 33.
37. Ibid.
38. Healey is quoted by Chalmers M. Roberts, "Will the Western Alliance Muddle Through?" *Washington Post,* November 21, 1974.
39. Quoted by Paul Dickson in *The Official Rules* (New York: Delacorte, 1978), p. 53.
40. *Special Analyses,* p. 10.
41. Office of Management and Budget, "Current Budget Estimates, March 1978," press release, March 13, 1978, pp. 2 and 3.
42. Brewer's remark is from a talk he gave at Duke University on December 3, 1973.
43. Aaron Wildavsky, "Policy Analysis Is What Information Systems Are Not," *Zero-Base Budget Legislation,* Hearings before the Task Force on Budget Process of the Committee on the Budget, House of Representatives, 94th Congress, 2nd Sess. (Washington, D.C.: U.S. Government Printing Office, 1971), p. 256.
44. U.S., Congress, House, Committee on Appropriations, *Second Supplemental Appropriations Bill, 1971,* 92d Cong., 1st sess. (Washington, D.C.: U.S. Government Printing Office, 1971), p. 256.
45. For a discussion of how business managers interpret the words *optimistic* and *pessimistic* differently when making sales estimates, thus "compounding uncertainty," see Donald H. Woods, "Improving Estimates That Involve Uncertainty," *Harvard Business Review* 44, no. 4 (July–August 1966): 92–93.
46. Paul A. Samuelson, "Policy Advising in Economics," *Challenge* 21, no. 1 (March–April 1978): 40.
47. See, for example, Robert L. Ludke, Fred F. Stauss, and David H. Gustafson, "Comparison of Five Methods for Estimating Subjective Probability Distributions," *Organizational Behavior and Human Performance* 19, no. 1 (June 1977): 162–179; and Robert L. Winkler, "The Assessment of Prior Distributions in Bayesian Analysis," *Journal of the American Statistical Association* 62, no. 319 (September 1967): 776–800.
48. As is reported in one literature review, "the research does not provide an adequate answer to the question . . . : What is the best way to assess probabilities?" Paul Slovic, Baruch Fischhoff, and Sarah Lichtenstein, "Behavioral Decision Theory," *Annual Review of Psychology* 28 (1977): 20.
49. Robin M. Hogarth, "Cognitive Processes and the Assessment of Subjective Probability Distributions," *Journal of the American Statistical Association* 70, no. 350 (June 1975): 284.
50. One could, of course, first assess a cumulative probability distribution (see chapter 9) and then read the median, upper quartile, and lower quartile off this curve. But as Winkler, "Assessment of Distributions," p. 793, observes, there exists a "tendency for the distributions corresponding to the direct techniques to be more dispersed than the distributions corresponding to the indirect techniques." Given the problem of overly narrow distributions, this observation provides a further reason for employing a direct technique.

Seaver et al. found that their subjects produced more dispersed distributions if they were asked to assess uncertainty measures (probabilities and odds) for specified values of the uncertain quantity, rather than asked to assess values of the uncertain quantity to go with specified probabilities. In other words, rather than asking for the 50th-percentile value of the uncertain quantity, the subjects were asked, for example, "What is the probability (or odds) that the uncertain quantity is above 50,000?" Unfortunately, this question immediately suggests that 50,000 is a reasonable number. But the results of our almanac questions, discussed later in this chapter, suggest that people have a difficult time determining what a reasonable number is. As Seaver et al. note, when giving a specific number and asking for a probability, "some information was necessarily transmitted." See David A. Seaver, Detlof von Winterfeldt, and Ward Edwards, "Eliciting Subjective Probability Distributions on Continuous Variables," *Organizational Behavior and Human Performance* 21, no. 3 (June 1978): 379–391.

Moreover, it is difficult to develop a method for assessing your own uncertainty about an uncertain quantity using the process of asking for probabilities to go with specific values. Where do you get the values to ask the probabilities about? Still, such a process might negate the anchoring and adjustment heuristic if it consisted of the following steps.

1. Develop upper and lower bounds between which you are absolutely convinced the uncertain quantity lies. The process of creating extreme scenarios to get extreme estimates would be helpful here. (Seaver et al. asked five of their colleagues to provide such bounds and then used the highest upper bound and the lowest lower bound to get the range from which they selected the quantities used in their probability questions.)
2. Assess probabilities (or odds) for different numbers in that range.
3. Determine an uncertainty curve (or cumulative probability distribution) from those assessments.
4. Obtain quartile (or other) estimates needed for decision-making purposes from that curve.

Of course, the success of this process depends upon the two extreme estimates obtained in step 1. If the upper and lower bounds aren't even in the ball park, the resulting estimate will be very poor.

51. This process is similar to what Winkler, "Assessment of Distributions," calls "assessment of fractiles," and what Ludke, et al., "Five Methods," call the "bisection method."
52. Amos Tversky and Daniel Kahneman, "Judgment under Uncertainty: Heuristics and Biases," *Science* 185, no. 4157 (September 27, 1974).
53. Ibid. Also see Tversky and Kahneman, "Anchoring and Calibration in the Assessment of Uncertain Quantities," *Oregon Research Institute Research Bulletin* 12, no. 12, April 1972.
54. Hogarth reports: "It has frequently been shown that man is often strongly influenced by his first hypothesis and requires much information to change this." "Cognitive Processes," p. 284. See also D. G. Pruitt, "Informational Requirements in Making Decisions," *American Journal of Psychology* 74 (September 1961): 433–439; and G. F. Pitz, "Subjective Probability Distributions for Imperfectly Known Quantities," in L. W. Gregg, ed., *Knowledge and Cognition* (New York: John Wiley, 1974), pp. 29–41.
55. Sarah Lichtenstein, Baruch Fischhoff, and Lawrence D. Phillips, "Calibration of Probabilities: The State of the Art," in H. Jungermann and G. de Zeeuw, eds., *Decision Making and Change in Human Affairs* (Dordrecht, Holland: D. Reidel Publishing Co., 1977), p. 314. A revised version of this paper appears as "Calibration of Probabilities: The State of the Art to 1980," in Daniel Kahneman, Paul Slovic, and Amos Tversky, eds., *Judgment Under Uncertainty: Heuristics and Biases* (New York: Cambridge University Press, 1981).
56. See ibid.
57. Daniel Kahneman and Amos Tversky, "Intuitive Predictions: Biases and Corrective Procedures," *TIMS Studies in Management Science* 12 (1979): 313–327. Also see Don Lyon and Paul Slovic, "Dominance of Accuracy Information and Neglect of Base Rates in Probability Estimation," *Acta Psychologica* 46 (1976): 287–298.
58. Kahneman and Tversky, "Intuitive Predictions."
59. Ibid.
60. Those familiar with Bayesian statistics will observe that what is recommended here is nothing more than a back-of-the-envelope approach to Bayesian updating, with the background, distributional information being the prior, which is then adjusted to reflect information about the particular case. Kahneman and Tversky offer a more detailed procedure; ibid. For some specifics on Bayesian statistics, see the appendix to chapter 10.
61. Amos Tversky and Daniel Kahneman, "Availability: A Heuristic for Judging Frequency and Probability," *Cognitive Psychology* 5, no. 2 (September 1973): 207–232.
62. The work of Koriat et al. appears to provide some support for this approach. They argue that overconfidence in a conclusion can be reduced by consciously generating reasons why the conclusion is wrong. Similarly, consciously generating scenarios for extreme values of uncertain quantities should help reduce overconfidence in the median estimate. See Asher Koriat, Sarah Lichtenstein, and Baruch Fischhoff, "Reasons for Confidence," *Journal of Experimental Psychology: Human Learning and Memory* 6, no. 2 (March 1980): 107–118.
63. Carl S. Spetzler and Carl-Axel S. Staël von Holstein, "Probability Encoding in Decision Analysis," *Management Science* 22, no. 3 (November 1975): 340–358.
64. Tversky and Kahneman, "Availability," p. 230.
65. Ibid., p. 229.
66. For a discussion of how our thinking about probabilities causes us to overlook the wisdom of Murphy, see Robert D. Behn, "Why Murphy Was Right," *Policy Analysis* 6, no. 3 (Summer 1980): 361–363.

67. Kahneman and Tversky also discuss why people underestimate the time to complete a project in "Intuitive Predictions."
68. Tversky and Kahneman, "Availability," p. 230.
69. This is not true if the uncertain quantity is a sample drawn randomly from a population with a well-known distribution, such as the weight of the first child born tomorrow at Boston's Lying-In Hospital. See Ludke et al., "Five Methods."
70. For a discussion of calibration, see Lichtenstein et al., "Calibration."
71. A. H. Murphy and R. L. Winkler, "Subjective Probability Forecasting Experiments in Meteorology: Some Preliminary Results," *Bulletin of the American Meteorological Society* 55 (1974): 1206–1216; Murphy and Winkler, "The Use of Credible Intervals in Temperature Forecasting: Some Experimental Results," in H. Jungermann and G. de Zeeuw, *Decision Making.*
72. See Lichtenstein et al., "Calibration," (1977 and 1981), and Baruch Fischhoff, "Debiasing," in Kahneman et al., *Judgment.* Lichtenstein et al. (1981) argue that "receiving outcome feedback after every assessment is the best condition for successful training."
73. The interquartile index and surprise index are discussed in ibid.
74. These results came from assessments made by the following groups of Duke students: 33 undergraduates in October 1974, 76 undergraduates in February 1976, 16 graduate students in October 1976, 10 graduate students in October 1977, 13 graduate students in October 1978, and 21 graduate students in October 1979. The questionnaires (similar to figure 7–4) were distributed in one class and collected in the next, and the exact details of the instructions (both written and oral) and the extent of any prior discussion of assessing estimates of uncertain quantities varied from year to year. Nevertheless, the results from all four groups were very similar. For example, the surprise index was greater than 38 for all six groups.

These results reveal calibrations worse than those surveyed by Lichtenstein, Fischhoff, and Phillips, "Calibration." In part, this may be because the exercise was consciously designed less to train students in assessment techniques than to demonstrate to them how overconfident they were in assessing estimates of uncertain quantities. Students were given few training instructions other than an occasional hint that their ranges would be too narrow. Moreover, the almanac questions were selected with the expectation that the students' intuitions about these quantities would be vague or misleading.

One student suggested that this was cheating. If you had never heard, for example, of the Verrazano-Narrows Bridge—if you had absolutely no idea what type of bridge this was— then your median assessment should be your best guess at the median length of all bridges. Similarly, your upper extreme should be such that 99 percent of all bridges have lengths less than this estimate. In this situation, you would *have* to be surprised, since the Verrazano-Narrows Bridge is the longest suspension bridge in the world. We doubt, however, that many of the "surprises" were the result of students using only base-rate information to make their assessments. As Tversky and Kahneman, "Judgment," point out, people usually ignore base-rate information.

Also, one feature of the assessments may have worked to decrease the surprise index. In addition to the five estimates given in figure 7–4, the students were also asked to assess their 12.5th and 87.5th percentiles—what are called the *lower* and *upper octiles* (see chapter 9). Being required to make an additional estimate between their lower quartile and lower extreme and between their upper quartile and upper extreme may have forced many students to spread out their extremes more than they would have done otherwise.

75. Winkler, "Assessment of Distributions," p. 793.
76. The quote is reported by Karen House and Joseph Winski in "Educated Guess: Estimating U.S. Crop Is a Painstaking Job And an Important One," *Wall Street Journal,* August 11, 1975.
77. U.S. Department of Agriculture, Statistical Reporting Service, Crop Reporting Board, "Crop Production," August 11, 1977, p. A-9.
78. See Clyde H. Farnsworth, "Carter To Seek Cut in '78 Wheat Crop; Food Reserve Asked," *New York Times,* August 30, 1977; and William Robbins, "Carter Order To Cut Wheat Acreage Gets Wide Farm Support," *New York Times,* August 31, 1977.
79. The Statistical Reporting Service determines the percentage error of each year's forecast, as compared with the final estimate, and uses these errors to calculate the root mean square error. This number provides the 67-percent confidence interval and, by multiplying by 1.7, the 90-percent confidence interval. For example, "a Root Mean Square Error of 5.0 percent means that chances are about 2 out of 3 that the current production forecast will not differ

from the final estimate by more than 5.0 percent, and about 9 out of 10 that the difference will not exceed 8.6 percent." "Crop Production," p. A-6.

80. The specialist is quoted by William Robbins in "U.S. Experts Predict a Good Grain Harvest in Soviet This Year," *New York Times,* April 20, 1975.

81. The subsequent forecasts are reported in Dan Morgan, "CIA Data Show Soviet Grain Setback," *Washington Post,* August 9, 1975; Dan Morgan, "Crop Sale Freeze is Extended," *Washington Post,* August 12, 1975; and "U.S. Cuts Its Soviet Estimate," *New York Times,* October 26, 1976.

82. The final figure is reported by Christopher S. Wren in "Brezhnev Reports A Bumper Harvest; Defends Detente," *New York Times,* October 26, 1976.

83. See Todd Crowell, "Farmers Say U.S. Bungled Water Data," *Washington Post,* August 1, 1977.

84. The quotation and data are reported by David Gumpert in "Home Input: The Computer Moves From the Corporation To Your Living Room," *Wall Street Journal,* February 4, 1977.

85. The quotation is reported by David E. Rosenbaum in "Uncertain Yield of Carter Job Bill To Intensify Debate on Spending," *New York Times,* February 13, 1977.

86. Thomas Grubisich, "Dashing the Myths About Housing," *Washington Post,* May 2, 1981.

87. James L. Rowe, Jr., and Art Pine, "$22 Billion Outlay Shortfall Worries Carter and Congress," *Washington Post,* September 18, 1977.

88. Art Buchwald, "Hey, You Guys in HEW, Can't You Use Another $22 Billion?" *Washington Post,* October 18, 1977.

89. "News Conference," p. 3.

90. Press conference, August 4, 1977. Transcript made by Radio-TV Monitoring Service, Inc., p. 2.

91. Quoted by Alex Rubner, *Three Sacred Cows of Economics* (London: MacGibbon & Kee, 1970), p. 115.

92. Rex V. Brown, "Do Managers Find Decision Theory Useful?" *Harvard Business Review* 48, no. 3 (May–June 1970): 88.

93. J. Bronowski, *The Common Sense of Science* (Cambridge, Mass.: Harvard University Press, 1953), chap. 6, "The Idea of Chance."

94. James B. Ramsey, *Economic Forecasting—Models or Markets?* (London: The Institute of Economic Affairs, 1977), pp. 16 and 76.

95. Lester C. Thurow, "Economics 1977," *Daedalus* 106, no. 4 (Fall 1977): 85–86.

96. This is, again, simply the Bayesian process of combining the physician's prior judgment concerning the probability that the patient has a particular disease with the probabilistic data obtained from the diagnostic test to give a posterior probability that the patient has this disease. See the appendix to chapter 10 for a discussion of how judgment and probabilistic evidence can be combined. Note also that judgment enters the decision process when assessing preferences for the outcomes.

97. Harold Bursztajn and Robert M. Hamm, "Medical Maxims: Two Views of Science," *Yale Journal of Biology and Medicine* 52, no. 5 (September–October 1979): 483–486. These ideas are expanded in Harold Bursztajn, Richard I. Feinbloom, Robert M. Hamm, and Archie Brodsky, *Medical Choices, Medical Chances: How Patients, Families, and Physicians Can Cope with Uncertainty* (New York: Delacorte, 1981).

98. Skylab came down on July 11, 1979 (at 1637 Greenwich Mean Time plus or minus two minutes). After July 7, NORAD started making its median, 5th-percentile, and 95th-percentile predictions in hours and minutes as well as days. For example, its July 8 prediction was 5th percentile, July 10, 2328 GMT; median, July 11, 1428 GMT; 95th percentile, July 12, 0528 GMT. The actual outcome, reentry on July 11, might suggest that NORAD's March 14 prediction had a much too narrow 90-percent confidence interval. But since NASA undertook some maneuvers of *Skylab* between March 14 and July 11, in part to delay reentry, such a critique is difficult to make. The March 14 predictions were based on the orbit of *Skylab* at that time and could not take into account future orbital maneuvers that NASA might make.

99. "Skylab Advisory 9," obtained from the Office of Public Information Services of the National Aeronautics and Space Administration.

100. "Skylab Gets Extra Week Flight Time," *Durham Morning Herald,* June 8, 1979.

101. For example, the *Wall Street Journal* reported of NORAD's May 9 prediction:
    NORAD currently is predicting a 90% chance that Skylab will fall between June 20 and

July 4, with a 50% chance that it will happen *on* June 26. (Emphasis added)
Arlen J. Large, "NASA Advises Calm About Skylab's Fall—And Chews Its Nails," *Wall Street Journal,* May 16, 1979.
102. Thomas O'Toole, "NASA May Try to Delay Skylab Fall," *Washington Post,* June 28, 1979.
103. NASA press release, July 11, 1979.

Chapter 8

1. For background on RKO's dilemma, see "RKO Sells TV in Boston to Group with Major Black Involvement," *Broadcasting,* April 24, 1978, pp. 29–30; "FCC Lifts Three RKO Licenses; 13 Others are Now in Jeopardy," *Broadcasting,* January 28, 1980, pp. 27–28; and "Ferris Under Fire for RKO Decision," *Broadcasting,* March 10, 1980, pp. 27–28.
2. If the license were revoked, RKO would not be left with literally nothing. It would still have the station's equipment, which it could sell or donate to a university (taking a tax deduction). But compared to the $80 million value of the licensed station, this outcome is worth essentially zero.
3. This can be calculated from figure 8–1, using the process described in the appendix to chapter 6: $(0.4 \times 1.0) + (0.6 \times 0) = 0.4$.
4. For preference curve A, the preference-probability for $54 million is 0.96 or 0.97; for curve B it is 0.9; for curve C it is 0.84 or 0.85.
5. These preference-probabilities for the sell alternative can be calculated just as the preference-probability for the do-not-sell alternative was (see note 3). For example, using preference curve C, this preference-probability is $(0.6 \times 0.84) + (0.4 \times 0) = 0.504 \approx 0.5$.
6. This preference-probability can be determined through logic similar to that applied to determine that the preference-probability for $6 million was 0.25. Use the substitution principle to replace the $15 million outcome in figure 8–26a with a 0.5 reference gamble and then follow the probability rules (as in figure 8–5) to reduce the resulting uncertainty to a reference gamble. This indicates (see figure 8–26b) that RKO is indifferent between $30 million and a 0.75 reference gamble, which means the preference-probability for $30 million is 0.75.

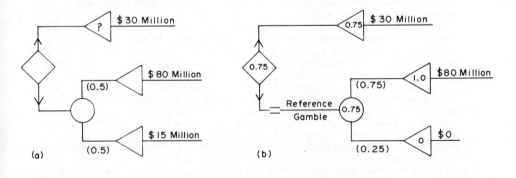

Figure 8–26. Assessing a Monetary Outcome with a 0.75 Preference-Probability.

7. The risk premium can provide a measure of risk aversion only when it is compared with the stakes of the gamble for which it was assessed. A risk premium of $1,000 indicates little risk aversion if it is for a 50-50 chance between $100,000 and nothing, but quite a bit of risk aversion if it is for a 50-50 chance between $3,000 and nothing. One way to make this comparison directly—to provide a measure of a decision maker's risk aversion—is with a *risk index.*

$$\text{risk index} = \frac{(EMV) - (CME)}{(EMV) - (\text{lowest monetary consequence of gamble})}$$

$$= \frac{\text{risk premium}}{(EMV) - (\text{lowest monetary consequence of gamble})}$$

The risk index compares the risk premium with the stakes of the gamble. For a 0.5 reference gamble, the risk index compares the risk premium to one-half the difference between the best and worst reference outcomes.

$$\text{risk index (for 0.5 reference gamble)} = \frac{\text{risk premium}}{(Best - Worst)/2}$$

For preference curve Z in figure 8–8, the risk index is the ratio of the length of the two arrows: $20 million/$50 million = 0.4.

For a 0.5 reference gamble, the risk index is the ratio of two horizontal (monetary) distances measured at the 0.5 preference-probability level:

$$\text{risk index} = \frac{\text{distance between EMV line and preference curve}}{\text{distance between EMV line and left-hand vertical axis}}$$

The first distance (numerator) is just the risk premium of the 0.5 reference gamble. The second distance (denominator) is the EMV of that gamble minus the *Worst* reference outcome. (Another way to look at the second distance is to note that the EMV of a 0.5 reference gamble is halfway between the two reference outcomes, or halfway between the two vertical axes. Thus, this second distance is nothing more than one-half the range of monetary values. The arrow of this second distance is drawn on figure 8–8 as one-half the range of monetary values along the bottom axis, solely as a matter of pictorial convenience.)

The risk index is a number between 0 and 1.0. If the risk premium is 0, the risk index is also 0. This is the case when the decision maker is not at all averse to the risk. He is willing to sacrifice absolutely nothing to avoid the risk; he is willing to make the decision on the expected-monetary-value criterion.

In contrast, if the risk index is 1.0, the decision maker is completely averse to the risk. If given the EMV of the gamble, he will pay it all back to avoid having to play the gamble. (Obviously, a risk index of 1.0 is a limiting case, not a real one. If the gamble is a 50-50 chance at $100 and $2,000—so that one is guaranteed $100 even if he "loses"—surely everyone would have a CME that was at least $100.01.)

Like the risk premium, the risk index is defined only in terms of a specific gamble; still, the risk index for a 0.5 reference gamble can provide a general measure of the decision maker's aversion to risk over the range between the two reference outcomes. Consider, for example, the $0-to-$100 million range for the preference curves in figure 8–8. The risk index for curve Z is 0.4 ($20 million/$50 million = 0.4). For curve Y, it is 0.7; for curve X, it is 0.9. For the EMV line, the risk index is 0. Thus, the risk index for the 0.5 reference gamble provides a direct measure of the amount of bend in a preference curve.

8. The series would be "worth less" if distributed by an independent "network" because it would then be shown on fewer stations, with smaller audiences, for the worth of the series is determined by the money that it earns. If RKO is unable to show the series on either one of the three major television networks or on its own independent network, the series is worth nothing.

9. David E. Bell and Howard Raiffa of the Harvard Business School distinguish between diminishing marginal value for money and risk aversion. They argue that a decision maker can have a *strength-of-preference* function that exhibits a diminishing marginal value for money and then a *utility* function for such a strength of preference that displays additional risk aversion. See Bell and Raiffa, "Marginal Value and Intrinsic Risk Aversion," Working Paper, #HBS 79-65, Division of Research, Graduate School of Business Administration, Harvard University. See also James S. Dyer and Rakesh K. Sarin, "Measurable Multiattribute Value Functions," *Operations Research* 27, no. 4 (July–August 1979): 810–822.

10. In mathematical language, this means that the second derivative is negative, or that the curve is concave downward.
11. To see why the shape of curve E above $15 million implies risk-seeking behavior, consider the choice between a certain $60 million and a 50-50 chance at $15 million and $80 million. For most people, such a choice would be pure fantasy—and thus difficult to comprehend. Nevertheless, note that this decision is equivalent to being given $15 million and then a choice between another (certain) $45 million, and a 50-50 chance at $0 and $65 million (more). (See figure 8–27.) Most people, even with their assets increased by a fantabulous $15 million, would prefer the certain $45 million to the 50-50 gamble for $65 million and nothing. (Those who find it impossible to think about numbers followed by the word "million"—particularly when it represents personal money rather than the government's—can replace "million" with "thousand." If you were given $15,000, would you rather have another $45,000, or a 50-50 chance at $65,000 or nothing? Now, one's own preference for the riskless alternative may be clearer.) But if the preference-probabilities defined by curve E (in figure 8–4) are used on either of two decision trees in figure 8–27, the preferred alternative is the gamble. This conflicting conclusion is a result of the risk-seeking behavior implied by curve E.

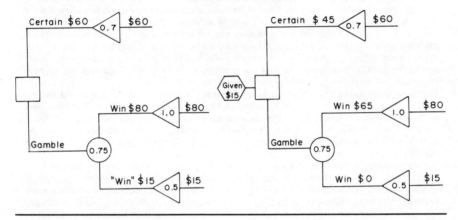

Figure 8–27. Two Different Ways of Thinking about the Same Decision (All Dollar Amounts in Millions or, If You Prefer, Thousands).

12. See, for example, the review by P.C. Fishburn and G.A. Kochenberger, "Two-Piece von Neumann-Morgenstern Utility Functions," forthcoming.
13. Daniel Kahneman and Amos Tversky, "Prospect Theory: An Analysis of Decision Under Risk," *Econometrica* 47, no. 2 (March 1979): 263–291.
14. Richard Thaler, "Toward a Positive Theory of Consumer Choice," *Journal of Economic Behavior and Organizations,* 1 (1980): 39–60.
15. See David Bell and Howard Raiffa, "Back from Prospect Theory to Utility Theory," unpublished manuscript; Fishburn and Kochenberger, "Two-Piece Functions"; and the references in Kahneman and Tversky, "Prospect Theory."
16. The desire to avoid the loser image does not, however, account for the risk-seeking attitude that many people exhibit when given choices that involve *only* losses. For example, if given a choice between losing a certain $500 and a 50-50 chance to lose $1,000 or $200, many people would pick the gamble.
17. Kahneman and Tversky, "Prospect Theory," p. 268.
18. Laurence H. Tribe, in his critique of the policy sciences in general and decision analysis in particular, writes that "the policy sciences . . . have taken an end-result position, focusing almost exclusively on ultimate outcomes, with no independent concern for the procedure whereby those outcomes are produced or for the history out of which they evolve." "Policy Science: Analysis or Ideology," *Philosophy & Public Affairs* 2, no. 1 (Fall 1972): 82. It may

be fair to criticize some decision analysts for such a "lack of concern for process," but there is nothing inherent in decision analysis that precludes an evaluation of the various outcomes in terms of the process by which they were obtained. The analyst can choose to evaluate his preferences for outcomes in terms of whatever consequences he decides are most important.

Thus, if Joe Sturdley believes that the process by which he ends up with $X + $600 in the bank is important, he merely includes that consequence on his decision tree by adding an additional consequence branch. Now, of course, the question becomes *How* important does Joe Sturdley think this process consequence is? Indeed, how can he specify the magnitude of its importance? Well, there is no absolute "scale of importance" that Sturdley can use to measure the value of "winning" or "losing." Rather, such a process consequence can be deemed important only in comparison with the other consequences involved in the various outcomes.

Thus, he faces a decision involving a trade-off between two consequences (process and money). To assess *how* important one consequence is, he must evaluate it in terms of the other consequence—he must think about what types of trade-offs he is willing to make between these two consequences. (For a discussion of how to make such trade-offs analytically, see chapter 11.) Some people may find making explicit trade-offs between money and nonmonetary consequences distasteful. But if that is the central reason why the decision is a dilemma—if the choice would be easy were there no trade-off between money and something else—then it is foolish to pretend that the trade-off does not exist. Even if one does not want to think explicitly about the trade-offs one is willing (and not willing) to make, the final choice will involve some implicit judgments about the relative importance of the two consequences. And, as with Joe Sturdley's choice, an explicit examination of the trade-offs may reveal exactly how important—or unimportant—one of those consequences really is.

19. Of course, if the stakes involved in the gamble were smaller, the $10 that Sturdley was willing to pay to avoid the loser image might appear more important. However, if the stakes involved in the gamble were smaller, the image consequence of losing would also be smaller. Thus, if the stakes are smaller, Sturdley will presumably be willing to pay much less to avoid the loser-image consequence, and thus this payment should still have very little impact upon the decision.

20. See, for example, Kahneman and Tversky, "Prospect Theory"; Sarah Lichtenstein and Paul Slovic, "Reversals of Preference Between Bids and Choices in Gambling Decisions," *Journal of Experimental Psychology* 89, no. 1 (1971): 46–55; and Baruch Fischhoff, Paul Slovic, and Sarah Lichtenstein, "Knowing What You Want: Measuring Labile Values," in T. Wallsten, ed., *Cognitive Processes in Choice and Decision Behavior* (Hillsdale, N.J.: Erlbaum, 1980), pp. 117–141.

21. Fischhoff, et al., ibid. (1980), p. 127.

22. Kahneman and Tversky, "Prospect Theory," p. 271.

23. See Kenneth R. MacCrimmon, "Descriptive and Normative Implications of the Decision-Theory Postulates," in Karl Borch and Jan Mossin, *Risk and Uncertainty* (London: Macmillan & Co., 1968), pp. 3–23. MacCrimmon confronted business executives with a variety of decision problems. The choices these executives made often violated the axioms of decision theory, including transitivity. But when confronted with the implications of their choices, the decision makers usually asserted that they had made "mistakes" and revised their choices to make them consistent with the basic postulates. See also MacCrimmon, "An Experimental Study of the Decision-Making Behavior of Business Executives," unpublished dissertation, University of California, Los Angeles, 1965; and ibid., p. 277.

24. Fischhoff, et al., "Knowing What You Want," p. 118.

25. Kahneman and Tversky, "Prospect Theory," p. 287.

26. It could be argued that this decision involved assets covering more than an $80 million range. The licenses that RKO had for several other stations were also under challenge, and if the FCC decided that RKO was not fit to operate WNAC-TV, the probability that it would decide not to renew the other licenses would increase. Thus, given that selling WNAC to NETV would increase the probability that the FCC would renew the license, the outcome of this decision could affect RKO's other corporate assets. As a first cut, however, it is reasonable to consider only first-order effects on corporate assets. If that simplification does not resolve the dilemma to the satisfaction of RKO's executives, they could undertake a second cut and include such factors.

27. This is due to the law of large numbers, from classical statistics: The more times the gamble is played, the closer the average is to the expected value. For example, if this gamble is played

100 times, there is only a 27-percent chance that it will be won more than 55 or less than 45 times.

28. For a discussion of how people think differently about real and hypothetical decisions, see Paul Slovic, "Differential Effects of Real Versus Hypothetical Payoffs on Choices Among Gambles," *Journal of Experimental Psychology* 80, no. 3 (1969): 434–437.

29. The "invention" of preference-probabilities or probabilistic utility theory is not as easy to date as the invention of the light bulb by Edison or even Archimedes' principle. Many decision analysts credit the mathematician John von Neumann and the economist Oskar Morgenstern with first explaining the concept in detail in *Theory of Games and Economic Behavior* (Princeton, N.J.: Princeton University Press, 1944). Nevertheless, credit must also go to an earlier work, by Frank P. Ramsey, "Truth and Probability," first published in 1926 and available in Henry E. Kyburg and Howard E. Smokler, eds., *Studies in Subjective Probability* (New York: John Wiley, 1954), and to a later book, by the statistician L. J. Savage, *The Foundations of Statistics* (New York: John Wiley, 1954).

30. Henry S. Rowen, "Policy Analysis as Heuristic Aid: The Design of Means, Ends, and Institutions," in Laurence H. Tribe, Corinne S. Schelling, and John Voss, eds., *When Values Conflict: Essays on Environmental Analysis, Discourse, and Decision* (Cambridge, Mass.: Ballinger, 1976).

31. For a discussion of the various types of costs, see Charles J. Christenson, Richard F. Vancil, and Paul W. Marshall, *Managerial Economics: Text and Cases,* rev. ed. (Homewood, Ill.: Richard D. Irwin, 1973), particularly chapter 1, on types of costs, and chapter 4, on decision analysis.

32. For a discussion of the failure of people to ignore sunk costs, see Thaler, "Positive Theory."

33. For a discussion of efforts to justify sunk costs, see Robert D. Behn, "Policy Analysis and Policy Politics," *Policy Analysis* 7, no. 2 (Spring 1981): 211–214.

Chapter 9

1. This median estimate differs from what is usually called an individual's life expectancy, which is the average, or mean, estimate. For this male, the mean estimate can be calculated from figure 9–7 to be approximately 70 or 71—slightly less than the median estimate of 72. If the uncertainty curve is "symmetrical" (that is, if the lower and upper quartiles are the same distance from the median, if the third and fifth octiles are the same distance from the median, etc.), then the mean and median are the same.

2. If in making the indirect assessments of the preference-probabilities in figure 9–8, none of the numbers were rounded-off, the preference-probability for the reject-settlement alternative would be 0.50625 instead of 0.51. Clearly, rounding does not affect the calculation or the resolution of the dilemma. Indeed, it verifies that simplification works.

3. The mean (or average) can also be used to indicate the center of the distribution of possible outcomes.

4. They do not all drop by exactly 5.00 percentage points. Rather, within the accuracy with which it is possible to read the preference curve, they all decrease by *approximately* 5 percentage points.

5. Sometimes, procrastination pays.

6. The preference-probability of 0.92 for the $825,000 payment is given to two significant figures to distinguish it from the preference-probability of 0.9 for the $750,000 payment.

7. This preference-probability of 0.85, which was obtained using a four-branch outcome fork, differs from the one of 0.86 obtained in the third-cut analysis (figure 9–3) using three two-branch outcome forks. The reason is the rounding conventions (as in 0.975 becoming 0.98). For the four-branch outcome fork (of figure 9–15c), the preference-probability assessed indirectly for a favorable verdict is $(1.0) \times (0.25) + (0.95) \times (0.25) + (0.9) \times (0.25) + (0.55) \times (0.25) = (1.0 + 0.95 + 0.9 + 0.55)/4 = 0.85$ (exactly).

  The calculation used in figure 9–3 had two stages, however, and the numbers were thus rounded-off twice. The preference-probability for a high award was $(1.0 + 0.95)/2 = 0.975 \approx 0.98$. The preference-probability for a low award was $(0.9 + 0.55)/2 = 0.725 \approx 0.73$. Thus, the preference-probability for the favorable verdict was $(0.98 + 0.73)/2 = 0.855 \approx 0.86$. Obviously, the difference is not at all significant.

8. This is usually, but not always, true. For example, if Phillips's uncertainty curve were skewed towards higher awards, the EMV obtained using a multibranch approximation would be higher than the median estimate. But using a risk-averse preference curve would tend to lower the preference-probability obtained with such an approximation. Consequently, which of these two tendencies would dominate is unclear; together they might raise or lower the preference-probability of the range of risk (compared to the preference-probability for the median estimate). Or they might just cancel each other out. It is always necessary to understand the nature of the problem, as well as the implications of the analytical tools being used, to be able to predict the impact of a more sophisticated approximation.

9. Due to rounding conventions, the preference-probability dropped by only four percentage points.

10. Usually these branches stand for equiprobable subranges, and thus there are as many branches above the median as below it. But this is not a rule. Consequently, if the reason that a decision is a dilemma suggests a different analytical approach, the branches need not stand for equiprobable subranges.

11. This is true for Phillips's problem, but it is not true in general. See note 8.

12. Ward Edwards, "Use of Multiattribute Utility Measurement for Social Decision Making," in David E. Bell, Ralph L. Keeney, and Howard Raiffa, eds., *Conflicting Objectives in Decisions* (Chichester, Great Britain: John Wiley, 1977), p. 251.

13. John D. Steinbruner, *The Cybernetic Theory of Decision* (Princeton, N.J.: Princeton University Press, 1974), p. 35.

14. Charles E. Lindblom, "The Science of 'Muddling Through,'" *Public Administration Review* 19, no. 2 (Spring 1959):84.

15. Hermann Bondi, "The Lure of Completeness," in Ronald Duncan and Miranda Weston-Smith, eds., *The Encyclopaedia of Ignorance* (New York: Pocket Books, 1978), p. 7.

16. R. A. Lyttleton, "The Nature of Knowledge," in Duncan and Weston-Smith, *Encyclopaedia,* p. 10.

17. Theodore Levitt, "A Heretical View of Management 'Science,'" *Fortune,* December 18, 1978, p. 50.

18. In most cases, the small probability of these extreme outcomes will not affect a decision. But being conscious of these very small probabilities can help avoid the common error (discussed in chapter 7) of being overconfident in the assessment of an uncertain quantity.

19. *Fiscal Year 1982 Budget Revisions* (Washington, D.C.: U.S. Government Printing Office, 1981), p. 11. President Carter's projection for FY 86 outlays was $1,050.3 billion; see *Budget of the United States Government: Fiscal Year 1982* (Washington, D.C.: U.S. Government Printing Office, 1981) p. 22. If you thought Carter's projection was more realistic than Reagan's target, you would (your political views notwithstanding) shift the uncertainty curves in figure 9–17 to the right.

Chapter 10

1. In the end, Edmisten decided not to run for the Senate, though not through the type of analysis described in this chapter. John R. Ingram, North Carolina's elected insurance commissioner, did decide to run and won the Democratic nomination, but he did not resign his state post. He lost to Jesse Helms in the general election.

2. The first four quotes are from "Under the Dome," *News and Observer,* September 11, 1977 (Raleigh, North Carolina). The last is from a private conversation with one of Edmisten's aides.

3. In the jargon of decision analysis, this is called *normal form.*

4. The classic books on dynamic programming are R. E. Bellman, *Dynamic Programming* (Princeton, N.J.: Princeton University Press, 1957); and R. E. Bellman and S. E. Dreyfus, *Applied Dynamic Programming* (Princeton, N.J.: Princeton University Press, 1962).

5. The study was prepared by Robert M. Veatch on the basis of an actual situation and was published in Robert M. Veatch, Sissela Bok, and Marc Lappé, "Options in Dealing with the Threat of Hemophilia," *Hastings Center Report* 4, no. 2 (April 1974) p. 8.

6. Ibid.

7. Actually, this complication becomes important only if it appears that the choice is between trying to adopt and becoming pregnant, with remaining childless a poor third. If an adopted

child is a better outcome than no child, it makes sense to undertake first the easier analysis of the choice between becoming pregnant and remaining childless; if remaining childless is the better of these (latter) two alternatives, then it makes sense to try to adopt (unless the psychological costs of attempting to adopt and failing are too high). If, however, an adopted child and becoming pregnant are both better than remaining childless, it is necessary to compare these two alternatives directly.

8. In the jargon of decision analysis, imperfect information is often called *sample information.*

9. Janice C. Simpson, "Light Beers Carve Out Growing Segment of Sales to Calorie-Conscious Drinkers," *Wall Street Journal,* March 8, 1978.

10. Quoted in "Anheuser-Busch Inc. Has Another Entry in 'Light Beer' Field," *Wall Street Journal,* February 13, 1978.

11. Ibid.

12. See Edgar A. Pessemier, *New Product Decisions: An Analytical Approach* (New York: McGraw-Hill, 1966), especially chapters 4 and 5.

13. "Edmisten Leans Toward Entering Race for Senate," *Durham Morning Herald,* October 23, 1977.

14. Thomas A. Preston, *Coronary Artery Surgery* (New York: Raven Press, 1977), p. 36.

15. For a more detailed examination of the use of decision analysis to decide whether to perform diagnostic tests, see Barbara J. McNeil and S. James Adelstein, "Determining the Value of Diagnostic and Screening Tests," *Journal of Nuclear Medicine* 17, no. 6 (June 1976): 439–448.

16. Two early books that focused on decisions to gather further information are Robert Schlaifer, *Probability and Statistics for Business Decisions* (New York: McGraw-Hill, 1959); and Howard Raiffa and Robert Schlaifer, *Applied Statistical Decision Theory* (Boston: Division of Research, Harvard Business School, 1961). For an excellent text that covers such problems, see Howard Raiffa, *Decision Analysis* (Reading, Mass.: Addison-Wesley, 1968).

17. This is often called Bayesian analysis, Bayesian updating, or Bayesian statistics. The Reverand Thomas Bayes discovered the formula, explained in the appendix to this chapter, on which such analyses are based. Consequently, such decision analysis is often called Bayesian decision analysis.

Chapter 11

1. These facts are reported by Jack Holmes, "RDU To Close To Jetliners For Fall Runway Work," *Durham Morning Herald,* April 28, 1976. The trade-offs made in this chapter, however, are obviously not those of the Raleigh-Durham Airport Authority.

2. Actually, the original independence principle, as set forth by L. J. Savage in *The Foundations of Statistics* (New York: John Wiley, 1954), concerned decision dilemmas complicated by uncertainty rather than conflicting consequences. As one of his basic axioms of decision theory, Savage argued that if two decision alternatives have the same chance of producing a certain outcome, then preferences for those alternatives should be independent of that outcome. For example, if both alternative A and alternative B result in a 35-percent chance of obtaining outcome Q (figure 11–29, p. 396), the decision is the same regardless of what Q is. That is, if you would choose A for $Q_1 = \$100$, you would also choose A for $Q_1 = \$1,000$, or $-\$25$, etc.

3. In special circumstances, the original value of a consequence does not affect the amount of that consequence that must be sacrificed to gain more of another (in other words, the compensating change in a consequence is the same regardless of the value of that consequence). This special condition is called *utility independence* by Kenney and Raiffa and *value independence* by Edwards. If this condition holds, it is legitimate to develop an additive or multiplicative *utility function.* Most of the research on decisions with conflicting consequences (or, as they are often called, problems with *multiple, competing objectives*) concerns such utility functions. Utility functions are more interesting to the mathematician, for they can be discussed and developed with much more rigor and elegance. Furthermore, utility functions can be of value in research projects that analyze, in depth, decisions of great complexity.

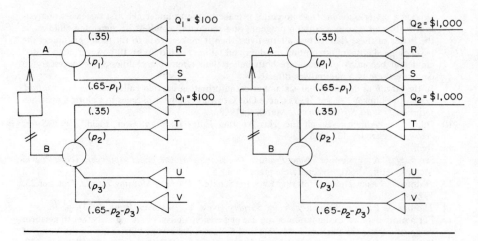

Figure 11–29. An Example of Savage's Independence Principle.

Trade-off analysis, however, is usually much more valuable for the busy decision maker. This chapter is devoted to trade-off analysis because:

1. Trade-off analysis requires the decision maker to be explicit about his willingness to make trade-offs between the key conflicting consequences that create his dilemma.
2. Utility functions obscure the potentially important effect of the original position on these trade-offs.
3. Utility functions make it more difficult to reanalyze the same trade-off from a slightly different perspective (using a different comparison consequence).
4. Trade-off analysis is the most direct and appropriate approach for the busy decision maker who, recognizing the inherent limitations of his own cognitive capabilities, wants to concentrate his analytical attention on the few, most significant consequences.

Furthermore, Charles L. Schultze argues that, because the values we hold are "quite subtle and complex, they are exceedingly difficult to specify" in the abstract. Consequently, it is very difficult to develop an all-purpose social-welfare (or utility) function; it makes much more sense to consider the specific decision to be made and to analyze the conflicting consequences involved with it. Writes Schultze:

We simply cannot determine in the abstract our ends or values and the intensity with which we hold them. We discover our objectives and the intensity that we assign to them only in the process of considering particular programs or policies. We articulate "ends" as we evaluate "means."

Indeed, Schultze argues that we cannot think seriously about trade-offs until we face particular choices—particular alternatives with particular consequences—and then sit down to analyze our willingness to make trade-offs among those consequences. For example, consider the dilemma created by the trade-off between transportation speed and transportation safety. Schultze argues that "no one can specify in advance the weight he attaches to traffic safety versus rapid transportation except when considering a specific traffic safety program and evaluating its particular impact on the transportation system." See Charles L. Schultze, *The Politics and Economics of Public Spending* (Washington, D.C.: The Brookings Institution, 1968), pp. 37–39.

Edwards argues that his "techniques for multi-attribute utility measurement . . . [have] the greater advantage of being easily taught to and used by a busy decision maker." But he also notes that "as a rule of thumb, 8 dimensions [consequences] is plenty and 15 is too many." But will a busy decision maker really want to worry about even eight different consequences? For a quick analysis, a careful examination of the trade-offs between the two or three consequences that create the dilemma seems most appropriate.

For researched analysis, however, utility functions may provide an appropriate analytical framework. For a discussion of utility functions, see Ralph L. Keeney and Howard Raiffa, *Decisions with Multiple Objectives: Preferences and Value Trade-Offs* (New York: John Wiley, 1976); and Ward Edwards, "How to Use Multi-Attribute Utility Measurement for Social Decision-Making," SSRI Research Report 76-3 (August 1976), Social Science Research Institute, University of Southern California. For an example of the use of such utility functions in researched analysis, see Ralph L. Keeney, "A Decision Analysis with Multiple Objectives: The Mexico City Airport," *Bell Journal of Economics and Management Science* 4, no. 1 (Spring 1973):101–117. An example of the use of utility functions to help make a group decision is James S. Dyer and Ralph F. Miles, Jr., *Trajectory Selection for the Mariner Jupiter/Saturn 1977 Project* (Pasadena, Cal.: California Institute of Technology, 1974), Jet Propulsion Laboratory Technical Memorandum 33-706.

4. Those familiar with the concept of *discounting* will recognize that it can make a difference when the airport authority must pay for the runway. People are not indifferent between an expenditure of $1 million made today and a $1 million expenditure made four years from now; they would prefer to surrender the $1 million in the future, for, in the meantime, they can invest the money in treasury bills or whatever so that after they pay off the $1 million debt they can still pocket the interest earned in the interim. Given the quick trade-off analysis being done to resolve the conflicting consequences confronting the airport authority, however, it hardly makes sense to introduce this complication. After all, if the airport authority really wants to consider its time preferences for various consequences, it will also have to consider how the benefits as well as the costs will change over time. A formal cost-benefit analysis would certainly consider this complication, but a quick analysis concentrates on the essence of the dilemma, and the timing of when the various consequences occur is not central to the airport authority's decision. Besides, it is quite reasonable to assume for the purposes of a quick analysis that the 6-year, $2 million runway will be financed by floating a $2 million bond. Then, each year, $333,333 of the principle plus the interest accrued on that amount will be paid back. In this case (if the appropriate discount rate is close to the rate at which the airport authority borrows funds), the present discounted value of the costs of each year of the runway is indeed $333,333.

For a discussion of discounting, time preferences, and trade-offs between consequences occurring in different time periods, see Keeney and Raiffa, *Multiple Objectives,* chapter 9, "Preferences Over Time," pp. 473–514.

5. Richard A. Musgrave, "Cost-Benefit Analysis and the Theory of Public Finance," *Journal of Economic Literature* 7 (September 1969): 800.

6. Robert Nozick, *Anarchy, State and Utopia* (New York: Basic Books, 1974), p. 297.

7. For a discussion of these types of personal trade-off dilemmas involving conflicting consequences, see Barrie S. Greiff and Preston K. Munter, *Tradeoffs: Executive, Family and Organizational Life* (New York: Simon and Schuster, 1979); and Paul Evans and Fernando Bartolome, *Must Success Cost So Much?* (New York: Basic Books, 1981).

8. A. Myrick Freeman III, "Project Design and Evaluation with Multiple Objectives," in Robert H. Haveman and Julius Margolis, eds., *Public Expenditure and Policy Analysis,* 2d ed. (Chicago: Rand McNally, 1977), p. 239.

9. For a discussion of the conflicting consequences involved in welfare reform, see Henry Aaron, *Why Is Welfare So Hard To Reform?* (Washington, D.C.: The Brookings Institution, 1973); and Martin Anderson, *Welfare: The Political Economy of Welfare Reform in the United States* (Stanford, Cal.: Hoover Institution Press, 1978).

10. Hatfield is quoted by Steven R. Weisman, "Capital Likes the Solo, but What About the Ensemble?" *New York Times,* November 23, 1980.

11. Nordhaus is quoted by Urban C. Lehner, "Work-Safety and Anti-Inflation Agencies Split Over Drive to Cut Regulatory Costs," *Wall Street Journal,* August 3, 1978.

12. Arthur M. Okun, *Equality and Efficiency: The Big Tradeoff* (Washington, D.C.: The Brookings Institution, 1975), pp. 1–2.

13. Udall is quoted by Dennis Farney, "House Panel Chairmen, Their Powers Reduced, Use Guile, Persuasion," *Wall Street Journal,* May 3, 1979.

14. Most of the work on both prescriptive and descriptive decision analysis has concentrated on decisions that are dilemmas because of uncertainty rather than because of conflicting consequences. Part of the reason is because prescriptive decision analysis was first developed in business schools, where the problems of uncertainty were seen to be more important than the problems of trade-offs. But also, human thinking about uncertainty is easier to study than is our thinking about trade-offs, for there are some objective ways of evaluating (over the long

run) how good we are at making judgments about uncertainty. Cognitive psychologists have given people a wide assortment of judgments and decisions to make involving uncertainty, have evaluated the results, and have concluded (based on objective, optimum results) that people think very poorly about uncertainty. For a review of this literature, see Paul Slovic, Baruch Fischhoff, and Sarah Lichtenstein, "Behavioral Decision Theory," *Annual Review of Psychology* 28 (1977): 1–39. Evaluating human thinking about trade-offs is more difficult, for although inconsistencies can be used to identify inadequate decision making, there is little objective basis on which to determine whether consistent decisions are good or bad.

15. For definitions of such measures of business performance, see Erich A. Helfert, *Techniques of Financial Analysis,* 4th ed. (Homewood, Ill.: Richard D. Irwin, 1977), chapter 2, pp. 51–87.

16. See, for example, Helfert, ibid., p. 123. Obviously, the concept of discounting (see note 4 above) can be used to help analyze such dilemmas involving conflicts over temporal differences in profit consequences.

17. Robert L. Banks and Steven C. Wheelwright, "Operations vs. Strategy: Trading Tomorrow for Today," *Harvard Business Review* 57, no. 3 (May–June 1979):113.

18. Ibid., p. 114.

19. Tim Metz, "American Bakeries Proxy Fight Pits Quick Profits vs. Longer-Term View," *Wall Street Journal,* April 14, 1981.

20. "American Bakeries Says Dissidents Won 4 of 12 Board Seats," *Wall Street Journal,* May 21, 1981.

21. Robert H. Hayes and William J. Abernathy, "Managing Our Way to Economic Decline," *Harvard Business Review* 55, no. 4 (July–August 1980):67 and 68.

22. Jones is quoted by Art Pine, "In Corporate Leadership An Era Ends at GE Co.," *Washington Post,* March 29, 1981.

23. Liz Roman Gallese, "Why Hartford Courant Turned Down Bid By Capital Cities to Take Over the Paper," *Wall Street Journal,* November 9, 1978.

24. Howard Raiffa, William B. Schwartz, and Milton C. Weinstein, "Evaluating Health Effects of Societal Decisions and Programs," *Analytical Studies for the U.S. Environmental Protection Agency: Decision Making in the Environmental Protection Agency* (Washington, D.C.: National Academy of Sciences, 1977).

25. Ibid.

26. Recall that how many years of runway life you need to compensate you for closing the airport depends upon how many runway-life years you can get without closing it. Similarly, the number of apples you are willing to give up may depend upon how many apples and oranges you have. If you have fifteen oranges and two apples, you may be willing to give up three oranges to get just one more apple; but if you have five oranges and twelve apples, you may be unwilling to give up three oranges unless you get ten apples in return.

27. Garrett Hardin, "The Tragedy of the Commons," *Science* 162, no. 3859 (December 13, 1968): 1244.

28. Raiffa, Schwartz, and Weinstein, "Evaluating Health Effects."

29. This phrase has been applied to the cognitive problems created by the task of "concept attainment" by Jerome S. Bruner, Jacqueline J. Goodnow, and George A. Austin in *A Study of Thinking* (New York: John Wiley, 1956). They examine some simplifying strategies people employ to eliminate various explanatory hypotheses so as to select the correct one.

30. Paul Slovic, "Toward Understanding and Improving Decisions," in W. C. Howell and E. A. Fleishman, eds., *Human Performance and Productivity:* vol. 2, *Information Processing and Decision Making* (Hillsdale, N.J.: Erlbaum, 1981).

31. Amos Tversky, "Elimination by Aspects: A Theory of Choice," *Psychological Review* 79, no. 4 (July 1972):281–299. Hogarth offers some other mental strategies that people use to avoid making explicit tradeoffs. There is the *conjunctive* approach: Establish minimum levels for each consequence and eliminate all alternatives that fall below these levels. There is the *disjunctive* approach: Evaluate each alternative in terms of its best consequence. And there is the *lexicographic* approach: Decide which consequence is most important and select the alternative that is best in terms of that consequence; if there is a tie, go to the second-most-important consequence, and continue until the tie is broken. Robin M. Hogarth, *Judgment and Choice: The Psychology of Decision* (Chichester, Great Britain: John Wiley, 1980), pp. 57–58.

32. Okun, *Equality and Efficiency,* p. 79.

33. John D. Steinbruner, *The Cybernetic Theory of Decision: New Dimensions of Political Analysis* (Princeton, N.J.: Princeton University Press, 1974), pp. 106 and 107.

34. "Environmental Protection Message," *Congressional Quarterly Weekly Report* 35, no. 22 (May 28, 1977):1059.
35. "Carter Environmental Message Text," *Congressional Quarterly Weekly Report* 37, no. 32 (August 11, 1979):1669.
36. Council on Environmental Quality, *The Good News About Energy* (Washington, D.C.: U.S. Government Printing Office, 1979), p. v.
37. Steven R. Weisman, "Most Support Tuition at City U. In Poll on Ways to Save Funds," *New York Times,* July 21, 1975.
38. Pinchot is quoted by Kenneth S. Fowler, "On Cutting Down Trees: Trade-Offs of Selected Harvest Policies," *Policy Analysis* 3, no. 3 (Summer 1977):342.
39. The mayor is quoted in "PostScript," *Washington Post,* September 18, 1978.
40. Laird is quoted in an Associated Press story, "Laird Defends U.S. Vietnam Tactics," *New York Times,* May 26, 1969.
41. Roger N. Shepard, "On Subjectively Optimum Selection among Multiattribute Alternatives," in Maynard W. Shell II, and Glenn L. Bryan, eds., *Human Judgments and Optimality* (New York: John Wiley, 1964), pp. 275 and 265.
42. Paul Slovic, "Choice Between Equally Valued Alternatives," *Journal of Experimental Psychology: Human Perception and Performance* 1, no. 3 (1975):280–287.
43. Shepard, "Optimum Selection," pp. 277 and 258.
44. "Post Card Request Seeks Long Answer," *Durham Morning Herald,* January, 1976.
45. Slovic performed another experiment "whose results should give pause to those who believe they are better off getting as much information as possible prior to making a decision." A number of expert horserace handicappers were given their choice of eighty-eight factors reflecting different horses' past performance. After picking and reviewing five of these factors, they predicted the winners of forty-five races. Then they did the same with ten, twenty, and forty factors of their choice. Reports Slovic, "The results indicated that, on the average, accuracy of prediction was as good with five variables as it was with 10, 20 or 40." Paul Slovic, "Toward Understanding."
46. Shepard, "Optimum Selection," p. 266.
47. This type of decision making is advocated by Laurence H. Tribe, "Policy Science: Analysis or Ideology?" *Philosophy & Public Affairs* 2, no. 1 (Fall 1972):107.
48. Hogarth, *Judgement and Choice,* p. 73.
49. Henry S. Rowen, "Policy Analysis as Heuristic Aid: The Design of Means, Ends, and Institutions," in Laurence H. Tribe, Corinne S. Schelling, and John Voss, eds., *When Values Conflict: Essays on Environmental Analysis, Discourse and Decision* (Cambridge, Mass.: Ballinger, 1976), p. 142.
50. Baruch Fischhoff, Paul Slovic, and Sarah Lichtenstein, "Knowing What You Want: Measuring Labile Values," in T. S. Wallsten, ed., *Cognitive Processes in Choice and Decision Behavior* (Hillsdale, N.J.: Erlbaum, 1980), pp. 137–138.

Chapter 12

1. Quoted by Richard E. Neustadt and Harvey V. Fineberg, *The Swine Flu Affair: Decision-Making on a Slippery Disease* (Washington, D.C.: U.S. Government Printing Office, 1978), p. 29.
2. More specifically, Epstein reports, the pharmaceutical companies insisted that "the United States [be] the sole party defendant in all suits" where a person "had been given the vaccine without being adequately warned of its possible adverse effects and had suffered injury." Richard Epstein, "Products Liability: The Gathering Storm," *Regulation* (September–October 1977): 15.
3. Stephen C. Schoenbaum, Barbara J. McNeil, and Joel Kavet, "The Swine-Flu Decision," *New England Journal of Medicine* 295, no. 14 (September 30, 1976):759–765.
4. Ibid., p. 760.
5. Ibid., p. 761.
6. Public Health Service Advisory Committee on Immunization Practice, "Influenza Vaccine—Supplemental Statement," *Morbidity and Mortality Weekly Report* 25, no. 28 (July 23, 1976): 221–222 and 227.

7. In October 1976, we assigned the following homework problem: "Use decision analysis to decide whether or not to get the swine flu shot." Many students used in their work a decision tree that explicitly included death as an outcome. Consequently, preference-probabilities had to be assessed with health and death as the reference outcomes. Unfortunately, too many students did this in an unthinking manner; using the brute-force and ignorance technique, they decided that catching the flu should have a preference-probability of 0.9 or even 0.8! A moment of concentration would reveal, however, that even a week in bed with the flu is far superior to a gamble involving a 10- or 20-percent chance of dying.

8. See, for example, Lennart Sjoberg, "Strength of Belief and Risk," *Policy Sciences* 11, no. 1 (August 1979):49.

9. James Boswell, *The Life of Samuel Johnson,* abridged by Bergan Evans (New York: Modern Library, 1967), p. 141.

10. John Rawls, *A Theory of Justice* (Cambridge, Mass.: Harvard University Press, 1971), p. 418.

11. Neustadt and Fineberg, *Swine Flu Affair,* p. 29.

12. Quoted by Arthur J. Viseltear, "A Short Political History of the 1976 Swine Influenza Legislation," in June E. Osborn, ed., *History, Science, and Politics: Influenza in America, 1918–1976* (New York: Prodist, 1977), p. 35.

13. Neustadt and Fineberg, *Swine Flu Affair,* p. 15.

14. Ibid., p. 20.

15. These two alternatives are essentially two of those considered by Schoenbaum, McNeil, and Kavet, "Swine-Flu Decision," but our quick analysis is quite different. Schoenbaum et al. consider the high-risk group to be all those over 65 plus individuals with "chronic cardiovascular disease, bronchopulmonary disease, renal disease and metabolic disease (diabetes mellitus and Addison's disease)," pp. 760–61.

16. Neustadt and Fineberg, *Swine Flu Affair,* p. 148.

17. Ibid., p. 11.

18. Ibid., p. 18.

19. Ibid., p. 88. This illustrates a point we made in chapter 1: Some decision makers, particularly scientists and engineers who have been rigorously trained in the use of objective statistical data, are reluctant to use judgmental probabilities. Report Neustadt and Fineberg (p. 88),

> Doctors, at least of the older generation, rarely think in probabilistic terms and, if asked, dislike it. . . . As scientists accustomed to thinking about experiments and "truth," they were uncomfortable expressing subjective estimates, even if based on expert knowledge and experience. . . . They think it is unprofessional to express judgments in terms they cannot call scientific, worse still to express them in the presence of laymen. They see placing precise numbers on uncertainties as an incitement to public misunderstanding.

Yet, might not knowing that public health experts thought the chances of an epidemic were between 2 and 20 percent have helped President Ford to think analytically about his decision?

20. Ibid., p. 19.

21. The probability of an epidemic would be the same whether or not there is a vaccination program. Even with a comprehensive program, only about two-thirds of the public would participate, and the vaccine would be effective for only about 75 percent of those who received it (Schoenbaum et al., "Swine-Flu Decision," pp. 760 and 761). Consequently, even a massive program would only protect about half the population, giving an epidemic the opportunity to spread almost as easily through the unprotected 50 percent. Moreover, the swine flu vaccination was less effective for children than for adults (Public Health Service Advisory Committee, "Influenza Vaccine"), and in "previous pandemics children had been the chief spreaders of disease" (Neustadt and Fineberg, *Swine Flu Affair,* p. 45). Consequently, any vaccination program could affect the number of people struck by a flu epidemic, but not the probability that an epidemic would occur.

22. The numbers used in the first two "considerations" are either taken or calculated from Schoenbaum et al., "Swine-Flu Decision."

23. Since all of us are going to die, the real issue is not the death but how prematurely the death occurs. See James W. Vaupel, "Early Death: An American Tragedy," *Law and Contemporary Problems* 40, no. 4 (Autumn 1976): 73–121. Thus, the more important consequence for public health decisions might be the number of years of life lost rather than the number of deaths. For the swine flu decision, however, the years-of-life-lost consequence is apt to vary in direct proportion to the number of deaths. Thus, a quick analysis using the death consequence will produce the same conclusion as one based on the years of life lost. When making decisions about the diseases on which to concentrate public health funds, however, thinking in terms of years of life lost may produce a different—and better—decision.

24. Not to everyone, however. On April 2, 1976, the chief epidemiologist of New Jersey said on the CBS evening television news, "We can soberly estimate that approximately fifteen percent of the entire population will suffer disability reaction" from a swine flu vaccination. Neustadt and Fineberg, *Swine Flu Affair,* p. 40.
25. If an epidemic occurred with no program, there would be 50,000 deaths, so that the expected number of deaths with no program would be 5,000. Consequently, the targeted program saves 5,000 − 3,900 = 1,100 lives at a cost of $24 million/1,100 = $22,000 per life saved. The general program saves an expected 500 lives at a cost of $100,000,000/500 = $200,000 per life saved.
26. *Statistical Abstract of the United States, 1980* (Washington, D.C.: U.S. Government Printing Office, 1980), p. 78.
27. Ibid.
28. The U.S. death rate in 1975 was 888.5 per hundred thousand (ibid.). Consequently, if a White House staffer had attempted in early 1976 to estimate the total number of deaths for that year, the result would have been 213 million people times 888.5 deaths per hundred thousand equals 1,892,505 deaths, or approximately 1,890,000 deaths.
29. Note that, in terms of expected number of deaths, both the targeted program and the general program entailed fewer deaths than the 5,000 expected deaths that would result from no program.
30. Neustadt and Fineberg, *Swine Flu Affair,* pp. 25, 26.
31. You could argue that the political consequence would increase faster than the number of people that die; that is, 20,000 people dying is more than twice as bad as 10,000 people dying. At the same time, however, you could argue the reverse, that above a certain threshold—say 10,000 deaths—the political consequence would be relatively fixed and not all that dependent upon the number of people who die. As a rough, first cut then, it might make sense to assume that the adverse political consequences would be proportional to the number of people who die.
32. Quoted by Philip M. Boffey, "Anatomy of a Decision: How the Nation Declared War on Swine Flu," *Science* 192, no. 4240 (May 14, 1976):637.
33. Ibid., p. 636.

INDEX

Abernathy, William J., on trade-offs in business, 334

accuracy: delusions of, 109, 162 (*see also* phoney precision); futile search for, 188–89, 265 (*see also* rounding-off); meaning of probabilistic, 88–89, 181 (*see also* calibration)

Adams, Brock, on uncertainties in budget, 167

addition rule of probability, 96–97; and flipping probability tree, 303, 306, 309–10; use of, 99, 142–43, 145–56, 303, 306, 309–10; *see also* probability rules

airport repair dilemma, 311–328, 311–20, 322–28, 329; decision trees for, fig. 11-1 (p. 312), fig. 11-2 (p. 313), fig. 11–14 (p. 323); first-cut analysis of, 313–20; and independence principle, 315–16; second-cut analysis of, 322–26; third-cut analysis of, 326–28; *see also* conflicting consequences; trade-off analysis

Allen, William McPherson, on cost predictability, 37

Allison, Graham T., on the motive for confident predictions, 92

almanac questions, 181–85, table 7-4 (pp. 182–83), table 7-5 (p. 185), 192–94, table 7-7 (p. 193)

Alsop, Joseph, on predictions and decisions, 38

alternative branch, 28

ambiguity, in language, 22

ambiguity, in probability words and phrases, 21, 74–78, table 4-1 (p. 76); and estimates of uncertain quantities, 173

American Bakery dilemma, 333–334

analysis, 3–10, 17; complete and comprehensive, 19, 267–68; derivation of, 17; and development of values, 342; and judgment, 20, 115, 268–69; purpose of, 148–49, 268–69, 376; scientific, 267–68; subjective nature of, 23, 148; value of, 221–23, 341–43; *see also* analytical thinking; decision analysis; dynamics of analysis; quick analysis; researched analysis

analytical thinking, 6, 16–24, 57, 264, 268; application of, 52–53; dynamics of, 374–76; five

concepts of, 16–24; *see also* dynamics of analysis

anchoring and adjustment heuristic, 83, 86, 177–179, 199

angina/bypass surgery dilemma, 26–37, 40–41; decision trees for, fig. 2-1 (p. 28), fig. 2-6 (p. 41); as compound dilemma, 298, 300

angiogram decision dilemma, 298, 300

appendectomy decision dilemma, 117–20

approximation, of range of risk, 136, 140–41, 173–76, 187–88, 239–43, 257–64; with four-branch outcome fork, 239–40; with point estimate, 136, 173–74, 187–88, 257–62; with ten-branch outcome fan, 262–64; with two-branch outcome fork, 140–41, 174–76; with uncertainty curve, 240–43; *see also* range of risk; simplification

arithmetic, the value of, 7, 17–18, 142, 160–62; and delusions of accuracy, 109

assets, and problem formulation; *see* total assets approach

availability heuristic, 179–81

backward induction of dynamic programming, 281

Ball, George W., on oil embargo, 74

Banks, Robert L., on trade-offs in business, 333

BART dilemma, *see* Bay Area Rapid Transit cable sheathing dilemma

base outcome, in trade-off analysis, 345

basic decision dilemma, 26–53 (chapter 2), 54–70 (chapter 3); analysis of, 30–37, 54–70; in business, 46–49; decision sapling for, fig. 2-7 (p. 41); in government, 39–40, 49–52, 54–70; sensitivity analysis for, 66–67; structure of, 27–30, 40–42; *see also* angina/bypass surgery dilemma; Bay Area Rapid Transit cable sheathing dilemma; corporate takeover dilemma; decision sapling; extra point dilemma; Mitsui petrochemical plant dilemma; Mount Baker evacuation dilemma; NASA shuttle abort system dilemma; prose-

Index

Index

gains and losses *(continued)*
RKO/FCC dilemma; RKO TV series dilemma; Sturdley's dilemma
Giaimo, Robert N., on uncertainty in budget estimates, 167
GNP, *see* gross national product
Good News About Energy, The (Council on Environmental Quality), and avoidance of trade-offs, 338
government decisions: and basic dilemma, 49–52; with conflicting consequences, 331–32; with uncertainty, 37–38, 71, 187; *see also* airport repair dilemma; Bay Area Rapid Transit cable sheathing dilemma; earthquake/natural disaster dilemma; Mount Baker evacuation dilemma; NASA's shuttle abort system dilemma; swine flu dilemma, President Ford's; traffic safety dilemma; veto dilemma; volcano/natural disaster dilemma
Greenspan, Alan, on public policy and forecasts, 71
gross national product, impact of spending shortfall on, 164

Hamm, Robert M., on probabilistic thinking in medicine, 190
Hammett, Dashiell, *The Maltese Falcon,* 39
Hansen, Julia Butler, on estimating project costs, 172
Hardin, Garrett, on incommensurables, 336
Hartford Courant dilemma, 334–35
Hartzog, George B., on estimating project costs, 172
Hatfield, Mark, on trade-offs in the budget, 331
Hayes, Robert H., on trade-offs in business, 334
Healey, Denis, on budget estimates, 171
Heisenberg's uncertainty principle, 190
Helms, Jesse A., and Edmisten's campaign, 273
hemophilia dilemma, 281–93, 298, 301, 302–10; and conflicting consequences, 283; decision tree for, fig. 10-7 (pp. 286–87); and flipping probability tree, 302–10; resolution of, 288–92; structure of, 284–85
"Heretical View of Management Science, A" (Levitt), 267–68
heuristics, 83, 86, 177–81, 221, 227
Hogarth, Robin M.: on assessing median and quartile estimates, 177; on human information processing capacity, 341
human mind, 17–25, 337–41; and analytical thinking, 16–25; and bounded rationality, 18–19; and cognitive strain, 337–38; and complexity, 18–20, 43, 337, 339–41; and im-

perative of simplification, 19–20, 339–41; and information processing capability, 18, 341; limits of, 18–20, 24–25; and need for decision making tools, 24–25, 341; and quick analysis, 24–25; *see also* analytical thinking, cognitive psychology, intuition, psychological decision theory
hypothetical decisions, 30–32, 82–84; and subjunctive thinking, 227–28; *see also* preference-probability, specification of; probability, specification of; reference gamble
hypothetical indifference decisions, *see* indifference relation
hypothetical indifference outcomes, *see* indifference outcome, and trade-off analysis
hypothetical probabilities and subjunctive thinking, 227

ideal probability generator, 6, 81–86, 99, 102, 198; *see also* probability, specification of
Ilacqua, R. S., on oil decontrol, 71
independence principle, 315, 319, 321, 326, 328, 345, 347; Savage's, 395n2 fig. 11-29 (p.396)
indifference consequence, and trade-off analysis, 317–20, 328
indifference outcomes: and certain monetary equivalents, 196–201, and trade-off analysis, 316, 321–22, 344–45
indifference probability, 33, 44, 105, 151, 161, 197; *see also* probability, specification of; preference-probability
indifference relation, and trade-off analysis, 315–16, 318–19, 321, 323–24, 327
indirect assessment: of preference-probability, 144–49; of probability, 94–100, 302–10
information: collection of, 16, 294–95, 298–301; and future-first principle, 301; human processing of, 16, 18, 341; and pD > C rule, 364–65; value of additional, 399n45
information collecting dilemma, 294–301; decision tree for, fig. 10-11 (p. 294); and pD > C rule, 364–65
interjacent outcome, 31, 42–45, 104–7, 111–13, 116, 289, 351
interquartile index, 182–84, 194
interquartile range, 174–75, 180, 184, 187, 246
intransitive choices, 222
intuition: and compound decision dilemma, 281; and decision making, 6, 268–69; and probabilities, 96, 100; quick analysis, and role of, 6, 20, 23

407

Index

Index

probabilistic midpoint, 175–76, 243–44; and outcome fan, 262–64; *see also,* median; quartile; octile

probabilistic prediction, 30–31, 58–61, 72–78, 86, 172–94, 228, 281; accuracy of, 88–89, 181–85, 188–94; and calibration, 91, 181–85, 192–94; and ideal probability generator, 81–85; misinterpretation of, 190–92; overconfidence in, 89–90, 178–81, 184–85; practice in making, 86–87, 172–85; vs. point estimates, 187–88, 257–62; for Skylab reentry, 190–92; *see also* probability; uncertainty

probabilistic thinking, 189–92, 228

probabilistic utility theory, *see* preference-probability

probability: and accuracy, 88–89, 181–85, 188–94; and analysis of dilemmas, 30–31, 58–61 *(see also specific dilemmas);* ambiguous phrases for, 21, 75–78; conditional, 94–95; and decision making, 38, 80; and ideal probability generator, 81–85; interpretations of, 78–81; intuition about, 100; joint, 95; judgmental, 6, 30–31, 60–61, 65, 80–1, 228; and knowledge, 87–88; and probability trees, 97–100, 302–10; relative frequency, 79–80, 85; rules of, 95–97; specification of, 30–31, 58–60, 81–85, 102–3, 172–81, 239–43; thinking with, 60–61; unconditional, 94–95; working with, 94–100, 302–10; *see also* preference-probability; probability rules; switch probability; uncertainty

probability distribution, 178; *see also* uncertainty curve

probability phrases and words, ambiguous, 21, 72–78, 173, table 4-1 (p. 76)

probability rules, 95–97; intuitive nature of, 100; and flipping probability tree, 303–4, 306–7, 309–10; use of, 97–100, 108, fig. 6-6b (p.139), 142–43, 145–46, 147, 149, 303–4, 306–7, 309–10

probability tree, 94–100; flipping of, 302–10

process, as consequence, 391–92*n* 18

product development dilemma, *see* new product dilemma

project assets, 229–31

prosecutor's dilemma, 38–40, 156

psychological decision theory, 9

public disaster dilemmas, 382–83*n* 14; *see also* natural disaster dilemma; swine flu dilemma, President Ford's

public policy decisions, *see* government decisions

publisher's dilemma: as basic dilemma, 48–49; and point estimate, 188; as range-of-risk dilemma, 156–57

quartile, 174–76, 177–85, 192–94, 234, 258–61; in second-cut analysis, 175–76, 234

quick analysis, 3–10, 14, 22–23, 24–25, 52–53, 65–66; and decision analysis, 5–6; as decision-making tool, 24–25; and decision theory, 9–10; dynamics of, 6, 56–58, 374–76; fundamentals of, 65–66; and intuition, 23, 268–69; methods of, 6; practicing, 46, 53, 68; and probability assessment, 177; purpose of, 7, 8, 148–49, 268–69, 376; and researched analysis, 3–5; subjective nature of, 7, 23, 148; and trade-offs, 329–30; value of, 18, 125–26, 360, 369–70, 374–75, 376

radioactive decay, and probabilistic laws of science, 189

Raiffa, Howard, on trade-offs, 335–36

Raleigh-Durham Airport decision, *see* airport-repair dilemma

Ramsey, James B., on uncertainty in economics, 190

range of risk: and approximation by median, 172–74; and approximation by median and quartiles, 172–76; and approximation by median, quartiles, and octiles, 239–40; and approximation by outcome fan, 262–64; and approximation by uncertainty curve, 240–43; point estimate and multi-branch estimate compared, 260–65

range-of-risk dilemma, 131–270 (Part II); and business investment dilemmas, 152–55; and legal decisions, 155–56; and risk aversion, 205–8; final-cut analysis of, 243–46; first-cut analysis of, 135–40; second-cut analysis of, 140–44; sensitivity analysis of, 246–57; third-cut analysis of, 237–239; *see also* McDonnell Douglas's new product dilemma; new product dilemma; oil-drilling dilemma; out-of-court settlement dilemma; Ventron Corporation's plant-investment dilemma

Rawls, John, on additional analysis, 24, 362

RDU, *see* Raleigh-Durham Airport

Reagan, Ronald, *Fiscal Year 1982 Budget Revisions,* 269–70

reference gamble, 6, 43–44, fig. 2-8 (p. 43), fig. 2-9 (p. 44), 63, 110–11, fig. 6-4 (p. 137), 149–52; for assessing preference curve, 197–99, 202–5; for assessing preference-probability, 104–11, 137–40, 141–44, 144–49, 160–62, 356–57; characteristics of, 118, 137; decisions as a choice between two of, fig. 2-4 (p. 35), fig. 5-7 (p. 109), fig. 5-10 (p. 113), fig. 5-16 (p. 120), fig. 6-6b (p. 139), fig. 6-9d (p.

Index

sensitivity *(continued)*
safety dilemma, 66–67; for risk aversion, 211, 250–54; value of, 114–16, 127, 256–57; *see also* switch curve; switch point

sequential trade-off technique, *see* trade-off analysis

Sencer, David J., and President Ford's swine flu dilemma, 365, 367, 368

second-cut analysis, 24, 40, 188, 264–65, 342, 375; of airport repair dilemma, 322–26; of out-of-court settlement dilemma, 140–44; of personal swine flu dilemma, 351–57; *see also* dynamics of analysis; simplification

Shakespeare, William, on uncertainty, 93

Shaw, George Bernard, on logarithms and square roots, 9

Shepard, Roger N., on human cognitive capabilities, 339–40, 341

Sherlock Holmes phenomenon, 90; *see also* overconfidence

short-term/long-term trade-off in business, 333–34

shuttle abort system dilemma, *see* NASA shuttle abort system dilemma

Silk, Leonard, on uncertainty, 91

Simon, Herbert A.: on human simplification process, 20; on principle of bounded rationality, 18, 19

simplification, 19–20, 22, 29, 52, 60, 65, 135, 136, 140, 141, 176, 234–70 (chapter 9), 312, 322, 339–41, 360; and analytical thinking, 19–20, 52, 268, 375; vs. complication, 266–69, 375–76; and conflicting consequences, 339–41; imperative of, 19–20, 22, 339–41; importance of, 339–41; and probability tree, 97–100; and quick analysis, 65, 375–76; resistance to, 19–20, 340–41; value of, 262–65, 268–69; value of decision tree for, 29, 60; why it works, 262–65

Skylab, probabilistic predictions for reentry, 190–92

Slovic, Paul: "Behavioral Decision Theory," 24; on cognitive strain, 337; on avoiding uncertainty, 92–93; on gambles and losses, 221; on human inability to make trade-offs, 340; on human decision-making capabilities, 24–25; on types of decisions, 6; on using multiple perspectives to analyze decisions, 342

Sox, Red, 81, 219

Spade, Sam, on district attorneys, 39

specification, 20–23, 29, 52, 60, 102, 136, 201, 208, 316, 335–36, 349, 376; of ignorance, 163–94 (chapter 7); and phoney precision, 171–72; value of decision tree for, 29, 60; *see*

also preference-probability, specification of; probability, specification of

spending shortfall, 163–171, 188–89; economic effect of, 164–65

Spetzler, Carl S., on assessments of uncertain quantities, 180

spurious specificity, 172; *see also* phoney precision; delusions of accuracy

Staël von Holstein, Carl-Axel S., on assessments of uncertain quantities, 180

statistical data, and probability assessment, 21, 60, 79–80, 300–1; *see also* relative-frequency probability

Steinbruner, John D.: on analysis, 267; on complex decisions, 377n5; on psychological pain of trade-offs, 337–38

structure, *see* decision sapling; decision tree; decomposition; simplification; structuring a decision analysis

structuring a decision analysis: for basic decision dilemma, 27–30, 40–42, 349; for complex analyses, 40–41, 351–53, 357–85; for compound dilemma, 273–74, 277–80, 284–87, 294–301; for conflicting consequences dilemma, 311–13, 320–22, 343–47; for double-risk dilemma, 101–02, 366–67, 370–71; importance of, 221–26; for range-of-risk dilemma, 134–35, 140–41, 152–53, 234, 237–39, 243–46; *see also* decision sapling; decision tree; decomposition; simplification

Strunk, William, Jr., *Elements of Style*, 21

Sturdley, Joe, *see* losses, preferences for

subjective probability, *see* judgmental probability

subjectivity: and judgment, 378n19; of judgmental probability, 85–86, 181; and preference-probabilities, 162; in quick analysis, 23–24, 148; and relative frequency probability, 85; and trade-offs, 336

subjunctive thinking, 227–28

substitution principle, 34–36, 45, 65, 107, 137, 142–43, 160, 268, 324–36; and indirect assessment of preference-probability, 34–36, 45, 65, 107–11, 127, 138–40, 144–49, 160, 202, 210, 238; logic of, fig. 2-4 (p. 35), 107, fig. 6-11 (p. 146), fig. 6-12 (p. 147), fig. 11-18 (p. 325); and resolution of specific dilemmas, 34–36, 64, 107, 118, 138–40, 142–44, 245, 354; and trade-off analysis, 315–16, 319, 324–26, 328, 347

sunk costs: and Mitsui petrochemical plant dilemma, 47–48; and RKO TV series dilemma, 229–33; why they don't count, 229–33

surprise index, 182–85, 194

413

Index

Index